X

The College of West Anglia

ookbook™

Tennyson Avenue • King's Lynn • PE30 2QW • Tel: (01553) 815306

LEARNING *Resource Centre*
• *Library* • *IT* • *Media Services* •

The card holder is responsible for the return of this book
Fines will be charged on ALL late items

The College of West Anglia

Other resources from O'Reilly

SECOND EDITION

CSS Cookbook™

Christopher Schmitt

O'REILLY®

Beijing · Cambridge · Farnham · Köln · Paris · Sebastopol · Taipei · Tokyo

CSS Cookbook™, Second Edition

by Christopher Schmitt

Copyright © 2007, 2004 O'Reilly Media, Inc. All rights reserved.
Printed in the United States of America.

Published by O'Reilly Media, Inc., 1005 Gravenstein Highway North, Sebastopol, CA 95472.

O'Reilly books may be purchased for educational, business, or sales promotional use. Online editions are also available for most titles (*safari.oreilly.com*). For more information, contact our corporate/institutional sales department: (800) 998-9938 or *corporate@oreilly.com*.

Editor: Tatiana Apandi
Production Editor: Philip Dangler
Copyeditor: Nancy Reinhardt
Indexer: Reg Aubry

Cover Designer: Karen Montgomery
Interior Designer: David Futato
Illustrators: Robert Romano and Jessamyn Read

Printing History:

August 2004:	First Edition.
October 2006:	Second Edition.

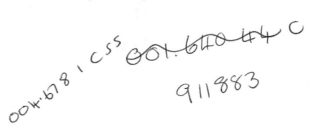

 This book uses RepKover™, a durable and flexible lay-flat binding.

ISBN-10: 0-596-52741-1
ISBN-13: 978-0-596-52741-9
[C]

For Dad

Table of Contents

Preface

Every book tells a story—even books on web design. Yet, the story of this book doesn't contain any hidden meanings or staggering cliffhangers. You won't read about people waiting for someone named Godot or a rugged archaeologist saving religious artifacts from a German army. While those books have their place, this book is for web designers and developers and for them it tells a different tale.

This book is about Cascading Style Sheets, or CSS as it's commonly abbreviated. CSS is a simple standardized syntax that gives designers extensive control over the presentation of their web pages and it is an essential component of Web design today. Compared to 1990s-era development techniques, web designers have greater control over a web site's design and can spend less time editing and maintaining web sites. CSS also extends beyond the traditional web design as well to design and control the look of a web page when it is printed.

The simplicity of Cascading Style Sheets is that you don't need any special hardware or software to use CSS. The basic requirements are a computer, a modern browser like Firefox, Safari, or Internet Explorer for Windows (to name a few), and your favorite web page editor. A web page editor can be anything from a simple text editor like Window's Notepad or Macintosh's TextEdit to a full-fledged WYSIWYG tool like Adobe Dreamweaver set in code view.

Now you know what the book is about, let me tell you the story of this book.

It's about history.

Some would say web design officially began when Tim Berners-Lee, inventor of the World Wide Web, put together the first set of web pages. Others would say it began when the center tag came about due to Netscape's own extension of HTML.

It's with a generous amount of humility and irony, I happen to believe that the web design really started with books. The books that helped lead the way to the dot-com boom in the 1990s started with Lynda Weinman's first full-color book about web graphics, *Designing Web Graphics*, which was published in January of 1996, and then David Siegel's *Creating Killer Web Sites* was published several months later that same year. These two books helped kick off the web revolution as much as those who invented the technologies that made them possible. However, the methods written in those books, while cutting edge for their time, are out-of-date in today's context.

As I write these pages, it's been 10 years since those initial books came out and a lot has changed. Another tidbit loaded with irony is that CSS was first introduced in 1996—the same year Wienman and Siegel's first books about web design came out.

While neither robust nor implemented in modern browsers at the time, CSS has come a long way. Over 10 years of development have been put into CSS and it's only now, with the advent of the Internet Explorer 7 for Windows in 2006 that web designers, developers, and everyday users of browsers will be able to utilize CSS to its intended potential.

The *CSS Cookbook*, a collection of CSS-based solutions to common web design problems, helps web designers and developers accomplish the many designs and techniques possible with CSS.

If you are serious about building today's usable and cutting-edge web sites, use CSS and the *CSS Cookbook*. This is the book is one to use when you are creating your own bit of web design history.

Audience

This book is for web designers and developers struggling with the problems of designing with CSS. With this book, web builders can solve common problems associated with CSS-enabled web page designs.

CSS Cookbook is ideal for people who have wanted to use CSS for web projects, but have shied away from learning a new technology. If you are this type of reader, use the solutions in the book one or a few at a time. Use it as a guidebook, and then come back to it when you are ready or need to learn another technique or trick.

Even if you consider yourself an expert with CSS, but not an expert in basic design knowledge, this book is useful to have by the side of your computer. It covers elements of design from web typography to page layouts and a motivational chapter called "Designing with CSS" is included.

Assumptions This Book Makes

This book makes several assumptions about you, the reader. One assumption is that you possess some web design or development experience either as a hobbyist, student, or professional.

CSS Cookbook is neither an introduction to CSS nor is it a book that goes into great detail on how CSS should work in browsers, so people at the start of their web design or development education may find this book a bit more challenging than a general or complete book on the theory of CSS. If you are looking for a book that delves into such topics about the CSS specification, you should look into *Cascading Style Sheets: The Definitive Guide,* also from O'Reilly Media, which serves as a solid complement to this book.

If you makes use of programs like Adobe Dreamweaver only in its WYSIWG or "design" mode and rarely if ever touch the markup in "code" view, you may have trouble getting the most out of this book right away. To get an introduction to hand-coding HTML, look into *Learning Web Design* by Jennifer Niederst Robbins (O'Reilly Media).

While WYSWIYG tools allow for CSS-enabled designs, some of the tools have not caught up with some of the unorthodox approaches recommended in this book and may cause some trouble if you attempt to implement them by editing solely in WYSIWG mode. To benefit from this book, you must be able to edit HTML and CSS by hand. Some of the code in this book can be recreated by using dialog-box driven web page building applications, but you may run into some problems along the way.

Another assumption is that web designers and developers practicing their craft with HTML table-based layouts, font tags, and single pixel GIFs will find this book both helpful and frustrating. Web designers practicing or more familiar with these old production methods are going to find CSS challenging. The "browser hell" often associated with cross-browser development where browser vendors tended to interpret the CSS specification differently or didn't implement the CSS specification completely still exists. This frustration is a natural part of the learning process. Learning how to design with CSS should be approached with patience and a good sense of humor.

The good news is that the major browser vendors seem to have solved the problems. The recent version releases of browsers appear to have implemented CSS correctly, however, attempting cross-browser support for the older or less-popular browsers may still be a challenging exercise. Yet the benefits of CSS, including greater control over the look and feel of web pages and easier maintenance over multipage web sites, outweigh the hardships associated with "browser hell."

To use the handful of solutions that make use of JavaScript, this book assumes that your have a general knowledge of the scripting language as well as the ability to successfully include JavaScript code into a web document. If this is a hurdle, we recommend that you download the code from the publisher's web site to get a first-hand look at a working example. On the other hand, if you were looking for a solution-focused book that deals with recipes where CSS plays a minor role compared to Java-Script, that book would be *JavaScript & DHTML Cookbook* by Danny Goodman (O'Reilly Media).

The final assumption is that you desire a resource that provides fast answers to common CSS-based web design problems. The solutions in this book, covering everything from web-based typography to multi-column layouts, are geared for the modern browsers with version numbers greater or equal to 5 with the exception of Safari, which doesn't have a version greater than 2 as of the writing of this book.

Whenever possible, I mention when a technique may cause problems in version 5 or higher browsers. While there is a chapter on hacks and workarounds to hide style sheets from browsers with poor implementations of the complete CSS specification, this book makes no assurances that you are going create pixel-perfect designs in every browser. Even with traditional web design methods from the 1990s, this has never been the case.

Contents of This Book

For me, the best use for a book like this would be to crack it open from time to time when trying to solve a particular problem, which I have done with the first edition when refreshing my memory. To that end, this book will serve well on or nearby a web builder's desk—always within reach to resolve a problem about CSS or web design. However, feel free to read the book from its first page to its last.

The following paragraphs review the contents of each chapter:

Chapter 1, *General*
> Discusses the basics of CSS as well some techniques associated with best practices in development.

Chapter 2, *Web Typography*
> Discusses how to use CSS to specify fonts in a web page, headings, pull quotes, and indents within paragraphs as well as other solutions.

Chapter 3, *Images*
> Discusses CSS techniques directly related to manipulating styles and properties related to web graphics.

Chapter 4, *Page Elements*
> Covers a loose collection of items that don't necessarily fit in every chapter, but that all carry a theme of affecting the design of the overall page. Solutions in this chapter include centering elements, setting a background image, placing a border on a page, and other techniques.

Chapter 5, *Lists*
> Describes how to style the basic list items in various ways. Solutions include cross-browser indentation, making hanging indents, inserting custom images for list markers, and more.

Chapter 6, *Links and Navigation*

Shows how to use CSS to control the presentation of a link and sets of links. Solutions range from the basic like removing an underline from links, to the more complex such as dynamic visual menu.

Chapter 7, *Forms*

Discusses ways to work around the basic ways browsers render forms. Solutions reviewed in this chapter include setting styles to specific form elements, setting a Submit once-only button, and styling a login form.

Chapter 8, *Tables*

Shows how to style HTML tables. Although CSS can help eliminate HTML table-based designs, sometimes you need to style tabular data like calendars and statistical data. This chapter includes solutions for things such as: setting cell-padding, removing gaps in table cells with images, and styling a calendar.

Chapter 9, *Page Layouts*

Talks about how CSS can be used to engineer layouts. The solutions in this chapter include methods for one-column layouts to multicolumn layouts.

Chapter 10, *Print*

Provides information on how to set styles that are used when printing web pages. Solutions discussed in this chapter include adding a separate print style sheet to a web page, setting styles for web forms, and inserting URLs after links.

Chapter 11, *Hacks, Workarounds, and Troubleshooting*

Covers solutions on how to hide style sheets that cannot be handled by certain browsers. Recipes include hiding style sheets for browsers like Netscape Navigator 4, Internet Explorer 5 for Windows, and other browsers.

Chapter 12, *Designing with CSS*

Is an inspirational chapter. Focusing on the notion that CSS is merely a tool that implements design, this chapter covers things like playing with enlarging type sizes, working with contrast, and building a panoramic presentation.

Appendix A, *Resources*

Is a collection of links and web sites related to learning more about CSS.

Appendix B, *CSS 2.1 Properties and Proprietary Extensions*

Is a listing of CSS properties that help define the look and feel or, in some cases, the sound of HTML elements on a web page.

Appendix C, *CSS 2.1 Selectors, Pseudo-Classes, and Pseudo-Elements*

Is a listing of selectors available within CSS.

Appendix D, *Styling of Form Elements*

Is a look at how various modern browsers handle the display of form elements.

Conventions Used in This Book

The following typographical conventions are used in this book:

Plain text

> Indicates menu titles, menu options, menu buttons, and keyboard accelerators (such as Alt and Ctrl).

Italic

> Indicates new terms, URLs, email addresses, filenames, file extensions, pathnames, directories, and Unix utilities.

`Constant width`

> Indicates commands, options, switches, variables, attributes, keys, functions, types, classes, namespaces, methods, modules, properties, parameters, values, objects, events, event handlers, XML tags, HTML tags, macros, the contents of files, or the output from commands.

`Constant width bold`

> Shows commands or other text that should literally be typed by the user.

`Constant width italic`

> Shows text that should be replaced with user-supplied values.

 This icon signifies a tip, suggestion, or general note.

 This icon indicates a warning or caution.

Using Code Examples

This book is here to help you get your job done. In general, you may use the code in this book in your web pages and design. You do not need to contact us for permission unless you're reproducing a significant portion of the code. For example, writing a program that uses several chunks of code from this book does not require permission. Selling or distributing a CD-ROM of examples from O'Reilly books does require permission. Answering a question by citing this book and quoting example code does not require permission. Incorporating a significant amount of example code from this book into your product's documentation does require permission.

We appreciate, but do not require, attribution. An attribution usually includes the title, author, publisher, and ISBN. For example: "*CSS Cookbook*, Second Edition, by Christopher Schmitt. Copyright 2007 O'Reilly Media, Inc., 978-0-596-52741-9."

If you feel your use of code examples falls outside fair use or the permission given above, feel free to contact us at *permissions@oreilly.com*.

How to Contact Us

Please address comments and questions concerning this book to the publisher:

O'Reilly Media, Inc.
1005 Gravenstein Highway North
Sebastopol, CA 95472
800-998-9938 (in the United States or Canada)
707-829-0515 (international or local)
707-829-0104 (fax)

We have a web page for this book, where we list errata, examples, and any additional information. You can access this page at:

http://www.oreilly.com/catalog/cssckbk2

To comment or ask technical questions about this book, send email to:

bookquestions@oreilly.com

For more information about our books, conferences, Resource Centers, and the O'Reilly Network, see our web site at:

http://www.oreilly.com

Safari Enabled

 When you see a Safari® Enabled icon on the cover of your favorite technology book, it means the book is available online through the O'Reilly Network Safari Bookshelf.

Safari offers a solution that's better than e-books. It's a virtual library that lets you easily search thousands of top technology books, cut and paste code samples, download chapters, and find quick answers when you need the most accurate, current information. Try it for free at *http://safari.oreilly.com*.

Acknowledgments

First, thanks to David Siegel and Lynda Weinman for their inspiration and support from the beginning of web design.

I wouldn't be writing any books for an industry I love so very much without the support and friendship of Molly Holzschlag.

A lot of appreciation and respect to fellow web builders for pushing CSS-enabled web designs forward: Douglas Bowman, Tantek Çelik, Dan Cenderhlem, Mike Davidson, Ethan Marcotte, Eric A. Meyer, Mark Newhouse, Dave Shea, and Jeffrey Zeldman.

Special thanks go to the technical editors, Erik J. Barzeski, Liza Daly, and John Allsopp, and as well as the copy editor, Nancy Reinhardt, for their time, expertise and patience.

To my friend, Porter Glendinning, who seems to have a knack for not only being able to read W3C specifications and see their implications two or three steps ahead of most web developers, but also articulates those thoughts in such a way as to make me believe that even my grandmother could understand what he's talking about. Your translation services and thoughts are truly appreciated.

Special thanks to Tatiana Apandi. Tatiana did a great job of making sure my questions were answered and guiding me throughout the life of the project. This writing process has been my most challenging, but most rewarding experience to date. And, frankly, I wouldn't have wanted it any other way with any other publisher.

Thanks to my friends who know me as the web geek I truly am: Katrina Ferguson, Kelly and Nathan Hensley, Trueman Muhrer, Eric Ellis, Jessica Lorenzi, Ansley Simmons, Mark Trammell, and Ryan Yordon.

Thanks to my family for the love and appreciation. Your support through good times and bad has been a rock. As always, I'm looking forward to our next reunion.

CHAPTER 1

General

1.0 Introduction

Cascading style sheets (CSS) provides a simple way to style the content on your web pages. CSS may look complicated to the first-time CSS user, but this chapter shows how easy it is to use CSS. The recipes provide the basics to get you started with CSS. After you write a few lines of HTML page, add a little CSS and you immediately see the results.

Here's an exercise with the traditional "Hello, world!" example. First, open a text editor or a favorite web page editing tool and enter the following:

```
<html>
 <head>
  <title>CSS Cookbook</title>
 <head>
 <body>
  <p>Hello, world!</p>
 </body>
</html>
```

Save the file and view it in your web browser. This line is nothing special as you can see in Figure 1-1.

Figure 1-1. Default rendering of HTML text without CSS

To change the style of the HTML text from to sans serif, add a bit of the following CSS (see Figure 1-2):

```
<p style="font-family: sans-serif;">Hello, world!</p>
```

Or, keeping the default font, change the font size to 150% font-size, using the following example that you see in Figure 1-3:

```
<p style="font-size: 150%">Hello, world!</p>
```

Figure 1-2. The font is changed to sans-serif through CSS

Figure 1-3. The size of the text gets larger

In this chapter, you'll learn about selectors and properties, organizing style sheets, and positioning. These general recipes prepare you for fancier recipes in upcoming chapters.

1.1   Using CSS with HTML

Problem

You want to use CSS in your web pages.

Solution

Start with a blank page in Notepad, your favorite text processor, or web development software like Macromedia Dreamweaver or Microsoft Expression.

Add the following HTML between the body tags and save the file as cookbook.html (see Figure 1-4):

```
<html>
 <head>
  <title>CSS Cookbook</title>
 </head>
 <body>
  <h1>Title of Page</h1>
  <p>This is a sample paragraph with a
  <a href="http://csscookbook.com">link</a>.</p>
 </body>
</html>
```

Figure 1-4. Default rendering of HTML in the browser

Then add the following code changes in order to redefine the style for links, bulleted lists, and headers, and then check out Figure 1-5:

```
<html>
 <head>
  <title>CSS Cookbook</title>
  <style type="text/css">
  <!--
  body {
   font-family: verdana, arial, sans-serif;
  }
  h1 {
   font-size: 120%;
  }
  a {
   text-decoration: none;
  }
  p {
   font-size: 90%;
  }
  -->
  </style>
```

```
 </head>
 <body>
  <h1>Title of Page</h1>
  <p>This is a sample paragraph with a
<a href="http://csscookbook.com">link</a>.</p>
 </body>
</html>
```

Figure 1-5. Page is rendered differently after adding CSS

Discussion

CSS contain rules with two parts: selectors and properties. A *selector* identifies what portion of your web page gets styled. Within a selector are one or more properties and their values. The *property* tells the browser what to change and the *value* lets the browser know what that change should be.

For example, in the following declaration block example, the selector tells the browser to style the content marked up with the h1 element in the web page to 120% of the default size:

```
h1 {
  font-size: 120%;
}
```

Table 1-1 breaks out the CSS by selector, property, and value used in the solution. The result column explains what happens when you apply the property and value to the selector.

Table 1-1. Breakdown of selectors, properties, and values from the solution

Selector	Property	Value	Result
h1	font-size	120%	Text size larger than default size.
a	text-decoration	none	Links don't have any decorations, including underlining
p	font-color	blue	Text appears in blue
p	font-size	90%	Text size smaller than default size.

The standard for writing CSS syntax includes the selector, which is normally the tag you want to style followed by properties and values enclosed within curly braces:

```
selector { property: value; }
```

However, most designers use the following format to improve readability:

```
selector {
 property: value;
}
```

Both are valid approaches to writing CSS. Use whatever method is more comfortable for you.

Also, CSS allows selectors to take on more than one property at a time to create more complex visual presentations. In order to assign multiple properties within a selector, use a semicolon to separate the properties as shown below:

```
selector {
 property: value;
 property: value, value, value;
 property: value value value value;
}
selector, selector {
 property: value;
}
```

See Also

Recipe 1.2 for more information about CSS selectors; and Appendix C, "CSS 2.1 Selectors, Pseudo-classes, and Pseudo-elements," for a listing of selectors.

1.2 Using Different Selectors to Apply Styles

Problem

You want to use selectors to apply unique styles to different parts of a web page.

Solution

Use different kinds of selectors to target different portions of web pages that you want to style (see Figure 1-6):

```
<html>
 <head>
  <title>CSS Cookbook</title>
  <style type="text/css">
  <!--
  * {
   font-family: verdana, arial, sans-serif;
  }
   h1 {
   font-size: 120%;
```

```
      }
      #navigation {
       border: 1px solid black;
       padding: 40px;
      }
      li a {
       text-decoration: none;
      }
      p {
       font-size: 90%;
      }
      -->
      </style>
    </head>
    <body>
     <h1>Title of Page</h1>
     <p>This is a sample paragraph with a
<a href="http://csscookbook.com">link</a>. Lorem ipsum dolor sit amet,
consectetuer adipiscing elit, sed diam nonummy nibh euismod tincidunt ut
laoreet dolore magna <em class="warning">aliquam erat volutpat</em>. Ut
wisi enim ad minim veniam, quis nostrud exerci tation ullamcorper suscipit
lobortis nisl ut aliquip ex ea commodo consequat.<p>
       <ul id="navigation">
       <li><a href="http://csscookbook.com">Apples</a></li>
       <li><a href="http://csscookbook.com">Bananas</a></li>
       <li><a href="http://csscookbook.com">Cherries</a></li>
      </ul>
    </body>
   </html>
```

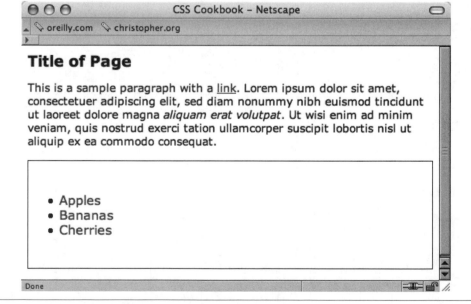

Figure 1-6. Web page with CSS styles

Discussion

CSS allows for many, and sometimes ingenious, ways to pinpoint which elements of a web page should be styled.

To better understand how to select portions of a web page to use selectors, a developer needs to recognize that content marked up with HTML creates a structure. Although the elements used in an HTML may look like the jumbled order shown in Figure 1-7, there is a structure.

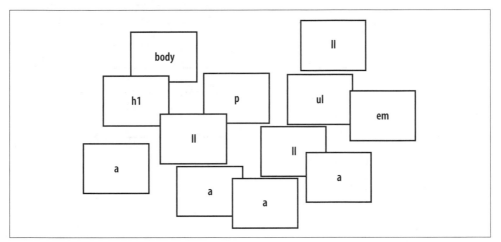

Figure 1-7. Elements used in the solution

This structure may be invisible to the visitor visiting the web page, but it's a crucial part of the rendering process that a browser goes through.

When a browser pulls a web page from the server and begins to display the page, the elements of the page are placed in a structure that is assembled by the browser software. Although this process of placing the elements in an organizational structure is more programming oriented, a good visual representation would be to view the structure much like an organizational chart at a company.

Using the HTML in the solution, Figure 1-8 shows what the organizational chart would look like.

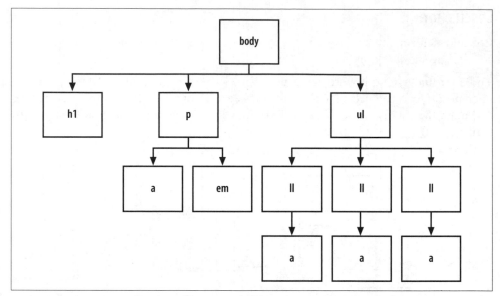

Figure 1-8. Elements used in the web page arranged in a top-down structure

Type selectors

Type selectors are selectors that name the element or HTML tag to style. The following rules would apply font styles to the h1 and p elements within a web page (see Figure 1-9):

```
h1 {
  font-size: 120%;
}
p {
  color: blue;
}
```

 Note that some elements inherit their parent's property values. For example, the text in the paragraph is set to blue, as is the em element.

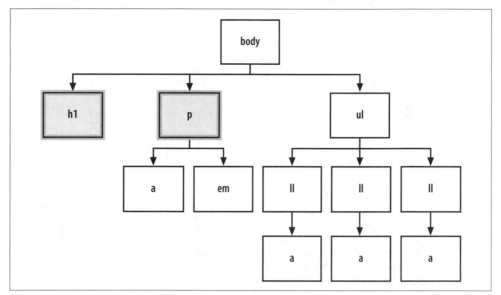

Figure 1-9. The elements selected from the CSS rules

Class selectors

When you want to apply the same CSS rule many times to different elements, use the class selector.

For example, class selectors can be used to identify warnings with red color in a paragraph, as well as in a list item.

First, create a warning class selector preceded with a period, ".", which is also known as full stop:

```
<html>
 <head>
  <title>CSS Cookbook</title>
  <style type="text/css">
  <!--
  * {
   font-family: verdana, arial, sans-serif;
  }
  body {
  }
  h1 {
   font-size: 120%;
  }
  #navigation {
   border: 1px solid black;
   padding: 40px;
```

```
  }
  li a {
   text-decoration: none;
  }
  p {
   font-size: 90%;
  }
  .warning {
   font-weight: bold;
  }
  -->
  </style>
 </head>
 <body>
  <h1>Title of Page</h1>
  <p>This is a sample paragraph with a
<a href="http://csscookbook.com">link</a>. Lorem ipsum dolor sit amet,
consectetuer adipiscing elit, sed diam nonummy nibh euismod tincidunt
ut laoreet dolore magna <em class="warning">aliquam erat volutpat</em>.
Ut wisi enim ad minim veniam, quis nostrud exerci tation ullamcorper suscipit
lobortis nisl ut aliquip ex ea commodo consequat.<p>
   <ul id="navigation">
    <li><a href="http://csscookbook.com">Apples</a></li>
    <li><a href="http://csscookbook.com">Bananas</a></li>
    <li><a href="http://csscookbook.com">Cherries</a></li>
   </ul>
 </body>
</html>
```

Then add the `class` attribute to a link and a list item to style those elements, as you see in Figure 1-10:

```
<html>
 <head>
  <title>CSS Cookbook</title>
  <style type="text/css">
  <!--
  * {
   font-family: verdana, arial, sans-serif;
  }
h1 {
   font-size: 120%;
  }
  #navigation {
   border: 1px solid black;
   padding: 40px;
  }
  li a {
   text-decoration: none;
  }
  p {
   font-size: 90%;
  }
  .warning {
```

```
    font-weight: bold;
  }
  -->
  </style>
</head>
<body>
  <h1>Title of Page</h1>
  <p>This is a sample paragraph with a
<a href="http://csscookbook.com" class="warning">link</a>. Lorem ipsum dolor
sit amet, consectetuer adipiscing elit, sed diam nonummy nibh euismod tincidunt
ut laoreet dolore magna <em class="warning">aliquam erat volutpat</em>. Ut wisi
enim ad minim veniam, quis nostrud exerci tation ullamcorper suscipit lobortis
nisl ut aliquip ex ea commodo consequat.<p>
    <ul id="navigation">
     <li class="warning"><a href="http://csscookbook.com">Apples</a></li>
     <li><a href="http://csscookbook.com">Bananas</a></li>
     <li><a href="http://csscookbook.com">Cherries</a></li>
    </ul>
 </body>
</html>
```

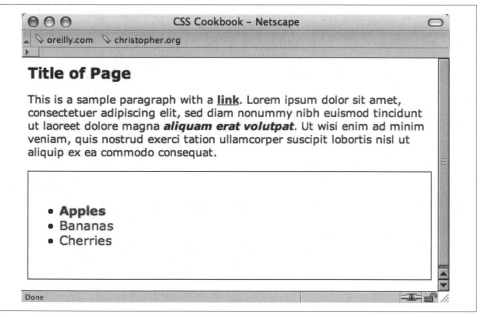

Figure 1-10. The modified CSS rules on the web page

Look at these selectors in the structure of the web page; it would look like
Figure 1-11.

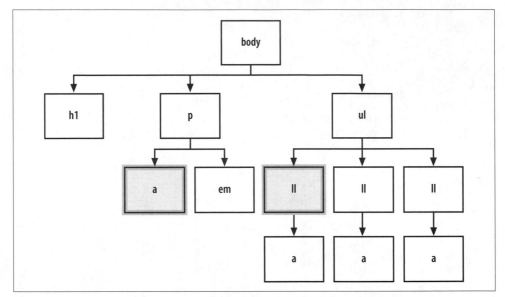

Figure 1-11. The styled elements within the page structure

ID selectors

ID selectors resemble class selectors except that according to the specification they appear only once in the document. Often they appear in a div, but they can be used elsewhere. To create an ID selector, use the hash, "#", and then immediately place a label or name:

```
#navigation {
   border: 1px solid black;
   padding: 40px;
   }
```

Then add an id attribute with the value of navigation (see Figure 1-12):

```
<ul id="navigation">
 <li class="warning"><a href="http://csscookbook.com">Apples</a></li>
 <li><a href="http://csscookbook.com">Bananas</a></li>
 <li><a href="http://csscookbook.com">Cherries</a></li>
</ul>
```

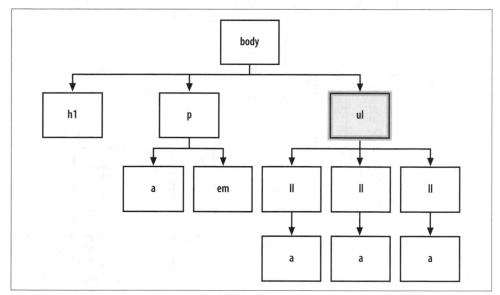

Figure 1-12. The unordered list element is styled

Descendant selectors

Descendant selectors come next in line and override the type and class selector styles. They typically have two elements with the second element being a descendant of the first:

```
li a {
  text-decoration: none;
}
```

Add the HTML in which a appears within li as you see in Figure 1-13:

```
<ul id="navigation">
<li class="warning"><a href="http://csscookbook.com">Apples</a></li>
<li><a href="http://csscookbook.com">Bananas</a></li>
<li><a href="http://csscookbook.com">Cherries</a></li>
</ul>
```

Child selectors

A child selector means that an element is styled if it is the *direct* descendant of its parent element. A child selector is signified by right-angled bracket often set between two type selectors as shown here:

```
p > strong {
  text-decoration: underline;
}
```

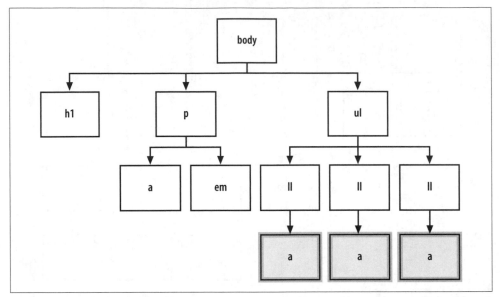

Figure 1-13. The links within the list items are selected

Only the strong element that isn't contained within another element, the p element in this case, is underlined (see Figure 1-14):

```
<div>
 <p>Nothing happens to this part of the sentence because this
<strong>strong</strong> isn't the direct child of div.</p>
 However, this <strong>strong</strong> is the child of div.
Therefore, it receives the style dictated in the CSS rule.
</div>
```

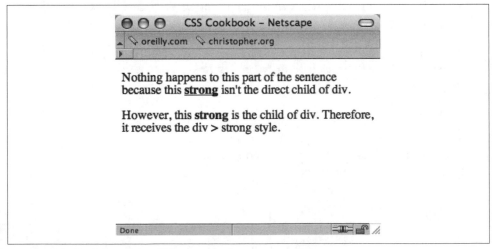

Figure 1-14. The affect of the child selector rule

To see which elements are affected by this CSS rule in an organizational chart, take a look at Figure 1-15.

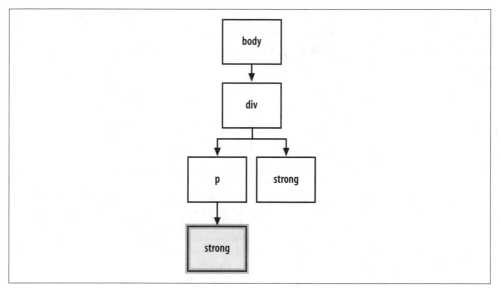

Figure 1-15. The child selector highlighted in the markup structure

In Figures 1-14 and 1-15, the reason the first strong element is not underlined is because it was placed within the p element. If the direct parent-to-child relationship is not present, then the style won't hold. This is an easy, but powerful, difference between a child selector and descendent selector.

Universal selectors

Universal selectors are represented with an asterisk (*) and apply to all elements (see Figure 1-16). In the following code, every element containing HTML text would be styled with a Verdana, Arial, or some other sans-serif font:

```
* {
  font-family: Verdana, Arial, sans-serif;
}
```

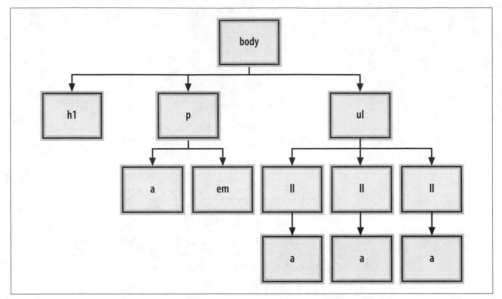

Figure 1-16. Every element gets styled with the universal selector

Adjacent sibling selectors

Adjacent siblings describe the relationship between two elements that are placed side-by-side within the flow of a web page's markup.

An adjacent sibling can be seen by the plus sign as shown here:

```
li + li {
  font-size: 200%;
}
```

The effect of this adjacent sibling rule is seen in Figure 1-17. Notice that only the second and third list item are styled since the second and third list item are placed side-by-side with another list item.

To see which elements are affected by this CSS rule showcasing adjacent sibling selectors in an organizational chart, take a look at Figure 1-18.

> Note that adjacent sibling selectors are not widely supported in modern browsers, most notably Internet Explorer 6 for Windows. Adjacent sibling selectors are supported in Mozilla, Firefox, Opera 5+, and Safari.

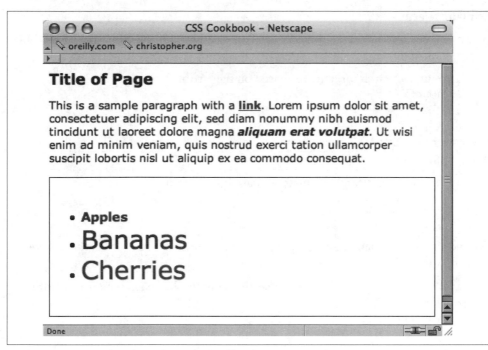

Figure 1-17. Adjacent sibling selectors only affect the ordered list because it appears after the unordered list

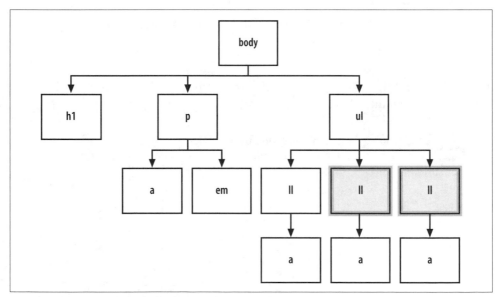

Figure 1-18. Showing which elements are being styled

Attribute selectors

Attribute selectors have four ways to find an element that has a matching attribute. Take a look at examples of each option:

[attribute] - Search for matches based on the attribute.

```
a[href] {
  text-decoration: none;
}
```

Whenever href attribute appears within an a element in the HTML, the link won't have an underline.

[attribute=val] - Search for matches based on the value.

```
a[href="csscookbook.com"] {
  text-decoration: none;
}
```

Whenever a link that points to csscookbook.com appears in the HTML, the link won't have an underline.

[attribute~=val] - Search for matches that contain the space-separated attribute somewhere in the value.

```
a[title~="digital"] {
  text-decoration: none;
}
```

Whenever "digital" appears in the title attribute of an anchor element, the link won't have an underline.

[attribute|=val] - Search for matches that contain the attribute with a hyphen.

```
a[href|="digital"] {
  text-decoration: none;
}
```

Also, whenever "digital-" appears in the href attribute of an anchor element, the link won't have an underline.

Note that attribute selectors are not widely supported in modern browsers, most notably Internet Explorer 6 for Windows. Attribute selectors are supported in Mozilla, Firefox Opera 5+, and Safari.

Pseudo-classes

You may want to add style to items that aren't based on elements' name, attributes, or content. This example of pseudo-classes creates rollover effects:

```
a:link {
 color: blue;
}
a:visited {
 color: purple;
}
a:hover {
 color: red;
}
a:active {
 color: gray;
}
```

In this setup, a basic link appears in blue. As soon as the mouse pointer hovers over the link, it changes to red. During the clicking of the link, the link appears gray. When returning to the page with the link after visiting, the link appears purple.

Three other pseudo-classes include :first-child, :focus, and :lang(n).

Pseudo-elements

With most selectors, a developer makes use of elements and their arrangement within a web document to style a document. However, sometimes a developer can style an item within a web document that's not marked up by elements through the use of pseudo-elements. Pseudo-elements consist of :first-letter, :first-line, :before, and :after.

You can see an example of the following pseudo-element in :first-letter in Figure 1-19:

```
p:first-letter {
 font-size: 200%;
 font-weight: bold;
}
```

Or you can use :first-line (see Figure 1-20) to style the entire first line. If the first line isn't a complete sentence or includes the start of a second sentence, :first-line still only impacts the first line.

```
p:first-line {
 font-size: 200%;
 font-weight: bold;
}
```

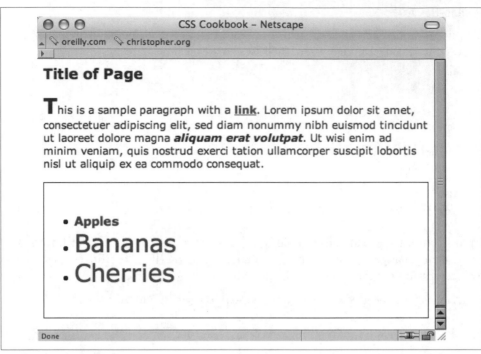

Figure 1-19. The first letter is styled

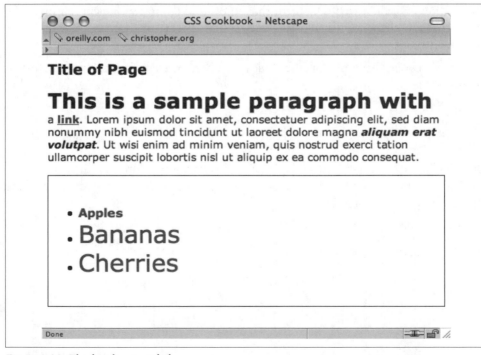

Figure 1-20. The first line is styled

See Also

The CSS 2.1 specification for selectors at *http://www.w3.org/TR/CSS21/selector.html*; Selectutorial, a tutorial of CSS selectors (*http://css.maxdesign.com.au/selectutorial/*); westciv browser selector support (*http://westciv.com/style_master/academy/browser_support/selectors.html*) shows the browsers that do and do not support specific selectors; and Appendix C for a listing of selectors.

1.3 Determining When to Use Class and ID Selectors

Problem

You want to determine the best use for class and ID selectors.

Solution

Use `class` selectors when you need to apply a style multiple times within a document and ID selectors for one-time only appearances of a style within a document.

In the following style sheet, #banner, #sub_banner, #nav1, #nav2, #footer, and #content are ID selectors and .title and .content are class selectors.

```
body {
  margin: 0;
  font-family: Verdana, Arial, Helvetica, sans-serif;
  font-size: .75em;
  padding: 0;
}
#banner {
  margin-top: 0;
  margin-bottom: 0;
  background-color: #900;
  border-bottom: solid 1px #000;
  padding: 5px 5px 5px 10px;
  line-height: 75%;
  color: #fff;
}
#sub_banner {
  background-color: #ccc;
  border-bottom: solid 1px #999;
  font-size: .8em;
  font-style: italic;
  padding: 3px 0 3px 10px;
}
#content {
  position: absolute;
  margin-left: 18%;
  width: 40%;
  top: 100px;
  padding: 5px;
}
```

```
#nav1 {
 position: absolute;
 width: 30%;
 left: 60%;
 top: 100px;
 padding: 5px;
}
#nav2 {
 position: absolute;
 padding: 5px 5px 5px 10px;
 top: 100px;
 width: 15%;
}
#footer {
 text-align: center;
 padding-top: 7em;
}
.warning {
 font-weight: bold;
 color: red;
}
.title {
 font-size: 120%;
}
.content {
 font-family: Verdana, Arial, sans-serif;
 margin-left: 20px;
 margin-right: 20px;
}
.footer {
 font-size: 75%;
}
```

Apply the ID and class selectors into the HTML code:

```
<!DOCTYPE html PUBLIC "-//W3C//DTD XHTML 1.0 Transitional//EN"
"http://www.w3.org/TR/xhtml1/DTD/xhtml1-transitional.dtd">
<html>
 <head>
  <title>CSS Cookbook</title>
  <link href="1-2.css" rel="stylesheet" type="text/css" />
 </head>
 <body>
 <div id="header">
  <h1>CSS Collection</h1>
  <h2>Showcase of CSS Web Sites</h2>
 </div>
 <div id="content">
  <h3>Content Page Title</h3>
  <p class="title">Content Item Title</p>
  <p class="content">Content goes here.</p>
 </div>
 <div id="navigation">
  <h3>List Stuff</h3>
```

```
    <a href="http://csscookbook.com/">Submit a site</a><br />
    <a href="http://csscookbook.com/">CSS resources</a><br />
    <a href="http://csscookbook.com/">RSS</a><br />
    <h3>CSS Cookbook Stuff</h3>
    <a href="http://csscookbook.com/">Home</a><br />
    <a href="http://csscookbook.com/">About</a><br />
    <a href="http://csscookbook.com/">Blog</a><br />
    <a href="http://csscookbook.com/">Services</a><br />
  </div>
  <div id="blipverts">
   <h3>Ads go here.</h3>
  </div>
  <div id="siteinfo">
    <p class="footer">Copyright 2006</p>
  </div>
 </body>
 </html>
```

Discussion

The ID selectors identify unique attributes that have one instance in the document tree, whereas class selectors can be used frequently throughout the web page. Remember that ID selectors use a hash, "#", while class selectors begin with a period, ".".

Typically, web developers will use ID selectors to mark off unique sections of a web page. In the previously shown solution, notice that the page is divided into the following sections:

- header
- content
- navigation
- blipverts
- siteinfo

By assigning these sections their own ID selector, designers are able to apply customized styles to those areas of the page, while keeping those same styles away from the other sections. This is accomplished through the combination of descendent selectors with ID selectors.

In the following example, the different h3 elements get different CSS rules:

```
#content h3 {
 font-size: 2em;
 font-weight: bold;
}
#navigation h3 {
 font-size: 0.8em;
 font-wieght: normal;
 text-decoration: underline;
}
```

See Also

The CSS 2.1 specification for ID selectors at *http://www.w3.org/TR/CSS21/selector. html#id-selectors*; the CSS 2.1 specification for class selector at *http://www.w3.org/TR/ CSS21/selector.html#class-html*.

1.4   Understanding CSS Properties

Problem

You want to learn more about CSS properties.

Solution

Recipes in this chapter cooked up popular properties such as `color`, `font-family`, `font-size`, and `text-decoration`. Properties fall between the brackets and their values immediately follow as shown here in a generic example:

```
selector {
 property: value;
}
```

A real-world example might look like the following:

```
li {
 list-style-type: square;
}
```

Any time `li` appears in the document, the bullet appears as a square rather than a traditional bullet.

Discussion

Selectors identify what should be styled within a web document, while properties and selectors identify the what and how that portion of the web document should be modified.

For example, the `color` property means the element's color will change, but not what color. That's the job for value. Table 1-2 showcases a few more properties, values, and what they do.

Table 1-2. A short listing of CSS properties

Property	Value	Result
font-weight	bold	Adds bold to text
border-color	Color name or color hexadecimal HTML value (e.g., #000000 for black and #ffffff for white)	Adds color to border

Table 1-2. A short listing of CSS properties (continued)

Property	Value	Result
border-style	solid	Adds solid line
	dotted	Adds dotted line
	dashed	Adds dashed line
	double	Adds two lines
text-align	left	Aligns text to the left
	center	Aligns text in the center
	right	Aligns text to the right
	justify	Fully expands text from left to right

For a more complete rundown of available CSS properties, see Appendix B.

See Also

W3C full property table at *http://www.w3.org/TR/CSS21/propidx.html*; HTML Dog CSS Properties at *http://www.htmldog.com/reference/cssproperties/*; a detailed look at the border property in Recipe 4.4; a complete listing of CSS properties in Appendix B.

1.5 Understanding the Box Model

Problem

You want to better understand the box model and how margins, borders, and padding work around content.

Solution

Every block level element, like a p or div element, contains a top, right, bottom, and left edge. These sides of block elements are composed of three layers surrounding the content. So, therefore each block element contains four sections:

content
> Actual content such as text, images, Java applets, and other objects. The content area is in the middle of the box.

padding
> Surrounds the content area.

border
> Next outer layer that surrounds padding and makes up the box border.

margin
> Transparent box that begins at the edge of the border and expands beyond.

The default margin value is 0, which lines up with the edge of the border. A border with a value of 0 lines up with the padding edge.

Obviously, a padding value of 0 lines flush against the content. Values above 0 expand the boxes. Take a look at Figure 1-21 to see views of a box model.

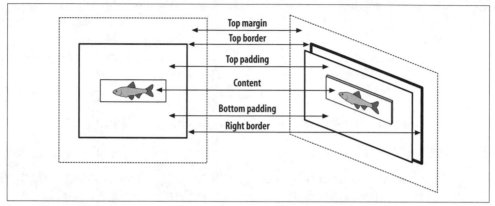

Top margin
Top border
Top padding
Content
Bottom padding
Right border

Figure 1-21. Box model viewed straight on and off to the side

Discussion

For a mental image of the box model, picture a cardboard box on the floor. Looking down at the box and you see its four sides: top, right, bottom, and left. The box can be big or small as you can modify the height and width properties.

```
div {
  height: 150px;
  width: 150px;
}
```

Add as many books as you want into the box until you fill the space with the contents that you see in Figure 1-22:

```
<div>
 <li>Moby Dick</li>
 <li>The Red Badge of Courage</li>
 <li>The Catcher in the Rye</li>
</div>
```

To help see the edges of the box, I'll place a thin border around the box (see Figure 1-23):

```
div {
  border: thin solid #000000;
  height: 150px;
  width: 150px;
}
```

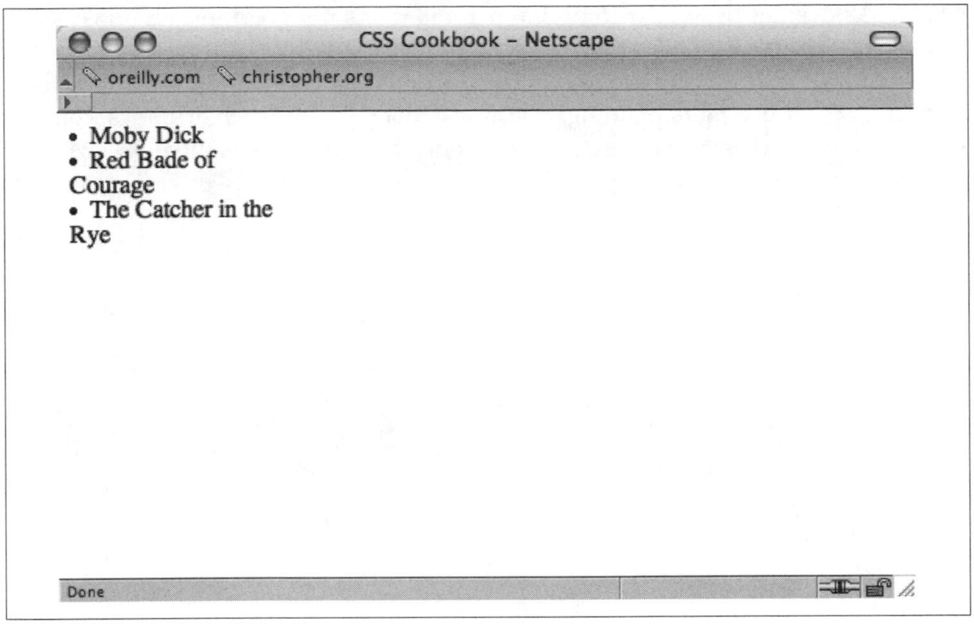

Figure 1-22. Content placed within a block level element

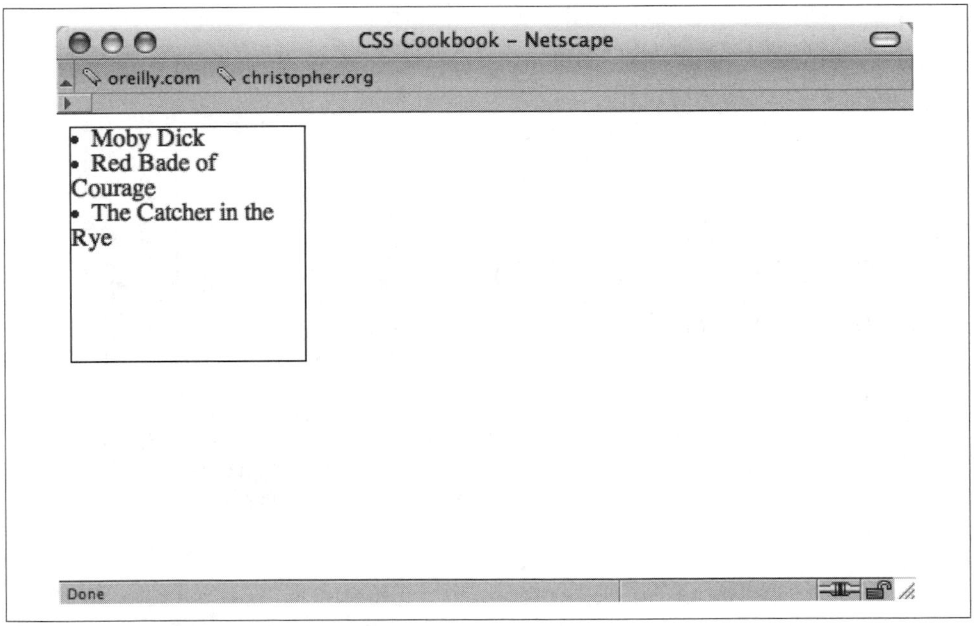

Figure 1-23. A border is placed around the content

The books overlap or sit next to each other and that's not good for the books especially since, in this example, they're collector's items. So, I'll add *padding* between the books and the box with the `padding` property for a little breathing room and protection. As you use more padding, you also reduce the number of books you can place into the box. Some padding has been added to the example in Figure 1-24:

```
div {
  border: thin solid #000000;
  height: 150px;
  width: 150px;
  padding: 10px;
}
```

Figure 1-24. *Padding is added*

Adding padding changes the overall box size, despite being set to width and height of 150 pixels. With the addition of the padding on all sides of the box, the new width is 170 pixels (padding of 10 pixels is placed on both the right and left sides). Also the height is now 170 pixels, too.

You need another box to fit the contents that didn't fit in the first box. So create another box, and enter the rest of the books or contents. Put the new box next to the original (see Figure 1-25):

```
<div>
<li>Moby Dick</li>
<li>The Red Badge of Courage<li>
```

```
<li>The Catcher in the Rye</li>
</div>
<div>
<li>The Red Queen</li>
<li>The Awakening</li>
<li>The Scarlet Letter</li>
</div>
```

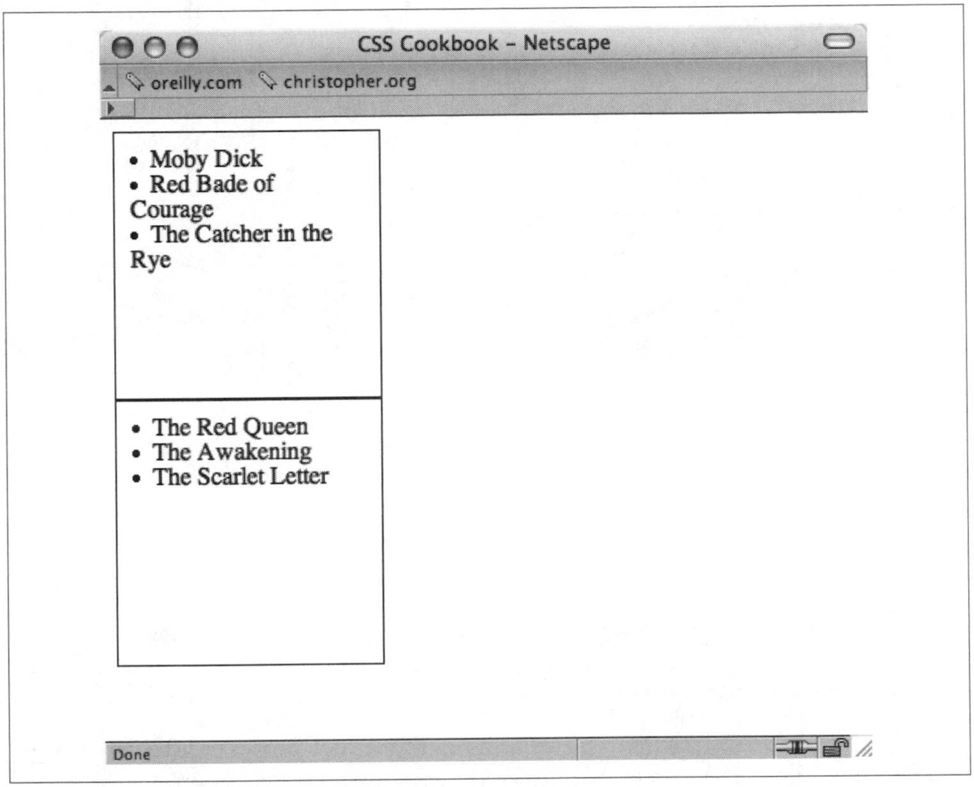

Figure 1-25. An additional listing of books is added

However, you want to space out the boxes so that they aren't on top of each other. So, modify the space between the boxes by using the margin property (see Figure 1-26):

```
div {
  border: thin solid #000000;
  height: 150px;
  width: 150px;
  padding: 10px;
  margin: 25px;
}
```

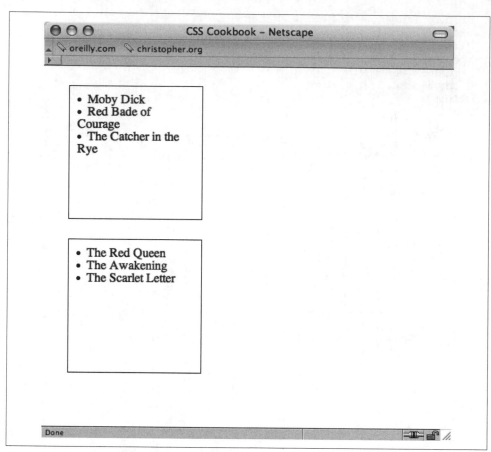

Figure 1-26. Adding margins to the block level elements

To help you distinguish the two boxes, modify the `border` property. Like the margin and padding, the border can be as thick or thin as you want (see Figure 1-27):

```
div {
  border: 5px double #000000;
  height: 150px;
  width: 150px;
  padding: 10px;
  margin: 25px;
}
```

At this point, you've modified the box model fairly consistently across two elements. You've adjusted the margin, padding, and borders around each side. However, you can also modify specific edges of the box model.

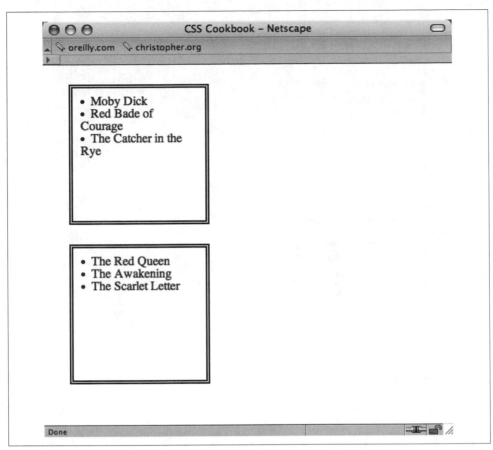

Figure 1-27. Border increased to five pixels

For example, if you want to adjust the right side of the div element (see Figure 1-28), but keep the same values for the other sides, the code could look something like the following:

```
div {
  border: 5px solid #000000;
  height: 150px;
  width: 150px;
  padding: 10px;
  margin: 0px;
  border-right: 1px solid #000000;
  padding-right: 1px;
  margin-right: 1px;
}
```

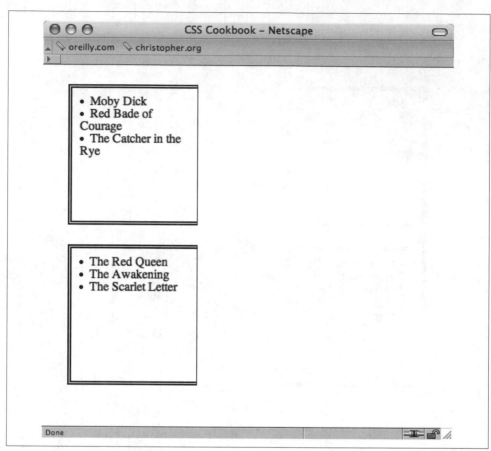

Figure 1-28. Adjustments to the right side of the box

You could also modify the other sides of the edges specifically as well. For example, using the margin property, the code might look like the following:

```
div {
  margin-top: 1px;
  margin-right: 1px;
  margin-bottom: 1px;
  margin-left: 1px;
}
```

By adjusting the sides and different properties of the box model, developers are able to better format the presentation of their web pages.

 Microsoft instituted its own box model in their browser, Internet Explorer for Windows. For more information about that box model and how to work around it, see Recipe 11.2.

See Also

The CSS 2.1 box model *http://www.w3.org/TR/CSS21/box.html*; the Brain Jar box model at `http://www.brainjar.com/css/positioning/default.asp`; and the interactive CSS Box Model at *http://www.redmelon.net/tstme/box_model/*.

1.6   Understanding DOCTYPES and Effects on Browser Layout

Problem

You want to make your web page standard-compliant and valid.

Solution

HTML 4.01 has three document types: strict, transitional, and frameset. XHTML 1.1 has one document type, but XHTML 1.0 has three document types, like HTML 4.01. Only one document type definition (DTD) appears in the HTML document, using any one of the following:

HTML 4.01 Strict DTD:
```
<!DOCTYPE HTML PUBLIC "-//W3C//DTD HTML 4.01//EN"
"http://www.w3.org/TR/html4/strict.dtd">
```
HTML 4.01 Transitional DTD:
```
<!DOCTYPE HTML PUBLIC "-//W3C//DTD HTML 4.01 Transitional//EN"
"http://www.w3.org/TR/1999/REC-html401-19991224/loose.dtd">
```
HTML 4.01 Frameset DTD:
```
<!DOCTYPE HTML PUBLIC "-//W3C//DTD HTML 4.01 Frameset//EN"
" http://www.w3.org/TR/1999/REC-html401-19991224/frameset.dtd">
```
XHTML 1.0 Strict DTD:
```
<!DOCTYPE html PUBLIC "-//W3C//DTD XHTML 1.0 Strict//EN"
"http://www.w3.org/TR/xhtml1/DTD/xhtml1-strict.dtd">
```
XHTML 1.0 Transitional DTD:
```
<!DOCTYPE html PUBLIC "-//W3C//DTD XHTML 1.0 Transitional//EN"
"http://www.w3.org/TR/xhtml1/DTD/xhtml1-transitional.dtd">
```
XHTML 1.0 Frameset DTD:
```
<!DOCTYPE html PUBLIC "-//W3C//DTD XHTML 1.0 Frameset//EN"
"http://www.w3.org/TR/xhtml1/DTD/xhtml1-frameset.dtd">
```
XHTML 1.1 DTD:
```
<!DOCTYPE html PUBLIC "-//W3C//DTD XHTML 1.1//EN"
"http://www.w3.org/TR/xhtml11/DTD/xhtml11.dtd">
```

Here's a basic page with the XHTML 1.1 DTD and the required head, body, and html tags.

```
<!DOCTYPE html PUBLIC "-//W3C//DTD XHTML 1.1//EN"
"http://www.w3.org/TR/xhtml11/DTD/xhtml11.dtd">
<html>
 <head>
  <title>XHTML DTD</title>
```

```
  </head>
  <body>
   <p>XHTML requires having a DTD in every document otherwise it won't pass muster
  with the validators.</p>
  </body>
  </html>
```

Discussion

DOCTYPE, short for DTD, defines an HTML or XHTML document's building blocks and tells the browsers and validators which version of HTML or XHTML your document is using.

The DOCTYPE declaration must appear at the beginning of every web page document before the html element to ensure your markup and CSS are standards compliant, and that browsers handle the pages based on the appropriate DTDs.

XHTML requires DOCTYPE, otherwise the pages won't validate and the browsers fall back on *quirks* mode, treating the pages as if they were written in invalid markup and therefore need to be improperly rendered in modern browsers even if the code may be perfect XHTML and CSS.

The W3C provides an HTML validator and a CSS validator so you can verify document validity. If there's no DOCTYPE, the validator chokes, as you see in Figure 1-29.

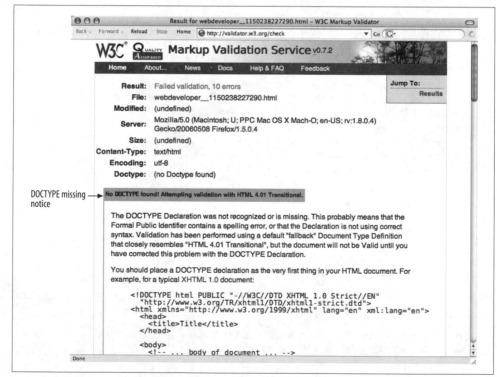

Figure 1-29. Screenshot of W3C's validator

A page without DOCTYPE, an older DOCTYPE, or an incorrectly coded DOCTYPE renders in *quirks* mode, in which a browser treats the page as buggy. In some cases, depending on the browser, some content will render according to W3C guidelines.

Figures 1-30 and 1-31 show how a web document with the same markup, a table contained within a div with a width of 100% goes into quirks mode in Internet Explorer 6.0 and how the page should look in standards mode.

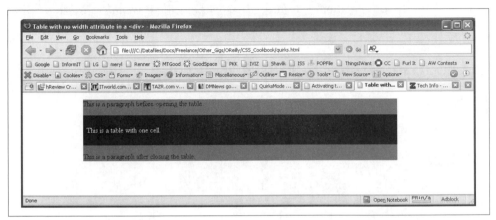

Figure 1-30. Table width in Internet Explorer 6.0 in quirks mode with no DOCTYPE included

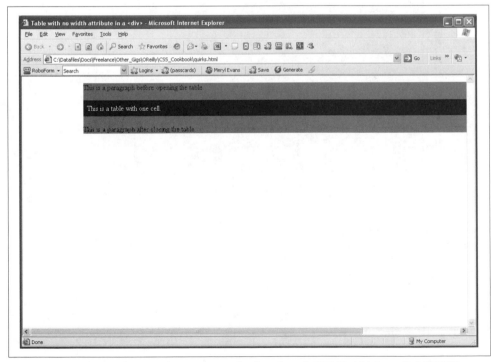

Figure 1-31. Table width in Firefox 1.5 in standard mode with HTML 4.01 Strict DOCTYPE

See Also

The HTML 4.01 specification for DTD at *http://www.w3.org/TR/html401/intro/ sgmltut.html#h-3.3*; W3C validators at *http://www.w3.org/QA/Tools/#validators*; "A List Apart" article on DOCYTPES at *http://www.alistapart.com/stories/doctype/*; "QuirksMode" article at *http://www.quirksmode.org/index.html?/css/quirksmode.html*; Mozilla's quirks Mode information explains the differences between the modes and how it handles quirks mode at *http://developer.mozilla.org/en/docs/Mozilla%27s_ Quirks_Mode*; Opera's DOCTYPE page at *http://www.opera.com/docs/specs/doctype/*.

1.7   Associating Styles to a Web Page

Problem

You want to know about the different ways of adding styles to a web page.

Solution

You can apply styles in three ways: *external*, *internal*, and *inline*. An internal style sheet appears near the top of the HTML document within the head.

```
<style>
<!--
#header {
 width: 100%;
 height: 100px;
 font-size: 150%
}
#content {
 font-family: verdana, arial, sans-serif;
 margin-left: 20px;
 margin-right: 20px
}
.title {
 font-size: 120%
}
-->
</style>
```

Note the use of HTML comments immediately after the style element. Comments are placed there to hide the CSS content and keep it from showing up in the web page layout or from being rendered by the browser in some unwanted fashion.

External style sheets are stored in a separate file, which become associated with the HTML file through linking. The following code is saved in its own file:

```
/* CSS Document */
h1 {
  font-size: 150%;
}
h2 {
  font-size: 120%;
}
p {
  font-family: Verdana, Arial, Helvetica, sans-serif;
}
```

 Notice that the style element is not present in the external style sheet. Also, HTML comments are not used in external style sheets.

In the web page, add the following line between the head tags to link to the external style sheet that contains the above styles:

```
<link href="screen.css" rel="stylesheet" type="text/css" media="screen" />
```

Inline styles work similarly to font in that they appear with the markup they affect.

```
<h1 style="font-family: verdana, arial, sans-serif;
font-size: 150%; color: blue;">Page Title</h1>

<p style="font-family: sans-serif; font-size: 90%;">Hello, world!</p>
```

Discussion

The three different types of style sheets are:

External
> All web pages link to the external style sheet that contains nothing but CSS styles. If you want to change the font color on all pages linked to this style sheet, just update the external style sheet. Link to the style sheet with the link tag.

Internal
> A unique web page may have its own style sheet so styles only affect the page and not all web pages. Define internal styles within the style tags.

Inline
> Inline styles work similarly to font with the style information applied to a specific tag within a web page. Designers rarely apply inline styles.

External and inline style sheets save time spent over inline styles on maintaining web sites.

For example, you inherit a web page where all the text is blue and use font to control the size. You receive orders to make change the text to black, so you search for every instance of <p> to change it from blue to black like the following:

```
<p><font size="2" color="blue">Text goes here</font></p>
```

To change all p from blue to black in an external style sheet takes two steps. Open the CSS file and change the color.

```
p {
  color: blue;
}
```

In an internal style sheet, changing the text from blue to black takes one step. Search for the style at the top of the page and replace blue with black.

```
<style>
<!--
p {
  color: blue
}
-->
</style>
```

When to use inline styles

However, with inline styles, changing the color takes as much time as fixing the original file with font tag:

```
<p style="font-color: blue">Test goes here.</p>
```

Why would anyone want to use inline styles considering it's time-consuming to make changes? It's rare, but you may have content that appears once in the whole web site that is in need of a special style. Rather than cluttering the external style sheet with the style for one item, you use inline styles instead.

When to use internal style sheets

As for internal and external style sheets, most sites use external style sheets. However, when starting to write CSS code for a web page design, it's best to start out with an inline style sheet. When you reach the point where the design is complete or starts to get a little unwieldy, move the style sheet to a separate file. Then make edits to the external style sheet as needed.

Also, you may have a special page that's not related to the web site or uses a special style. In this case, an internal style sheet could be easier to use as opposed to adding more clutter to the external style sheet.

See Also

The Style Sheets section in HTML 4.01 specification at *http://www.w3.org/TR/html401/present/styles.html*; W3Schools' "CSS How to Insert a Style Sheet" at *http://www.w3schools.com/css/css_howto.asp*.

1.8   How to Use Different Types of Style Sheets

Problem

You want to provide style sheets for different media types such as aural, print, and handheld.

Solution

Create separate external style sheets for the different media and name them by their media such as *print.css*, *screen.css*, and *handheld.css*. Then use the link element with the media type in the web page to link to these styles. Another option is to use the @media rule.

Here's *print.css*:

```
body {
  font: 10pt times, georgia, serif;
  line-height: 120%
}
```

A new file called *screen.css*:

```
body {
  font: 12pt verdana, arial, sans-serif;
  line-height: 120%
}
```

Then finally another file called *projection.css*:

```
body {
  font: 14pt;
  line-height: 120%
}
```

Then link to the three files from the web page with the following lines within the head section. Each link has a different media type:

```
<link rel="stylesheet" type="text/css" href="/css/print.css" media="print" />
<link rel="stylesheet" type="text/css" href="/css/screen.css" media="screen" />
<link rel="stylesheet" type="text/css" href="/css/projection.css" media="projection" />
```

You could use the @media rule instead to specific the different media rules within the same style sheet:

```
<style type="text/css">
<!--
@media print {
  body { font: 10pt times, georgia, serif }
}

@media screen {
  body { font: 12pt verdana, arial, sans-serif}
}
```

```
@media projection {
  body { font-size: 14pt }
}

@media screen, print, projection {
  body { line-height: 120% }
}
-->
</style>
```

Discussion

When creating the styles for printing, add them to *print.css* and then only these styles are applied during printing. This ensures the page prints without wasting space or ink from printing the images.

Only devices supporting the specific media type will see its related media CSS styles. The media style sheets don't affect the appearance of other media or the web page itself.

The @media rule allows you to put all the media in one style sheet.

Figure 1-32 shows how the web page looks in its original screen format. Users don't need to print the side items, so copy the *screen.css* style sheet and save it as a new one called *print.css*. Rather than starting from scratch, modify *screen.css* to optimize the web page for printing. The following items in *screen.css* have been changed in *print.css*.

```
#sub_banner {
  background-color: #ccc;
  border-bottom: solid 1px #999;
  font-size:.8em;
  font-style: italic;
  padding: 3px 0 3px 5px;
}
#nav1 {
  position: absolute;
  width: 30%;
  left: 60%;
  top: 100px;
  padding: 5px 5px px 5px 0;
}
#nav2 {
  position: absolute;
  width: 15%;
  left: 1%;
  top: 100px;
  padding: 5px 5px px 5px 0;
}
h1 {
  text-align: left;
  color: #fff;
  font-size: 1.2em;
```

```
  text-align: left;
  margin-bottom: 5px;
  margin-top: 5px;
}
.entry {
  padding-bottom: 20px;
  padding: 5px;
  border: solid 1px #999;
  background-color: #fcfcfc;
  margin-bottom: 25px;
}
```

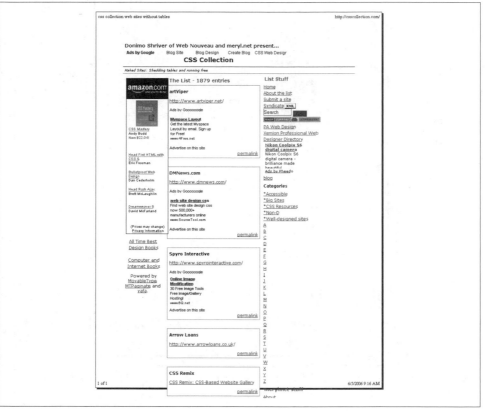

Figure 1-32. This is how the page would look if printed without print.css

Figure 1-33 shows how they now appear with *print.css*:

```
#sub_banner {
  display: none
}
#nav1 {
  display: none
}
#nav2 {
```

```
  display: none
}
h1 {
  display: none
}
.entry {
  padding: 5px;
}
```

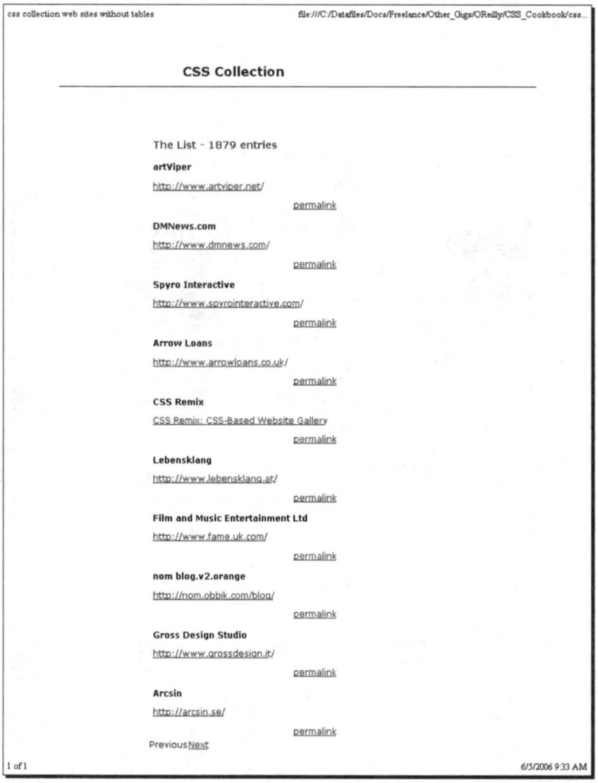

Figure 1-33. After creating print.css and adding a link to the style sheet, the web page is printer-friendly

This takes out the `sub-banner` with the tagline and hides the two navigation columns. The `h1` element wasn't necessary to have and removing it saved space at the top. The entries have a light gray box, a big waste of ink, so they've been simplified to show only the padding between entries.

Remember to add the `link` element in the HTML page:

```
<link rel="stylesheet" type="text/css" href="/css/print.css" media="print" />
<link rel="stylesheet" type="text/css" href="/css/screen.css" media="screen" />
```

That's all there is to it. CSS simplifies many things including design for different media. Table 1-3 lists the current media types that appear in the CSS 2.1 specification.

Table 1-3. Listing of media types

Media Type	Devices
all	Users for all devices
aural	Used for speech and sound synthesizers
braille	Used for Braille tactile feedback devices
embossed	Used for Braille printers
handheld	Used for handheld or small devices like PDAs and smartphones
print	Used for printers and print preview
projection	Used for projected presentations
screen	Used for color monitors
tty	Used for fixed-pitch character grid such as teletypes, terminals, and portable devices with limited characters
tv	Used for television and WebTV

See Also

Chapter 10 for setting up styles for printing; media types section in CSS 2.1 specification at *http://www.w3.org/TR/CSS21/media.html*; "ALA's New Print Styles" at *http://www.alistapart.com/articles/alaprintstyles*; and "Pocket-Sized Design: Taking Your Website to the Small Screen" at *http://www.alistapart.com/articles/pocket*.

1.9 Adding Comments Within CSS

Problem

You want to organize and keep track of the CSS with comments.

Solution

Add /* and */ anywhere in the styles to show the start and end of a comment.

```
/* This is a comment */
a {
 text-decoration: none;
}
/* This is also a comment */
h1, h2 {
 font-size: 100%;
 color: #666666;
}
```

Discussion

You may look at old code and not remember why you took certain steps with that code. Comments can explain and organize code to help with reviewing at a later time. Comments also help those who don't create the original code understand its purpose. Browsers ignore content that appears between the /* and */.

As you break up your code by section, comments come in handy in identifying each section such as header, footer, primary navigation, subnavigation, and so on. Comments provide a great way to test your web pages. If you're not sure about a style rule or how it affects the page, add a comment around the style to turn it off.

```
/*
a {
  text-decoration: none;
}
*/
```

The style rule for text-decoration won't take affect with the comments taking it out of circulation. Unless there are other styles for a, the underline appears under links until the comment is removed.

See Also

The CSS 2.1 specification on comments, online at *http://www.w3.org/TR/CSS21/ syndata.html#comments*.

1.10 Organizing the Contents of a Style Sheet

Problem

You want to know how effectively to organize contents within a style sheet for easier management.

Solution

Managing CSS can be accomplished by grouping common visual elements of a web page together. The following list shows a suggestion of the order of items grouped in a style sheet:

- Elements (h1–h6, p, a, list, links, images)
- Typography
- Page layout (header, content, navigation, global navigation, subnavigation, sidebar, footer)
- Form tags (form, fieldset, label, legend)
- Content (post, events, news)

Here are the comments from three style sheets with each organizing the CSS differently:

```
/* Typography & Colors
------------------------------------ */
[css code ]

/* Structure
------------------------------------ */
[css code ]

/* Headers
------------------------------------ */
[css code ]

/* Images
------------------------------------ */
[css code ]

/* Lists
------------------------------------ */
[css code ]

/* Form Elements
------------------------------------ */
[css code ]

/* Comments
------------------------------------ */
[css code ]

/* Sidebar
------------------------------------ */
[css code ]

/* Common Elements
------------------------------------ */
[css code ]
```

Discussion

What works for one person may not work for another. This setup from the solution is a recommendation based on a combination of experience and best practices that should work best for small- to medium-size web sites.

For different projects and your own personal preference, you may find a way that works better for you. Visit your favorite web sites and review their style sheets to study how they're organized.

See Also

Doug Bowman's "CSS Organization Tip 1: Flags," a method for finding rules in your CSS files, at *http://www.stopdesign.com/log/2005/05/03/css-tip-flags.html*; Recipe 1.11 on how to organize style sheet files; and Recipe 11.7 on how to set up an intelligent hacking system.

1.11   Organizing Style Sheet Files

Problem

You want to effectively manage and organize your CSS files.

Solution

Manage CSS files by placing them in their own directory. The following CSS files live in their own `css` directory.

```
/_assets/css/print.css
/_assets/css/screen.css
```

For a large or complex sites, rather than having one CSS file for each type (print, screen, and so on), break out CSS by function. These are in the same directory as the simple version.

```
/_assets/css/layout.css
/_assets/css/color-imagery.css
/_assets/css/type.css
```

Then, in the HTML file, link to these files by placing the following in the `head` element:

```
<link rel="stylesheet" type="text/css" media="print"
href="/_assets/css/print.css" />
<link rel="stylesheet" type="text/css" media="screen"
href="/_assets/css/screen.css" />
```

For the large sites, the `screen.css` would include methods for importing the separate CSS files that dictate the design for screen delivery. Here's what the `screen.css` would look like in this solution:

```
/* import style sheets */
@import url("/_assets/css/layout.css");
@import url("color-imagery.css");
@import url("type.css");
```

Discussion

If you are using external style sheets (Recipe 1.6) for smaller or easily managed sites, breaking out style sheets by media type (print, screen, and so on) does the job nicely.

Taking this approach with larger or more complex site can make it difficult to search the files to see how the CSS is set up.

Currently, there isn't a standard or recommended approach for managing CSS-related files. Like the previous recipe, you may discover another approach that works better for you. Experiment with file and content organization until you find one that works well.

See Also

See Recipe 1.7 for more information on external style sheets.

1.12 Working with Shorthand Properties

Problem

You want to use shorthand properties in style sheets.

Solution

Begin with a properly marked up section.

```
<h3>Shorthand Property</h3>
<p>Combine properties with shorthand and save time, typing, and a
few bytes. Your style sheets will also be easier to read.</p>
```

Then use just one instance of font property instead of three: font-style, font-size, and font-family:

```
h3 {
 font: italic 18pt verdana, arial, sans-serif;
}
p {
 border: 2pt solid black;
}
```

Discussion

Several CSS properties can be tossed in favor of shorthand properties.

The border property is a shorthand property, which combines three properties into one. The border property can cover the values from the following properties:

- border-color
- border-width
- border-style

The font property is a shorthand property, which combines three properties into one. The font property can cover the values from the following properties:

- font-style
- font-size/line-height
- font-family
- font-weight
- font-variant

Enter the values just as you would with any other property except for font-family and font-size/line height. With font-family, enter the fonts in the order you wish for them to have priority and use a comma between each.

If you use both font-size and line height, then separate their values with a forward slash:

```
h3 {
  font: italic 18pt/20pt verdana, arial, sans-serif
}
```

For a rundown on the shorthand properties available to web developers, see Table 1-4.

Table 1-4. Shorthand properties

Property	Values	Example
background	background-color background-image background-repeat background-attachment background-position	background: url(book.gif) #999 no-repeat top;
border border-left border-right border-top border-bottom	border-width border-style border-color	border: thin solid #000;
font	font-style font-variant font-weight font-size/line-height font-family caption icon menu message-box small-caption status-bar	font: 14px italic Verdana, Arial, sans-serif;
list-style	list-style-type list-style-position list-style-image	list-style: circle inside;

Table 1-4. Shorthand properties (continued)

Property	Values	Example
margin	margin-top margin-right margin-bottom margin-left	margin: 5px 0px 5px 10px; margin: 5px;
padding	padding-top padding-right padding-bottom padding-left	padding: 5px 10%;

See Also

The CSS 2.1 specification for border shorthand properties at *http://www.w3.org/TR/CSS21/box.html#border-shorthand-properties* and font shorthand properties at *http://www.w3.org/TR/CSS21/about.html#shorthand*; and see Appendix B for a full listing of CSS properties.

1.13   Setting up an Alternate Style Sheet

Problem

You want to provide other style options for users who may want larger text or a different color scheme.

Solution

Use the link element with a title and link it to the alternate style sheets. The title lets the user see what options are available when viewing the list of available styles. In Firefox, click View → Page Styles to see the list.

```
<link href="default.css" rel="stylesheet" title="default styles"
type="text/css" media="screen" />
<link href="green.css" rel="stylesheet" title="green style"
type="text/css" media="screen" />
<link href="blue.css" rel="stylesheet" title="blue style"
type="text/css" media="screen" />
```

Unfortunately, this solution doesn't work in Internet Explorer 6.0 or Safari.

Discussion

Alternate style sheets work similarly to the media type style sheets in Recipe 1.7. Instead of creating styles for media, you're providing users with multiple choices of styles for the screen. Furthermore, this technique doesn't require using JavaScript. Some users have disabled JavaScript, which would affect a style sheet switcher.

All you have to do is make a copy of your default style sheet and rename it. Make the changes to the style sheet and add the link element with a title (see Figure 1-34).

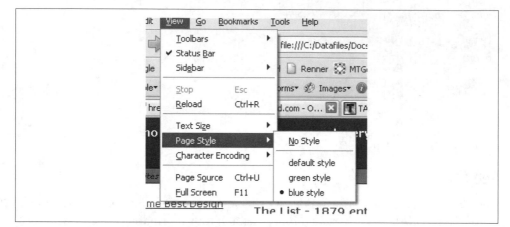

Figure 1-34. Switching style sheets within the browser options

See Also

The article "Invasion of the Body Switchers" by Andy Clarke and James Edwards shows how to create a JavaScript style switcher at *http://www.alistapart.com/articles/bodyswitchers*; and Amit Ghaste's CSS Style Switcher tutorial at *http://ghaste.com/pubs/styleswitcher.html*.

1.14   Using Floats with Images

Problem

You want to place an image on the left or the right side with text wrapping around the image instead of appearing above or below the image (see Figure 1-35).

Solution

First create class selectors for the images:

```
.leftFloat {
 float: left
}
.rightFloat {
 float: right
}
```

Then add the class selector to the markup and see how it works in Figure 1-36:

```
<img src="csscookbook.gif" class="leftFloat" alt="cover" />
<p>This is the book cover for the <em>CSS Cookbook</em>.</p>
<img src="csscookbook.gif" class="rightFloat" alt="cover" />
<p>This is the book cover for the <em>CSS Cookbook</em>.</p>
```

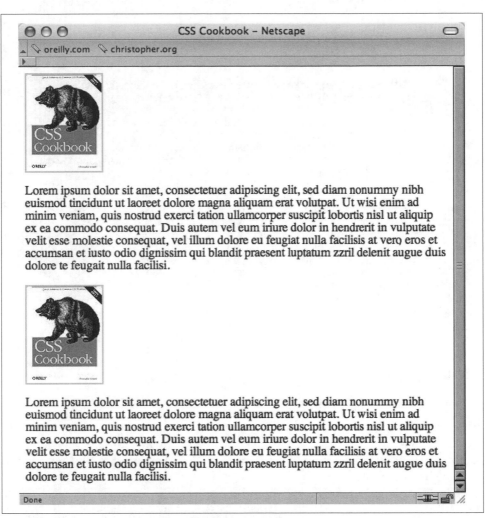

Figure 1-35. Images do not wrap around the text by default

Discussion

In the times before there were any compliant standards, designers used the `align` attribute with the `img` element to move images to the side with text wrapping. W3C deprecated `align` and now recommends using `float` instead.

Floats can be used with elements other than images to shift an item left or right within its current place. In Figure 1-36, the second image overlaps with the paragraph referencing the first image. This looks confusing and needs to be fixed. To work around that, use `clear`:

```
p {
  clear: left;
}
```

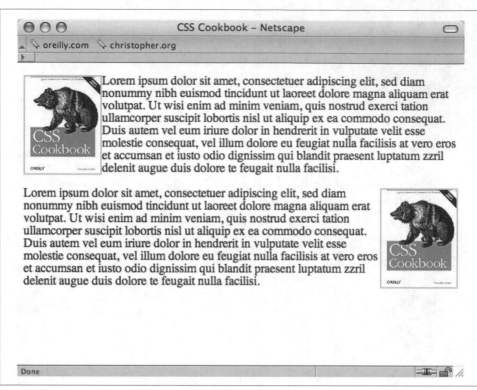

Figure 1-36. With float, the text wraps around the images

The clear property tells the paragraph to appear after the end of the image flow. At the second img, the clear properties push the image down to the first line after the previous ends. Instead of lining up with the second p element, the image waits for a new line before showing up.

See Also

W3C 2.1 specification on floats at *http://www.w3.org/TR/CSS21/visuren.html#floats*; Chapter 9 provides three recipes on using float with page columns; and Eric Meyer's CSS/edge covers floats at *http://meyerweb.com/eric/css/edge/*.

1.15   Using Absolute Positioning

Problem

You want to position an element based on the window rather than on the element's default position.

Solution

Use the `position` property with the `absolute` value in the style sheet. Also use `bottom`, `left`, or both properties to indicate where to position an element:

```
.absolute {
  position: absolute;
  bottom: 50px;
  left: 100px;
}
```

Discussion

Designing with `absolute` places the content *out of the natural flow of the page layout* and puts it exactly where the CSS properties tell it to go within the current box or window. The sample code used in the solution tells the browser to position the element with the `absolute` class exactly 40 pixels down from the top and 20 pixels over from the left edge of the window.

Look at the natural flow of an image and a paragraph in Figure 1-37.

Next, apply the absolute positioning to the div that encompasses the content by adding the `class` attribute and the `absolute` value and take a look at Figure 1-38:

```
<div class="absolute">
 <img src="csscookbook.gif" alt="cover" />
<p>Lorem ipsum dolor sit amet, consectetuer adipiscing elit,
sed diam nonummy nibh euismod tincidunt ut laoreet dolore
magna aliquam erat volutpat...
 </p>
</div>
```

You can also use `right` and `bottom` properties for changing the absolute position. Bottom represents the bottom of the window not matter how big or small you make the window. Beware that right and bottom aren't supported in Internet Explorer 5 and Netscape 6.0.

Figure 1-37. Default rendering of the content

Absolute positioning of elements was used to shift a block of content around to demonstrate how it works. However, the practice needs to be used with care because absolutely positioned elements will remain in place even as flexible web page layouts change due to flexible browsers and/or text resizing.

Figure 1-38. Absolute positioning places an element based on its location within a window

See Also

Recipe 9.8 for a discussion about using absolute positioning for creating a layout; W3C 2.1 specification on absolute positioning at *http://www.w3.org/TR/CSS21/ visuren.html#absolute-positioning*; and W3Schools tutorial on positioning at *http:// www.w3schools.com/css/css_positioning.asp*.

1.16   Using Relative Positioning

Problem

You want to place content based on its position in the document. In other words, the element's position is modified relative to its natural position as rendered by the browser.

Solution

Use the position property with the relative value in the style sheet. Also add top, left or both properties to indicate where to position an element.

Using the following CSS rule on the image, the image was able to move over the paragraph content in Figure 1-39:

```
.relative {
 position: relative;
 top: 100px;
 left: 20px;
}
```

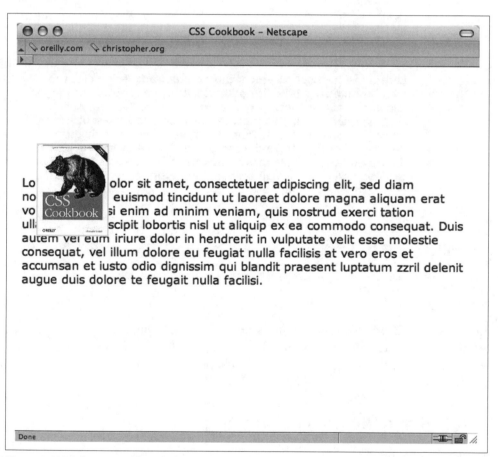

Figure 1-39. Relative positioning places an element based on its location within the document's natural flow

Discussion

Unlike absolute positioning, the sample code doesn't start at the top and left edges of the window. Instead, it begins where p elements would be if left alone. The code tells the browser to position the paragraph 100 pixels down from the top and 20 pixels over from the left edge of the original paragraph's position instead of from the edge of the window. With absolute, the content is placed exactly where the properties tell it to go from the edges in the current box.

See Also

W3C 2.1 specification on relative positioning at *http://www.w3.org/TR/CSS21/visuren.html#relative-positioning* and W3Schools tutorial on positioning at *http://www.w3schools.com/css/css_positioning.asp*.

1.17   Using CSS in Adobe Dreamweaver

Problem

You use Dreamweaver for creating and editing web pages and want to use its CSS features.

Solution

Use the CSS Styles Panel to create, edit, delete, and view CSS styles (see Figures 1-40 and 1-41). You have several ways to work with styles sheets. While editing an HTML page, you can attach an external style sheet through the CSS Styles panel or start a new CSS document (click File → New and then choose Basic page and CSS).

Another option is to use the Code or Split view and enter the CSS directly into the code for inline and internal style sheets.

1. To attach an external style sheet to any web page in Dreamweaver, click the Attach icon on the CSS Styles Panel (see Figure 1-42).
2. Click File → New and choose Basic page and CSS to start a blank CSS document.
3. Edit the web page like a word document, Dreamweaver automatically adds internal styles.
4. Enter styles in Code view.

You can view CSS properties by categories, such as font, background, and border. You can switch to List view, an alphabetical list of properties.

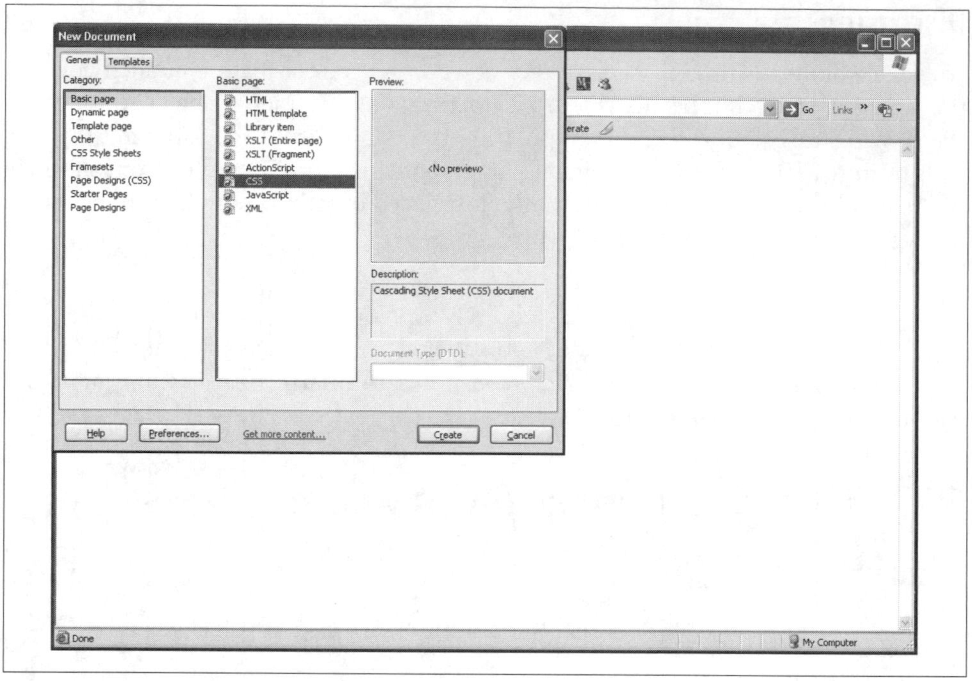

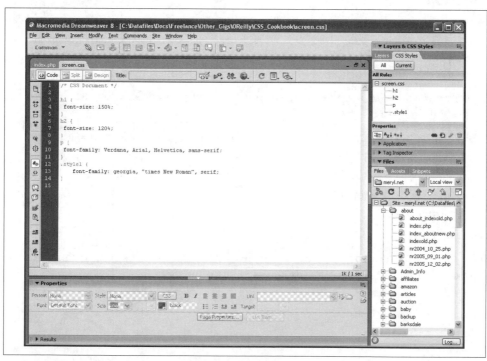

Figure 1-40. Start a new CSS file in Dreamweaver

Figure 1-41. Enter and edit styles in Dreamweaver's CSS document

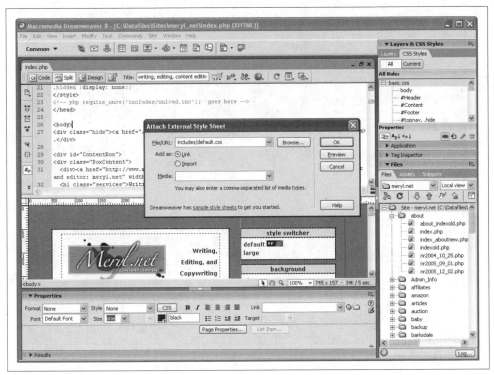

Figure 1-42. Use Dreamweaver's CSS Panel to attach an external style sheet

Discussion

If you add styles to content within an HTML page in Dreamweaver, using Properties, the application automatically adds inline CSS (see Figure 1-43). As you select
fonts and color to selected text, Dreamweaver creates an internal style sheet rather
than use font element. In older versions of Dreamweaver, the code would look like
the following:

```
<font face="georgia, times new roman, serif" color="#ff0000"
size="2">This is text.</font>
```

You can review the style sheet generated by Dreamweaver (see Figure 1-44).

See Also

Adobe's Best Practices of CSS selectors *http://www.adobe.com/products/dreamweaver/
bestpractices/css/* and Dreamweaver home at *http://www.adobe.com/products/
dreamweaver/*.

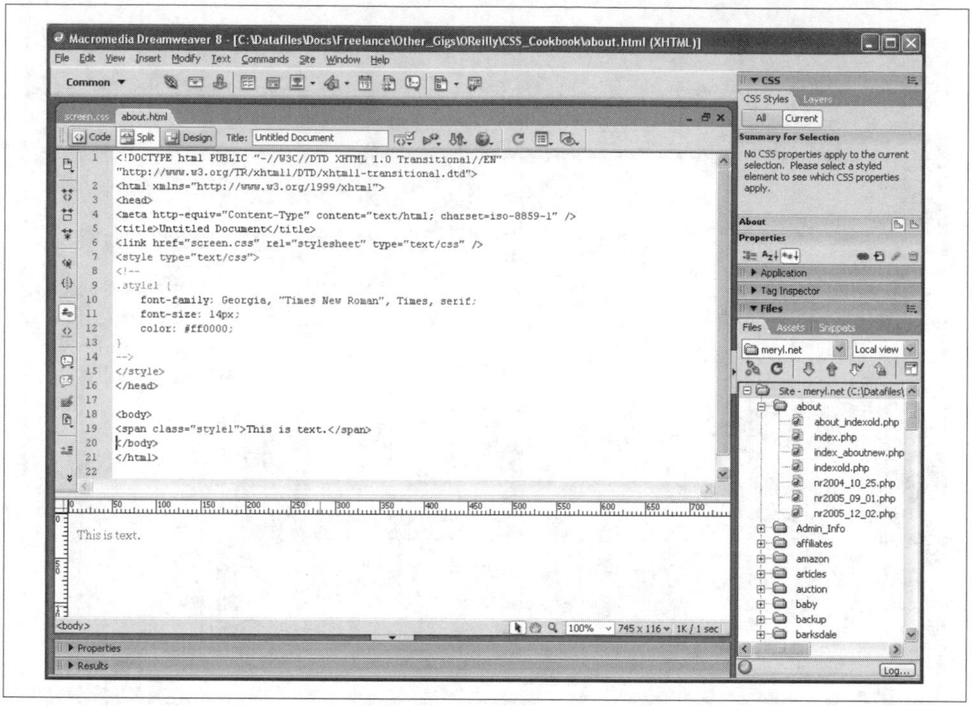

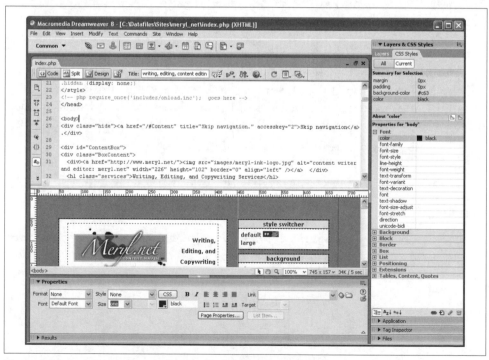

Figure 1-43. Dreamweaver automatically creates new styles when assigning font and colors to text

Figure 1-44. Review the current document's styles in the CSS panel

1.18 Using CSS in Microsoft Expression Web Designer

Problem

You use Microsoft Expression Web Designer to design web pages and want to take advantage of its CSS features.

Solution

Like Dreamweaver, Microsoft Expression Web Designer allows you to attach an external style sheet, create a new one from scratch, and add styles within the HTML page as you can see in Figures 1-45 through 1-47. Here are a few ways to add CSS:

- To attach an external style sheet to any web page in Microsoft Web Expression, click Attach Style Sheet in the Apply Styles task pane.

- Click the New Document icon, and then click CSS to start a new CSS document with a blank page.

- Edit the web page like a Word document; Expression Web Designer automatically adds internal styles.

- Enter styles in the Code view.

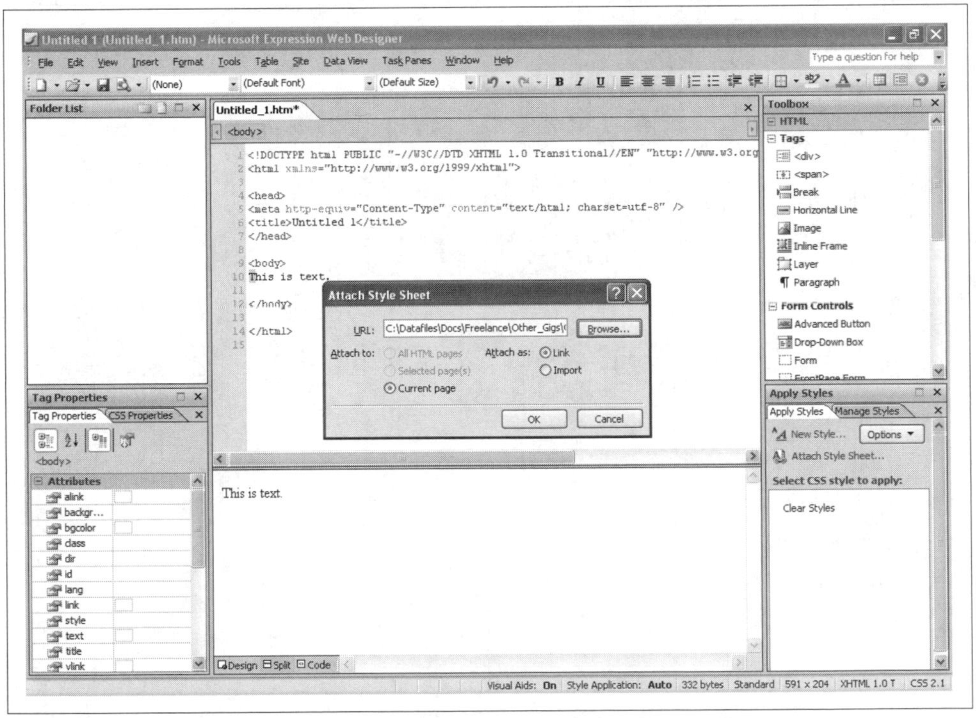

Figure 1-45. Use Microsoft Expression Web Designer Apply Styles task pane to attach an external style sheet

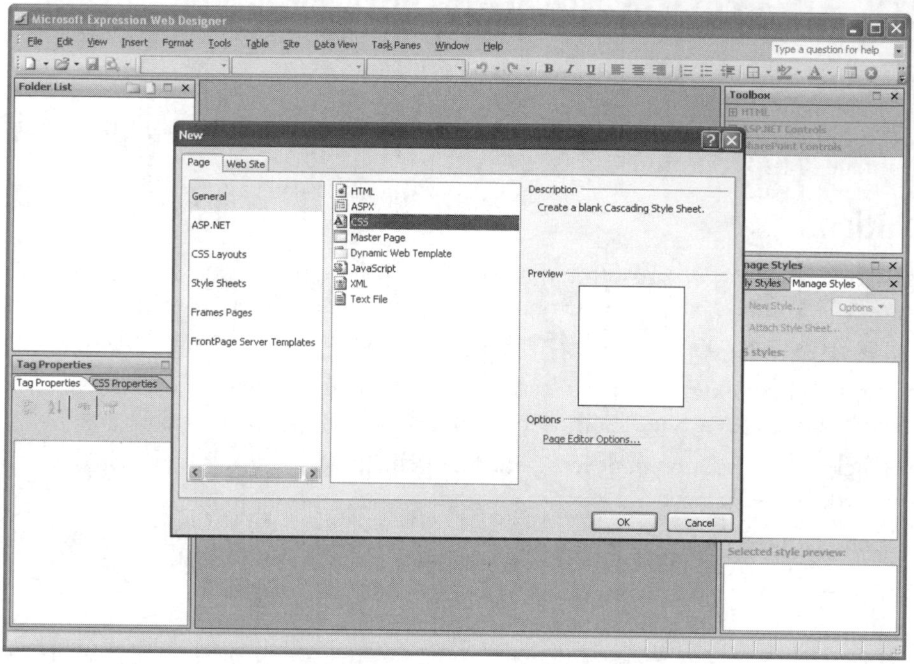

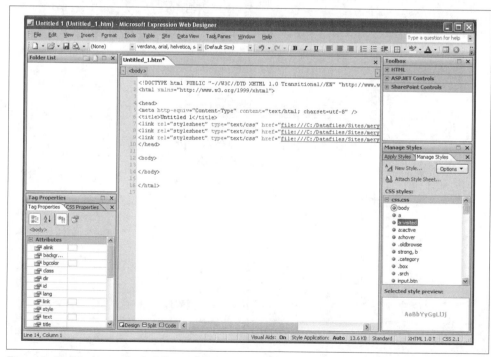

Figure 1-46. Start a new CSS file in Microsoft Expression Web Designer

Figure 1-47. Manage styles in Microsoft Expression Web Designer in its Manage Styles task pane

Discussion

Microsoft Expression Web Designer has made strides in CSS support over FrontPage, its predecessor. After adding styles to a web page, refer to the Manage Styles task pane to list current styles and to switch styles from external CSS to internal CSS and vice versa.

If you add styles to content within an HTML page in using the Formatting toolbar, the application automatically adds inline CSS. As you select fonts and color to selected text, Expression Web Designer creates an internal style sheet rather than use <font>. In FrontPage, the code would look like the following:

```
<font face="georgia, times new roman, serif" color="#ff0000"
size="2">This is text.</font>
```

If you made changes to the code in FrontPage, the application often doubled-up on the code, such as the following:

```
<font face="georgia, times new roman, serif" color="#ff0000"
size="2"><font face="times new roman, serif">This is text.</font></font>
```

This led to bloated pages that rarely rendered correctly in browsers other the Internet Explorer. Expression Web Designer doesn't have double code trouble as you can see in Figure 1-48. Furthermore, styles can be categorized by order or type for easier reviewing.

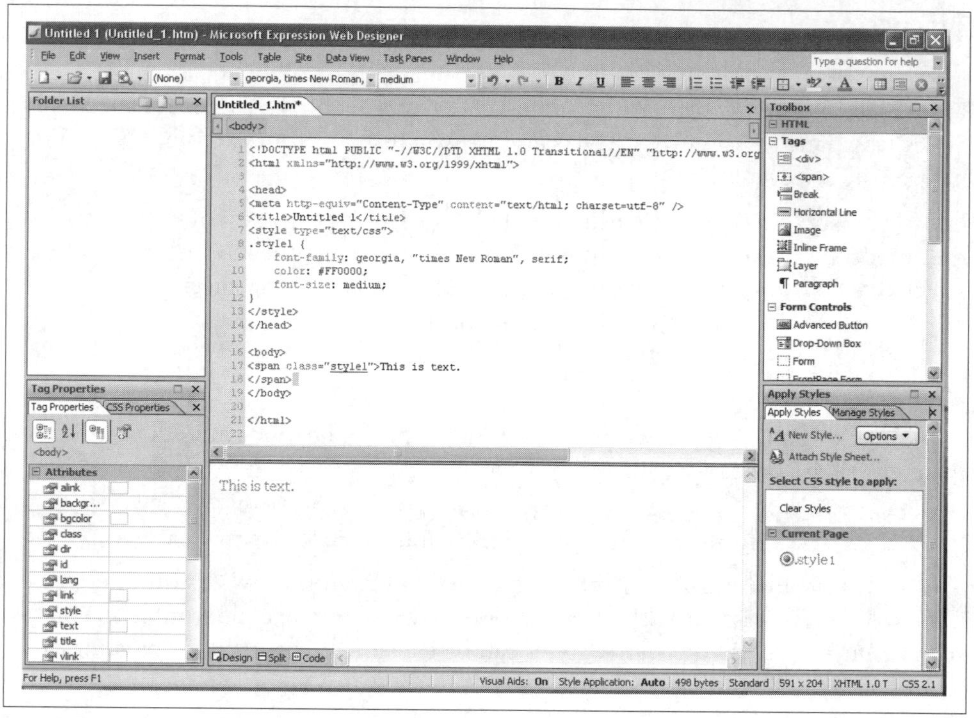

Figure 1-48. When adding style to text, Expression Web Designer creates internal styles

See Also

The Microsoft Expression Web Designer CSS Tours at *http://www.microsoft.com/ products/expression/en/web_designer/demos.mspx*.

CHAPTER 2

Web Typography

2.0   Introduction

Before CSS, web developers used font tags to set the color, size, and style of text on different parts of a web page:

```
<font face="Verdana, Arial, sans-serif" size="+1" color="blue">
Hello, World!
</font>
```

Although this method was effective for changing the appearance of type, the technique was limiting. Using multiple font tags across many, many pages resulted in time-consuming updates, inflated the overall file size of the web document, and increased the likelihood that errors would occur in the markup. CSS helps to eliminate these design and maintenance problems.

As a quick demonstration, first set content within a p element:

```
<p>Hello, World!</p>
```

Then set styles in the head of the document to dictate the look of the paragraph:

```
<style type="text/css" media="all">
 p {
  color: blue;
  font-size: small;
  font-family: Verdana, Arial, sans-serif;
 }
</style>
```

Now through this technique, the paragraph's structure and its visual presentation are separated. Because of this separation, the process of editing and maintaining a web site's design, including typography, is simplified immensely. Modifications to the style can be done in a style sheet without having to make changes at the content level.

Web developers not only get greater editing ease over previous techniques, but also typography control. In addition to discussing setting the color, style, and size of fonts, this chapter also covers techniques for setting initial caps, creating visually compelling pull quotes, modifying leading, and more.

2.1   Specifying Fonts

Problem

You want to set the typeface of text on a web page.

Solution

Use the font-family property:

```
body {
  font-family: Georgia, Times, "Times New Roman", serif;
}
```

Discussion

You can specify the fonts you want the browser to render on a web page by writing a comma-delimited list for the value of the font-family property. If the browser can't find the first font on the list, it tries to find the next font, and so on, until it finds a font.

If the font name contains spaces, like Times New Roman, enclose the name with single or double quotation marks.

At the end of the list of font choices, you should insert a generic font family. CSS offers five font family values to choose from, listed in Table 2-1.

Table 2-1. CSS font families

Generic font family values	Font examples
serif	Georgia, Times, Times New Roman, Garamond, and Century Schoolbook
sans-serif	Verdana, Arial, Helvetica, Trebuchet, and Tahoma
monospace	Courier, MS Courier New, and Prestige
cursive	Lucida Handwriting and Zapf-Chancery
fantasy	Comic Sans, Whimsey, Critter, and Cottonwood

All web browsers contain a list of fonts that fall into the five families shown in Table 2-1. If a font is neither chosen via a CSS rule nor available on the user's computer, the browser uses a font from one of these font families.

The most problematic generic font value is fantasy because this value is a catchall for any font that doesn't fall into the other four categories. Designers rarely use this font because they can't know what symbols will be displayed! Another problematic generic value is cursive because some systems can't display a cursive font. If a browser can't use a cursive font, it uses another default font in its place. Because text marked as cursive may not actually be displayed in a cursive font, designers often avoid this generic font value as well.

If you want to use an unusual font that may not be installed on most peoples' machines, the rule of thumb is to set the last value for the font-family property to serif, sans-serif, or monospace. This will maintain at least some legibility for the user viewing the web document.

You don't have to set the same properties for every tag you use. A child element *inherits*, or has the same property values of, its parent element if the CSS specification that defines a given property can be inherited. For example, if you set the font-family property to show a serif font in a paragraph that contains an em element as a child, that text in the em element is also set in a serif font:

```
<p style="font-family: serif;">The water fountain
with the broken sign on it is <em>indeed</em> broken.</p>
```

Inheritance doesn't occur under two circumstances. One is built into the CSS specification and concerns elements that can generate a box. Elements such as h2 and p are referred to as *block-level elements* and can have other properties such as margins, borders, padding, and backgrounds, as you see in Figure 2-1.

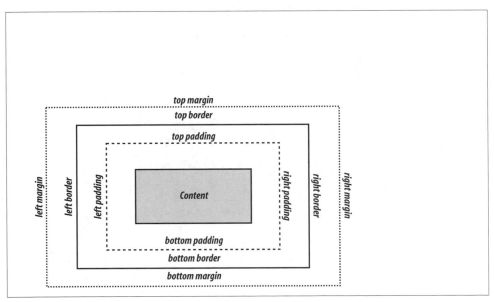

Figure 2-1. The box model for a block-level element

Because these properties aren't passed to child block-level elements, you don't have to write additional rules to counter the visual effects that would occur if they were passed. For example, if you applied a margin of 15% to a body element, that rule would be applied to every h2 and p element that is a child of that body element. If these properties were inherited, the page would look like Figure 2-2.

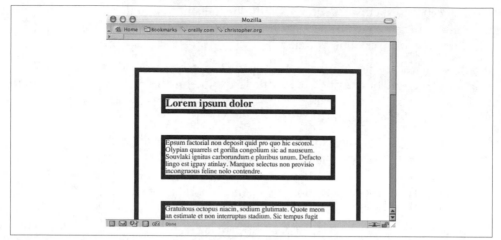

Figure 2-2. Hypothetical mock-up of margins and border properties being inherited

Because certain properties are defined to be inheritable and others aren't, the page actually looks like the one shown in Figure 2-3 in a modern CSS-compliant browser.

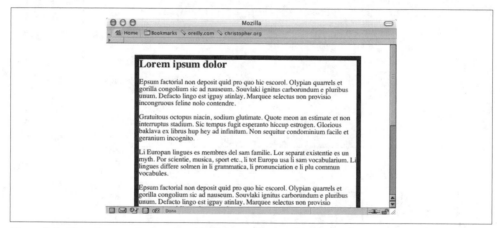

Figure 2-3. How the page looks when block-level elements don't inherit certain properties

The other circumstance under which inheritance doesn't work is, of course, if your browser doesn't follow the CSS specification. For example, in Netscape Navigator 4, child elements may not inherit the font-family and color values set in a body type selector. To work around this problem, explicitly set the font-family and color values for block-level elements:

```
body {
  font-family: Georgia, Times, "Times New Roman", serif;
  color: #030;
}
```

```
h1, h2, h3, h4, h5, h6, p, td, ul, ol, li, dl, dt, dd, {
  font-family: Georgia, Times, "Times New Roman", serif;
  color: #030;
}
```

See Also

The CSS 2.1 specification for inheritance, online at *http://www.w3.org/TR/CSS21/ cascade.html#inheritance*; the CSS 2.1 specification for font-family values at *http:// www.w3.org/TR/CSS21/fonts.html#propdef-font-family*; more about CSS and Netscape 4 issues at *http://www.mako4css.com/cssfont.htm*.

2.2   Specifying Font Measurements and Sizes

Problem

You want to set the size of type used on a web page.

Solution

Set the values of fonts by using the font-size property:

```
p {
  font-size: 0.9em;
}
```

Discussion

The font-size property can take on different values and use several units. In the solution, em units were used. There are other units like percentages.

Setting the size of the font with percentages causes the browser to calculate the size of the font based on the size of the parent element. For example, if the font size for the body is set to 12 pixels and the font size for p element is set to 125%, the font size for the text in paragraphs is 15 pixels.

You can use percentages, length units, and font-size keywords to set type size.

Length units

Length units fall into two categories: absolute and relative. Absolute length units include the following:

* Inches (in)
* Centimeters (cm)
* Millimeters (mm)
* Points (pt)
* Picas (pc)

A point, in terms of the CSS specification, is equal to 1/72nd of an inch and a pica is equal to 12 points.

Relative units

Relative units set the length of a property based on the value of another length property. Relative length units include the following:

- Em
- X-height (ex)
- Pixels (px)

Em units refer to the default font size set in the preference of the user's browser, while *x-height* (ex) refers to the height of the lowercase letter *x* in the font.

Pixels are the smallest dot that can be made on a computer screen.

Setting the size of fonts to zero or a negative value

The CSS specification doesn't dictate how browser vendors should treat text when the `font-size` property is set to a value of zero. Therefore different browsers interpret the value unpredictably.

For example, such text isn't visible in the Firefox or Mozilla browser. In Internet Explorer for Macintosh and Safari, the text isn't hidden, but, rather, is displayed at the default value of the font size. The Opera browser displays the text at a smaller, but still legible, size. And Internet Explorer for Windows sets the type size to a small, illegible, but still visible line of text that appears to be equal to the size of 0.1em, as you can see in Figure 2-4.

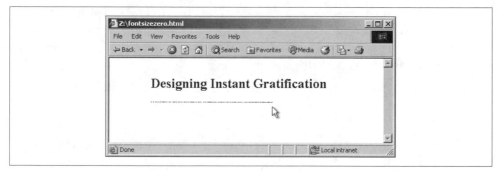

Figure 2-4. Internet Explorer for Windows showing illegible type when the font size is set to zero

If you want to make text invisible, use the CSS properties `visibility` or `display` instead of setting the size of fonts to zero.

```
p {
  display: none;
}
```

A negative value for length, such as `-25cm`, for the `font-size` property isn't allowed.

See Also

The CSS 2.1 specification on `font-size` property at *http://www.w3.org/TR/CSS21/fonts.html#font-size-props*.

2.3   Gaining More Control over Font Sizes

Problem

You want the size of type to be consistent across different browsers and operating systems.

Solution

Set the `font-size` in the body element to 62.5%:

```
body {
  font-size: 62.5%;
}
```

Then set the `font-size` in the inherited form and table elements to `1em` For Internet Explorer for Windows:

```
input, select, th, td {
  font-size: 1em;
}
```

Now your font sizes in your document will be equivalent to 10 pixels for each 1 em unit. For example, if you add the body declaration in the first part of the solution, then the following rule sets the font size for a paragraph to 19 pixels:

```
p {
  font-size: 1.9em // displays text as 19 pixels
}
```

Discussion

Because browser displays vary due to different operating systems and video settings, setting type in a *fixed* (or *absolute*) value doesn't make much sense. In fact, it's best to avoid absolute measurements for web documents, unless you're styling documents for fixed output. For example, when you create a style sheet to print a web document, absolute length units are preferred. For more on creating style sheets for printing, see Chapter 10.

Using pixels

Although pixels appear to consistently control the size of typography in a web document across most platforms and browsers, it's not a good idea to use pixels when designing for the following browsers:

- Netscape Navigator 4.*x*, which doesn't display pixel size values correctly
- Opera 5 for the Macintosh, which displays pixel lengths smaller than the size set in the style sheet

If most visitors to your site use browsers other than Netscape Navigator 4.7x and Opera 5 for the Mac, you can safely use pixels to set the size of your type.

Accessibility and web typography

The main issue in regard to setting type size in pixels isn't one of accurate sizing, but of accessibility. People with poor vision may want to resize the type to better read the document. However, if you use pixels to set the type on your web page, people who are using Internet Explorer for Windows will be unable to resize the type. Because Internet Explorer for Windows is the most commonly used browser on the planet, the use of pixels to set type size becomes a problem for most users who need to resize the type in their browsers.

If you do require an absolute size measurement, pixels should be used rather than points, even though print designers are more accustomed to point measurements. The reason is that Macintosh and Windows operating systems render point sizes differently, but pixel size typically stays the same.

 Even though pixels are technically a relative, unit, designers refer to pixels as absolute units. A pixel is relative in terms of its actual physical size but it is absolute in terms of its size ratio on a web page, which is what is important to a designer.

If accessibility is a concern, switch to em units. In the solution, we set the text in a paragraph to 1.9em units. This value is equivalent to setting the font size to 90% of the default font size set in the browser's preference.

However, the use of em units raises another concern. This time the problem pertains to usability. Although you may be able to resize the type in a web page, if you set a font to a size that is smaller than the default text size of the browser (for example, to 0.7em), Internet Explorer for Windows will display small, almost illegible lines of text, (see Figure 2-5). So, the lesson here is: be careful with relative sizes, as it is easy to make text illegible.

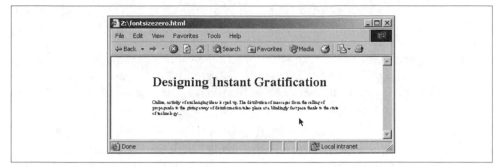

Figure 2-5. Almost illegible type set with em units

Using font keywords

This brings up the possibility of another solution: the use of font-size keywords. The CSS 2.1 specification has seven font keywords for absolute sizes that you can use to set type size (see Figure 2-6): xx-small, x-small, small, medium, large, x-large, xx-large.

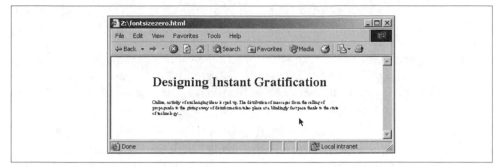

Figure 2-6. The font-size keywords on display

There are two other font-size keywords for relative measurements: larger and smaller. If a child element is set to larger, the browser can interpret the value of the parent's font-size value of small and increase the text inside the child element to medium.

Font-size keywords provide two benefits: they make it easy to enlarge or reduce the size of the text in most browsers, and the font sizes in browsers never go smaller than 9 pixels, ensuring that the text is legible. If you do set text to a small size, use a sans-serif font such as Verdana to increase the chances for legibility.

The main drawback with font-size keywords is that Internet Explorer 4–5.5 sets the small value as the default setting instead of the recommended medium setting. Because of this decision, Internet Explorer actually maps all the font-size keywords to one level lower than other browsers. In other words, the value for xx-large in IE 4–5.5 is every other browser's x-large, x-large in IE is large in another browser, and so on. Another drawback is that in Netscape 4, the smaller sizes are sometimes illegible because they aren't rendered well by the browser.

The workaround for these drawbacks is to first create a separate style sheet that contains the font-size keywords for the web document. Then use the @import method for associating a style sheet, as explained in Recipe 10.1 and as you see here (this step keeps Navigator 4 from rendering illegible type):

```
<link href="/_assets/basic.css" media="all"
rel="stylesheet" />
<style type="text/css" media="screen">
 @import url(/_assets/fontsize.css);
</style>
```

To keep Internet Explorer 5 and 5.5 for Windows from displaying the wrong sizes for the font-size keywords, use the voice-family workaround for delivering alternative values in Internet Explorer, as explained in Recipe 11.2 and as you see here:

```
#content {
 /*
  font-size workaround for WinIE 5:
  1) WinIE 5/5.5 value first:
 */
 font-size: x-small;
 voice-family: "\"}\"";
 voice-family: inherit;
 /*
  2) Then the correct value next 2 times:
 */
 font-size: small;
}
html>#content
 font-size: small;
}
```

Using em units to control type

Although using font keywords allows general control over the size of the typography, designers typically want more choices than the several that keywords provide. The solution offered in this recipe, developed by Richard Rutter (*http://www.clagnut.com/*), delivers this kind of control.

Browsers set the default value of 16 pixels for web typography, which is equal to the medium keyword. By setting the font-size in the body element to 62.5%, the default value of 16 pixels reduces to 10 pixels:

```
(16 pixels)62.5% = 10 pixels
```

As discussed earlier, an em unit is the default font size of the user's browser. With the manipulation of the default font size on the body element, one em unit is now set to 10 pixels.

```
1em = 10px
```

This solution then allows the web developer that desires pixel-sized control over their fonts to have that control, without the browser limitations manifested in the use of pixels as a value.

For example, if a web developer wants to set the size of heading to 24 pixels while the text in a paragraph is 15 pixels, the rule sets based on this solution would look like the following:

```
body {
  font-size: 62.5%;
}
input, select, th, td {
  font-size: 1em;
}
h2 {
  font-size: 2.4em;
}
p {
  font-size: 1.5em;
}
```

Another of benefit of this solution is the inherit nature of the solution. The use of relative units does not hinder the usability and accessibility issues that other solutions do.

See Also

The original article by Richard Butter detailing the solution, which is online at *http://www.clagnut.com/about/*; the article "CSS Design: Size Matters," written by Todd Fahrner (an invited member to the W3C CSS Working Group) available at *http://www.alistapart.com/articles/sizematters/*; Recipe 12.1 for enlarging text to gain attention; the CSS 2.1 specification at *http://www.w3.org/TR/CSS21/cascade.html#q1* for more on how a browser determines values; the CSS 2 specification for length units at *http://www.w3.org/TR/REC-CSS2/syndata.html#length-units*; the section "Font Size" in Chapter 5 of *Cascading Style Sheets: The Definitive Guide*, Second Edition by Eric A. Meyer (O'Reilly Media).

2.4   Enforcing Font Sizes

Problem

You want to override control over font sizes.

Solution

Use the !important rule to override a user's style sheet rules:

```
p {
 font-size: 12px !important;
}
```

Discussion

The !important rule consists of an exclamation mark (!) followed immediately by the word *important*.

In some browsers, a user can have a style sheet set up for browsing the Web that enables him to set font sizes (and other CSS properties) to his liking. However, as a designer of a web document, you may want to make sure your designs render in the manner you planned. The !important rule gives you a little insurance that your designs remain intact. (However, the nature of the medium means that designs are never precise or "pixel-perfect" from one display to another.)

Although you, as the designer, write the !important CSS rules, the user can also write these rules in his own style sheet. And in the CSS 2 specification, !important rules that the user writes override any !important rules the designer writes.

See Also

The CSS 2.1 specification on !important rules at *http://www.w3.org/TR/CSS21/cascade.html#important-rules*.

2.5   Centering Text

Problem

You want to center text within a paragraph or a heading.

Solution

Use the text-align property with the value set to center:

```
h3 {
 text-align: center;
}
p {
 text-align: center;
}
```

Discussion

The center value for the text-align property is designed to control the alignment of inline content within a block element.

See Also

The CSS 2.1 specification for `text-align` property at *http://www.w3.org/TR/CSS21/ text.html#alignment-prop*; for information about centering various items in a web page, see Recipe 4.3.

2.6 Setting Text to Be Justified

Problem

You want to align text to be justified on both the left and right sides, as in Figure 2-7.

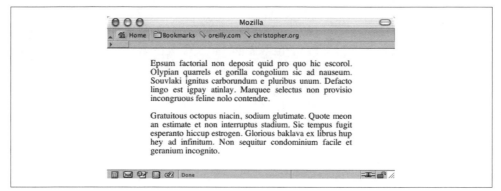

Figure 2-7. The paragraph justified on both sides

Solution

Use the `text-align` property:

```
P {
 width: 600px;
 text-align: justify;
}
```

Discussion

How well does web-based text justification work? According to the CSS 2.1 specification, it depends on the algorithms developed by the engineers who made the browser being used to view the web page. Because there isn't an agreed-upon algorithm for justifying text, the look of the text varies from browser to browser, even though the browser vendor technically supports justification.

Browser support for the property is good in Internet Explorer 4+ for Windows, Internet Explorer 5 for Macintosh, Safari, and Opera 3+. In those browsers, justified text looks pleasing to the eye. In other browsers, justified text may look bad; for example, it may have a lot of whitespace between words.

See Also

The CSS 2.1 specification about the text-align property at *http://www.w3.org/TR/ REC-CSS2/text.html#alignment-prop*.

2.7   Removing Space Between Headings and Paragraphs

Problem

You want to reduce the space between a heading and a paragraph.

Solution

Set the margin and padding for both the heading and paragraph to zero:

```
h2 {
  margin: 0;
  padding: 0;
}
p {
  margin: 0;
  padding: 0;
}
```

Discussion

Browsers have their own internal style sheet that dictate the default values for HTML elements. These styles include predetermined values for margin and padding of elements for headings and paragraphs.

These default values makes it easy for people to read non-styled documents, but are often not desired by web developers.

To remove the default spacing between the viewport (sometimes referred as the browser window) and the elements within a web page, set the margin and padding of the body element to a value of zero.

See Also

Review CSS 2.1 specification's default style sheet for HTML 4 at *http://www.w3.org/ TR/CSS21/sample.html*.

2.8   Setting a Simple Initial Cap

Problem

You want a paragraph to begin with an initial cap.

Solution

Mark up the paragraph of content with a p element:

```
<p>Online, activity of exchanging ideas is sped up. The
distribution of messages from the sellin of propaganda to the
giving away of disinformation takes place at a blindingly fast
pace thanks to the state of technology &hellip;</p>
```

Use the pseudo-element :first-letter to stylize the first letter of the paragraph (see Figure 2-8):

```
p:first-letter {
 font-size: 1.2em;
 background-color: black;
 color: white;
}
```

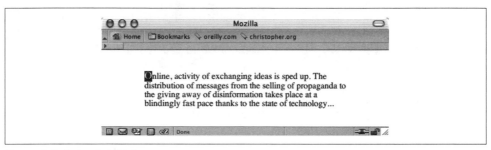

Figure 2-8. A simple initial cap

Discussion

The CSS specification offers an easy way to stylize the first letter in a paragraph as a traditional initial or drop cap: use the :first-letter pseudo-element.

:first-letter is supported in common modern browsers such as Internet Explorer 6 for Windows, Firefox, Safari, and Opera. For other browsers, a different approach may be needed.

Wrap a span element with a class attribute around the first letter of the first sentence of the first paragraph:

```
<p><span class="initcap">O</span>nline, activity of exchanging ideas is sped
up. The distribution of messages from the selling of propaganda
to the giving away of disinformation takes place at a blindingly
fast pace thanks to the state of technology &hellip;</p>
```

Then set the style for the initial cap:

```
p .initcap {
 font-size: 1.2em;
 background-color: black;
 color: white;
}
```

Initial caps, also known as *versals*, traditionally are enlarged in print to anything from a few points to three lines of text.

See Also

The CSS 2.1 specification for the `:first-letter` pseudo-element at *http://www.w3.org/TR/CSS21/selector.html#x52*; for more information on initial caps in general, see *http://fonts.lordkyl.net/fonts.php?category=vers*.

2.9   Setting a Larger, Centered Initial Cap

Problem

You want to place a large initial cap in the center of a paragraph.

Solution

Wrap a `span` element with a `class` attribute around the first letter of the first sentence of the first paragraph:

```
<p><span class="initcap">O</span>nline, activity of exchanging ideas is sped
up. The distribution of messages from the selling of propaganda
to the giving away of disinformation takes place at a blindingly
fast pace thanks to the state of technology&hellip;</p>
```

In conjunction with styling the initial letter through the span tag with a class selector, create the decoration that sets the text indent for the paragraph (see Figure 2-9):

```
p {
  text-indent: 37%;
  line-height: 1em;
}
p span.initcap {
  font-size: 6em;
  line-height: 0.6em;
  font-weight: bold;
}
```

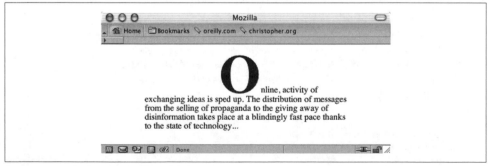

Figure 2-9. A larger, centered initial cap

Discussion

This solution works due to the interaction of three CSS properties. The first is the text-indent property, which moves the first line toward the middle of the paragraph. The value is set to 37%, which is a little bit more than one-third the distance from the left side of the paragraph, (see Figure 2-10), but not enough to "center" the initial cap.

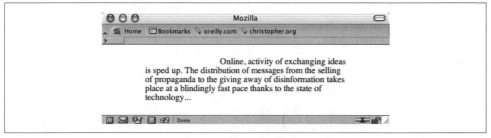

Figure 2-10. The indented text

The next property that helps is the font-size property. Setting the size to 6em makes the font six times (or 600%) larger than the default size set for fonts in the browser (see Figure 2-11).

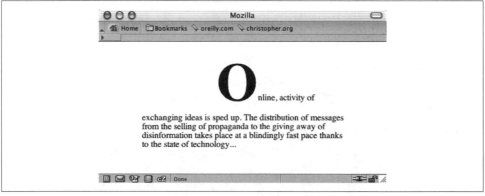

Figure 2-11. The initial cap enlarged six times its normal height

Because the font size is six times as large as the rest of the type, the leading on the first line is now deeper than it is on the remaining lines. To help adjust that, set the line height for the span element to 0.6em.

Note that this recipe centering the initial cap works, technically, when the character's width is equal to 26% of the paragraph's width. In other words, if the letter for the initial cap or the width of the paragraph is different for your own work, adjustments to the values in the CSS rules are necessary to move the initial cap to the center.

See Also

Recipe 2.23 for adjusting leading with line height; the CSS 2.1 specification for text-indent at *http://www.w3.org/TR/CSS21/text.html#propdef-text-indent*.

2.10 Setting an Initial Cap with Decoration (Imagery)

Problem

You want to use an image for an initial cap.

Solution

Wrap a span element around the first letter of the first sentence of the first paragraph:

```
<p><span class="initcap">O</span>nline, activity of exchanging
ideas is sped up. The distribution of messages from the selling of
propaganda to the giving away of disinformation takes place at a
blindingly fast pace thanks to the state of technology&hellip;</p>
```

Set the contents inside the span to be hidden:

```
span.initcap {
 display: none;
}
```

Then set an image to be used as the initial cap in the background of the paragraph (see Figure 2-12):

```
p {
 line-height: 1em;
 background-image: url(initcap-o.gif);
 background-repeat: no-repeat;
 text-indent: 35px;
 padding-top: 45px;
}
```

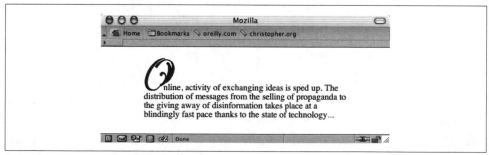

Figure 2-12. An image used as an initial cap

Discussion

The first step of this solution is to create an image for use as the initial cap. Once you have created the image, make a note of its width and height. In this example, the image of the letter measures 55 × 58 pixels (see Figure 2-13).

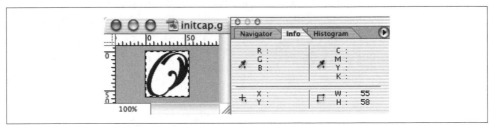

Figure 2-13. The image of the initial cap

Next, hide the first letter of the HTML text by setting the display property to none. Then put the image in the background of the paragraph, making sure that the image doesn't repeat by setting the value of background-repeat to no-repeat:

```
background-image: url(initcap-o.gif);
background-repeat: no-repeat;
```

With the measurements already known, set the width of the image as the value for text-indent and the height of the image as the padding for the top of the paragraph (see Figure 2-14):

```
text-indent: 55px;
padding-top: 58px;
```

Figure 2-14. Adjusting the space for the initial cap

Then change the text-indent and padding-top values so that the initial cap appears to rest on the baseline (refer to Figure 2-12).

Note that users with images turned off aren't able to see the initial cap, especially since the solution doesn't allow for an alt attribute for the image. If you want to use an image but still have an alt attribute show when a user turns off images, use an image to replace the HTML character:

```
<p><img src="initcap-o.gif" alt="O" />nline, activity of exchanging
ideas is sped up. The distribution of messages from the selling
of propaganda to the giving away of disinformation takes place at
a blindingly fast pace thanks to the state of technology&hellip;</p>
```

Note also that while the alt attribute is displayed in this solution, the ability to kern the space between the initial cap and the HTML text is lost. The HTML text begins exactly at the right side of the image and can't be moved closer to the letter being displayed in the graphic itself.

See Also

Recipe 2.8 for setting a simple initial cap.

2.11 Creating a Heading with Stylized Text

Problem

You want to use CSS properties to design a heading that is different from the default. For example, you want to put the heading in Figure 2-15 into italics, as you see in Figure 2-16.

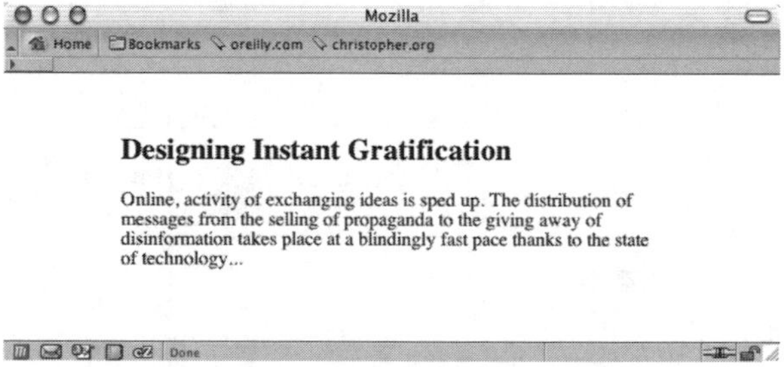

Figure 2-15. The default rendering of a heading

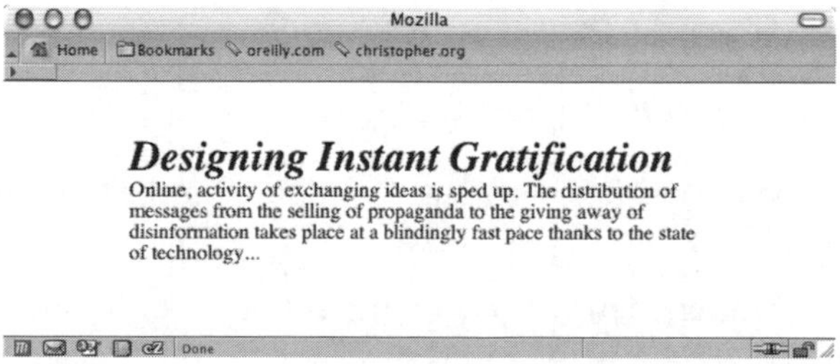

Figure 2-16. The stylized text of a heading

Solution

First, properly mark up the heading:

```
<h2>Designing Instant Gratification</h2>
<p>Online, activity of exchanging ideas is sped up. The
distribution of messages from the selling of propaganda to the
giving away of disinformation takes place at a blindingly fast
pace thanks to the state of technology&hellip;</p>
```

Then, use the font shorthand property to easily change the style of the heading:

```
h2 {
  font: bold italic 2em  Georgia, Times, "Times New Roman", serif;
  margin: 0;
  padding: 0;
}
p {
  margin: 0;
  padding: 0;
}
```

Discussion

As described in Recipe 1.12, *shorthand property* combines several properties into one. The font property is just one of these timesavers. One font property can represent the following values:

- font-style
- font-variant
- font-weight
- font-size/line-height
- font-family

The first three values can be placed in any order, while the others need to be in the order shown.

When you want to include the line-height value, put a forward slash between the font-size value and the line-height value:

```
p {
  font: 1em/1.5em Verdana, Arial, sans-serif;
}
```

When setting the style headings, remember that browsers have their own default values for padding and margins of paragraphs and heading tags. These default values are generally based on mathematics, not aesthetics, so don't hesitate to adjust them to further enhance the look of your web document.

See Also

The CSS 2.1 specification for the font shorthand property at *http://www.w3.org/TR/CSS21/fonts.html#propdef-font*.

2.12 Creating a Heading with Stylized Text and Borders

Problem

You want to stylize the borders on the top and bottom of a heading (see Figure 2-17).

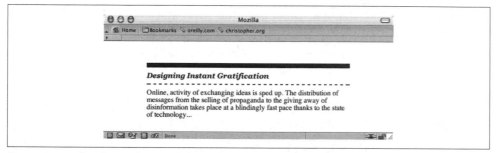

Figure 2-17. A heading stylized with borders

Solution

Use the `border-top` and `border-bottom` properties when setting the style for the heading:

```
h2 {
  font: bold italic 2em Georgia, Times, "Times New Roman", serif;
  border-bottom: 2px dashed black;
  border-top: 10px solid black;
  margin: 0;
  padding: 0.5em 0 0.5em 0;
  font-size: 1em;
}
p {
  margin: 0;
  padding: 10px 0 0 0;
}
```

Discussion

In addition to top and bottom borders, a block-level element also can have a border on the left and right sides via the `border-left` and `border-right` properties, respectively. The `border-top`, `border-bottom`, `border-left`, and `border-right` properties are shorthand properties that enable developers to set the width, style, and color of each side of a border.

Without the two shorthand border declarations in the solution, the CSS rule for the heading would be expanded by four extra declarations:

```
h2 {
  font: bold italic 2em Georgia, Times, "Times New Roman", serif;
  border-bottom-width: 2px;
```

```
    border-bottom-style: dashed;
    border-bottom-color: black;
    border-top-width: 10px;
    border-top-style: solid;
    border-top-color: black;
    margin: 0;
    padding: 0.5em 0 0.5em 0;
    font-size: 1em;
}
```

Also available is a shorthand property for the top, bottom, left, and right shorthand properties all together: border. The border property sets the same style for the width, style, and color of the border on each side of an element:

```
h2 {
  border: 3px dotted #33333;
}
```

When setting the borders, make sure to adjust the padding to put enough whitespace between the borders and the text of the heading. This aids in readability. Without enough whitespace on a heading element, the text of the heading can appear cramped.

See Also

Recipe 4.4 for more information on styles of borders and the shorthand border property.

2.13   Stylizing a Heading with Text and an Image

Problem

You want to place a repeating image at the bottom of a heading, like the grass in Figure 2-18.

Solution

Use the background-image, background-repeat, and background-position properties:

```
h2 {
  font: bold italic 2em Georgia, Times, "Times New Roman", serif;
  background-image: url(tall_grass.jpg);
  background-repeat: repeat-x;
  background-position: bottom;
  border-bottom: 10px solid #666;
  margin: 10px 0 0 0;
  padding: 0.5em 0 60px 0;
}
```

Figure 2-18. A background image used with a heading

Discussion

Make a note of the height of the image used for the background. In this example, the height of the image is 100 pixels (see Figure 2-19).

Figure 2-19. An image of tall grass

Set the `background-repeat` property to a value of `repeat-x`, which will cause the image to repeat horizontally:

```
background-image: url(tall_grass.jpg);
background-repeat: repeat-x;
```

Next, set the `background-position` property to bottom:

```
background-position: bottom;
```

The `background-position` can take up to two values corresponding to the horizontal and vertical axes. Values for background-position can be a length unit (such as pixels), a percentage, or a keyword. To position an element on the *x*-axis, use the keyword values `left`, `center`, or `right`. For the *y*-axis, use the keyword values `top`, `center`, or `bottom`.

When the location of the other axis isn't present, the image is placed in the center of that axis, like in Figure 2-20.

```
background-position: bottom;
```

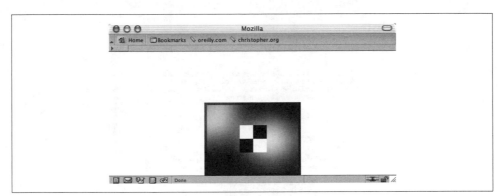

Figure 2-20. The image aligned on the bottom of the y-axis and in the middle of the x-axis

So, in this solution, the image is placed at the bottom of the *y*-axis but is repeats along the *x*-axis.

See Also

Recipe 3.3 for setting a background image in an entire web page.

2.14   Creating a Pull Quote with HTML Text

Problem

You want to stylize the text for a pull quote so that it is different from the default. Undifferentiated quotes aren't obviously from another writer (see Figure 2-21), whereas stylized quotes are (see Figure 2-22).

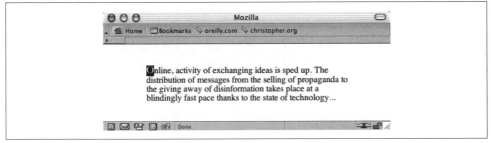

Figure 2-21. The default rendering of the text for a pull quote

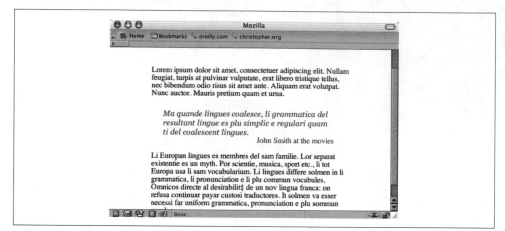

Figure 2-22. The stylized pull quote

Solution

Use the blockquote element to indicate the pull quote semantically in the markup:

```
<blockquote>
 <p>Ma quande lingues coalesce, li grammatica del resultant
 lingue es plu simplic e regulari quam ti del coalescent
lingues.</p>
 <div class="source">John Smith at the movies</div>
</blockquote>
```

With CSS, apply the margin, padding, and color values to the blockquote element:

```
blockquote {
 margin: 0;
 padding: 0;
 color: #555;
}
```

Next, set the style for the p and div elements nested in the blockquote element:

```
blockquote p {
 font: italic 1em Georgia, Times, "Times New Roman", serif;
 font-size: 1em;
 margin: 1.5em 2em 0 1.5em;
 padding: 0;
}
blockquote .source {
 text-align: right;
 font-style: normal;
 margin-right: 2em;
}
```

Discussion

A pull quote is used in design to grab a reader's attention so that he will stick around and read more. One easy way to create a pull quote is to change the color of a portion of the main text. Improve on this by adding contrast: change the generic font family of the pull quote so that it is different from that of the main text. For example, if the main text of a web document is set in sans-serif, set the pull quote text to a serif font.

See Also

Recipe 2.15 and Recipe 2.16 for more information on designing pull quotes with CSS.

2.15   Creating a Pull Quote with Borders

Problem

You want to stylize a pull quote with borders on the top and bottom, as in Figure 2-23.

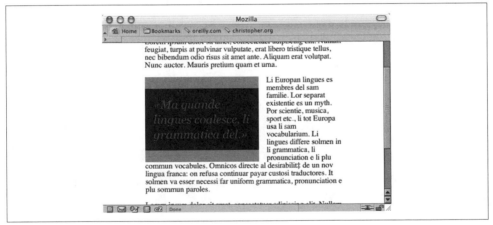

Figure 2-23. A stylized pull quote using borders

To put borders on the left and right, instead of the top and bottom, use the `border-left` and `border-right` properties:

```
border-left: 1em solid #999;
border-right: 1em solid #999;
```

Solution

Use the blockquote element to mark up the pull quote content:

```
<blockquote>
 <p>&laquo;Ma quande lingues coalesce, li
grammatica del.&raquo;</p>
</blockquote>
```

Next, set the CSS rules for the border and text within the pull quote:

```
blockquote {
 float: left;
 width: 200px;
 margin: 0 0.7em 0 0;
 padding: 0.7em;
 color: #666;
 background-color: black;
 font-family: Georgia, Times, "Times New Roman", serif;
 font-size: 1.5em;
 font-style: italic;
 border-top: 1em solid #999;
 border-bottom: 1em solid #999;
}
blockquote p {
 margin: 0;
 padding: 0;
 text-align: left;
 line-height: 1.3em;
}
```

Discussion

Set the float property as well as the width property for the blockquote element. These two CSS properties allow the main content to wrap around the pull quote:

```
float: left;
width: 200px;
```

Contrast the pull quote with the surrounding text by changing the quote's foreground and background colors:

```
color: #666;
background-color: black;
```

Use the border-top and border-bottom properties to match the color of the text in the pull quote:

```
border-top: 1em solid #999;
border-bottom: 1em solid #999;
```

See Also

Chapter 9 for several page-layout techniques that take advantage of the float property; Recipe 2.12 for styling headings with borders; Recipes 12.3 and 12.4 for more on designing with contrast.

2.16 Creating a Pull Quote with Images

Problem

You want to stylize a pull quote with images on either side, such as the curly braces in Figure 2-24.

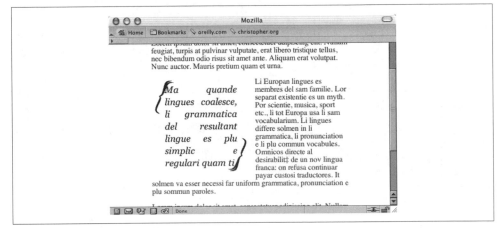

Figure 2-24. A pull quote with images

Solution

Use the blockquote element to mark up the pull quote content:

```
<blockquote>
 <p>Ma quande lingues coalesce, li grammatica del resultant
lingue es plu simplic e regulari quam ti.</p>
</blockquote>
```

Then set the style for the pull quote, placing one image in the background of the blockquote element and another in the background of the p:

```
blockquote {
 background-image: url(bracket_left.gif);
 background-repeat: no-repeat;
 float: left;
 width: 175px;
 margin: 0 0.7em 0 0;
 padding: 10px 0 0 27px;
 font-family: Georgia, Times, "Times New Roman", serif;
 font-size: 1.2em;
 font-style: italic;
 color: black;
}
blockquote p {
 margin: 0;
 padding: 0 22px 10px 0;
```

```
      width:150px;
      text-align: justify;
      line-height: 1.3em;
      background-image: url(bracket_right.gif);
      background-repeat: no-repeat;
      background-position: bottom right;
   }
```

Discussion

For this solution, the bracket images for the pull quote come in a pair, with one at the upper-left corner and the other at the bottom-right corner. Through CSS, you can assign only one background image per block-level element.

The workaround is to give these images the proper placement; put one image in the background of the blockquote element and the other in the p element that is a child of the blockquote element:

```
blockquote {
  background-image: url(bracket_left.gif);
  background-repeat: no-repeat;
  float: left;
  width: 175px;
}
blockquote p {
  background-image: url(bracket_right.gif);
  background-repeat: no-repeat;
  background-position: bottom right;
}
```

Then adjust the padding, margin, and width of the blockquote and p elements so that you have an unobstructed view of the images:

```
blockquote {
  background-image: url(bracket_left.gif);
  background-repeat: no-repeat;
  float: left;
  width: 175px;
  margin: 0 0.7em 0 0;
  padding: 10px 0 0 27px;
}
blockquote p {
  margin: 0;
  padding: 0 22px 10px 0;
  width: 150px;
  background-image: url(bracket_right.gif);
  background-repeat: no-repeat;
  background-position: bottom right;
}
```

A benefit of this solution is that if the text is resized (see Figure 2-25), the images (brackets) reposition themselves.

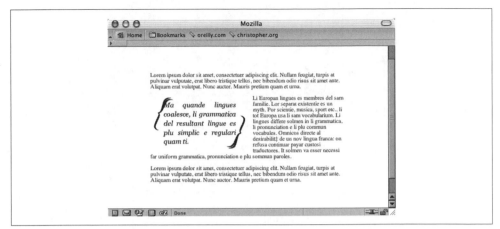

Figure 2-25. The background images stay in the corners as the text is resized

See Also

Recipe 6.15 for another example of the rubber-band technique. If you stretch a rubber band on both ends, the rubber band stays intact, just like the presentation of the images stay intact even if you resize the text.

2.17   Setting the Indent in the First Line of a Paragraph

Problem

You want to place an indent in the first line of each paragraph, turning the paragraphs in Figure 2-26 into the paragraphs in Figure 2-27.

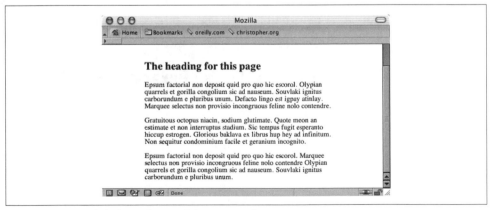

Figure 2-26. The default rendering of the paragraphs

Figure 2-27. The paragraphs with first lines indented

Solution

Use the text-indent property to create the indent:

```
p {
  text-indent: 2.5em;
  margin: 0 0 0.5em 0;
  padding: 0;
}
```

Discussion

The text-indent property can take absolute and relative length units as well as percentages. If you use percentages, the percentage refers to the element's width and not the total width of the page. In other words, if the indent is set to 35% of a paragraph that is set to a width of 200 pixels, the width of the indent is 70 pixels.

See Also

The CSS 2.1 specification for more on the text-indent property at *http://www.w3.org/TR/CSS21/text.html#propdef-text-indent*.

2.18 Setting the Indent of Entire Paragraphs

Problem

You want to indent entire paragraphs, turning Figure 2-28 into Figure 2-29.

Solution

To achieve the desired effect, use class selectors:

```
p.normal {
  padding: 0;
```

```
  margin-left: 0;
  margin-right: 0;
}
p.large {
  margin-left: 33%;
  margin-right: 5%;
}
p.medium {
  margin-left: 15%;
  margin-right: 33%;
}
```

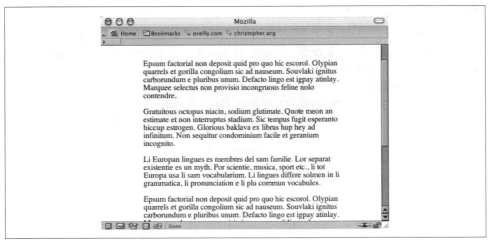

Figure 2-28. The paragraphs as the browser usually renders them

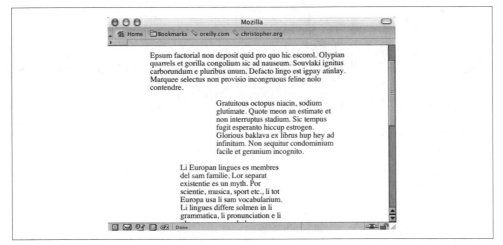

Figure 2-29. Indented paragraphs

Then place the appropriate attribute in the markup:

```
<p class="normal">Lorem ipsum dolor sit amet, consectetuer
adipiscing elit,  sed diam nonummy nibh euismod tincidunt ut
laoreet dolore magna al iquam erat volutpat.</p>
<p class="large">Epsum factorial non deposit quid pro quo hic
escorol. Olypian quarrels et gorilla congolium sic ad nauseum.
Souvlaki ignitus carborundum e pluribus unum.</p>
<p class="medium ">Li Europan lingues es membres del sam
familie. Lor separat existentie es un myth. Por scientie, musica,
sport etc., li tot Europa usa li sam vocabularium</p>
```

Discussion

Class selectors pick any HTML element that uses the class attribute. The difference between class and type selectors is that type selectors pick out every instance of the HTML element. In the following two CSS rules, the first selector is a type selector that signifies all content marked as h2 be displayed as red while the following CSS rule, a class selector, sets the padding of an element to 33%:

```
h2 {
   color: red;
}
.largeIndent {
   padding-left: 33%;
}
```

Combining both type and class selectors on one element gains greater specificity over the styling of elements. In the following markup, the third element is set to red and also has padding on the left set to 33%:

```
<h2>This is red.</h2>
<h3 class="largeIndent">This has a rather large indent.</h3>
<h2 class="largeIndent">This is both red and indented.</h2>
```

Another solution that can be used instead of class selectors is to apply the indent, using margins, and then use adjacent sibling selectors to apply the style to the paragraphs:

```
p, p+p+p+p {
 padding: 0;
 margin-left: 0;
 margin-right: 0;
}
p+p, p+p+p+p+p {
 margin-left: 33%;
 margin-right: 5%;
}
p+p+p, p+p+p+p+p+p {
 margin-left: 15%;
 margin-right: 33%;
}
```

This method takes advantage of the adjacent sibling selectors, which are represented by two or more regular selectors separated by plus sign(s). For example, the h2+p selector stylizes the paragraph *immediately following* an h2 element.

For this recipe we want to stylize certain paragraphs in the order in which they appear on-screen. For example, p+p selects the paragraph element that follows another paragraph. However, when there are more than two paragraphs, the third paragraph (as well as others after the third paragraph) is rendered in the same style as the second paragraph. This occurs because the third paragraph is immediately followed by a paragraph.

To separate the styles from the second and third paragraphs, set up another CSS rule for the third paragraph that selects three paragraphs that follow each other:

```
p+p+p {
  margin-left: 15%;
  margin-right: 33%;
}
```

Then, build off of these CSS rules by *grouping* the selectors. Instead of writing two CSS rules to stylize the third and sixth paragraphs, separate the selectors by a comma and a space:

```
p+p+p, p+p+p+p+p+p {
  margin-left: 15%;
  margin-right: 33%;
}
```

The main problem with adjacent sibling selectors is that they aren't supported by all versions of Internet Explorer for Windows. Therefore, these users will not see the paragraphs indented. Adjacent sibling selectors are supported in Safari, Firefox, Netscape Navigator 6+, and Opera 5+.

See Also

The CSS 2.1 specification about class selectors at *http://www.w3.org/TR/CSS21/selector.html#class-html*; the CSS 2.1 specification about adjacent sibling selectors at *http://www.w3.org/TR/CSS21/selector.html#adjacent-selectors*.

2.19   Creating a Hanging Indent

Problem

You want to create a hanging indent.

Solution

Use a negative value for the text-indent property:

```
p.hanging {
  text-indent: -5em;
}
```

Discussion

The typographic treatment of a hanging indent is already commonplace in most browsers in definition lists. With this simple code, a series of hanging indents (see Figure 2-30) is created without breaking a proverbial sweat.

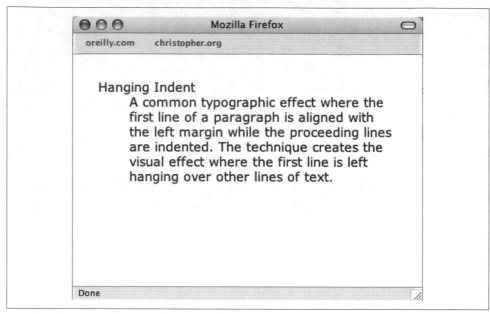

Figure 2-30. Definition lists render hanging indents by default

```
<dl>
 <dt>Hanging Indent</dt>
 <dd>A common typographic effect where the first line of a paragraph is aligned
with the left margin while the proceeding lines are indented.  The technique
creates the visual effect where the first line is left hanging over other lines of
text.</dd>
 </dl>
```

When you want a hanging indent on just a paragraph (not a list), the use of definition list markup will not suffice. The straightforward approach shown in the solution involves the use of the text-indent property in CSS.

Hanging indents safely

Before putting the text-indent property into a style sheet, make sure the code is implemented the right way. For example, by putting just the text-indent property into a CSS rule along with some basic font styling properties, that hanging indent could cause a legibility issue.

In Figure 2-31, note that the hanging indent extends to the left of the viewport. A reader may be able to determine the words being cropped off through the context of the rest of the paragraph, but that's simply an unneeded burden to place on them.

In order to work around this situation, check out Figure 2-31; apply a value equal to the indent to the left margin of the paragraph. The hanging indent then extends over the area already made clear by the margin ensuring that that text in the hanging indent remains visible.

```
p.hanging {
  text-indent: -5em;
  margin-left: 5em;
}
```

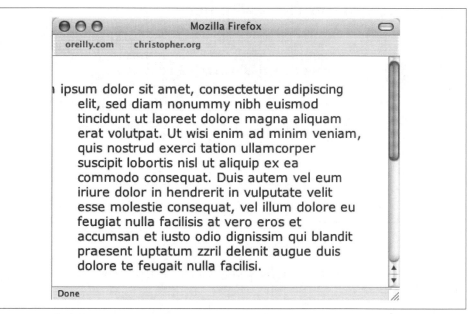

Figure 2-31. The hanging indent exits stage left

The paired hanging indent

In addition to having just the first line indent, moving a heading to the left as well results in a paired hanging indent (see Figure 2-32):

```
#content p.hanging {
  text-indent: -60px;
  margin: 0 0 0 60px;
  padding: 0;
}
#content h3 {
  text-indent: -60px;
  margin: 0 0 0 60px;
  padding: 0;
}
```

The HTML markup for this effect is:

```
<div id="content">
 <h3>Once more time with feeling</h3>
 <p class="hanging">
Lorem ipsum dolor sit amet, consectetuer adipiscing elit, sed diam nonummy
nibh euismod tincidunt ut laoreet dolore magna aliquam erat volutpat&hellip;</p>
</div>
```

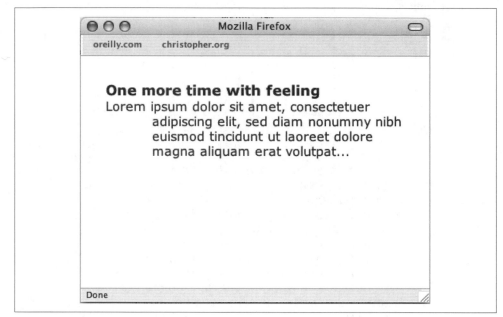

Figure 2-32. Double stacking the hanging indent

Or with some slight adjustment, have only the heading become the hanging indent like in Figure 2-33:

```
#content p {
 margin: 0;
 padding: 0 0 0 60px;
}
#content h3 {
 text-indent: -60px;
 margin: 0 0 0 60px;
 padding: 0;
}
```

The refined HTML markup follows:

```
<div id="content">
 <h3>Once more time with feeling</h3>
 <p>
Lorem ipsum dolor sit amet, consectetuer adipiscing elit, sed diam nonummy
nibh euismod tincidunt ut laoreet dolore magna aliquam erat volutpat&hellip;</p>
</div>
```

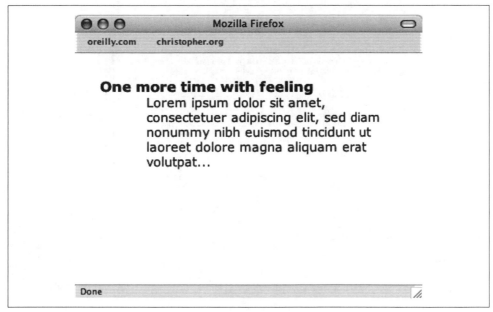

Figure 2-33. Hanging indent headline

See Also

See the CSS 2.1 specification regarding the text-indent property at *http://www.w3.org/ TR/CSS21/text.html#propdef-text-indent*.

2.20 Styling the First Line of a Paragraph

Problem

You want to set the first line of a paragraph in boldface, as in Figure 2-34.

Solution

Use the :first-line pseudo-element to set the style of the first line:

```
p:first-line {
 font-weight: bold;
}
```

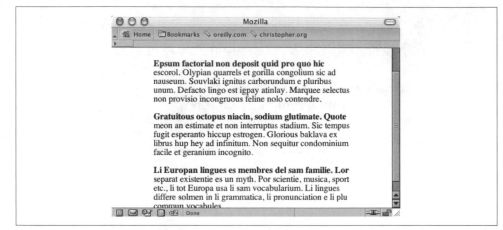

Figure 2-34. The first line set to bold

Discussion

Just like a class selector, a *pseudo-element* enables you to manipulate the style of parts of a web document. Unlike a class selector, however, resizing a browser window or changing the size of the font can change the area marked by a pseudo-element. In this solution, the amount of text in the first line can change if the browser is resized (see Figure 2-35).

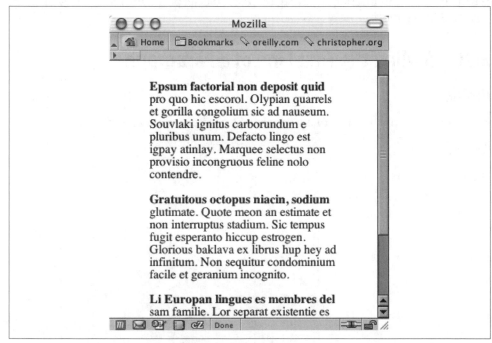

Figure 2-35. The amount of text changes when the browser is resized

See Also

The CSS 2.1 specification for the :first-line pseudo-element at *http://www.w3.org/TR/CSS21/selector.html#first-line-pseudo*.

2.21 Styling the First Line of a Paragraph with an Image

Problem

You want to stylize the first line of a paragraph and include an image; for example, see Figure 2-36.

Figure 2-36. The first line with a background image

Solution

Use the background-image property within the :first-line pseudo-element:

```
p:first-line {
  font-size: 2em;
  background-image: url(background.gif);
}
```

Discussion

Through the :first-line pseudo-elements, styles can only be applied to the first line of text of an element and not the width of the element itself.

In addition to the background-image property, the :first-line pseudo-element also supports the following properties allowing for greater design control:

```
font
color
background
word-spacing
```

```
letter-spacing
text-decoration
vertical-align
text-transform
text-shadow
line-height
clear
```

See Also

The CSS 2.1 specification for the `:first-line` pseudo-element at *http://www.w3.org/TR/CSS21/selector.html#first-line-pseudo*.

2.22   Creating a Highlighted Text Effect

Problem

You want to highlight a portion of the text in a paragraph, as in Figure 2-37.

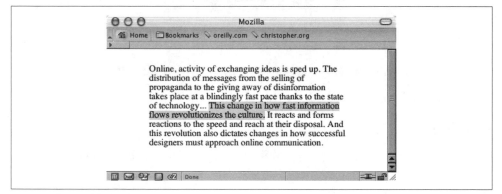

Figure 2-37. Highlighted text

Solution

Use the strong element to mark up the portions of text you want to highlight:

```
<p>The distribution of messages from the selling of propaganda
to the giving away of disinformation takes place at a blindingly
fast pace thanks to the state of technology&hellip; <strong>This
change in how fast information flows revolutionizes the
culture.</strong></p>
```

Then set the CSS rule to set the highlighted:

```
strong {
 font-weight: normal;
 background-color: yellow;
}
```

Discussion

Although the strong element is used in this solution, you also can use the em element instead of the strong element to mark highlighted text. The HTML 4.01 specification states that em should be used for marking *emphasized* text, while strong "indicates stronger emphasis."

Once the text has been marked, set the highlighter color with the background-color property. Because some browsers apply a bold weight to text marked as strong, set the font-weight to normal. When using the em element, be sure to set the font-style to normal as this keeps browsers from setting the type in italic, as shown in the next code listing.

```
em {
  font-style: normal;
  background-color: #ff00ff;
}
```

See Also

The HTML specification for strong and em at *http://www.w3.org/TR/html401/struct/text.html#edef-STRONG*.

2.23   Changing Line Spacing

Problem

You want to leave more or less space between lines. Figure 2-38 shows the browser default, and Figure 2-39 shows paragraphs with half again as much space.

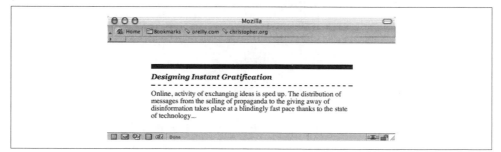

Figure 2-38. The default leading of a paragraph

Solution

Use a line-height value:

```
p {
  line-height: 1.5em;
}
```

Figure 2-39. Increased leading between the lines of text

Discussion

As the line-height value increases, the distance between the lines of text grows. As the value decreases, the distance between the lines of text shrinks and eventually the lines overlap each other. Designers notice a similarity to line height and *leading*.

A line-height value can be a number and a unit such as points, just a number, or a number and a percentage symbol. If the line-height value is just a number, that value is used as percentage or a scale unit for the element itself as well as for child elements.

Negative values aren't allowed for line-height.

The following example effectively sets the font-size to 12px and the line-height to 14.4px (10px * 1.2) * 1.2px = 14.4px):

```
body {
  font-size: 10px;
}
p {
  font-size: 1.2em;
  line-height: 1.2;
}
```

You also can set the line-height property with the shorthand font property when paired with a font-size value. The following line transforms any text in a p element to have a font size of 1em, to have a line-height of 1.5em, and to display in a sans-serif typeface:

```
p {
  font: 1em/1.5em sans-serif;
}
```

See Also

The CSS 2.1 specification on the line-height property at *http://www.w3.org/TR/ CSS21/visudet.html#propdef-line-height*; Recipe 2.10 for more information on the font property.

2.24   Adding a Graphic Treatment to HTML Text

Problem

You want to apply a repeating graphic treatment on top of HTML text, such as worn edges or the stripes in Figure 2-40.

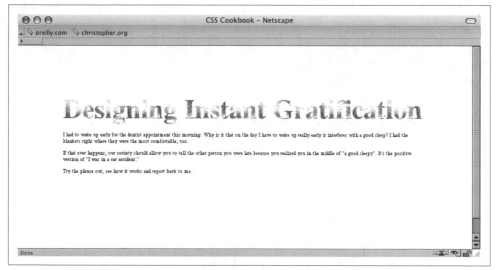

Figure 2-40. A striped image repeats over HTML text

Solution

Place a span element between after the opening tag of a heading element, but before the HTML text:

```
<h2><span></span>Designing Instant Gratification</h2>
```

Next, use a version of the *Gilder/Levin image replacement* technique (see Recipe 3.9) to place a GIF file with seamless pattern over the HTML text:

```
h2 {
 font:3em/1em Times, serif;
 font-weight: bold;
 margin:0;
 position: relative;
 overflow: hidden;
```

```
  float: left;
  }
h2 span {
  position: absolute;
  width: 100%;
  height: 5em;
  background: url(striped.gif);
  }
p {
  clear: left;
  }
```

Discussion

The text within the heading element is set to float to the left. This technique is to allow the background image, placed in the span element, to be placed over the HTML text through absolute positioning.

Normally, when floating an element the heading would move to the left and have the content wrap on the right side. However, the clear property placed on the paragraph stops this from happening.

The height property is set to 5em and overflow property is set to a value of hidden to keep the background image from spilling out of the heading element and onto the other portions of the web document.

See Also

The Gilder/Levin image replacement technique page at *http://www.mezzoblue.com/tests/revised-image-replacement/#gilderlevin*; read more about the technique at *http://www.khmerang.com/index.php?p=95.*

2.25   Placing Shadow Behind Text

Problem

You want to place a shadow behind the text in a heading, as shown in Figure 2-41.

Figure 2-41. Instant drop shadows on HTML text

Solution

Use the `text-shadow` property to set the color and placement of the shadow:

```
h1 {
  font-size: 2.5em;
  font-family: Myriad, Helvetica, Arial, sans-serif;
  width: 66.6%;
  text-shadow: yellow .15em .15em .15em;
  margin: 0 0 0.1em 0;
}
```

Discussion

The first value of the text-shadow property sets the color. The first length unit value, .15em, moves the shadow on the *x*-axis relative to the position of the HTML text. The next value moves the shadow on the *y*-axis. The last value is the blur radius of the shadow. The larger the value the more disperse the shadow.

The only known browser that supports the `text-shadow` property is Safari.

 Imagery used for this effect should be able to tile seamlessly, but also provide enough contrast so that the text is still legible.

See Also

Read more about the CSS 2.1 specification for `text-shadow` at *http://www.w3.org/TR/REC-CSS2/text.html#text-shadow-props*.

2.26   Adjusting the Spacing Between Letters and Words

Problem

You want to adjust the space between letters and words within HTML text as in Figure 2-42.

Solution

To adjust the space between the letters use the `letter-spacing` property (see Figure 2-43):

```
h2 {
  font: bold italic 2em "Helvetica Nue", serif;
  margin: 0;
  padding: 0;
  letter-spacing: -0.1em;
}
```

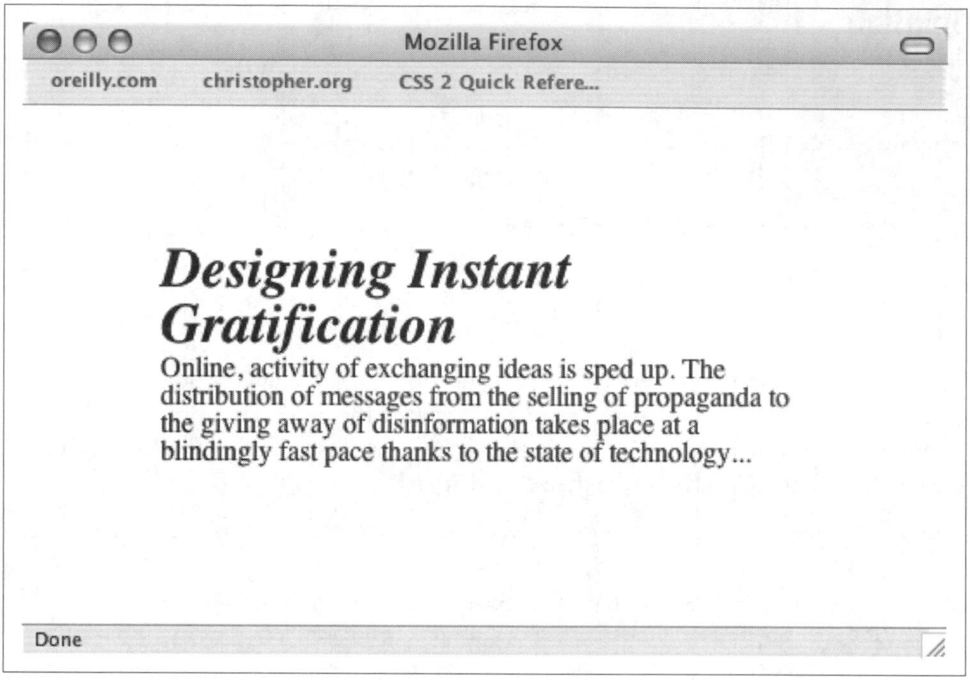

Figure 2-42. Default spacing between letters and words in HTML text

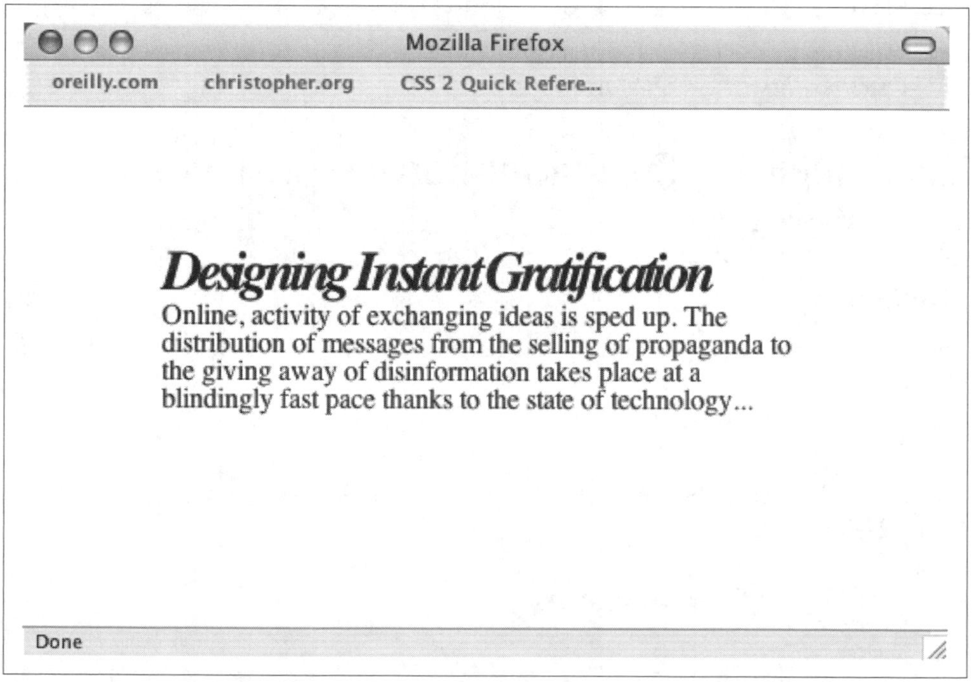

Figure 2-43. The adjusted letter spacing of the text in the heading

To adjust the space between words, use the word-spacing property (see Figure 2-44):

```
h2 {
  font: bold italic 2em "Helvetica Nue", serif;
  margin: 0;
  padding: 0;
  word-spacing: 0.33em;
}
```

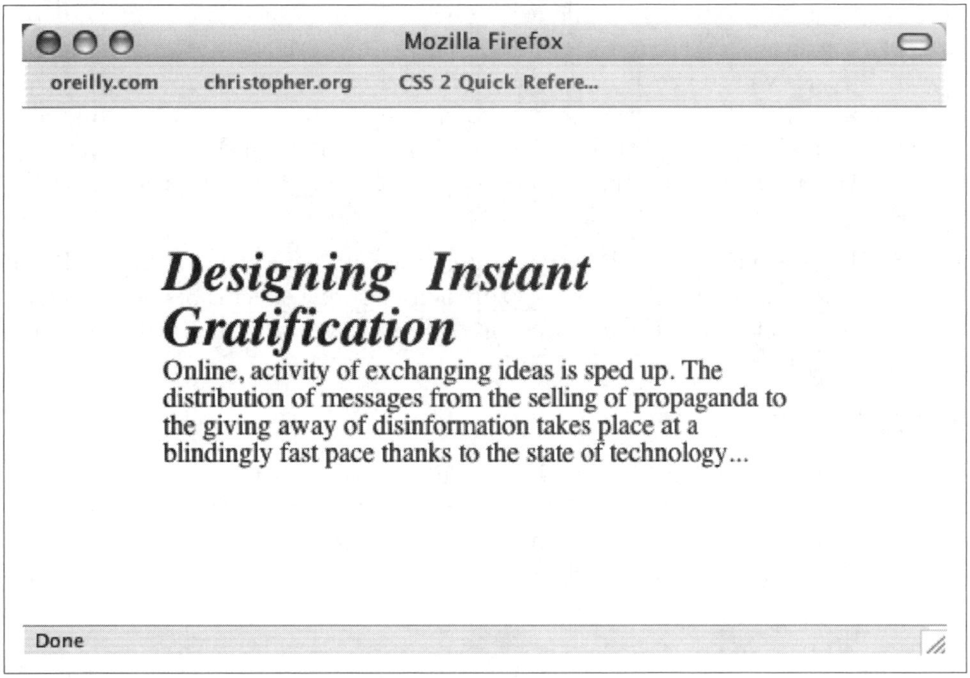

Figure 2-44. Words in the heading are spaced farther apart

Discussion

One of the main strengths of CSS is how the technology handles web typography. Web designers and developers had to use a puzzling array of nested font, b elements, and SPGs to create compelling text treatments. An effect like adjusting the space between two letters or separating whole words within a paragraph is something that CSS can render with ease.

The adjustment of the space between letters to create a better aesthetic is an old tradition in graphic design. There are two terms that describe how the change in the space is adjusted onto text: kerning and tracking.

Kerning is a design term used to describe the changing of the space between a pair of letters to create a better visual effect. An example of kerning is adjusting just the space between an uppercase letter *T* and a lowercase letter *i*. *Tracking* is defined as adjusting the space between letters in a large amount of text, not just between a pair of letters.

The `word-spacing` property is supported in Firefox, Internet Explorer for Windows 6+, Internet Explorer for the Macintosh 4+, Netscape Navigator 6+, Opera 3.5+, and Safari.

For best practices, the unit values of `letter-spacing` and `word-spacing` should be set in relative unit sizes instead of absolute length units. Since users can redefine the font sizes of their browsers, a fixed width value of 5 points originally intended for font size at 12 pixels will still be 5 points even if the user resizes the text to a larger value. In other words, the 5 point spacing between letters is barely going to be noticeable when the font size is set to 72 pixels or larger. With relative units like em, however, a value of `1.5em` for the letter-spacing property scales along with the resizing of the text.

Also, it's best to employ the text effects so that the text being styled is still legible. If communication is important to you or your client, a subtle effect is better than creating esoteric text elements. If the text becomes illegible, you may annoy the very people you are trying to reach.

See Also

Read the CSS 2.1 specification for `letter-spacing` at *http://www.w3.org/TR/CSS2/text.html#propdef-letter-spacing* and `word-spacing` at *http://www.w3.org/TR/CSS2/text.html#propdef-word-spacing*; learn more about kerning and tracking at *http://desktoppub.about.com/cs/typespacing/a/kerningtracking.htm*.

CHAPTER 3

Images

3.0   Introduction

When Marc Andreessen, founder of Netscape, allowed for the inline display of images back in the early 1990s, it helped kick start not only a global discussion, but added enticing visuals. Shared documents no longer were doomed to be text-laden academic papers allowing designers the initial foothold to begin the field of web design.

In this chapter, many recipes regarding CSS interactions with images are discussed. Recipes include dealing with borders, manipulating background images, rounding corners on boxes, replacing HTML text with images and much more.

3.1   Placing a Border Around an Image

Problem

You want to place a border around an image.

Solution

Use the border property on the img element (see Figure 3-1):

```
img {
 width: 300px;
 border: 6px double #666;
 background: #fff;
 padding: 6px;
}
```

Figure 3-1. A border is placed around an image

Discussion

If you make an image a link, there's a possibility of creating a more complex presentation with the border property. Using the :hover pseudo-class, the style of the border can be changed when a user rolls over the image (see Figure 3-2):

```
img {
  width: 30px;
  border: 4px double #666;
  background: #fff;
  padding: 4px;
}
a:hover img {
  border-style: solid;
  background: #999;
}
```

While the border acts like a frame around the image, the border style and color can be changed when a user rolls over the image. The padding of 4 pixels set in the img declaration block allows for color change inside this frame as well. So, a simple move of rolling over an image creates a rich visual with only two declaration blocks.

See Also

Recipe 3.2 for removing borders from images.

Figure 3-2. Combining background color with border styles creates an interesting rollover effect

3.2 Removing Borders Set on Images by Default in Some Browsers

Problem

You want to remove borders on images that are clickable like the one in Figure 3-3.

Solution

Set the border for images to zero (see Figure 3-4):

```
a img {
  border: 0;
}
```

Discussion

Before CSS, web developers would set the border of images through the border attribute of the img element:

```
<a href="http://csscookbook.com">
 <img src="file.jpg"  border="0" alt="logo" />
</a>
```

Figure 3-3. An image with a border

Figure 3-4. Now all images that are links will no longer have a border

With the advent of CSS, developers separate the presentation from the content and that includes the border property. While including the border attribute in the HTML element is no longer required, this method can lead to a complication.

See Also

Recipe 3.1 for applying a border on an image.

3.3 Setting a Background Image

Problem

You want a background image that doesn't repeat.

Solution

Use the background-image and background-repeat properties to control the display of an image (see Figure 3-5):

```
body {
  background-image: url(bkgd.jpg);
  background-repeat: no-repeat;
}
```

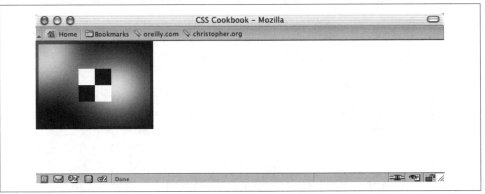

Figure 3-5. The background image displayed once in the upper-left corner

Discussion

You can place text and other inline images over a background image to create a sense of depth on a web page. Also, you can provide a framing device for the web page by tiling a background image along the sides of a web browser.

See Also

Recipe 3.4 for repeating background images in a line either horizontally or vertically.

3.4 Creating a Line of Background Images

Problem

You want a series of background images to repeat vertically or horizontally.

Solution

To tile the background image horizontally, or along the *x*-axis, use the following CSS rule (see Figure 3-6):

```
body {
  background-image: url(bkgd.jpg);
  background-repeat: repeat-x;
}
```

Figure 3-6. The background image tiled horizontally

To have the background image repeat along the vertical axis, use the `repeat-y` value for `background-repeat`.

See Also

Recipe 3.5 for placing a background image at a specific location in a web page.

3.5 Placing a Background Image on a Web Page

You want to position a background image in a web page.

Solution

Use the `background-position` property to set the location of the background image. To place an image that starts 75 pixels to the right of and 150 pixels below the upper-left corner of the viewport (see Figure 3-7), use the following CSS rule:

```
body {
  background-image: url(bkgd.jpg);
```

```
    background-repeat: no-repeat;
    background-position: 75px 150px;
}
```

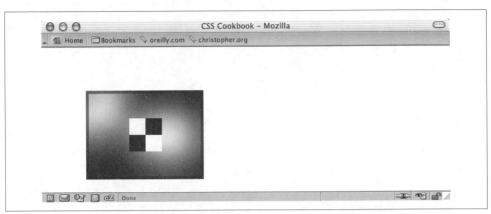

Figure 3-7. The background placed precisely 75 pixels from the right and 150 pixels from the upper-left corner of browser's viewport

Discussion

The background-position property contains two values separated by a space. The first value of the pair sets the origin point along the *x*-axis, while the second value sets the point on the *y*-axis. If only one value is given, that value is used for the horizontal position and the vertical position is set to 50%.

The solution used pixel units to determine the placement of the background image; however, you also can use percentages. A value of 50% for background-position means that the browser places the image in the dead center of the viewport, like the one in Figure 3-8, while the values 0% and 100% place the image in the upper-left and lower-right corners, respectively.

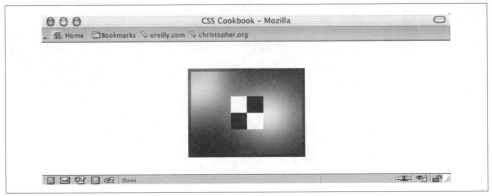

Figure 3-8. The background image centered in the browser window

Along with percentages, you can use the values top, center, and bottom for the *y*-axis and left, center, and right for the *x*-axis. Using combinations of these values, you can place the background image at the eight points around the edges of the viewport (in the corners and in between), as well as in the middle of the viewport. For example, to recreate the value of 50% in Figure 3-8, you can use this CSS rule instead:

```
body {
  background-image: url(bkgd.jpg);
  background-repeat: no-repeat;
  background-position: center;
}
```

To place a background image in the lower-right corner (see Figure 3-9), you can use the following CSS rule:

```
body {
  background-image: url(bkgd.jpg);
  background-repeat: no-repeat;
  background-position: bottom right;
}
```

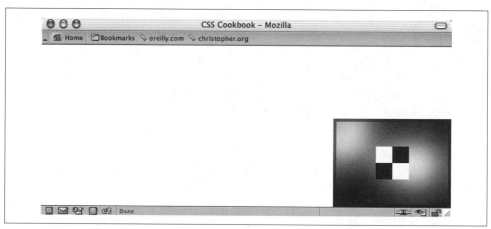

Figure 3-9. The background image placed in the lower-right corner

You also can use the `background-position` and `background-repeat` properties for background images that tile but aren't chained to the sides of the viewport. For example, the following CSS snippet creates a web page design such as the one in Figure 3-10:

```
body {
  background-image: url(montage.jpg);
  background-repeat: repeat-x;
  background-position: 55px 100px;
}
h1 {
  font-size: 75px;
  font-family: Verdana, Helvetica, Arial, sans-serif;
```

```
    text-align: center;
    margin: 0;
    padding: 0 0 125px 0;
}
p {
    line-height: 1.5em;
    font-family: Verdana, Helvetica, Arial, sans-serif;
    margin: 0 15%;
}
```

Figure 3-10. A repeating montage created using the CSS properties background-repeat and background-position

 Netscape Navigator 4 doesn't support background-position, and it's impossible to work around this limitation through CSS.

See Also

Recipe 3.7 for setting a non-scrolling image; CSS 2.1 specification for background-position at *http://www.w3.org/TR/CSS21/colors.html#propdef-background-position*.

3.6 Using Multiple Background Images on One Selector

Problem

You want to place more than one background image within one CSS selector.

Solution

As of this writing, Safari for Macintosh has implemented the CSS 3 specification for layering multiple background images in one selector.

In CSS 3, the shorthand background property can accept multiple sets of background image information as long as commas separate them (see Figure 3-11):

```
h2 {
  padding-top: 72px; /* enough padding for the images */
  text-align: center;
  background: url(plane.gif) center no-repeat,
   url(mail.gif) top center no-repeat,
   url(printer.gif) 40% 24px no-repeat,
   url(gift.gif) 60% 24px no-repeat;
}
```

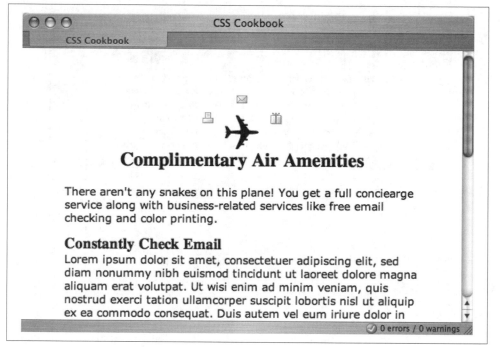

Figure 3-11. Individual icons are placed as background images in the heading

Discussion

Like most shorthand properties, the shorthand code for multiple backgrounds can be split out into separate CSS declaration blocks.

```
h2 {
  padding-top: 72px; /* enough padding for the images */
  text-align: center;
  background: url(plane.gif), url(mail.gif), url(printer.gif), url(gift.gif);
```

```
    background-position: center, top center, 40% 24px, 60% 24px;
    background-repeat: no-repeat, no-repeat, no-repeat, no-repeat;
}
```

Since all the backgrounds in the CSS rule do not repeat, one no-repeat value can be placed in the code and applied to all background images:

```
h2 {
    padding-top: 72px; /* enough padding for the images */
    text-align: center;
    background: url(plane.gif), url(mail.gif), url(printer.gif), url(gift.gif);
    background-position: center, top center, 40% 24px, 60% 24px;
    background-repeat: no-repeat;
}
```

This reduction of similar values can be applied to all CSS background-related properties making sure that it's desired that the background images share the same value.

For the time being, introducing new elements and applying background images to these new elements is the only way to achieve the technique of multiple images across all modern browsers. For more information and examples on these techniques, see Recipes 3.15 and 3.16 that produce rounded corners with additional markup.

See Also

For more information on the CSS 3 specification for layering multiple images, see *http://www.w3.org/TR/2005/WD-css3-background-20050216/#layering*.

3.7   Creating a Stationary Background Image

Problem

You want a background image to remain in the browser window, even as the user scrolls down a web page.

Solution

Use the background-attachment property set with a fixed value, like so:

```
body {
    background-image: url(bkgd.jpg);
    background-repeat: no-repeat;
    background-attachment: fixed;
}
```

Discussion

By using this technique, you are locking down the background image. So, even if a visitor scrolls, the image remains where you placed it originally. Another acceptable value for background-attachment is scroll, which is the default value. So, even if you don't specify scroll, the background image moves up with the rest of the document as the visitor scrolls down.

For example, imagine that you want to post a photo of a recent trip on your web page, and you want the photo positioned on the left side of the page and your text on the right. As the reader scrolls down to read more about the trip, the photo from the trip stays in place (see Figure 3-12). Here's the code:

```
body {
  background-image: url(bkgd2.jpg);
  background-repeat: no-repeat;
  background-attachment: fixed;
  background-position: -125px 75px;
  margin: 75px 75px 0 375px;
}
h1, h2, h3 {
  padding-top: 0;
  margin-top: 0;
  text-transform: uppercase;
}
p {
  text-align: justify;
}
```

To take this further, you can lock down the image on block-level elements other than body. For example, try the heading elements when designing a review for a movie or concert. The following CSS rule can create the interesting surfing experience:

```
h1, h2, h3 {
  font-size: 200%;
  background-image: url(bkgd2.jpg);
  background-repeat: no-repeat;
  background-attachment: fixed;
  background-position: center;
  padding: 1.5em;
  text-align: center;
  color: white;
}
```

Because of the padding and light color on the headings, there is enough room to see the background image "through" the elements as well as to read the headlines. As the visitor scrolls the web page reading the review, she will see the rest of the image (see Figure 3-13).

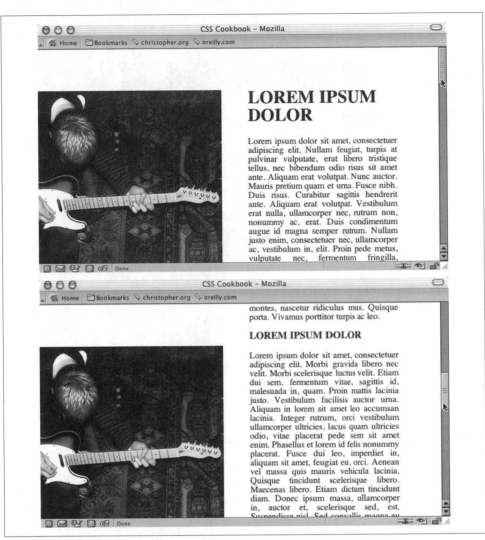

Figure 3-12. The photo staying in place as the visitor scrolls

At press time, only Mozilla, Firefox, Safari, and Netscape 6+ supported the application of background images as fixed attachments to block-level elements like the header elements used in this solution. Internet Explorer 5.x and 6 for Windows repeat the background image in each header element.

Figure 3-13. The photo coming through the headings instead of the body element

See Also

Recipe 3.5 to position a background image; Recipe 11.4 for a hack to fix Internet Explorer for Windows' lack of support for background-fixed; the CSS 2.1 specification for background-attachment at *http://www.w3.org/TR/CSS21/colors.html#propdef-background-attachment*.

3.8 Overlaying HTML Text on an Image

Problem

You want to position HTML text over an image.

Solution

Set the image within the background, and then position and style the HTML text accordingly.

First, wrap the text around a div element with an id attribute (see Figure 3-14):

```
<div id="frame">
 <div id="banner">
  <h1>White House Confidential <br /><span>
Classified Lawn Care Secrets</span></h1>
 </div><!-- end #banner -->
 <p>...</p>
</div><!-- end #frame -->
```

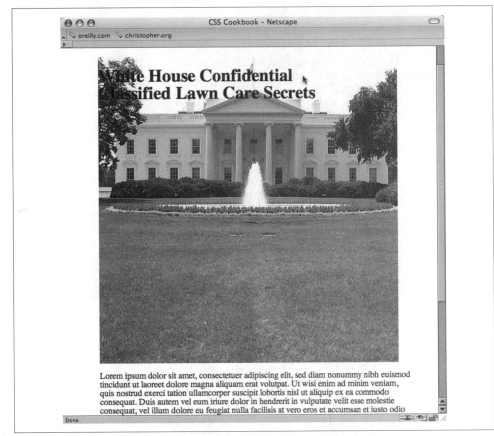

Figure 3-14. The photo coming through the headings instead of the body element

Insert the image through the `background-image` property making sure to set the width and height:

```
#banner {
 width: 550px;
 height: 561px;
 overflow: hidden;
 background-image: url(whitehouse.jpg);
 background-position: 0;
 background-repeat: no-repeat;
}
```

Then adjust the type to the desired style (see Figure 3-15):

```
h1 {
 margin: 0;
 padding: 0;
 font-family: Verdana, Arial, sans-serif;
 margin-top: 325px;
 margin-left: 25px;
```

```
/* room around text */
padding-left: 25px;
padding-bottom: 25px;

/* bring in the translucent background image */
background-image: url(white-banner.png);
background-position: bottom;
background-repeat: no-repeat;
}
h1 span {
  font-size: .8em;
}
```

Figure 3-15. The photo coming through the headings instead of the body element

Discussion

Instead of bringing in an image and having it be inline or be part of the content of a web page when its purpose is strictly decorative, use the background-image property to display the image. This method allows the content of the page to have more integrity, but still maintain the intended visual.

See Also

Recipe 3.9 for replacing HTML text with an image.

3.9   Replacing HTML Text with an Image

Problem

You want to replace HTML text like a heading as shown in Figure 3-16 with an image that contains visually rich imagery or typography.

Figure 3-16. The default rendering of the heading text

Solution

Use the Gilder/Levin image replacement technique.

First, introduce a span element before the HTML text:

```
<h1>
 <span></span>
 Replacement Text Is Here
</h1>
```

Then set the width and height for the replacement image on the h1 selector as well as setting the positioning of the element to relative:

```
h1 {
  width: 216px;
  height: 72px;
  position: relative:
}
```

Next, by setting the positioning of the span element to absolute and adjusting the width and height of the span inside the h1 element, the span element now overlaps the HTML text. The last step is to bring in the replacement image through the background property (see Figure 3-17):

```
h1 span {
  background: url(replacementimage.jpg) no-repeat;
  position: absolute;
  width: 100%;
  height: 100%;
}
```

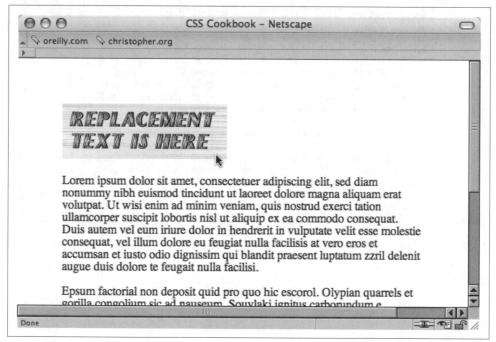

Figure 3-17. The HTML text is now replaced by a graphic

Discussion

There are several image replacement techniques in web development and all seem to have their own benefits and drawbacks.

Origin of the image replacement method

Todd Fahrner is one of the persons credited with the original concept of image replacement technique.

The markup for the Farhner Image Replacement (FIR) technique also introduces a nonsemantic span element, except that the span element is wrapped around the content:

```
<h1>
 <span>
  Replacement Text Is Here
 </span>
</h1>
```

Then the CSS rules bring in the replacement image through the selector for the h1 element while hiding the text:

```
h1 {
  background: url(replacementimage.jpg) no-repeat;
  width: 216px;
  height: 72px;
}
h1 span {
  display: none;
}
```

Problem with the FIR method

The easy implementation of the FIR technique made it quite popular in web development. However, screen readers used by people with disabilities would often skip over the reading of the HTML text because the span element set the text to be hidden from view. Thus important text would be lost to those members of a site's audience.

Phark image replacement method

Both the FIR and the Gilder/Levin image replacement methods use an unsemantic span tag to achieve their results. Another image replacement technique created by Mike Rundle from phark.net removes the need for the span tag.

First, adjust the HTML by removing the span tag:

```
<h1>
 Replacement Text Is Here
</h1>
```

For the CSS rules, use a negative value for the text-indent property instead of using the display property to hide the text:

```
h1 {
  text-indent: -9000em;
  background: url(replacementimage.jpg) no-repeat;
  width: 216px;
  height: 72px;
}
```

Like the other methods, the Phark image replacement method works very well. Its main drawback is that the HTML text does not appear if a site visitor has turned off images from being viewed in their browser.

CSS 3 approach to image replacement

The CSS 3 specification has an easy method for image replacement, if browsers were to implement it. For example, to replace text within an h1 element all the CSS that would be required would be one declaration block:

```
h1 {
 content: url(logo.gif);
}
```

The specification also makes no limits on what kind of multimedia can be supported with the content property. In theory, a web developer could place a QuickTime movie instead of an animated GIF:

```
h1 {
 content: url(logo.mov);
}
```

However, at the time of this writing, support for the CSS 3 specification is not in modern browsers. Also, the CSS 3 specification is still under development.

See Also

Levin Alexander's web page about the Gilder/Levin image replacement technique at *http://levin.grundeis.net/files/20030809/alternatefir.html*; information on the inserting content with CSS 3 at *http://www.w3.org/TR/css3-content/#inserting3*.

3.10   Replacing HTML Text with Flash Text

Problem

You want to replace HTML text with more typography choices, but without the hassle of having to manually update static images (as discussed in Recipe 3.9).

Solution

Use the Scalable Inman Flash Replacement (sIFR) technique.

Download the JavaScript and other components used for the technique at *http://www.mikeindustries.com/sifr/*.

Using Flash, open the sifr.fla file. Click on the white canvas area (it will appear as though there isn't anything present) to bring up the Properties palette (shown in Figure 3-18).

Select the font you wish to use on your web site design (see Figure 3-19).

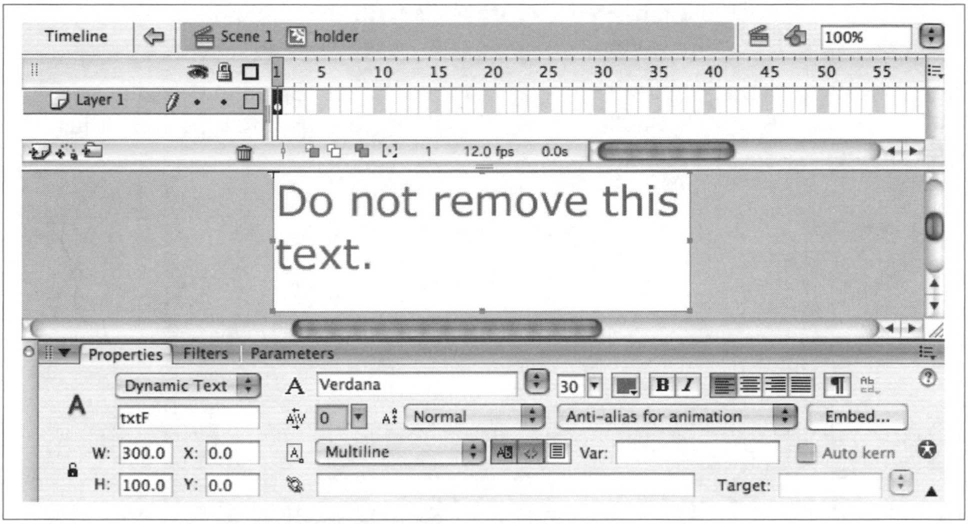

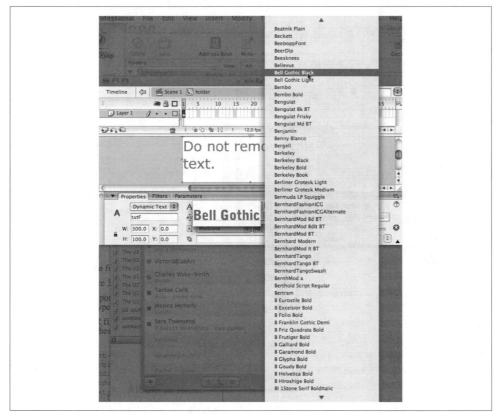

Figure 3-18. Bring up the Flash Properties palette

Figure 3-19. Pick the typeface from the Flash Properties palette

Next, export the file and name the exported file with the name of the typeface. For example, the Bell Gothic typeface would be named `bellgothic.swf`.

The sFIR files include a set of CSS rules that need to be copied and pasted onto the site's CSS files. Be sure to include these files. To bring up the typeface, adjust the CSS rules to include, for example:

```
h1 {
  font-family: "Bell Gothic", Arial, Verdana, sans-serif;
  margin: 0 0 .3em 0;
  padding: 0 0 .3em 0;
  border-bottom: 2px solid #666;
  text-align: left;
  font-size: 2em;
}
```

Finally, upload the files to view results like the headline in Figure 3-20.

Figure 3-20. The headline appears in Bell Gothic

Discussion

In 2004, web developer Shaun Inman created the Inman Flash Replacement method. While lightweight and direct in scope, it accomplished the job of replacing typical HTML text with Flash-based text.

Another web developer Mike Davidson used Inman's technique as the basis for a more robust system that allowed for text resizing and multiline text.

The sFIR method is used primarily for replacing heading text and not text-based links. Although it's possible to replace the text-based links, it's not recommended as users won't be able to right- or middle-click the links to open the pages in a new browser.

Since the technique makes heavy use of JavaScript and Flash, visitors to your site may notice that the browser is taking longer than usual to render the sFIR text.

Another issue is that although most modern browsers like Internet Explorer for Windows, Opera 8+, Safari, and Firefox support Flash transparency, the ability for the browsers to render background images through the transparency is a CPU intensive. Users on slower machines may notice a sluggish surfing experience.

See Also

More information Shaun Inman's sFIR at *http://www.shauninman.com/plete/2004/04/ ifr-revisited-and-revised.*

3.11   Using Multiple PNGs with Transparency

Problem

You want to use multiple PNGs with alpha transparency.

Solution

Use Drew McLellan's updated Sleight script for triggering alpha transparency in Internet Explorer 5.5–6.

You can write the code into a separate JavaScript file or download the code from McLellan's site at *http://allinthehead.com/code/samples/bgsleight.js*:

```
if (navigator.platform == "Win32" &&
 navigator.appName == "Microsoft Internet Explorer" &&
 window.attachEvent) {
   window.attachEvent("onload", fnLoadPngs);
}

function fnLoadPngs() {
 var rslt = navigator.appVersion.match(/MSIE (\d+\.\d+)/, '');
 var itsAllGood = (rslt != null && Number(rslt[1]) >= 5.5);
 for (var i = document.all.length - 1, obj = null;
  (obj = document.all[i]); i--) {
   if (itsAllGood &&
 obj.currentStyle.backgroundImage.match(/\.png/i) != null) {
   this.fnFixPng(obj);
   obj.attachEvent("onpropertychange",
 this.fnPropertyChanged);
  }
 }
}
```

```
function fnPropertyChanged( ) {
  if (window.event.propertyName == "style.backgroundImage") {
   var el = window.event.srcElement;
   if (!el.currentStyle.backgroundImage.match(/x\.gif/i)) {
     var bg = el.currentStyle.backgroundImage;
     var src = bg.substring(5,bg.length-2);
     el.filters.item(0).src = src;
     el.style.backgroundImage = "url(x.gif)";
   }
  }
}

function fnFixPng(obj) {
 var bg = obj.currentStyle.backgroundImage;
 var src = bg.substring(5,bg.length-2);
 obj.style.filter =
"progid:DXImageTransform.Microsoft.AlphaImageLoader(src='"
 + src + "', sizingMethod='scale')";
 obj.style.backgroundImage = "url(x.gif)";
}
```

Attach the JavaScript file to the web page by placing the following code in between the head elements:

```
<script src="/_assets/js/bgsleight.js" type="text/javascript"></script>
```

 Make sure to reference the JavaScript correctly. In this example, the JavaScript is located in the js folder that is placed in the _assets folder.

Be sure to upload single pixel transparent GIF (listed as x.gif in the script) to the web server and update the location reference the file location in the script for your needs.

Discussion

Support for alpha transparency in modern browsers is almost commonplace. Browsers that include native support for PNGs include Netscape Navigator 6+, Opera, Safari, and Internet Explorer for Windows 7. However, this list does not include the currently popular Internet Explorer for Windows 6.

To work around this, Aaron Boodman created a piece of JavaScript that used Microsoft's proprietary filter property to activate Internet Explorer for Windows 5.5–6 support for inline PNGs with alpha transparency, without interfering with the other browsers that support PNGs natively.

Drew McLellan built off of Boodman's work and modified the JavaScript used in the solution to make the script work not only for inline images, but also for background images (see *http://allinthehead.com/retro/69/sleight-of-hand*).

As a page is loaded, McLellan's JavaScript is executed. The script goes through the HTML markup looking for img elements that point to images with the png extension.

Once it finds such an `img` code, the script dynamically rewrites the HTML on the fly. The first part of the revision is to replace the PNG image with a single pixel GIF that is transparent.

Next, the PNG file is set in Internet Explorer's `filter` property in order to trigger the alpha transparency in that browser. Since the only way this can be done, the PNG gets set in the background.

Thus, the PNG is shown in the background behind the transparent GIF.

 When you code the page, be sure to set the width and height of the PNG image in the CSS with the `width` and `height` properties. Otherwise, the script will not execute properly.

See Also

The original posting of the Sleight script at *http://www.youngpup.net/2001/sleight*; more information about Microsoft's `filter` property at *http://msdn.microsoft.com/ workshop/author/filter/reference/filters/alpha.asp*.

3.12   Building a Panoramic Image Presentation

Problem

You want to create the appearance that the width of an image to increases or decreases as a user resizes his browser window, like the one in Figure 3-21.

Solution

Place an image element that refers to a panoramic image into the background of a block-level element (see Figure 3-22).

```
<h1>Visit France City!</h1>
 <div><img src="frenchtown.jpg" alt=" " /></div>
<h2>The quaint and charming little destination in France</h2>
```

Position the image element in the upper-right corner of the block-level element, and then hide the image by setting the `display` to none:

```
div {
 background-image: url(frenchtown.jpg);
 background-repeat: no-repeat;
 background-position: top right;
 height: 300px;
 border: 1px solid black;
 max-width: 714px;
}
div img {
 display: none;
}
```

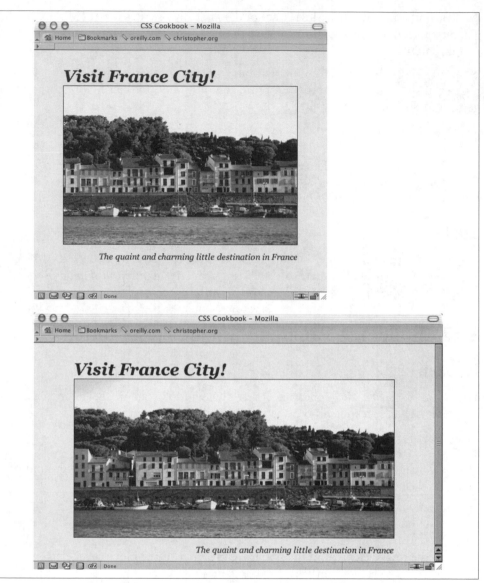

Figure 3-21. Browser window increased in size to show more of the panoramic image

When the image is placed as a background image, it will be resized based on the size of the browser window.

Discussion

To create a panoramic presentation, you need a wide photograph. You then need to position the image element in the upper-right corner of the block-level element so that the image will grow or shrink depending on the size of the browser window. The

Figure 3-22. Panoramic photo placed on a web page

use of max-width property constrains the width of the div element from expanding beyond the width of the image itself.

In this solution, the same image is used in both the HTML and CSS. The rationale behind this approach is to make sure the image (or content) displays, even if the user agent rendering the page doesn't understand CSS.

See Also

http://www.creighton.edu/~jaypl/oldpage/panhow.html for more information on how to create panoramic pictures; the CSS 2.1 specification for max-width property at *http://www.w3.org/TR/CSS21/visudet.html#propdef-max-width*.

3.13   Combining Different Image Formats

Problem

You want to combine two different image formats into one presentation. For example, you want to combine GIF and JPEG images into one graphical presentation (see Figure 3-23).

Figure 3-23. Two different image formats combined into one

Solution

Place an image inside a block-level element such as a div or h2:

```
<h2><img src="headline_text.gif" alt="Headline image set in
GIF format" /></h2>
```

Use an image-editing program, to separate the elements of the image into separate file formats (see Figure 3-24).

Figure 3-24. Two images that will be used to create one image

Name one of the images the same as the image referred to in the src attribute for the img element. Place the other image in the background of the block-level element to merge both images into one presentation:

```
h2 {
  background-image: url(headline_bkgd.jpg);
  background-repeat: none;
  width: 587px;
  height: 113px;
}
```

Discussion

The two prevailing image formats on the Web are GIF and JPEG. Both compress images in different ways. Typically, images with flat areas of color compress better in the GIF format, while JPEG images are better for photos or images that contain fine color gradations.

In the example shown in Figures 3-23 and 3-24, the file size of the two separate images added together is actually less than the file size of the final, combined image. This occurs because part of the image would work against the compression scheme of one file format. If you saved the presentation as one GIF, the photographic portions of the image would create an inflated file size. And if you saved the image as a JPEG, the areas of flat color would inflate the size. By splitting up the images into different formats that leverage their respective compression schemes, you reduce file sizes overall.

Although the method in this solution uses background properties in CSS, you can accomplish the same effect by positioning block elements that contain inline images. For example, in Figure 3-25, you can see that the line art of the boat was overlaid on the photograph of the two children.

To make this method work, wrap the image elements in block-level div elements, as shown in the following HTML code:

```
<!DOCTYPE html PUBLIC "-//W3C//DTD XHTML 1.0 Transitional//EN"
    "http://www.w3.org/TR/xhtml1/DTD/xhtml1-transitional.dtd">
<html xmlns="http://www.w3.org/1999/xhtml">
 <head>
  <title>CSS Cookbook</title>
 </head>
 <body>
  <img src="kids.jpg" width="360" height="304"  alt="kids
playing" />
  <div id="boat"><img src="boat.gif" width="207" height="123"
   alt="boat" /></div>
  <div id="water"><img src="landscape.gif" width="315"
height="323"
   alt="landscape" /></div>
 </body>
</html>
```

Figure 3-25. Intricate combination of different image formats

Then, through CSS, set the position of the elements to absolute. By setting the position to absolute, you take the elements out of the normal flow of the web page, and instead assign values to the left, top, and z-index properties to determine their new placements:

```
#boat {
 position: absolute;
 width: 207px;
 height: 123px;
 z-index: 2;
 left: 264px;
 top: 0;
}
#water {
 position: absolute;
 width: 315px;
 height: 323px;
 z-index: 1;
 left: 359px;
 top: -20px;
}
```

The left and top properties indicate the placement of the images within their nearest positioned ancestor element or the initial containing block. In this case, it's the initial containing block to the div elements.

Furthermore, the body element's margin has a value of 0, meaning that the origin point is in the upper-left corner of the browser's viewport:

```
body {
  margin: 0;
}
```

Even though this method works, if the web document is later modified, exact positioning becomes a design liability. For example, adding a simple headline above the images in the HTML results in the anomaly you see in Figure 3-26:

```
<h2>Kids Welcome New Boat!</h2>
 <img src="kids.jpg" width="360" height="304"  alt="kids
playing" />
 <div id="boat"><img src="boat.gif" width="207" height="123"
   alt="boat" /></div>
 <div id="water"><img src="landscape.gif" width="315" height="323"
alt="landscape" /></div>
```

Figure 3-26. Presentation breaks with the addition of a heading

Because the image of the children has not been positioned with `absolute`, it moves down the flow of the document. The other image stays in place because it has been positioned within the initial containing block and is still in the same place it was before the headline was added.

By using the `background-positioning` method within block-level elements, you can create a self-containing module. Then, when content is added to and removed from

the web page, the presentation remains whole, as seen in Figure 3-27 and shown in
the following code:

```
<!DOCTYPE html PUBLIC "-//W3C//DTD XHTML 1.0 Transitional//EN"
    "http://www.w3.org/TR/xhtml1/DTD/xhtml1-transitional.dtd">
<html xmlns="http://www.w3.org/1999/xhtml">
 <head>
 <title>CSS Cookbook</title>
<style type="text/css">
body {
 margin: 5% 10% 0 10%;
}
#content {
 background-image: url(landscape.gif);
 background-repeat: no-repeat;
 background-position: bottom right;
 height: 400px;
 width: 674px;
}
h2 {
 margin: 0;
 padding: 0;
 background-image: url(kids.jpg);
 background-repeat: no-repeat;
 background-position: bottom left;
 height: 400px;
 width: 600px;
}
#boat {
 background-image: url(boat.gif);
 background-repeat: no-repeat;
 display: block;
 width: 207px;
 height: 123px;
 margin-left: 250px;
 margin-top: 75px;
}
</style>
 </head>
 <body>
  <div id="content">
   <h2>Kids Welcome New Boat!
    <span id="boat">
    </span>
   </h2>
  </div>
 </body>
</html>
```

See Also

Recipe 12.2 on creating unexpected incongruity between two elements; Recipe 12.3
on combining unlike elements.

Figure 3-27. A different approach to combining images

3.14   Rounding Corners with Fixed-Width Columns

Problem

You want to create rounded corners on columns that set with fixed-width columns.

Solution

Create two background images with one image containing the top corners and the other image containing the bottom corners (Figure 3-28).

Wrap a div element around the content that's within the column:

```
<div id="box">
 <h2>
  I Met a Girl I&#8217;d Like to Know Better
 </h2>
 <p>Lorem ipsum dolor sit amet, consectetuer adipiscing elit, sed diam
nonummy nibh euismod tincidunt ut laoreet dolore magna aliquam erat volutpat.
Ut wisi enim ad minim veniam.</p>
</div>
```

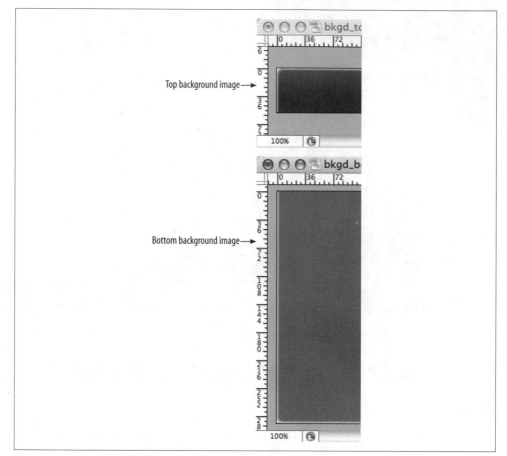

Figure 3-28. One image for the top corners and another for the bottom corners

Place the bottom background image in the div element (see Figure 3-29):

```
#box {
 width: 214px;
 background-image: url(bkgd_bottom.gif);
 background-position: bottom;
 background-repeat: no-repeat;
}
```

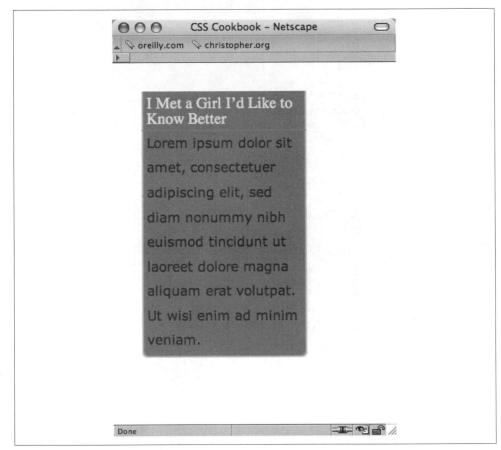

Figure 3-29. A background image is placed at the bottom of the column

Then place the top background image in the h2 element (see Figure 3-30):

```
h2 {
  background-image: url(bkgd_top.gif);
  backgroung-position: left top;
  background-repeat: no-repeat;
  padding: 7px 7px 3px 7px;
  margin: 0;
  border-bottom: 1px solid #999;
  font-size: 1.3em;
  font-weight: normal;
  color: #eee;
}
```

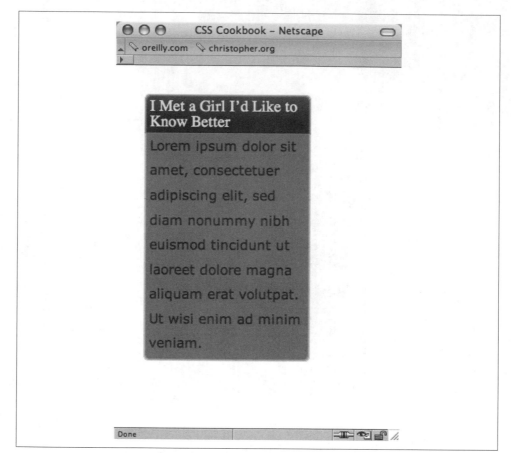

Figure 3-30. A background image is placed at the top of the column

Discussion

To compensate for different text sizes like the ones in Figure 3-31, make the background images extend for longer than just the space specified in the design. For example, the images used in this solution are 600 pixels tall, however it's not unheard of to have the lengths of the graphics to be more than 1,000 pixels to insure a page's design maintains its integrity with extreme font sizing.

By fixing the width of the column to a length unit like pixels, it's possible to place an image containing two corners in one image. With column widths that change when the user resizes the browser, however, the fixed-width solution falls apart.

See Also

Recipes 3.15, 3.16, and 3.17 for rounding corners with flexible widths.

Figure 3-31. As the text enlarges, the design keeps its integrity

3.15   Rounding Corners (Sliding Doors Technique)

Problem

You want to round corners in columns that have flexible widths.

Solution

Use the Sliding Doors technique that was made popular by web designer Douglas Bowman.

Create the design of the rounded corners (see Figure 3-32).

Figure 3-32. The basic design for the column

Then create separate graphics for the four corners like the ones in Figure 3-33.

Wrap the content that is in the column with additional div elements:

```
<div id="box">
 <div id="innerhead">
  <h2>
   I Met a Girl I&#8217;d Like to Know Better
  </h2>
 </div>
 <div id="content">
  <div id="innercontent">
   <p>Lorem ipsum dolor sit amet, consectetuer adipiscing elit, sed
diam nonummy nibh euismod tincidunt ut laoreet dolore magna aliquam
erat volutpat. Ut wisi enim ad minim veniam.</p>
  </div>
 </div>
</div>
```

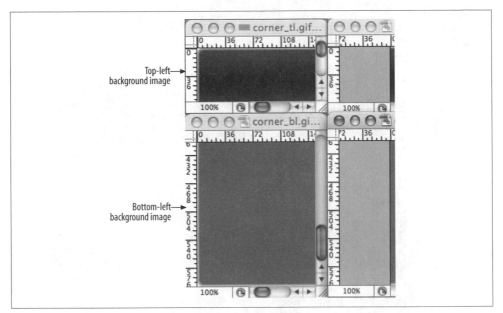

Figure 3-33. The column design split up into four graphics

Then place the background images through CSS (see Figure 3-34). The top-left corner goes in the "inner-head" id selector, the top-right corner slides into the preexisting h2 element, the "content" id selector gets the bottom-left selector, and the "inner-content" id selector houses the bottom-right graphic.

```
#innerhead {
 background-image: url(corner_tl.gif);
 background-position: top left;
background-repeat: no-repeat;
}
h2 {
 background-image: url(corner_tr.gif);
 background-position: top right;
 background-repeat: no-repeat;
 margin: 0;
 padding: 7px;
 border-bottom: 1px solid #999;
 font-size: 1.3em;
 font-weight: normal;
 color: #eee;
}
#content {
 background-image: url(corner_bl.gif);
 background-position: bottom left;
 background-repeat: no-repeat;
}
```

```
#innercontent {
 background-image: url(corner_br.gif);
 background-position: bottom right;
 background-repeat: no-repeat;
}
```

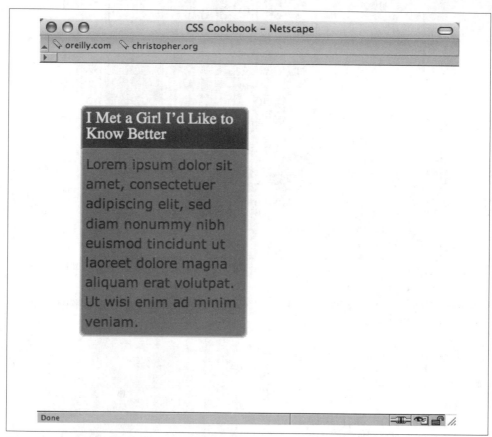

Figure 3-34. Rounded corners appear on the column

Discussion

The div and h2 elements act as hooks to add background images into all four corners of the column. As the browser resizes, the background images stay in their respective corners (see Figure 3-35).

To make sure that the design integrity is maintained as the column expands, further digital image editing is required. Manipulate one side, either left or right, and expand the two graphics both vertically and horizontally. For example, the top-left and bottom-left graphics (see Figures 3-36 and 3-37) were expanded for this solution.

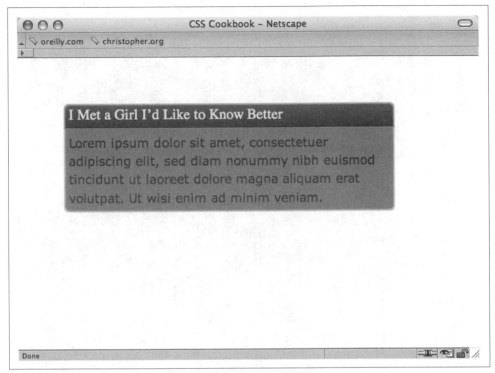

Figure 3-35. Rounded corners are maintained even though the column expands

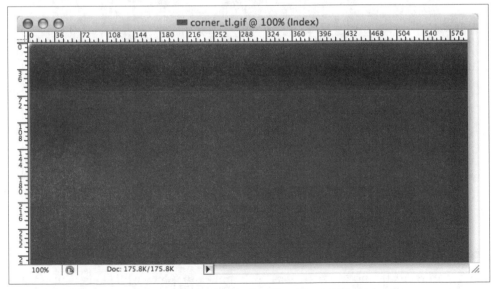

Figure 3-36. The bottom-right graphic is 600 pixels wide and over 250 pixels tall

Figure 3-37. The bottom-left graphic is 600 pixels wide and 600 pixels tall

See Also

Recipe 3.16 for a simple solution to rounding corners of a column.

3.16 Rounding Corners (Mountaintop Technique)

Problem

You want to create one set of graphics for rounded graphics while being able to display many background colors within the column.

Solution

Use the Mountaintop technique that was popularized by web designer Dan Cederholm.

Create a small graphic that will act as basis for the rounded corners (see Figure 3-38).

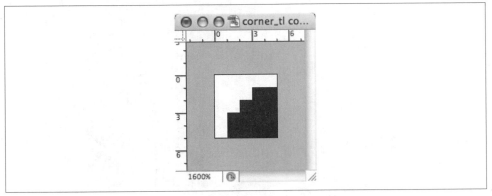

Figure 3-38. The top-left corner graphic

 Note that the black color in Figure 3-38 will be set to transparent when the image is exported as a GIF.

Export the image as a GIF with the filename of *corner_tl.gif*.

Then rotate the image 90 degrees (see Figure 3-39) and export as a GIF image, naming it *corner_tr.gif*. Repeat the last two steps to create the bottom corners, *corner_br.gif* and *corner_bl.gif*.

Add additional div elements around the column content:

```
<div id="box">
 <div id="head_outer">
  <div id="head_inner">
   <h2>
    I Met a Girl I&#8217;d Like to Know Better
   </h2>
  </div>
 </div>
 <p>Lorem ipsum dolor sit amet, consectetuer adipiscing elit, sed diam
nonummy nibh euismod tincidunt ut laoreet dolore magna aliquam erat
volutpat. Ut wisi enim ad minim veniam.</p>
</div>
```

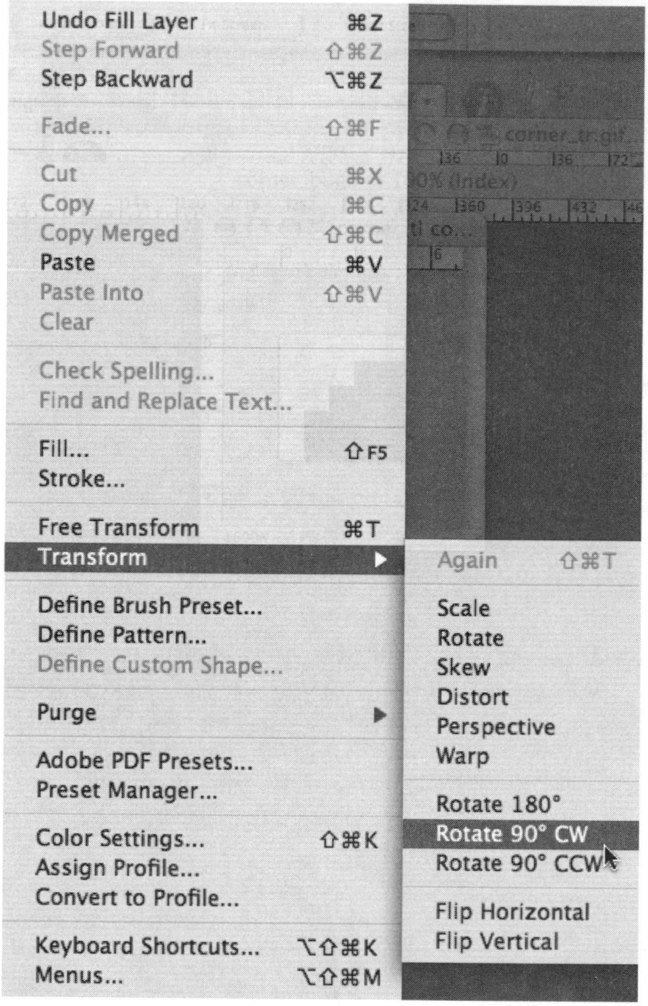

Figure 3-39. Rotating the image 90 degrees

Then place the four corner graphics within the id and p selectors (see Figure 3-40):

```
div#box {
 width: 55%;
 background-color: #999999;
 background-image: url(corner_bl.gif);
 background-repeat: no-repeat;
 background-position: bottom left;
}
#head_outer {
 background-image: url(corner_tl.gif);
 background-repeat: no-repeat;
}
```

```
#head_inner {
 background-image: url(corner_tr.gif);
 background-repeat: no-repeat;
 background-position: top right;
}
div p {
 margin: 0;
 padding: 7px;
 font-family: Verdana, Arial, Helvetica, sans-serif;
 font-size: 1.1em;
 background-image: url(corner_br.gif);
 background-position: bottom right;
 background-repeat: no-repeat;
 color: #333333;
 font-size: .8em;
 line-height: 1.5;
}
```

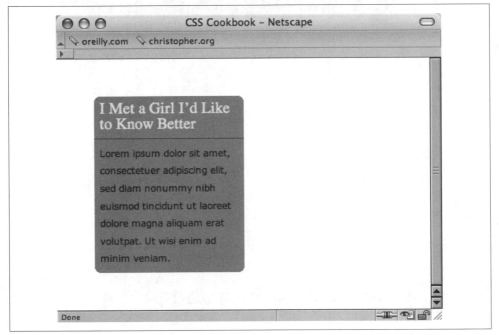

Figure 3-40. Mountaintop corner example

Discussion

The beauty of the mountaintop technique rests in its simplicity. Four small graphics are made with low file-sizes thanks to the GIF compression algorithms that are placed in the background of four block-level elements.

Also, there isn't the need to expand a couple of images to make sure the design integrity is maintained because the column resizes such as in the Solution for Recipe 3.15.

Plus, the Mountaintop technique allows for quickly changing the column's background color without revising the corner graphics as you see in Figure 3-41. However, the corner graphics *will* need to be changed if the background color of the web page or column's parent element changes.

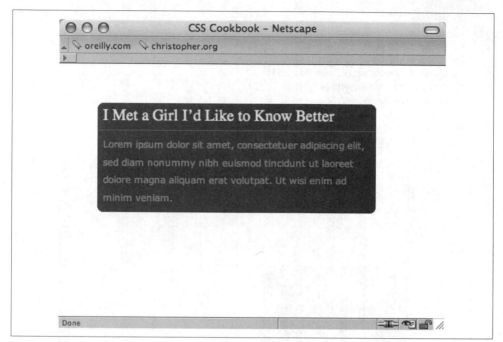

Figure 3-41. The column maintains integrity even with the color change and resizing

See Also

Recipe 3.17 for automatically adding corners on columns without custom-made images.

3.17   Rounding Corners with JavaScript

Problem

You want to include rounded corners on elements without the hassle of introducing new markup or images manually.

Solution

Use Nifty Corners Cube code by Alessandro Fulciniti.

First down the components of the Nifty Corners Cube solution, which include one CSS and one JavaScript file, at *http://www.html.it/articoli/niftycube/NiftyCube.zip*.

Upload both the JavaScript and CSS files associated with the Nifty Corners Cube solution. Then link the JavaScript to the web page by using the src attribute in the script element:

```
<script type="text/javascript" src="/_assets/js/niftycube.js"></script>
```

 You won't link directly to the CSS file because the JavaScript file does that. Also, make sure to reference the JavaScript correctly. In this example, the JavaScript is located in the js folder that is placed in the _assets folder.

Next modify the markup that will have rounded corners (see Figure 3-42) by giving it a unique value in the id attribute:

```
<div id="box">
<h2>Marquee selectus</h2>
<p>...<p>
</div>
```

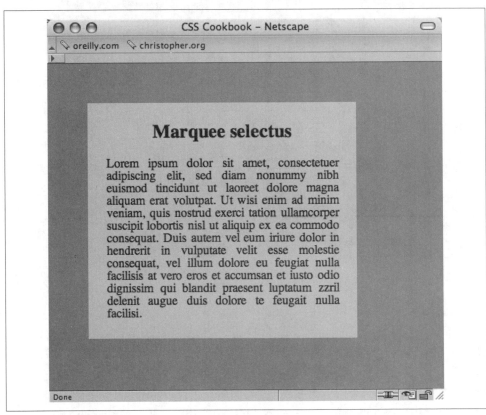

Figure 3-42. Default rendering of the column

Next, make a separate JavaScript call to tell the browser which element gets the rounded corners and then define the size of the rounded corners (see Figure 3-43):

```
<script type="text/javascript" src="niftycube.js"></script>
<script type="text/javascript">
 window.onload=function() {
  Nifty("div#box","big");
}
</script>
```

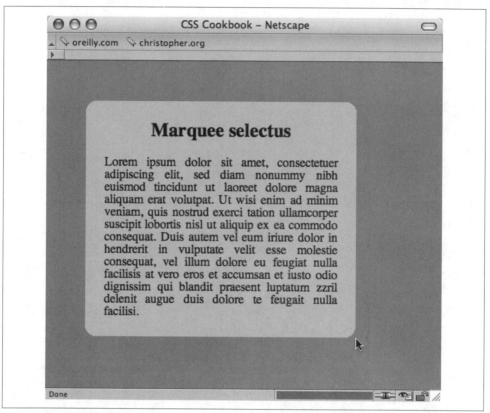

Figure 3-43. The rounded corners appear

Discussion

Since it's almost a completely worry-free method for creating rounded corners, the Nifty Corners Cube solution has been called more of a tool than a technique.

Different colors

Colors are detected automatically. The JavaScript automatically changes the colors to match the background color within the element as well as its parent element (usually the body of the web page). This means a developer only has to be worried with setting which element gets the curves and the size.

Different sizes

There are four keywords sizes written in to the Nifty Corners Cube JavaScript: none, small, normal (default), and big. Small is equal to the value of 2 pixels, normal is 5 pixels and big is 10 pixels.

For example, to adjust the corners so that they are small, the JavaScript call would look like:

```
<script type="text/javascript">
 window.onload=function( ) {
   Nifty("div#box","small");
 }
</script>
```

Different elements

Nifty Corners Cube accepts numerous selectors making it easier to dictate which elements should receive rounded corners; the selectors are listed in Table 3-1.

Table 3-1. Selectors understood by Nifty Corners Cube JavaScript

Selector	Example
Type	"div" "h3"
id	"div#box" "h3#main"
class	"div.box" "h3.box"
Descendent with id	"div#box h3" "h3#main div"
Descendent with class	"div.box h3" "h3.main div"
Grouping	"div, h3" "div, h3.main div, p"

For example, to apply rounded corners to multiple elements, the JavaScript function may look like this:

```
<script type="text/javascript">
 window.onload=function( ) {
   Nifty("div, h3.main div, p","small");
 }
</script>
```

Specific corners

The Nifty Corners Cube also makes allowances for developers who may *not* want to apply rounded edges to all the corners. Table 3-2 lists the keywords that allow developers to single out which corner or corners to round.

Table 3-2. Keywords understood by Nifty Corners Cube JavaScript

Keyword	Meaning
tl	Top-left corner
tr	Top-right corner
bl	Bottom-left corner
br	Bottom-right corner
top	Upper corners
bottom	Lower corners
left	Left corners
right	Right corners
all (default)	All the corners

For example, to apply rounded corners to just the top corners of multiple elements within a web page, the JavaScript function may look like the following:

```
<script type="text/javascript">
 window.onload=function() {
   Nifty("div, h3.main div, p","small top");
 }
</script>
```

See Also

For more information about Nifty Corners Cube at *http://www.html.it/articoli/niftycube/index.html*.

3.18   Placing a Drop Shadow Behind an Image

Problem

You want to place a drop shadow behind an image like the one in Figure 3-44.

Solution

Place the image element (see Figure 3-45) inside a div element with the class attribute set to imgholder:

```
<div class="imgholder">
 <img src="dadsaranick2.jpg" alt="Photo of Dad, Sara, Nick" />
 </div>
```

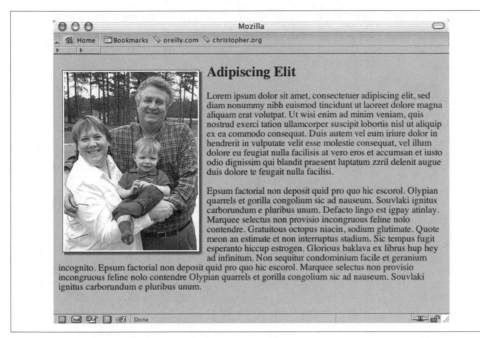

Figure 3-44. A drop shadow is placed behind the image

Figure 3-45. The image placed above the content

To the div element, set the image alignment to the left so that text wraps around the image. Next set the background image of the drop shadow in two background properties. In the first background property use an image with an alpha transparency like PNG:

```
div.imgholder {
 float:left;
 background: url(dropshadow.png) no-repeat bottom
  right !important;
 background: url(dropshadow.gif) no-repeat bottom right;
 margin: 10px 7px 0 10px !important;
 margin: 10px 0 0 5px;
}
```

As for the image itself, set the margin-right and margin-bottom properties to define how much of the drop shadow image shows through. Also set a border property as well as padding to create a more dramatic effect:

```
div.imgholder img {
 display: block;
 position: relative;
 background-color: #fff;
 border: 1px solid #666;
 margin: -3px 5px 5px -3px;
 padding: 2px;
}
```

Discussion

The first step is to create a drop shadow image in your image-editing program like Adobe Photoshop. It's best to create a background image sized 600×600 pixels or larger (see Figure 3-46). With the image that large, this technique can accommodate almost any image used in a web page.

The first image background property uses the !important rule to display the PNG file as a drop shadow. By using the PNG, the background color or image of the web document can be changed without affecting the drop shadow. For the other browsers that don't support this rule, like Internet Explorer for Windows, go to the next background property and use the GIF image as the drop shadow instead.

The margin-left and margin-bottom properties in the image element control the distance the drop shadow image appears out from the image. If your drop shadow distance on the right or left side is larger than five pixels (like the one used in this solution), change the value accordingly.

See Also

A List Apart article on creating CSS Drop Shadows, *http://www.alistapart.com/articles/cssdropshadows/*; Recipe 3.19 for creating smooth drop shadows behind an image.

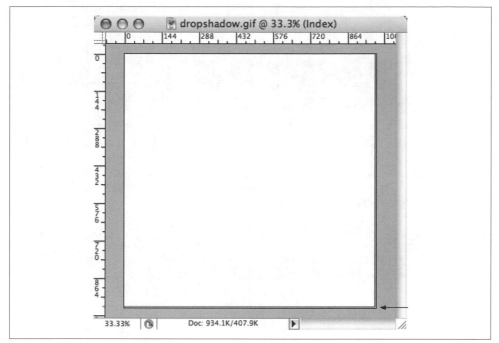

Figure 3-46. The drop shadow can be seen on the right and bottom sides

3.19   Placing a Smooth Drop Shadow Behind an Image

Problem

You want to have soft edges for an image's drop shadow.

Solution

Adding another unsemantic div wrapper around another background image allows for the creation of soft edges on the drop shadows.

First, create a new image in Adobe Photoshop that will act as a mask to soften the drop shadow image used in Recipe 3.18. Using the same dimensions as the drop shadow, delete the entire image content in the file leaving only a transparent background. Then using the gradient tool, pick the gradient option that will create a fade from Background Color to Transparent (see Figure 3-47).

Making sure that the background color in the toolbar will match the background color used in the web site, create a six pixel fade from the left edge of the canvas towards the right side of the image.

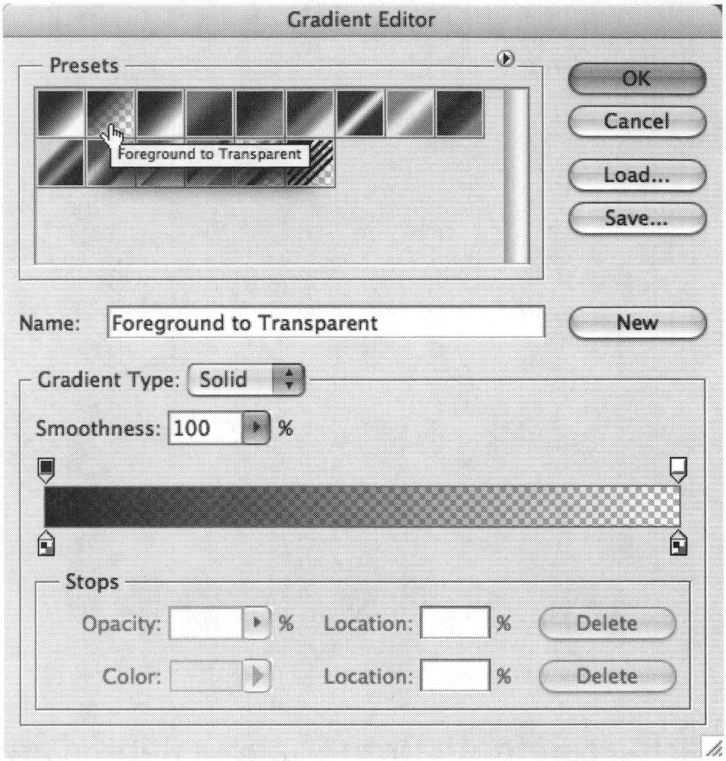

Figure 3-47. Selecting the right gradient fade

Then repeat the creation of the fade, but this time create the fade from the top of the canvas to the bottom.

Next, save the image as a PNG-24 image with transparency (see Figure 3-48):

With the images set up, adjust the HTML to include a new div wrapper:

```
<div class="imgholder">
 <div>
  <img src="dadsaranick2.jpg" alt="Photo of Dad, Sara, Nick" />
 </div>
</div>
```

Adjusting the CSS first image wrapper, float the image to the left, apply the drop shadow, and set some spacing between the image and the HTML content:

```
div.imgholder {
 float: left;
 background: url(dropshadow.gif) no-repeat bottom right;
 margin: 0 7px 7px 0;
}
```

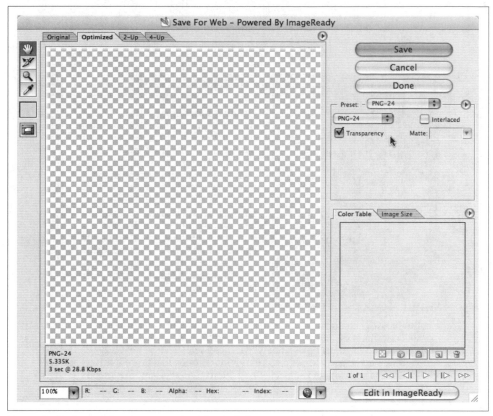

Figure 3-48. Saving the image as a PNG with alpha transparency

Next, bring in the mask that will soften the drop shadow background as well as make room to display both the drop shadow and the mask (see Figure 3-49):

```
div.imgholder div {
 background: url(shadowmask.png) no-repeat;
 padding: 0 6px 6px 0;
}
```

Finally, add some padding and a border to the image (see Figure 3-50):

```
div.imgholder img {
    display: block;
    position: relative;
    background-color: #fff;
    border: 1px solid #666;
    padding: 2px;
}
```

Figure 3-49. The smooth edges are now on the drop shadows

Discussion

The hard part of this solution is creating a PNG with alpha transparency that works with the drop shadow and matches the background of the web site.

Since Internet Explorer for Windows 5.5–6 does not natively support PNGs with alpha transparency, use the Solution from Recipe 3.11.

See Also

Recipe 3.18 for creating a simple drop shadow on an image.

3.20   Making Images Scalable

Problem

You want images to resize as the browser window resizes.

Figure 3-50. The image with drop shadow is styled a bit more

Solution

Define the width of images to percentages (see Figures 3-51 and 3-52):

```
img {
 border: 1px solid #cecece;
 width: 60%;
 float: left;
 margin-right: .7em;
 margin-bottom: .5em;
}
```

Modern browsers will scale the height of the images in the relative proportion to the width, so defining both the width and height is not necessary.

Discussion

When building fluid or flexible layouts, the HTML text set in columns is set to expand and retract as the browser resizes. However, images with dimensions that are commonly set in pixels retain their size.

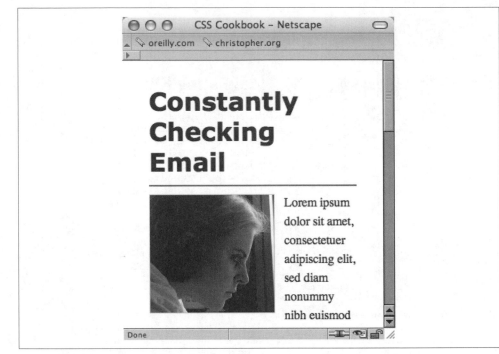

Figure 3-51. The image scaled down

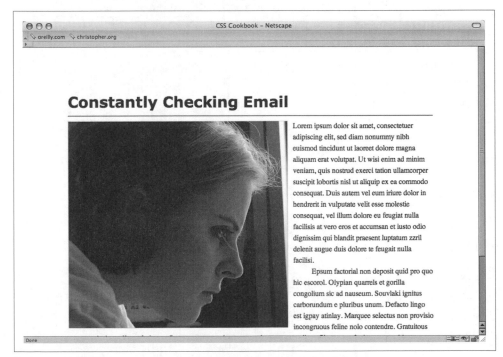

Figure 3-52. The image at a larger size since the browser window is larger

To make sure all the page elements are resized in proportion to each other in flexible layouts, developers may set the width and height to percentages.

When images are set to percentage-based dimensions, browsers may stretch images beyond the point where they retain image integrity. For example, artifacts that are nearly invisible in a JPEG start to show or the pixilation of a GIF image becomes apparent when they are expanded.

To keep the images from expanding beyond a defined width, use the `max-width` property with length units (see Figure 3-53):

```
img {
 border: 1px solid #cecece;
 width: 60%;
 max-width: 300px;
 float: left;
 margin-right: .7em;
 margin-bottom: .5em;
}
```

Constantly Checking Email

Lorem ipsum dolor sit amet, consectetuer adipiscing elit, sed diam nonummy nibh euismod tincidunt ut laoreet dolore magna aliquam erat volutpat. Ut wisi enim ad minim veniam, quis nostrud exerci tation ullamcorper suscipit lobortis nisl ut aliquip ex ea commodo consequat. Duis autem vel eum iriure dolor in hendrerit in vulputate velit esse molestie consequat, vel illum dolore eu feugiat nulla facilisis at vero eros et accumsan et iusto odio dignissim qui blandit praesent luptatum zzril delenit augue duis dolore te feugait nulla facilisi.

Epsum factorial non deposit quid pro quo hic escorol. Olypian quarrels et gorilla congolium sic ad nauseum. Souvlaki ignitus carborundum e pluribus unum. Defacto lingo est igpay atinlay. Marquee selectus non provisio incongruous feline nolo contendre. Gratuitous octopus niacin, sodium glutimate. Quote meon an estimate et non interruptus stadium. Sic tempus fugit esperanto hiccup estrogen. Glorious baklava ex librus hup hey ad infinitum. Non sequitur condominium facile et geranium incognito. Epsum factorial non deposit quid pro quo hic escorol. Marquee selectus non provisio incongruous feline nolo contendre Olypian quarrels et gorilla congolium sic ad nauseum. Souvlaki ignitus carborundum e pluribus unum.

Figure 3-53. The image expands only to the value of the max-width property

See Also

Recipe 9.4 and Recipe 9.6.

3.21 Making Word Balloons

Problem

You want to create a word-balloon effect like the one in Figure 3-54.

Figure 3-54. The word balloon

Solution

Mark up the content for a word balloon, and include both the text to appear in the word balloon as well as the name of the person cited as the source (see Figure 3-55):

```
<blockquote>
 <p>
  <span>
   Be bold, baby!
  </span>
 </p>
 <cite>
  Christopher Schmitt
 </cite>
</blockquote>
```

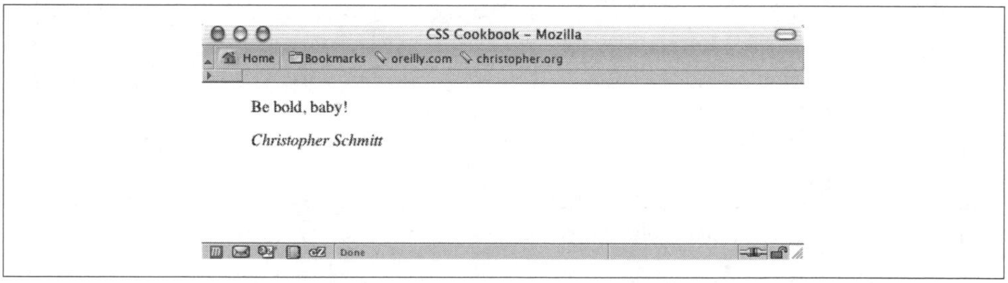

Figure 3-55. Structured content for a word balloon

Form the word balloon using the CSS border and background properties. Then align the cited text so that it falls underneath the balloon tail image:

```css
blockquote {
 width: 250px;
}
blockquote p {
 background: url(balloontip.gif);
 background-repeat: no-repeat;
 background-position: bottom;
 padding-bottom: 28px;
}
blockquote p span {
 display: block;
 padding:  0.25em 0.25em 0.5em 0.5em;
 border: 1pt solid black;
 border-bottom-width: 0;
 font-size: 3em;
 font-family: "Comic Sans MS", Verdana, Helvetica, sans-serif;
 line-height: 0.9em;
}
cite {
 text-align: right;
 display: block;
 width: 250px;
}
```

Discussion

To create a word balloon you need at least one image, which includes a balloon tail and one border of the balloon (see Figure 3-56). The image is available for download at this book's web site, mentioned in the Preface. Create the other three sides of the word balloon by setting the border in the span tag.

Figure 3-56. The word balloon tail

For a comic book look and feel, be sure to set the font family to Comic Sans MS, a free font from Microsoft:

```css
font-family: "Comic Sans MS", Verdana, Helvetica, sans-serif;
```

If you have a computer running the Windows OS, the font may be installed on your computer already. Although this is a common font, some users may not have it installed on their systems. If that is the case, the browser will look for the next font, in the order listed in the value, until it finds a font available to render the page.

You can create a more whimsical presentation using the word-balloon technique by adjusting the markup and CSS slightly. First, place a span element with a class attribute set to no around the name in the cite element:

```
<blockquote>
 <p>
  <span>
   Be bold, baby!
  </span>
 </p>
 <cite>
  <span class="no">
   Christopher Schmitt
  </span>
 </cite>
</blockquote>
```

Next, in CSS, add the following rule, which keeps the text from being displayed in the browser:

```
.no {
 display: none;
}
```

Place a photograph in the cite element through the background-position property to finish the effect (see Figure 3-57):

```
cite {
 margin: 0;
 padding: 0;
 background-image: url(baby.jpg);
 background-position: 0 0;
 height: 386px;
 text-align: right;
 display: block;
 width: 250px;
}
```

See Also

Background information about Comic Sans MS at *http://www.microsoft.com/ typography/web/fonts/comicsns/default.htm;* propaganda on why not to use Comic Sans MS at *http://www.bancomicsans.com.*

Figure 3-57. Word balloon coming from an image

3.22   Hindering People from Stealing Your Images

Problem

You want to make it difficult for people to copy your images from your web page.

Solution

Using a single pixel transparent GIF as a place marker, wrap a div element around the img tag:

```
<div class="slide">
 <img src="singlepixel.gif" alt="" />
</div>
```

Then bring in the image into the web page by using the background-property and making sure to set the width and height of the image in both the div and img elements:

```
div.slide {
 width: 500px;
 height: 468px;
 background-image: url(face.jpg);
 background-repeat: no-repeat;
```

```
}
.slide img {
  width: 500px;
  height: 468px;
}
```

Discussion

Having the single-pixel GIF as a placeholder is not necessary for the intended image to be displayed; in fact, you can do away with the img element altogether and still have the source image be displayed:

```
<div class="slide">
</div>
```

The purpose of the transparent image is to be used as a feint. The users will think they are downloading the image they desire, when in fact they are downloading an innocuous image.

Microsoft's Image toolbar

In Internet Explorer 6 for Windows, Microsoft includes a feature called the Image toolbar.

With this feature, a visitor to your site can easily email, download, or print your image with merely a click of the mouse. To keep the image toolbar from appearing on your web pages, add the following meta tags between the head elements:

```
<meta http-equiv="imagetoolbar" content="no" />
<meta http-equiv="imagetoolbar" content="false" / >
```

It's a slight a pain for developers to add code to their web page to keep someone else's product from stealing your images, but there is not much a developer can do since Microsoft produces the most popular browser.

No images are safe

Even with the solution and Image toolbar workaround implemented in your web page, no image is safe from being copied from your web site to a user's computer.

First, images are automatically stored by the visitor's browser and kept in temporary folder for quick reloading of web pages. These cached images are routinely deleted after a fixed amount of time or whenever a user clears their browser's cache.

However, the browser often renames these images automatically and most visitors don't even know where the cached files are located on their computer.

The most direct route a user can take is to simply take a screen capture of their desktop with your image displayed on a browser. With the screen capture taken, they can take the screenshot to their favorite digital imaging software application and crop the image.

Although these hindering methods may block out some visitors, they are not solutions that will work all the time.

See Also

More information on the Image toolbar at *http://www.microsoft.com/windows/ie/ie6/ using/howto/customizing/imgtoolbar.mspx#EXE*; a JavaScript-powered technique to make it harder for people to steal images at *http://javascript.internet.com/page-details/ no-right-click.html*.

3.23   Inserting Reflections on Images Automatically

Problem

You want to place a reflection of a header graphic automatically.

Solution

Download the JavaScript that powers the effect at *http://cow.neondragon.net/stuff/ reflection/*.

After uploading it to the web server, link the JavaScript file into the web page between the head element:

```
<script type="text/javascript" src="scripts/reflection.js">
</script>
```

Insert the image you want to apply the reflection to into the web page (see Figure 3-58):

```
<img src="christinaleaf.png" alt="christina m. huggins" />
```

Figure 3-58. The header graphic is displayed

To activate the reflection (see Figure 3-59), insert a `class` attribute with the value of reflect:

```
<img src="christinaleaf.png" alt="christina m. huggins" class="reflect" />
```

Figure 3-59. A reflection of the header graphic appears

Discussion

As a page is rendered in the site visitor's browser, the JavaScript reflection goes through the image elements of your web page looking for `class` attributes with the reflect value. Then the script uses the source of the image you want to reflect and creates a new image.

If the script finds any `image` elements that meet those criteria, the script copies the image, flips it and then applies the default values of 50% for both the opacity and height to this new reflected image.

Customization features

The reflection script allows two kinds of customizations: the height of the reflection and the opacity of the reflection.

To adjust the height of the reflection, add a new value, rheightXX, to the image's class attribute where XX is the percentage of the image's height should be duplicated in the reflection (see Figure 3-60):

```
<img src="christinaleaf.png" alt="christina m. huggins"
class="reflect rheight99" />
```

Figure 3-60. The reflection almost equals the height of the source image

As the percentage value increase the size of the reflection increases. For example, the value of `rheight99` means that 99% of the original image's height will be used in the reflection.

To adjust the opacity of the reflection, include a new value, `ropacityXX`, to the image's class attribute where XX is the percentage of the transparency of the reflected image (see Figure 3-61):

```
<img src="christinaleaf.png" alt="christina m. huggins"
class="reflect ropacity33" />
```

Figure 3-61. The reflection becomes more obscure

As the opacity value decreases the less visible the reflection becomes. For example, the value of `ropacity33` means that 33% of the original image's opacity will be used in the reflection.

Both the height and opacity features can be used at the same time to create more subtle effects like the ones in Figure 3-62:

```
<img src="christinaleaf.png" alt="christina m. huggins"
class="reflect rheight99 ropacity33" />
```

Figure 3-62. Both custom values for opacity and height are set

Known browser issues

Internet Explorer for Windows 5.5+, Firefox 1.5+, Opera 9+, and Safari support the reflection script. Animated images do not work with the reflection script except for Internet Explorer for Windows. Also, scaled images appear distorted in Internet Explorer for Windows.

See Also

The blog post announcing the reflection effect at *http://cow.neondragon.net/index.php/ 1025-Reflectionjs-Version-15*.

3.24   Using Image Sprites

Problem

You want to save on bandwidth by placing all or most icons onto one image.

Solution

Place the most-often-used images into one master image, making sure that there is plenty of space around each image (see Figure 3-63).

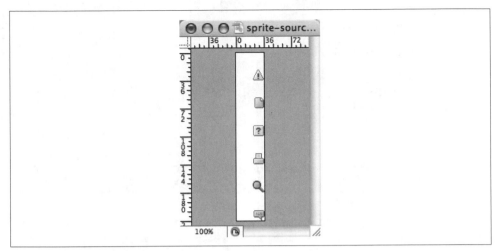

Figure 3-63. Icons are placed into one image

Create enough space for each icon's own space. For this example, one icon will be placed next to a heading (see Figure 3-64):

```
h2 {
 margin: 0;
 font-family: Verdana, Arial, Helvetica, sans-serif;
 padding: 0 0 0 24px;
 font-weight: normal;
}
```

Using id selectors, bring in each icon to the appropriate heading by using background-position property (see Figure 3-65):

```
h2#warning {
 background-image: url(sprite-source.gif);
 background-repeat: no-repeat;
 background-position: -16px 24px;
}
h2#questions {
 background-image: url(sprite-source.gif);
 background-repeat: no-repeat;
 background-position: -16px 60px;
}
h2#comment {
 background-image: url(sprite-source.gif);
 background-repeat: no-repeat;
 background-position: -16px 96px;
}
h2#document {
 background-image: url(sprite-source.gif);
 background-repeat: no-repeat;
 background-position: -16px 132px;
}
```

```
h2#print {
  background-image: url(sprite-source.gif);
  background-repeat: no-repeat;
  background-position: -16px 168px;
}
h2#search {
  background-image: url(sprite-source.gif);
  background-repeat: no-repeat;
  background-position: -16px 204px;
}
```

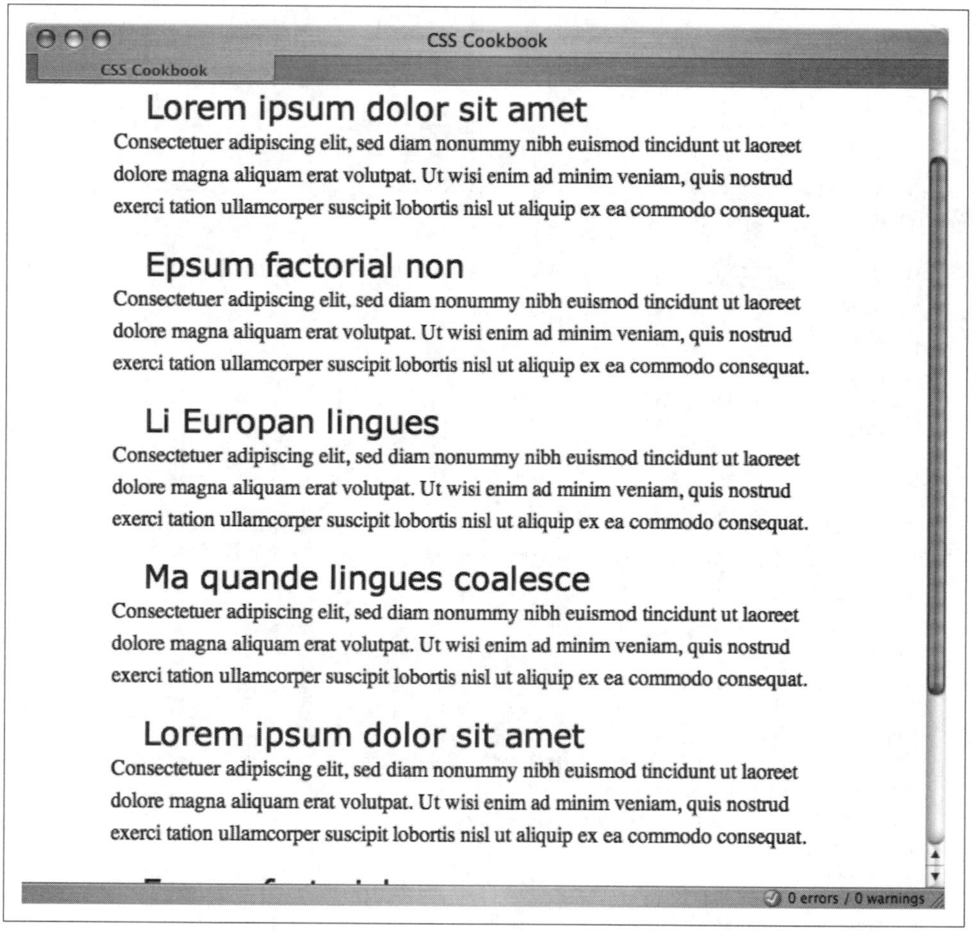

Figure 3-64. Making space in the design for the icons

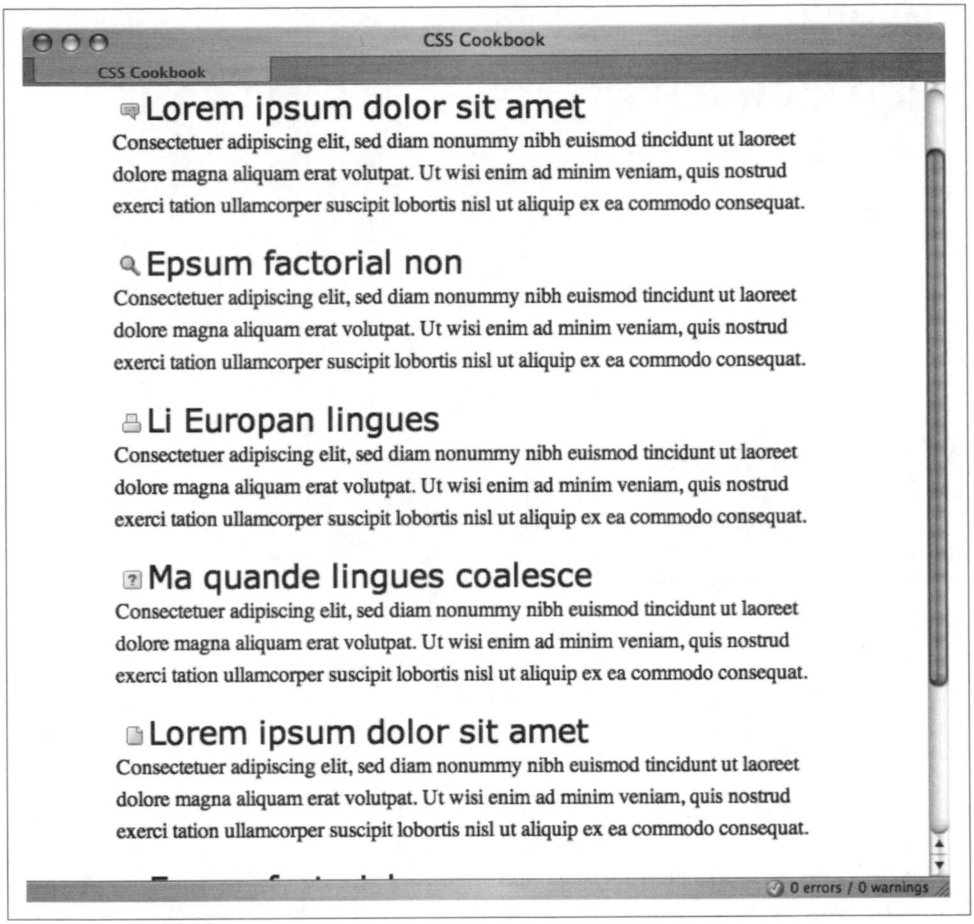

Figure 3-65. The icons are displayed from one single image

Discussion

In much the same way developers use the same image over and over again to make use of a browser's ability to cache an image, using sprites helps push that idea a bit further. By placing the separate graphic elements onto one image, web developers can reduce the amount of server calls to their machines from a browser. This solution would be more apt for sites receiving medium-to-large amounts of traffic.

See Also

The CSS Sprites article at *http://www.alistapart.com/articles/sprites*.

CHAPTER 4

Page Elements

4.0 Introduction

From the most obvious design choices, such as selecting the appropriate typography and imagery, to those that are often overlooked, such as adjusting leading and color schemes, every decision affects the how the message in a web site is conveyed to the visitor.

This chapter covers page elements that help to Frame a web page like a frame for a painting. *Page elements* are items that affect the appearance of a web page, but aren't necessarily thought of as comprising a web page's design. For example, the appearance of the scrollbar is a page element.

By manipulating elements such as the margins and borders surrounding the contents of a web page, developers can effectively frame the content of the page without actually styling the content. Such simple changes can affect the page's overall design in a profound way, or they can add a subtle detail that completes the design.

4.1 Eliminating Page Margins

Problem

You want to get rid of the whitespace around the edges of a web page and between the browser chrome and the contents of the page (see Figure 4-1).

Solution

Set the value of the `margin` and `padding` properties for the `html` and `body` elements to zero:

```
html, body {
  margin: 0;
  padding: 0;
  position: absolute;
```

```
  top: 0;
  left: 0;
}
```

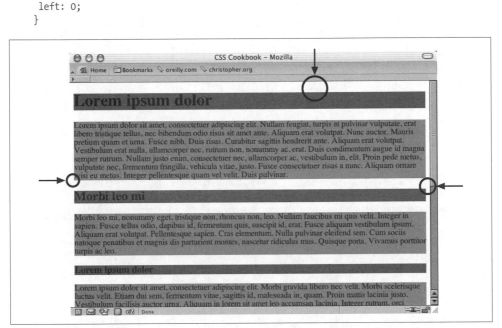

Figure 4-1. Page margins visible as the whitespace around the edges of a web page

Discussion

Setting the margin and padding properties of the body element to 0 helps create a *full-bleed* effect—in other words, it eliminates the whitespace around a web page (the units are unnecessary when specifying zero). Setting the position to absolute and the values for top and left to 0 helps remove the body margins in Netscape Navigator 4.

However, depending on the content of the web page, the margin and padding properties may not be all you need to change to get a full-bleed effect. Default properties on other elements can have unexpected side effects when you attempt to change the page margin For example, if h1 is the body element's first child element, some unintended whitespace will appear above the headline and below the top of the browser's viewport. Figure 4-2 shows this undesired effect; the background color of the headings and paragraphs is gray so that you can more clearly see the effect.

To ensure the full-bleed effect in this situation set the margin and padding of the offending element (in this case, h1, h2, h3) to 0 as well as the body's. This sets all the sides of the element's padding to 0. If that setup isn't possible (for example, if you need to have a value at the bottom padding or margin), set the margin-top and padding-top values to 0 to maintain the full-bleed effect:

```
html, body {
  margin: 0;
  padding: 0;
```

```
   position: absolute;
   top: 0;
   left: 0;
 }
h1, h2, h3 {
  margin-top: 0;
  padding-top: 0;
  background-color: #666;
}
p {
  background-color: #999;
}
```

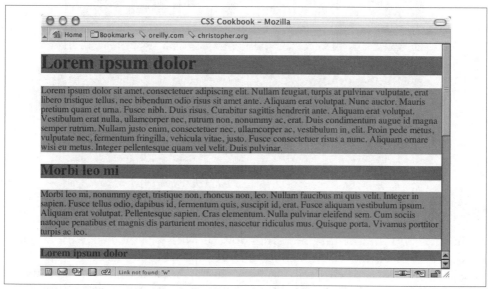

Figure 4-2. Whitespace above the heading and below the top of the browser's viewport

As you can see in Figure 4-3, this accomplishes the full-bleed effect. Notice how the gray background color of the first heading now touches the top of the browser's viewport.

See Also

Recipe 9.1 for writing one-column layouts by setting the margin and padding properties to a value other than 0.

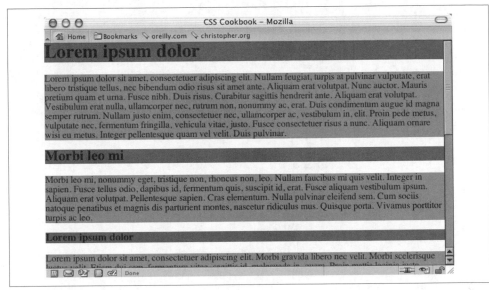

Figure 4-3. *Whitespace removed above the heading*

4.2 Coloring the Scrollbar

Problem

You want to adjust the color of the scroll bar on a browser's viewport, or the window on the browser.

Solution

Use the properties that manipulate scroll bar colors in browsers that support it:

```
body,html {
  scrollbar-face-color: #99ccff;
  scrollbar-shadow-color: #ccccff;
  scrollbar-highlight-color: #ccccff;
  scrollbar-3dlight-color: #99ccff;
  scrollbar-darkshadow-color: #ccccff;
  scrollbar-track-color: #ccccff;
  scrollbar-arrow-color: #000033;
}
```

 Because these properties aren't part of the W3C recommendations for CSS, browser vendors don't have to put in support for these properties. This solution works only on the KDE Konqueror browser and on Internet Explorer 5.5+ for Windows. Other browsers will simply skip over the rules. However these rules won't be validated by services such as *http://jigsaw.w3.org/css-validator/validator-uri.html*.

Discussion

Although you may think of a scroll bar as a simple tool, it's actually composed of several widgets that create a controllable 3D object. Figure 4-4 spotlights the different properties of a scroll bar. As you can see, to create a truly different color scheme for the scroll bar, you must alter the value of seven properties.

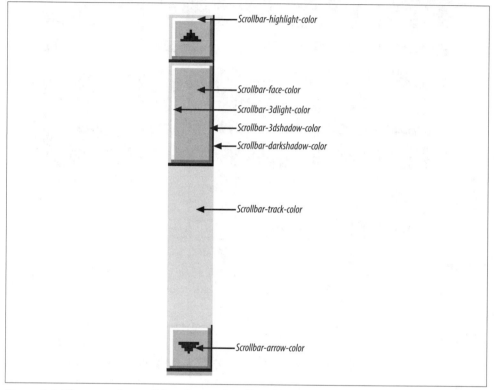

Figure 4-4. The parts of a scroll bar that can be affected by proprietary CSS for Internet Explorer for Windows

In addition to adjusting the scrollbar of the browser viewport, you also can adjust the colors of the scroll bar in the textarea for a web form, framesets, iframes, and generally anything with a scroll bar:

```
.highlight {
 scrollbar-face-color: #99ccff;
 scrollbar-shadow-color: #ccccff;
 scrollbar-highlight-color: #ccccff;
 scrollbar-3dlight-color: #99ccff;
 scrollbar-darkshadow-color: #ccccff;
 scrollbar-track-color: #ccccff;
 scrollbar-arrow-color: #000033;
}
```

```
<form>
 <textarea class="highlight"></textarea>
</form>
```

When rendering a page that doesn't contain a valid DOCTYPE, Internet Explorer for Windows experiences what is known as *quirks* (nonstandard behavior) mode and looks for the scrollbar properties in the body selector. When the page contains a valid DOCTYPE, Internet Explorer for Windows is in standards mode and it obeys the html selector. So, just in case the web document's DOCTYPE may change, it's best to ensure that the body and html selectors are grouped and applied in one CSS rule:

```
html .highlight, body .highlight {
  scrollbar-face-color: #99ccff;
  scrollbar-shadow-color: #ccccff;
  scrollbar-highlight-color: #ccccff;
  scrollbar-3dlight-color: #99ccff;
  scrollbar-darkshadow-color: #ccccff;
  scrollbar-track-color: #ccccff;
  scrollbar-arrow-color: #000033;
}
```

See Also

The MSDN Scrollbar Color Workshop at *http://msdn.microsoft.com/workshop/ samples/author/dhtml/refs/scrollbarColor.htm* to pick colors for a custom scroll bar.

4.3   Techniques for Centering Elements on a Web Page

Problem

You want to center parts of a web page, as in Figure 4-5.

Solution

To center text in a block-level element, use the text-align property:

```
h1, h2, h3 {
  text-align: center;
}
```

Discussion

By using text-align, you can center text inside block-level elements. However, in this example, the heading takes up the entire width of the body element, and if you don't apply a background color to the element, you probably won't even notice that this is happening. The gray background color in Figure 4-6 shows the actual width of the centered elements.

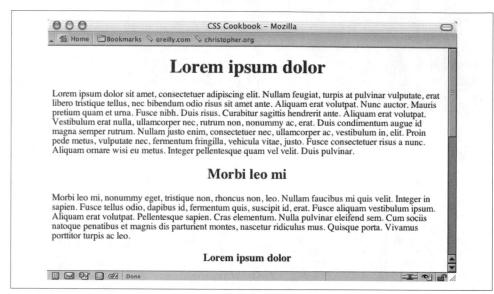

Figure 4-5. The headline text centered

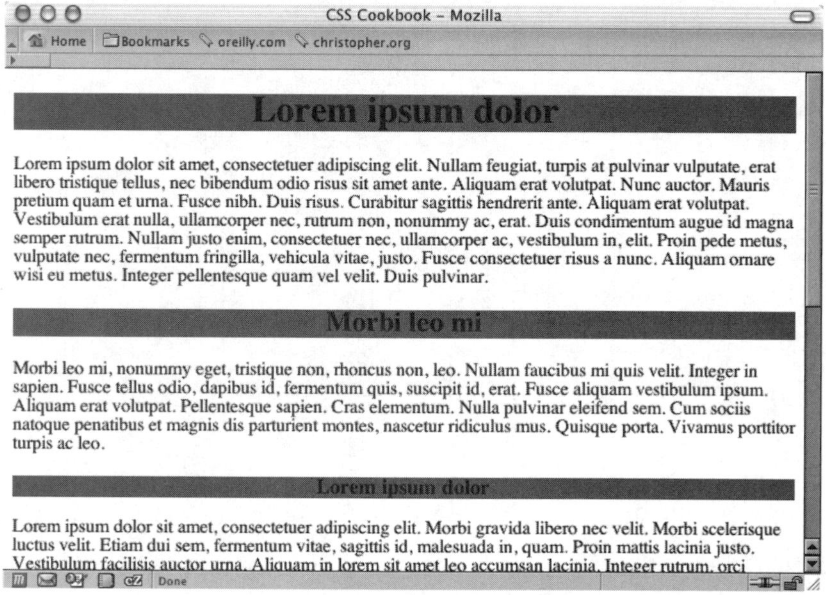

Figure 4-6. The actual width of the elements shown by the gray background color

An alternative approach is to use margins to center text within its container:

```
h1, h2, h3 {
  margin-left: auto;
  margin-right: auto;
}
```

When you set the `margin-left` and `margin-right` properties to `auto`, you center the element inside its parent element. However, older but still popular browsers won't render the presentation correctly. So, workarounds are needed for individual situations.

Tables

To center a table, place the table as the child of a div element:

```
<div class="center">
 <table width="50%" border="1" cellpadding="30">
  <tr>
   <td>This is the first cell</td>
   <td>This is the second cell</td>
  </tr>
  <tr>
   <td>This is the third cell, it's under the first cell</td>
   <td>This is the fourth cell, it's under the second cell.</td>
  </tr>
 </table>
</div>
```

Then write the following CSS rule:

```
.center {
  text-align: center;
}
.center table {
 width: 50%;
 margin-left: auto;
 margin-right: auto;
 text-align: left;
}
```

Although setting both sides of the margin to auto works in newer generations of browsers, it doesn't work in Internet Explorer 5 for Windows or Netscape Navigator 4. To catch those two browsers and tell them to "do the right thing," the center class selector uses the `text-align` technique. However, if that were all you did, the contents of the table cells would be centered as well. To counteract that effect, use a descendent selector, `.center table`, to align the contents in the table cell elements.

Note that if you use th elements in an HTML table, the content inside those cells is centered by default. Setting the `text-align` property to a value of `left` in the descendent selector `.center table` doesn't counter that effect. To left-align the content inside th, use this CSS rule:

```
th {
 text-align: left;
}
```

To save a line or two of CSS code, you may want to incorporate the shorthand version of the `margin` property, as shown here (although this works in most browsers, it fails in Internet Explorer 5 for Macintosh):

```
.center table {
  margin: 0 auto;
  text-align: left;
}
```

Images

If you want to center an image, wrap a `div` element around the `img` element first. This technique is required because an `img` element, like `em` and `strong`, is inline. It rests in the flow of the web page instead of marking off space like the `p` or `blockquote` block-level elements do. The markup looks like this:

```
<div class="flagicon"><img src="flag.gif" alt="Flag" width="160"
height="60" /></div>
```

And the CSS rule looks like this:

```
.flagicon {
  text-align: center;
}
```

To center elements with fixed widths, such as images, first set the value of the parent's `padding-left` property to 50%. Then determine half of the width of the element you are centering and set it as a negative value in the `margin-left` property. That prevents the element's left side from resting on the 50% line caused by its padding and makes it slide into the middle of the page. The markup for an image in a web page using this technique looks something like this:

```
<img src="wolf.jpg" width="256" height="192" alt="Photo of wolf.">
```

The CSS rule to produce the result you see in Figure 4-7 looks like this:

```
body {
  padding-left: 50%;
}
img {
  /* equal to the negative of half its width */
  margin-left: -138px;
}
```

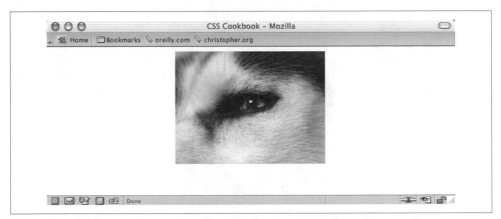

Figure 4-7. The image centered without the deprecated center element

Another way to center an image, but not as backwards compatible for Internet Explorer 5 for Windows, is to change the display and margin properties of the image.

First, apply a `class` attribute to the image that is going to be centered:

```
<img src="flag.gif" alt="Flag" width="160" height="60"
class="blockimg" />
```

Then create a CSS rule that positions the image in the center:

```
.blockimg {
 display: block;
 margin: 0 auto;
}
```

Vertical centering

With the element centered horizontally, you can take this technique one step further and center the image (or any other element) vertically as well. The difference with this method is that it uses the `position` property to make this work. The markup is the same as that used for the image element in the previous example, but this time the CSS rule is for just one selector (see Figure 4-8):

```
img {
 position: absolute;
 top: 50%;
 left: 50%;
 margin-top: -96px;
 margin-left: -138px;
 height: 192px;
 width: 256px;
}
```

With absolute positioning, you take the element out of the normal flow of the document and place it wherever you want.

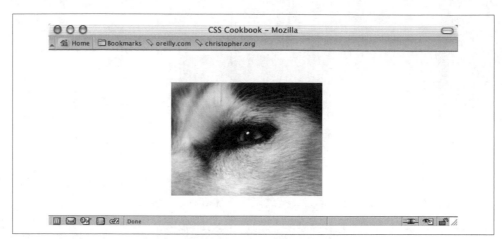

Figure 4-8. The image centered horizontally and vertically on the web page

If you want to center both text and an image (or other images) instead of just one image, enclose all the content with a div element:

```
<div id="centerFrame">
 <p>Epsum factorial non deposit quid pro quo hic escorol. Olypian
quarrels et gorilla congolium sic ad nauseum. Souvlaki ignitus
carborundum e pluribus unum. Defacto lingo est igpay atinlay.</p>
 <img src="wolf.jpg" width="256" height="192" alt="Photo of
wolf." />
 </div>
```

Then in the CSS rule, remove the height property and adjust the negative value of the top margin to compensate for the additional elements on the page:

```
#centerFrame  {
 position: absolute;
 top: 50%;
 left: 50%;
 /* adjust negative value until content is centered */
 margin-top: -150px;
 margin-left: -138px;
 width: 256px;
}
```

Keep the amount of content that you want centered short. This solution is only going to roughly center the text and the images because the text will render at different heights on different computers. If you have numerous images and long amounts of HTML text, users with small resolutions will have to scroll the page to see your centered content.

See Also

Chapter 9 for information on multicolumn layouts, which deal with the position of elements in a web page; the CSS 2.1 specification for text-align, online at *http://www.w3.org/TR/CSS21/text.html#propdef-text-align*.

4.4   Placing a Page Border

Problem

You want to place a visual frame or border around a web page, as in Figure 4-9.

Figure 4-9. A framed web page

Solution

Use the border property on the body element:

```
body {
 margin: 0;
 padding: 1.5em;
 border: 50px #666 ridge;
}
```

Discussion

The border property is a shorthand property, in that it enables you to set the width, color, and style of the border around an element in one step instead of three. If you didn't use this shorthand property in the preceding solution, you would have to replace the line that reads border: 50px #666 ridge; with the following three lines:

```
border-width: 50px;
border-color: #666;
border-style: ridge;
```

You can create a framing effect with other styles as well, such as dotted, dashed, solid, double, groove, inset, and outset (see Figure 4-10).

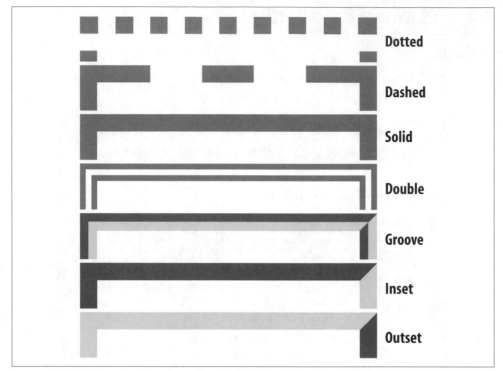

Figure 4-10. The available border styles in CSS

Note that groove style is the inverse of the shades of shadow as seen in the solution, which uses the `ridge` value.

 The only browser incompatibilities to worry about are in Internet Explorer 5 for Macintosh and Internet Explorer for Windows, where the dotted style appears as aliased circles, whereas in Netscape 6+, Firefox, Mozilla, and Safari, the dotted style appears as blocks.

You also can place a stylized border on images as well. Instead of having a default solid line, try experimenting in your designs with groove or double borders like the one in Figure 4-11:

```
img.left {
 float: left;
 margin-right: 7px;
 margin-bottom: 3px;
 border: 4px double #666;
}
```

See Also

Recipe 2.15 for creating pull quotes with different border styles.

Figure 4-11. A double border around an image

4.5   Customizing a Horizontal Rule

Problem

You want to change the look of a horizontal rule from the solid line in Figure 4-12 to something more interesting, for example the small centered rectangle in Figure 4-13.

Solution

Use a mixture of CSS properties on the hr element to obtain a desired effect:

```
hr {
  margin-left: auto;
  margin-right: auto;
  margin-top: 1.25em;
  margin-bottom: 1.25em;
  width: 10px;
  height: 10px;
  background-color: #777;
}
```

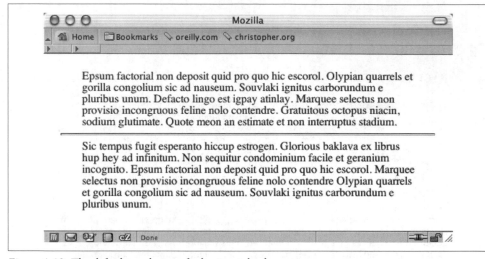

Figure 4-12. The default rendering of a horizontal rule

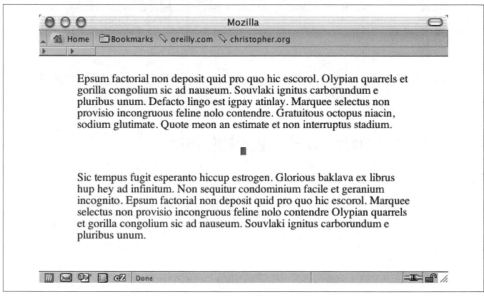

Figure 4-13. A stylized horizontal rule

Discussion

Before HTML 4.0, the presentation of horizontal rules could be manipulated through a set of four attributes: `align`, `width`, `size`, and `noshade`. Since HTML is intended to mark up content and not the look of the content, those values are no longer a part of the HTML specification. (Browser vendors may support the values, but your mileage will vary.) With CSS rules controlling the presentation, you have far greater control over the appearance of horizontal rules.

For example, you can set the height as well as the width properties for horizontal rules through CSS:

```
hr {
  width: 80%;
  height: 3px;
  margin-left: auto;
  margin-right: auto;
}
```

Setting the margin-left and margin-right to auto centers the horizontal rule in the web page for Safari, although it's not required for Mozilla, Firefox, Navigator, and Internet Explorer for Windows.

If you want to style an hr element with color (see Figure 4-14), use the following code:

```
hr {
  color: green;
  background-color: green;
  width: 80%;
  height: 3px;
  margin-left: auto;
  margin-right: auto;
}
```

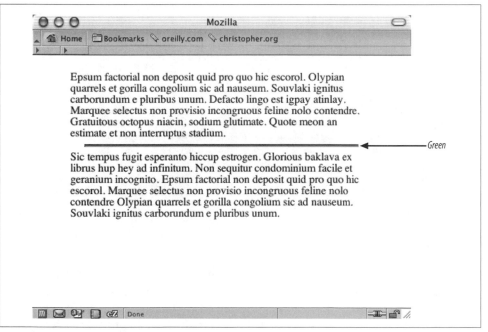

Figure 4-14. A centered, green horizontal rule

The first property, color, is understood by Internet Explorer for Windows while Safari, Mozilla, Firefox, and Netscape Navigator 6+ pick up the second property, background-color.

To place an image instead of a horizontal bar, use the background-image property:

```
hr {
  background-image: url(hr-decoration.gif);
  background-repeat: no-repeat;
  border: none;
  width: 76px;
  height: 25px;
  margin-left: auto;
  margin-right: auto;
}
```

However, Internet Explorer for Windows renders a border around the hr element in Figure 4-15 that can't be removed through CSS properties.

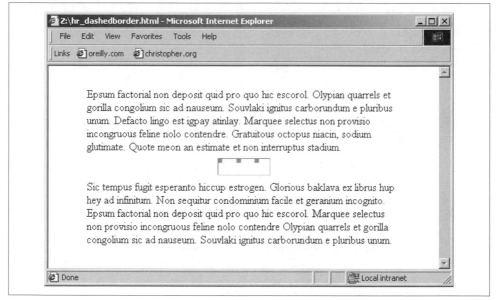

Figure 4-15. A border around a horizontal rule in Internet Explorer for Windows

See Also

The HTML 4.01 specification for hr elements at *http://www.w3.org/TR/html401/ present/graphics.html#edef-HR*; an overview of styling an hr element, online at *http:// www.sovavsiti.cz/css/hr.html*; another example of refining the presentation of horizontal rules at *http://www.sidesh0w.com/weblog/2004/03/17/sexily_styling_ horizontal_rules.html*.

4.6   Adding a Lightbox

Problem

You want to overlay images on top of a current web page (see Figure 4-16) without popping a new browser window.

Figure 4-16. The default page

Solution

Download the source code the lightbox effect from *http://www.huddletogether.com/projects/lightbox2/#download*.

Along with the Prototype Framework and Scriptaculous Effects JavaScript libraries, include a specialized JavaScript for overlaying images:

```
<title>Mr. McCool's Homepage</title>
<!-- Structure for Lightbox effect -->
<script type="text/javascript" src="prototype.js"></script>
<script type="text/javascript" src="scriptaculous.js?load=effects"></script>
<!-- Script for Lightbox -->
<script type="text/javascript" src="lightbox.js"></script>
```

Next, link to style sheet that renders the look-and-feel of the overlay effect:

```
<title>Mr. McCool's Homepage</title>
<script type="text/javascript" src="prototype.js"></script>
<script type="text/javascript" src="scriptaculous.js?load=effects"></script>
<script type="text/javascript" src="lightbox.js"></script>
<link rel="stylesheet" href="lightbox.css" type="text/css" media="screen" />
```

Within the web page content, include a link to an image making sure to include a `rel` attribute with a value of `lightbox`. A common link example would be to wrap a link around a thumbnail image:

```
<a href="trammell_shoes.jpg" rel="lightbox" title="Trammell shows off
his happy shoes."><img src="trammell_shoes_tn.jpg" alt="Mark Trammel
is happy with his shoes." /></a>
```

Clicking on the link activates the lightbox effect, as shown in Figure 4-17.

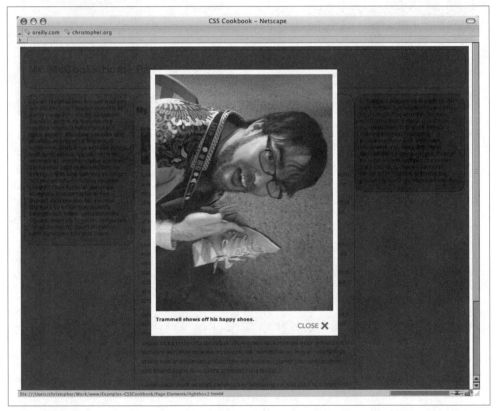

Figure 4-17. The lightbox appears on top of the page

Discussion

The lightbox effect is built on two core pieces: the Prototype JavaScript Framework and Scriptaculous.

Prototype creates a more object-oriented framework that allows developers to quickly build web-based applications based on JavaScript. For more information about Prototype, see the official site *http://prototype.conio.net/*.

Scriptaculous is a collection of JavaScript libraries. When used in conjunction of Prototype, Scriptaculous allows developers to build dynamic, Asynchronous JavaScript + XML (Ajax) interactions. For further information on Scriptaculous, see *http://script.aculo.us/*.

With the JavaScript foundations in place, web developer Lokesh Dhakar (see *http://www.huddletogether.com/*) developed a clever image viewer that displays a full-size image without having to leave the web page that displays the thumbnails.

Setting up the files

When you download and link the JavaScript files and a style sheet to a web page, make sure the files are properly linked. For example, if you place JavaScript and a style sheet in a separate folder locations, make sure the code reflect their locations:

```
<script type="text/javascript" src="/_assets/js/prototype.js"></script>
<script type="text/javascript" src="/_assets/js/scriptaculous.js?load=effects">
</script>
<script type="text/javascript" src="/_assets/js/lightbox.js"></script>
<link rel="stylesheet" href="/_assets/css/lightbox.css" type="text/css"
media="screen" />
```

In the lightbox JavaScript file, also make sure the locations of the images are correct. If you need to edit the location of the images, look towards the top of the JavaScript file for the following lines to modify:

```
var fileLoadingImage = "/_assets/img/loading.gif";
var fileBottomNavCloseImage = "/_assets/img/closelabel.gif";
```

The style sheet for the lightbox utilizes the background image property three times. Make sure those images referenced in the properties are also set to the correct locations:

```
#prevLink, #nextLink {
 width: 49%;
 height: 100%;
/* Trick IE into showing hover */
 background: transparent url(/_assets/img/blank.gif) no-repeat;
 display: block;
}
#prevLink:hover, #prevLink:visited:hover {
 background: url(/_assets/img/prevlabel.gif) left 15% no-repeat;
}
#nextLink:hover, #nextLink:visited:hover {
 background: url(/_assets/img/nextlabel.gif) right 15% no-repeat;
}
```

Making a slideshow

In addition to showcasing one image at a time, the lightbox can be set up to display a slideshow like the one in Figure 4-18.

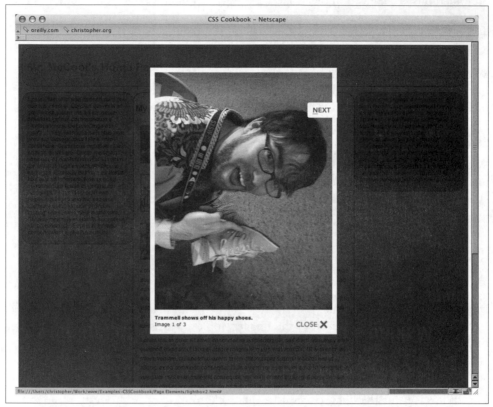

Figure 4-18. The lightbox can display a slideshow of images

In order to achieve this affect, modify the value of the rel element by using right-angle brackets after lightbox and inserting a gallery name. In the code example, I used the gallery name austin as I took the pictures in Austin, TX:

```
<ul>
 <li><a href="trammell_shoes.jpg" rel="lightbox[austin]"
title="Trammell shows off his happy shoes."><img src="trammell_shoes_tn.jpg"
alt="Mark Trammel is happy with his shoes." /></a></li>
 <li><a href="molly_andy.jpg" rel="lightbox[austin]" title="Molly and
Andy pose for a shot."><img src="molly_andy_tn.jpg" alt="Molly and Andy
pose for a shot." /></a></li>
 <li><a href="msjen.jpg" rel="lightbox[austin]" title="Ms. Jen at
breakfast."><img src="msjen_tn.jpg" alt="Ms. Jen at breakfast." /></a></li>
 </ul>
```

The gallery name needs to be the same in order for related images to be put into the same slideshow presentation.

Known browser issues

Since the lightbox effect is built on Prototype framework, the lightbox effect's support in browser is based on how many browsers Prototype supports. As of this writing the following browsers support Prototype:

- Microsoft Internet Explorer for Windows 6+
- Mozilla Firefox 1.0+
- Mozilla 1.7+
- Apple Safari 1.2+

The lightbox effect degrades gracefully. If a visitor's browser does not support the lightbox effect, the browser will follow the value of the href attribute.

```
<a href="trammell_shoes.jpg" rel="lightbox" title="Trammell shows off
his happy shoes."><img src="trammell_shoes_tn.jpg" alt="Mark Trammel
is happy with his shoes." /></a>
```

In this example, the browser pulls up the file trammel_shoes.jpg.

See Also

An overview of the Prototype JavaScript Library at *http://blogs.ebusiness-apps.com/jordan/pages/Prototype%20Library%20Info.htm*; an overview of Ajax at *http://adaptivepath.com/publications/essays/archives/000385.php*.

CHAPTER 5

Lists

5.0   Introduction

From a wife handing a husband a grocery list as he steps out the door to a music channel presenting their top 100 worst songs of all time, lists help people stay focused and organized. In web design, it's the same case: HTML lists facilitate the presentation of organized content to our site's visitors by grouping key elements together.

HTML lists are appealing in part because of the way they appear on the page. List items typically are indented and keyed off by a marker, usually by a filled circle for an unordered list or numbers for an ordered list (see Figure 5-1). With a few lines of HTML, a web coder can create a bulleted list on a web page without opening an image editor. With CSS, you can create even more visually compelling lists.

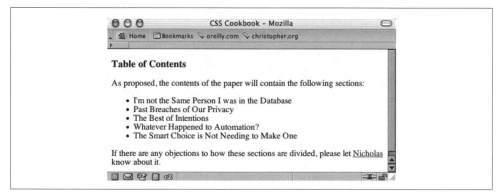

Figure 5-1. The default rendering of a list

Web developers can tailor the presentation of the list to complement the design of a web page instead of relying on the browsers' default styling. This chapter illustrates how to change the numbering of list items, use your own image for a list marker, create a hanging indent that doesn't use a list marker, and more.

5.1 Changing the Format of a List

Problem

You want to change the default list style; for example, to change the bullet or numbering, as in Figure 5-2.

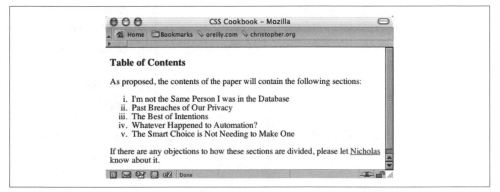

Figure 5-2. The list markers changed to lowercase Roman numerals

Solution

Use the `list-style-type` property to change the bullet or type of counter:

```
li {
  list-style-type: lower-roman;
}
```

Discussion

The CSS 2.1 specification offers several styles for numbering a list, as shown in Table 5-1. Browsers typically vary the bullet style from one level of nesting to the next. To stop lists from presenting this traditional system of setting the list marker, change the value of `list-style-type` for each child list.

Table 5-1. Bullet styles

Style/value	Description	Browser support
square	Usually a filled-in square, although the exact representation isn't defined.	All major browsers
disc	Usually a filled-in circle, although the exact representation isn't defined.	All major browsers
circle	Usually an unfilled circle, although the exact representation isn't defined.	All major browsers
decimal	Starts with 1 and continues with 2, 3, 4, etc.	All major browsers

Table 5-1. Bullet styles (continued)

Style/value	Description	Browser support
decimal-leading-zero	Starts with 01 and continues with 02, 03, 04, etc. The number of leading zeros may equal the number of digits used in a list. For example, 0001 may be used for a 5,876-item list.	All major browsers
lower-roman	Starts with lowercase roman numerals.	All major browsers
upper-roman	Starts with uppercase roman numerals.	All major browsers
lower-alpha	Starts with lowercase ASCII letters.	All major browsers
upper-alpha	Starts with uppercase ASCII letters.	All major browsers
lower-latin	Starts with lowercase ASCII letters.	All major browsers
upper-latin	Starts with uppercase ASCII letters.	All major browsers
lower-greek	Starts with classical Greek letters, starting with alpha and then beta, gamma, etc.	Safari, Mozilla, Netscape 6+
hebrew	Starts counting with traditional Hebrew.	Safari, Mozilla, Netscape 6+
hiragana	Starts counting with the Japanese hiragana system.	Mozilla, Netscape 6+
katakana	Starts counting with the Japanese traditional katakana system.	Mozilla, Netscape 6+
hiragana-iroha	Starts counting with the Japanese hiragana-iroha system.	Mozilla, Netscape 6+
katakana-iroha	Starts counting with the Japanese katakana-iroha system.	Mozilla, Netscape 6+
none	No marker is displayed.	All major browsers

See Also

Recipe 5.6 for using custom images for list markers; Chapter 12 in *Cascading Style Sheets: The Definitive Guide,* Second Edition by Eric A. Meyer (O'Reilly Media).

5.2   Writing Cross-Browser Indentation in Lists

Problem

Different browsers use different methods to indent lists. You want to specify left margins for your list that will render on all browsers.

Solution

Set the margin-left and padding-left properties for the ul element:

```
ul {
  margin-left: 40px;
  padding-left: 0px;
}
```

Discussion

Different browsers use different methods to pad or indent a list. Mozilla and Netscape 6+ browsers indent a list on the *padding*, while Internet Explorer and Opera pad a list through the *margin* of a list.

To gain cross-browser effectiveness, you need to set the values for *both* the left margins and the padding for the list. Keep the amount of the indentation in one of the properties. Splitting the amount into two different properties results in inconsistent presentation across the browsers.

If you set the margin and padding to zero while the list is contained by only the body element, the browser renders the markers outside the viewport, making them invisible to the user. To make sure the markers are visible, set the left margin or left padding of the ul to at least 1em.

See Also

Recipe 5.9 on creating hanging indents; CSS 2.1 specification for padding at *http://www.w3.org/TR/CSS21/box.html#propdef-padding*; CSS 2.1 specification for margin at *http://www.w3.org/TR/CSS21/box.html#propdef-margin*.

5.3   Place Dividers Between List Items

Problem

You want to create list dividers between list items.

Solution

Use the border property to create a visual divider.

```
li {
  border-top: 1px solid black;
  padding: .3em 0;
}
```

Then apply a border to the bottom of the ul element to create the bottom border (see Figure 5-3):

```
ul {
  margin-left: 40px;
  padding-left: 0px;
  border-bottom: 1px solid black;
  list-style: none;
  width: 36%;
}
```

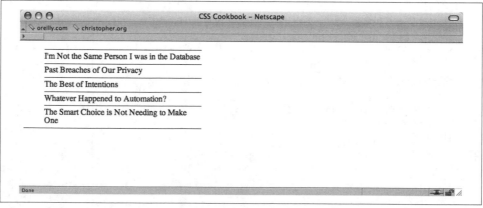

Figure 5-3. Dividers placed between list items

Discussion

To ensure consistency for the length of the dividers, apply only a value to the `margin-left` or `padding-left` property of the unordered list. Otherwise the length of the border on both the list items and the unordered list will be inconsistent. For example, if the list items are indented through the `padding-left` property, the bottom border is longer than the border for the individual list items (see Figure 5-4):

```
li {
  border-top: 1px solid black;
  padding: .3em 0;
}
ul {
  margin-left: 0px;
  padding-left: 40px;
  border-bottom: 1px solid black;
  list-style: none;
  width: 36%;
}
```

Figure 5-4. The bottom divider is longer than the other dividers

See Also

Recipe 5.2 for creating cross-browser indents for lists.

5.4   Creating Custom Text Markers for Lists

Problem

You want to use a custom text marker in a list.

Solution

Indent the first line of text and insert the custom text, along with the right-angle quotes acting as pointers, through autogenerated content (see Figure 5-5):

```
ul {
  list-style: none;
  margin: 0;
  padding: 0 0 0 1em;
  text-indent: -1em;
}
li {
  width: 33%;
  padding: 0;
  margin: 0 0 0.25em 0;
}
li:before {
  content: "\00BB \0020";
}
```

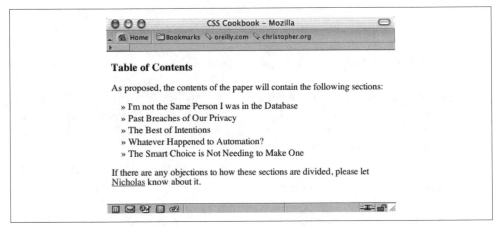

Figure 5-5. Text marker for a list

Discussion

Setting the list-style property to a value of none turns off the list marker usually associated with a list. Typically, a marker is appended to the left of each list item.

Instead of appending the marker to the list item, the custom text marker will be placed inline with the content of the item. Because the text marker is inside the list item, you need to push the marker out of the list item box. Indenting the first line of the marker with a negative value creates this push. The negative value for the text-indent property moves the first line to the left, whereas a positive value moves the indent to the right:

```
ul {
  list-style: none;
  margin: 0;
  padding: 0 0 0 1em;
  text-indent: -1em;
}
```

The :before pseudo-element generates the text marker. The content of simple keyboard characters can be easily inserted like so:

```
li:before {
  content: ">> ";
}
```

However, for embedding special characters, the CSS 2.1 specification calls for special characters to be Unicode (ISO 10646) values. So you need to write out the character in its *escaped Unicode hexadecimal equivalent* and not the usual HTML 4 entities like ».

You escape values in CSS by inserting a backslash before each Unicode hexadecimal value:

```
li:before {
  content: "\00BB \0020";
}
```

At press time, this solution worked in Mozilla, Firefox, Netscape 6+, Safari, and Opera browsers because they can handle the creation of autogenerated content. Unfortunately, this list omits Netscape 4 and Internet Explorer for Windows and Macintosh as they cannot do autogenerated content.

To create a cross-browser effect, don't use autogenerated content. Instead, insert the text marker manually before the list item:

```
<ul>
  <li>&#187; I'm not the Same Person I was in the Database</li>
  <li>&#187; Past Breaches of Our Privacy</li>
  <li>&#187; The Best of Intentions</li>
  <li>&#187; Whatever Happened to Automation?</li>
  <li>&#187; The Smart Choice is Not Needing to Make One</li>
</ul>
```

The main drawback with this approach is that you have two markers for every list item (the browser generated list marker and the manually inserted text marker) if CSS is turned off in the browser and the user see only the content. Although this isn't a mission-critical problem, it adds an unneeded design element to the web page.

See Also

The CSS 2.1 specification about escaping characters at *http://www.w3.org/TR/REC-CSS2/syndata.html#escaped-characters*; and hexadecimal values for ASCII and Unicode characters at *http://www.alanwood.net/demos/ansi.html*.

5.5 Creating Custom Image Markers for Lists

Problem

You want to use your own graphic for a list marker. For example, Figure 5-6 uses a diamond image.

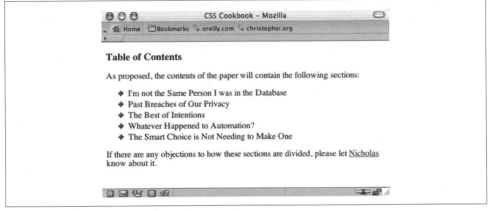

Figure 5-6. Custom-made image markers for a list

Solution

Use the list-style-image property to use a graphic for a bullet marker:

```
ul {
  list-style-type: disc;
  list-style-image: url(bullet.eps);
}
```

Discussion

Set the location of the image you want to use as a marker as the value of the list-style-image property. You can't control the size of the image used as a list marker through CSS, so the image you specify should already be at the correct size. Images that are too large may interfere with the legibility of the list item or the marker may not be displayed entirely in the viewport (see Figure 5-7). When creating custom bullets, make sure they are of the appropriate size to complement the design of your web page.

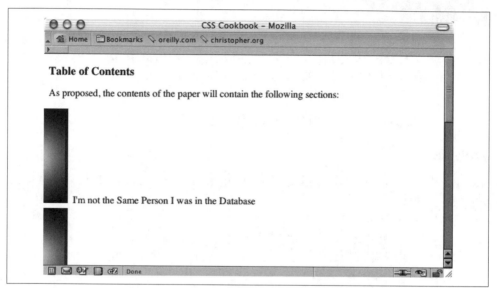

Figure 5-7. A large image used for a marker isn't fully displayed

The value for the image marker is *inherited*, meaning that nested lists pick up the image as the marker as does the parent. To stop this inheritance, the value of none needs to be set for the child lists.

```
ul {
  list-style-type: disc;
  list-style-image: url(bullet.eps);
}
ul ul {list-style-image: none;}
```

Always include the `list-style-type` property to provide a fallback should the image not be usable. In the solution, the list marker `disc` is used if the image, *bullet.eps*, can't be displayed.

See Also

Recipe 5.4 on creating custom text markers; the CSS 2.1 specification for `list-image-type` at *http://www.w3.org/TR/CSS21/generate.html#propdef-list-style-image*.

5.6 Inserting Large Custom Image Markers for Lists

Problem

You want to use a large custom graphic for a list marker without running into constraints by using `list-style-image` property.

Solution

First, remove default list marker through the `list-style` property (see Figure 5-8):

```
ul {
    margin-left: 40px;
    padding-left: 0px;
    list-style: none;
}
```

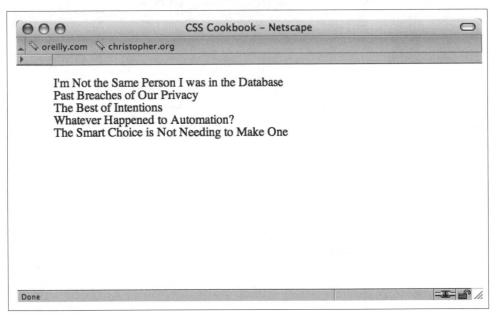

Figure 5-8. Default list markers are removed

Apply enough padding on the right side of the list item to allow the new image marker to be placed (see Figure 5-9):

```
ul {
  margin-left: 40px;
  padding-left: 0px;
  list-style: none;
}
li {
  padding: .3em 0 1em 40px;
  font: 1.1em/1.2 Verdana, Arial, Verdana, sans-serif;
}
```

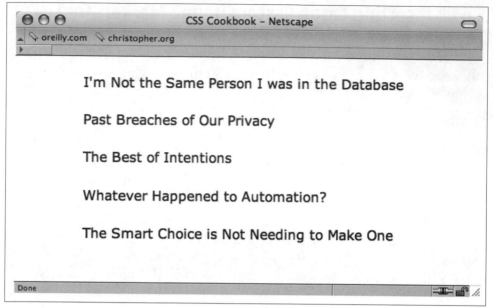

Figure 5-9. Extra padding is placed on the left side of the list

Then insert the new custom marker through the background property (see Figure 5-10):

```
ul {
  margin-left: 40px;
  padding-left: 0px;
  list-style: none;
}
li {
  padding: .3em 0 1em 40px;
  font: 1.1em/1.2 Verdana, Arial, Verdana, sans-serif;
  background: url(search_32.eps) no-repeat;
}
```

Discussion

Using the background property to create enhanced list presentation allows for greater flexibility than using the list-style-image property. With this technique, any size custom list marker can be used as long as there is enough padding set to the left of the list item.

See Also

Recipe 5.7 for a more complex version of this Solution.

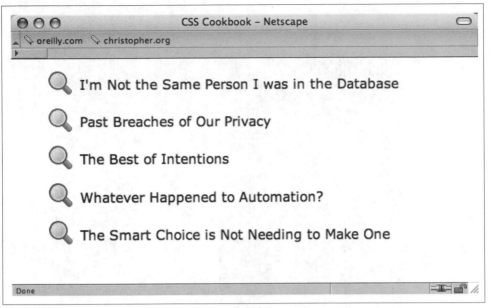

Figure 5-10. A large image used for a marker isn't fully displayed

5.7   Making a List Presentation Rich with Imagery

Problem

You want to create added attention to a list with rich imagery.

Solution

Integrate the background images for both the ul and li element.

First, create a background image for the unordered list set and an image for the list marker (see Figure 5-11):

Next, set up the unordered list element to bring in the background image. Also, include the width property set to the same width as the background image (see Figure 5-12):

```
ul {
    background: url(list-bkgd.gif) bottom;
    width: 298px;
    list-style: none;
    padding: 0 0 12px;
    margin: 0;
}
```

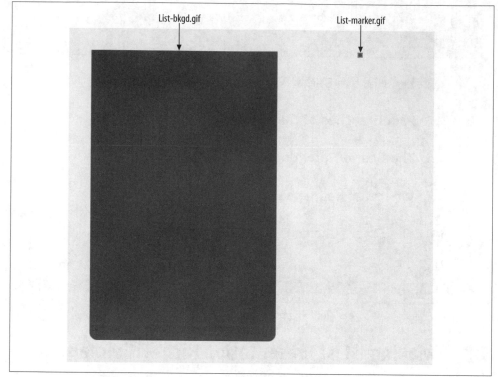

Figure 5-11. The two images used for our custom list presentation

Next, include the list marker through the list item. Also, place borders at the bottom to act as dividers between the list items (see Figure 5-13):

```
ul {
    background: url(list-bkgd.gif) bottom;
    width: 298px;
    list-style: none;
    padding: 0 0 12px;
    margin: 0;
}
li {
    color: #eee;
    font-family: Verdana, Arial, Verdana, sans-serif;
    padding: 7px 7px 7px 20px;
    border-bottom: 1px solid #888;
    background: url(list-marker.gif) no-repeat 5px .8em;
}
```

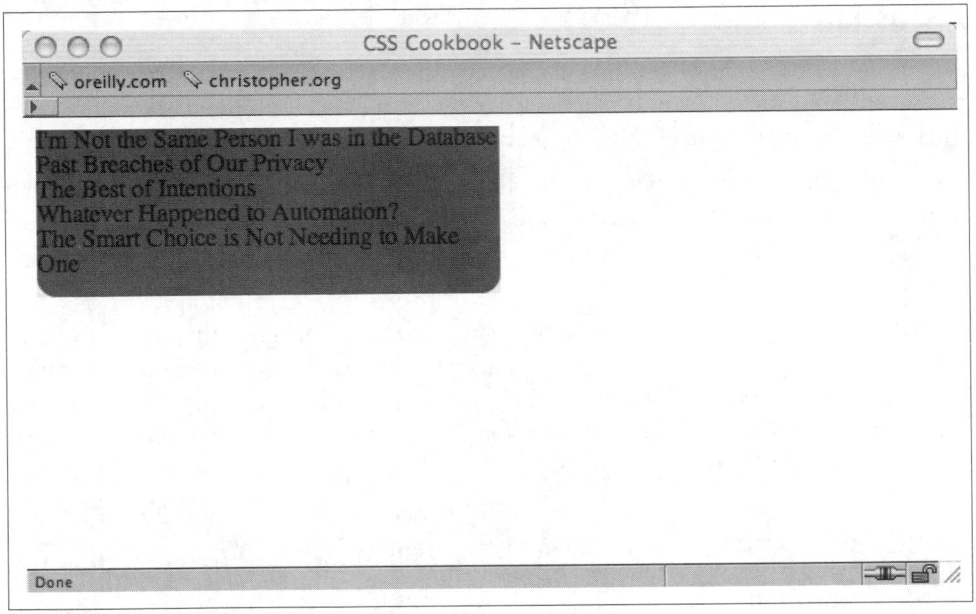

Figure 5-12. Background image for the entire list is set

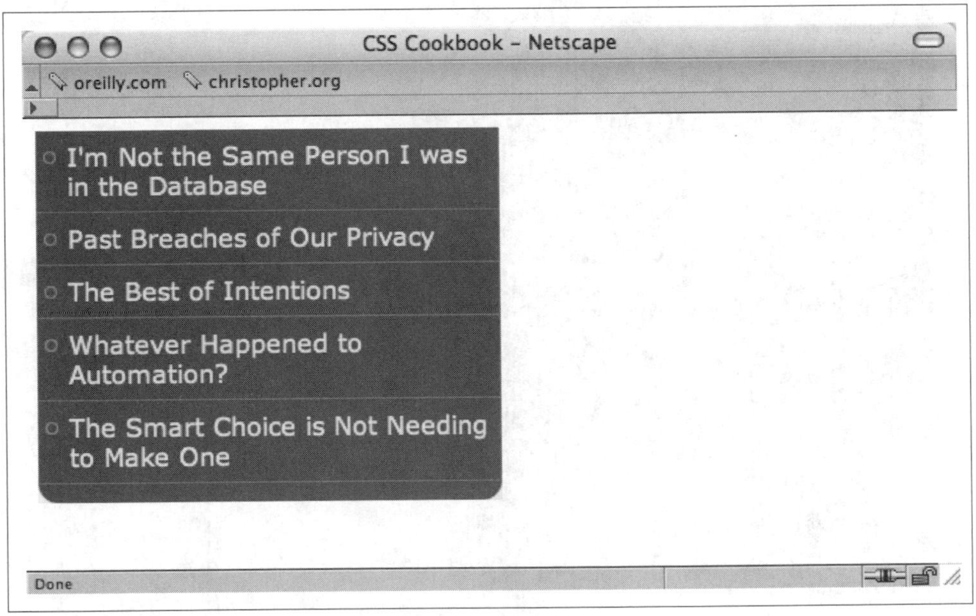

Figure 5-13. The styled list items complete the presentation

Discussion

A number of different techniques come together to achieve this solution. The first part of the solution deals with placing a background image into the ul element. Since the image has a set width and height, make sure to set the width through CSS.

For the height, there are many issues that keep web developers from setting that property. A user might increase the size of the default text making the text larger or smaller. Also, the style for the list may be used for lists with a high or a low number of items.

In order to compensate for almost any situation, the background image needs to have a large height. In this solution, the background image is set to 465 pixels, which is more than enough space for normal view of a handful of items. However, in case someone's browser has set the fonts to a large size, the design solution is still intact, as shown in Figure 5-14.

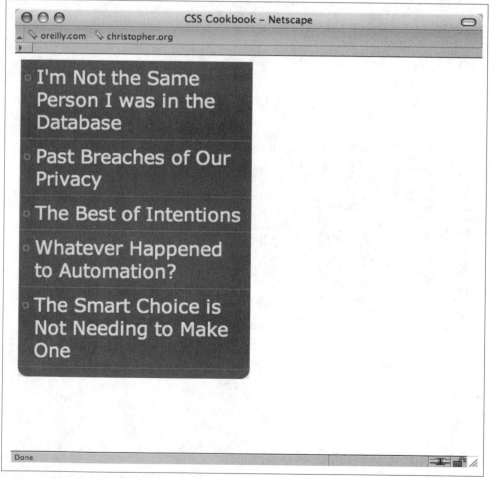

Figure 5-14. The design holds together as text size increases

Since the background image has curved edges on the bottom, padding of 12 pixels was applied to the bottom so that the list items would not cover it up. Also, the positioning of the background image was set to bottom. This allowed the background image to always display the curves even if the text size expands or the number of list items increases.

Next, the list items involve a couple of techniques. First, dividers are placed between the list items. Unlike in Recipe 5.3, a divider isn't needed on the bottom of the ul element. Second, the list markers are inserted by using the technique from Recipe 5.6.

See Also

Chapter 6 for ways to translate this text into a working navigation menu.

5.8 Creating Inline Lists

Problem

You want to list items to be displayed within a paragraph, as in Figure 5-15, in which the bold, comma-separated list was generated from an HTML ul list.

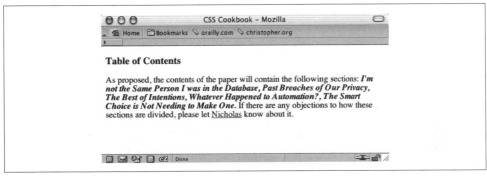

Figure 5-15. The list formatted to appear inside a paragraph

Solution

Set the paragraphs before (and, if needed, after) the list:

```
<h3>
 Table of Contents
</h3>
<p>
 As proposed, the contents of the paper will contain the
following sections:
</p>
<ul>
 <li>I'm not the Same Person I was in the Database</li>
 <li>Past Breaches of Our Privacy</li>
```

```
<li>The Best of Intentions</li>
<li>Whatever Happened to Automation?</li>
<li class="last">The Smart Choice is Not Needing to Make One</li>
</ul>
<p>
If there are any objections to how these sections are divided,
please let <a href="nick@heatvision.com">Nicholas</a> know about
it.
</p>
```

Through CSS, set the paragraph to display as inline elements, and then use autogenerated content to show the commas between items and the period at the end of the list:

```
ul, li {
  display: inline;
  margin: 0;
  padding: 0;
  font-weight: bold;
  font-style: italic;
}
li:after {
  content: ", ";
}
li.last:after {
  content: ".";
}
p {
  display: inline;
}
```

Discussion

Through this method you retain the structure of lists and paragraphs, but you stretch CSS' capability to present the list inside a paragraph. However, you hide the obvious visual appearance of a list in favor of having the contents placed inside a paragraph.

The critical part of this solution is setting the display property to inline on the list items and paragraphs. By using the inline value, the elements are placed on the same line instead of being separated by whitespace above and below each element.

 Note that Internet Explorer for Windows does not support autogenerated content.

See Also

The CSS 2.1 specification about the display property at *http://www.w3.org/TR/CSS21/visuren.html#propdef-display*.

5.9   Making Hanging Indents in a List

Problem

You want the first line of a list item to begin further to the left than the rest of the list, thereby creating a hanging indent as in Figure 5-16.

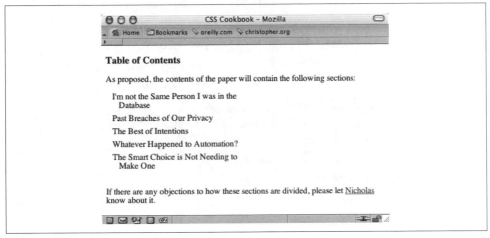

Figure 5-16. Hanging indents on a list

Solution

Use a negative value for the text-indent property:

```
ul {
  width: 30%;
  padding: 0 0 0.75em 0;
  margin: 0;
  list-style: none;
}
li {
  text-indent: -0.75em;
  margin: 0.33em 0.5em 0.5em 1.5em;
}
```

Discussion

Although list markers (numeric, image, or text) help to call attention to the actual list, sometimes you may not want to add those kinds of design elements to a list. Instead of relying on markers to carry off the list design, use a hanging indent.

In this solution, you indent the list by three-quarters of an em unit, creating a visible but almost subtle hanging indent effect. You can push this design technique from subtle to the foreground by reducing the text-indent value further, or by increasing the font size of the text in the list item.

See Also

Recipe 2.18 on setting indents in paragraphs; the CSS 2.1 specification for text-indent at *http://www.w3.org/TR/CSS21/text.html#propdef-text-indent*.

5.10   Moving the Marker Inside the List

Problem

You want the list marker to be pulled inside the border of the list items, as in Figure 5-17. This creates an effect in which the text wraps around the marker.

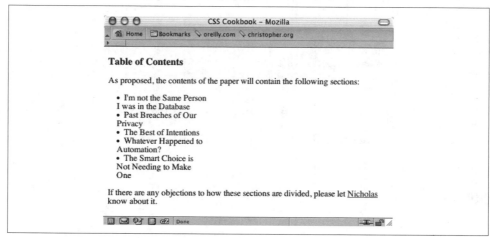

Figure 5-17. Moving the marker inside the list item

Solution

Use the list-style-position property and set the value to inside:

```
li {
  list-style-position: inside;
  width: 33%;
  padding: 0;
  margin: 0;
}
ul {
  margin: 0;
  padding: 0 0 0 1em;
}
```

Discussion

Normally the list marker stands outside the text and the result is a very distinctive list. Some designs, however, may require the marker to appear as part of the text. A designer may choose to keep the marker inside, for example, to eliminate the need to have enough whitespace on the left side. Also, replacing the list marker with your own custom marker can visually enhance this recipe. For example, Figure 5-18 shows arrows rather than the default bullet.

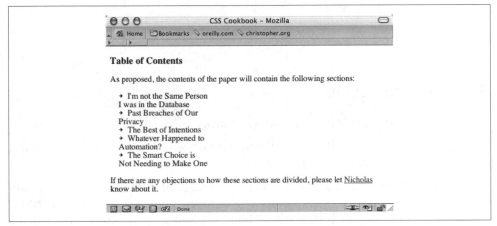

Figure 5-18. Custom marker inside the list item

See Also

The CSS 2.1 specification for list-style-position at *http://www.w3.org/TR/CSS21/generate.html#propdef-list-style-position*.

Links and Navigation

6.0   Introduction

Without links, the point of the Web would be lost.

Links let you to follow a trail of information from one web page to another, from one idea to another, regardless of where in the world the site's server is located.

In 1996, web usability expert Jakob Nielsen listed the use of nonstandard link colors as one of the top ten mistakes in web design (see *http://www.useit.com/alertbox/9605.html*). However, his advice to use blue for the link color for pages that the user hasn't visited and to use purple or red links to represent previously visited pages, came from consistency concerns, not aesthetics.

With CSS, the Web isn't an either-or proposition. Links being an essential part of the World Wide Web can be *both* consistent *and* visually pleasing.

This chapter shows you how to improve aesthetics by changing the link styles. You'll learn everything from how to remove the underline from links to how to change cursors, create rollovers without the need for JavaScript, create a horizontal tab menu, and much more.

6.1   Removing Underlines from Links (and Adding Other Decorations)

Problem

Links in a web document are underlined. You want to remove the underlining (see Figure 6-1).

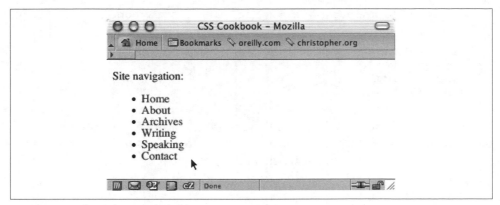

Figure 6-1. Links without underlines

Solution

Use the `text-decoration` property with the pseudo-class selector for unvisited and visited links:

```
a:link, a:visited {
 text-decoration: none;
}
```

Discussion

Use the :link and :visited pseudo-classes to apply styles to links within a web document. The :link pseudo-class applies to links that the user has not visited. The :visited pseudo-class corresponds to links that the user has visited.

The text-decoration property can take up to five settings; they are listed in Table 6-1.

Table 6-1. Text-decoration settings

Text-decoration values	Result
underline	A line is placed beneath the text.
overline	A line is placed above the text.
blink	The text flashes.
line-through	A line is placed through the middle of the text.
none	No effect is associated with the text.

These text-decoration properties are often used to enhance the presentation of a web page. Instead of having all the links in a document underlined, designers set text-decoration to none along with changing the link's background color, text color, or both:

```
a:link, a:visited {
  text-decoration: none;
  background-color: red;
  color: white;
}
```

In order to complement the design for those site visitors who may be color-blind and therefore may not be able to determine a link color from the default color of regular HTML text, designers also set the weight of the font to bold:

```
a:link, a:visited {
  font-weight: bold;
  text-decoration: none;
  color: red;
}
```

The value of line-through may be an interesting element to add to a page design and use to indicate that a link has already been visited by a user, like an item scratched off a to-do list (see Figure 6-2):

```
a:link {
font-weight: bold;
text-decoration: none;
color: red;
}
a:visited {
  font-weight: bold;
  text-decoration: line-through;
  color: black;
}
```

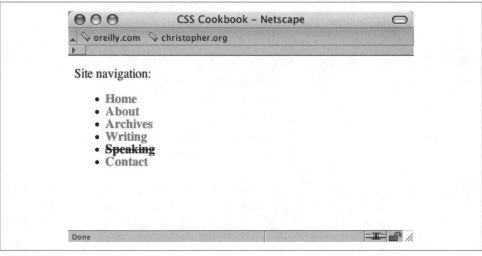

Figure 6-2. Visited link is crossed out

See Also

The CSS 2.1 specification for the text-decoration property at *http://www.w3.org/TR/CSS21/text.html#propdef-text-decoration*, Jakob Neilson's updated "Design Guidelines for Visualizing Links" at *http://www.useit.com/alertbox/20040510.html*.

6.2 Changing Link Colors

Problem

You want to change the colors of the links.

Solution

Use these pseudo-classes in this order: :link, :visited, :hover, and :active:

```
body {
 color: #99ffff;
}
a:link {
 color: #33ccff;
}
a:visited {
 color: #cecece;
}
a:hover {
 color: #336666;
}
a:active {
 color: #339999;
}
```

Discussion

The hyperlink pseudo-classes are equal in terms of priority within the cascade, so avoid the conflict by listing the selectors in the order: link, visited, hover, and active. The mnemonic device commonly used to remember the order is "LoVe/HAte."

A visited or an unvisited link can enter hover and active state at the same time. Since hyperlink pseudo-classes have the same ranking, the one listed last is what the user sees and that's why in some cases :hover won't work. When :hover appears before :active or :visited, then these hide the hover state based on the cascading rules.

See Also

The CSS 2.1 specification for the dynamic pseudo-classes: :hover, :active, and :focus at *http://www.w3.org/TR/CSS21/selector.html#dynamic-pseudo-classes*; Eric Meyer on link specificity at *http://www.meyerweb.com/eric/css/link-specificity.html* 7.

6.3   Changing Link Colors in Different Sections of a Page

Problem

You want to apply different links to the main text and the navigation.

Solution

First, wrap sections of the page with `div` elements and different attribute values:

```
<div id="nav">
 [...]
</div><!-- end -->
<div id="content">
 [...]
</div><!-- end -->
```

Then use descendant selectors with `ID` selectors along and the LV/HA method discussed in Recipe 6.2 to isolate different link styles to different areas of a web page:

```
/* navigation link design */
#nav a:link {
 color: blue;
}
#nav a:visited {
 color: purple;
}
/* content link design */
#content a:link {
 color: white;
}
#content a:visited {
 color: yellow;
}
```

Discussion

The use of the `ID` selector to identify sections of the web page opens the door for applying different styles to the same elements or selectors. Rely on the same selectors to create links with different styles by section. For more on `ID` selector, see Recipe 1.2. Applying LV/HA mnemonic order to the links also ensures your links operate as expected.

See Also

The W3Schools Tutorial on CSS Pseudo-classes at *http://www.w3schools.com/css/css_pseudo_classes.asp*, or the Backstage tutorial on multiple link colors at *http://www.metalusions.com/backstage/articles/2/*.

6.4   Placing an Icon at the End of the Link

Problem

You to display icons at the end of an inline link like the ones in Figure 6-3.

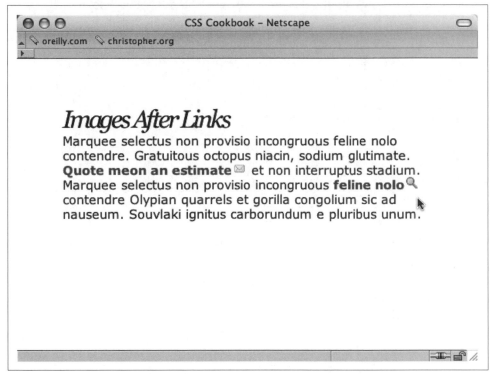

Figure 6-3. Icons are placed at the end of the links

Solution

Adding a class attribute to the links, place two values for the attributes. One value is icon while the other value describes the nature of the link. In this case, the links are for an email address and a search engine:

```
<a href="mailto:orders@csscookbook.com" class="icon email">Quote me on an estimate</a>
<a href="http://www.google.com/" class="icon search">feline nolo</a>
```

Provide room for the icons at the end of the links by using a class selector and the :after pseudo-class with the width, margin and height properties:

```
a {
 text-decoration: none;
 font-weight: bold;
}
```

```
#content a.icon:after {
 display: block;
 width: 17px;
 height: 15px;
 margin: 2px;
}
```

To place images at the end of links, use a different CSS rule for each icon.

Using the `class` selector and `:after` pseudo-class, the icons of an envelope and a magnifying glass are placed at the end of the links in two CSS rules:

```
#content a.email:after {
 content: url(email.gif);
}
#content a.search:after {
 content: url(search.gif);
}
```

Discussion

The setup for this solution allows for the easy editing of the design. If an icon (for email, it's a Word document icon) needs to be added at the end of a link, first add the value `document` within the `class` attribute:

```
<a href="/_assets/report.pdf" class="icon document">feline nolo</a>
```

Then add a new CSS rule to place the icon:

```
#content a.document:after {
 content: url(doc.gif);
}
```

There is another method that wouldn't require the additional markup of a class attribute and value. For example, use attribute selectors as discussed in Recipe 1.2 to place icons for email addresses at the end of links:

```
#content a[href|="mailto"]:after {
 content: url(email.gif);
}
```

However, support for attributes selectors is limited. Also, since the solution uses content generation, it's not suitable for Internet Explorer for Windows.

See Also

Dave Shea's presentation on adding an icon with a background image in an inline link at *http://www.mezzoblue.com/presentations/2006/sxsw/css/q1.html*; and an explanation about why this fails in IE at *http://www.brunildo.org/test/InlineBlockLayout.html*.

6.5 Changing Cursors

Problem

You want to change the cursor to an icon representation of a timepiece when the mouse pointer rolls over a link, as in Figure 6-4.

Figure 6-4. The cursor changes to a timepiece

Solution

Use the cursor property to change the cursor:

```
a:link, a:visited {
 cursor: move;
}
```

Discussion

The cursor property can take multiple values, as listed in Table 6-2. However, support for these values varies from browser to browser. Opera 7 and Internet Explorer for Windows 5.5+ support the cursor property. Although Netscape Navigator 6+ supports most values, the browser doesn't support the uri. Also, in Navigator, the cursor property isn't inherited to child elements from the parent.

Table 6-2. Cursor property values

Value	Description	Sample
auto	The cursor changes to an image that is determined by the browser.	
crosshair	Two perpendicular lines intersecting in the middle; this is similar to an enlarged plus sign.	+
default	Platform-dependent cursor that in most browsers is rendered as an arrow. Browser vendors or computer operating systems may dictate a different cursor style.	

Table 6-2. Cursor property values (continued)

Value	Description	Sample
pointer	Used to illustrate that the mouse pointer is over a link; sometimes rendered as a hand with an extended index finger. Browser vendors or computer operating systems may dictate a different cursor style.	
move	Illustrates that an element can be moved; sometimes rendered as a crosshair with arrowheads on the tips or a five-fingered hand.	
e-resize, ne-resize, nw-resize, n-resize, se-resize, sw-resize, s-resize, w-resize	An arrow illustrating the direction in which a side can be moved; for example, se-resize indicates a southeast direction.	
text	Illustrates that text can be selected; sometimes rendered like an I-beam commonly used in word processing programs.	
wait	Illustrates that the computer is busy; sometimes rendered as an hourglass.	
progress	Illustrates that the computer is busy, but the user still can interact with the browser.	
help	Illustrates that information or help is available, often at the destination of the link; sometimes rendered as a question mark or an arrow with a question mark.	
<uri>	The cursor can be swapped with an externally defined cursor like an image, Windows cursor file, SVG cursor, etc.	N/A

The code to include a custom cursor is similar to that used to set a background image on an element:

```
a.help:link, a.help:visited{
  cursor: url(bewildered.gif);
}
```

While employing different cursors, most users will find changes to their routine surfing habits somewhere between a whimsical annoyance and an extreme aggravation, depending on how excessive your implementation is. Therefore, change the cursor a user is accustomed to seeing at your own risk.

See Also

The CSS 2.1 specification for the cursor property at *http://www.w3.org/TR/CSS21/ui.html#propdef-cursor*; and examples of the various cursors in action at *http://www.zimmertech.com/tutorials/css/20/changing-cursors-tutorial.php*.

6.6   Creating Rollovers Without JavaScript

Problem

You want to create a simple rollover effect without using JavaScript to swap images.

Solution

Use the :hover and :active pseudo-classes to create the rollover:

```
a:link {
 color: #777;
 text-decoration: none;
}
a:visited {
 color: #333;
 text-decoration: none;
}
a:link:hover, a:visited:hover {
 color: #777;
 background-color: #ccc;
}
a:link:active, a:visited:active {
 color: #ccc;
 background-color: #ccc;
}
```

Discussion

The :hover pseudo-class mimics the common JavaScript event onmouseover. Instead of executing a function in JavaScript, when a user rolls over a link with :hover, a different set of styles is applied to the link.

With the selectors having the same specificity, selectors written out of order may stop one of the other styles from appearing. Avoid this common problem with LV/HA.

Although :hover and :active can be applied to any element, they are commonly used on links. Note that browser support for :hover and :active is nonexistent in Netscape Navigator 4.

In the solution, the two pseudo-classes make sure that the rollover effects occur only on anchor links. Without :hover and :active, modern browsers could legally apply the rollover effects on any anchor elements, as you see in this code and in Figure 6-5:

```
<h2><a name="europan">Li Europan lingues</a></h2>
```

The College of West Anglia

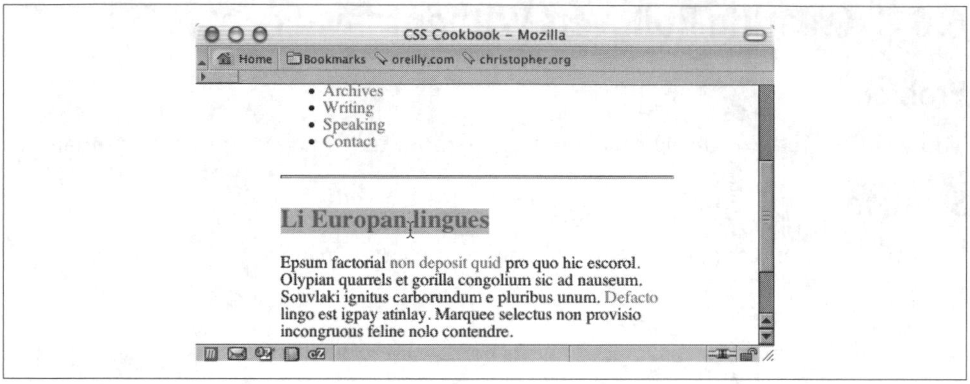

Figure 6-5. An unwanted rollover effect on a heading

See Also

The CSS 2.1 specification for :active and :hover at *http://www.w3.org/TR/CSS21/ selector.html#x36;* an explanation about links and specificity at *http://www. meyerweb.com/eric/css/link-specificity.html.*

6.7   Creating Text Navigation Menus and Rollovers

Problem

You have a list of links, but want to build an elegant menu like the one in Figure 6-6.

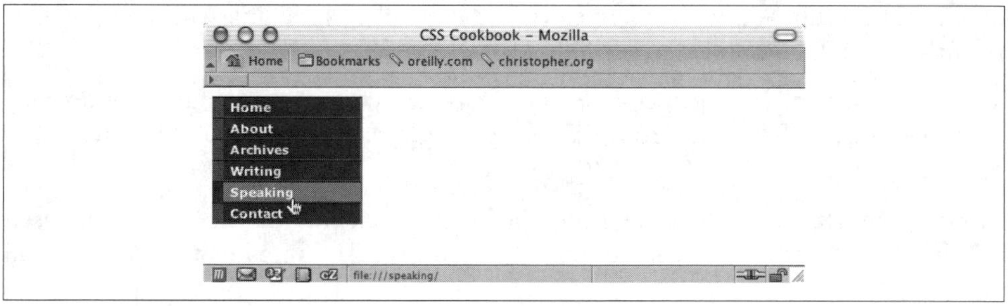

Figure 6-6. Set of stylized links

Solution

First, mark up the list of links in an unordered list so that they wrap around a div element with an id attribute:

```
<div id="navsite">
 <p>Site navigation:</p>
 <ul>
  <li><a href="/">Home</a></li>
```

```
      <li><a href="/about/">About</a></li>
      <li><a href="/archives/">Archives</a></li>
      <li><a href="/writing/">Writing</a></li>
      <li><a href="/speaking/">Speaking</a></li>
      <li><a href="/contact/">Contact</a></li>
    </ul>
  </div>
```

Next, use the border property on the anchor elements to create the bulk of the design:

```
#navsite p {
 display: none;
}
#navsite {
 font-family: Verdana, Helvetica, Arial, sans-serif;
 font-size: 0.7em;
 font-weight: bold;
 width: 12em;
 border-right: 1px solid #666;
 padding: 0;
 margin-bottom: 1em;
 background-color: #9cc;
 color: #333;
}
#navsite ul {
 list-style: none;
 margin: 0;
 padding: 0;
}
#navsite ul li {
 margin: 0;
 border-top: 1px solid #003;
}
#navsite ul li a {
 display: block;
 padding: 2px 2px 2px 0.5em;
 border-left: 10px solid #369;
 border-right: 1px solid #69c;
 border-bottom: 1px solid #369;
 background-color: #036;
 color: #fff;
 text-decoration: none;
 width: 100%;
}
html>body #navsite ul li a {
 width: auto;
}
#navsite ul li a:hover {
 border-left: 10px solid #036;
 border-right: 1px solid #69c;
 border-bottom: 1px solid #369;
 background-color: #69f;
 color: #fff;
}
```

Discussion

A menu makes it easier for visitors to navigate your site. To help the user find the navigation menu, stylize the links so they stand out from the regular text. Do this by using the id selector when writing the CSS rules. As the solution shows, successfully creating the menu requires some browser bug workarounds as well as straightforward CSS design implementation.

In the division marked with the div, one line of text labels the set of links as navigational links:

```
<p>Site navigation:</p>
```

If the user's browser doesn't have CSS support, the line of text is visible. To hide the text from CSS-enabled browsers, set the display to none:

```
#navsite p {
  display: none;
}
```

The next step is to stylize the div element that encapsulates the set of menu links. In this CSS rule, styles are set for the links to inherit properties set on the div element. Also, set the values of the width, border-right, padding, and margin-bottom properties to keep the menu from bunching up:

```
#navsite {
  font-family: Verdana, Helvetica, Arial, sans-serif;
  font-size: 0.7em;
  font-weight: bold;
  width: 12em;
  border-right: 1px solid #666;
  padding: 0;
  margin-bottom: 1em;
}
```

The next CSS rule eliminates any potential problems with the indentation of lists (see Recipe 5.2) by setting the margin and padding to 0 as well as by eliminating any list markers:

```
#navsite ul {
  list-style: none;
  margin: 0;
  padding: 0;
}
```

In the following rule you're making sure margins aren't applied to each list item. This CSS rule also places a one-pixel border at the top of the list item. This design element helps reinforce the separation of the list items:

```
#navsite ul li {
  margin: 0;
  border-top: 1px solid #003;
}
```

The next rule sets the styles for the links. By default, links are inline elements. The links need to be rendered as block-level elements so that the entire part of the "link design" becomes clickable, and not just the text. Setting the display property to block accomplishes this transformation.

Use the following declarations to stylize the appearance of the borders, text color, text decoration, and width:

```
#navsite ul li a {
  display: block;
  padding: 2px 2px 2px 0.5em;
  border-left: 10px solid #369;
  border-right: 1px solid #69c;
  border-bottom: 1px solid #369;
  background-color: #036;
  color: #fff;
  text-decoration: none;
  width: 100%;
}
```

The final declaration for the links sets the width at 100%. This rule was set to make sure Internet Explorer for Windows makes the entire area clickable. The drawback with this rule is that it causes problems in Internet Explorer 5 for Macintosh and in Netscape Navigator 6+. To work around this problem, use the child selector, which Internet Explorer for Windows can't process (see Recipe 11.2), to reset the width of the link:

```
html>body #navsite ul li a {
  width: auto;
}
```

The last CSS rule states the styles for the rollover effect of the links:

```
#navsite ul li a:hover {
  border-left: 10px solid #036;
  border-right: 1px solid #69c;
  border-bottom: 1px solid #369;
  background-color: #69f;
  color: #fff;
}
```

An unordered list is a perfect way to structure a menu of links in both theory and practical application. On the one hand, a set of links *is* a set of unordered items. And using unordered lists for navigation creates a solid structure for your web document based on both logic and semantically correct markup.

On the other hand, with the links set in an unordered list, it's easier to style the links into a menu presentation than it is to style a series of div elements:

```
<div id="navsite">
<p>Site navigation:</p>
<div><a href="/">Home</a></div>
<div><a href="/about/">About</a></div>
<div><a href="/archives/">Archives</a></div>
```

```
<div><a href="/writing/">Writing</a></div>
<div><a href="/speaking/">Speaking</a></div>
<div><a href="/contact/">Contact</a></div>
</div>
```

See Also

"CSS Design: Taming Lists" by Mark Newhouse at *http://www.alistapart.com/articles/ taminglists/*; the article/tutorial "Semantics, HTML, XHTML, and Structure" by Shirley E. Kaiser at *http://brainstormsandraves.com/articles/semantics/structure/*.

6.8   Building Horizontal Navigation Menus

Problem

You want to create a horizontal navigation menu out of an unordered set of links; Figure 6-7 shows the default, and Figure 6-8 shows what you want.

Figure 6-7. The default appearance of the links

Solution

First create a properly constructed set of unordered links:

```
<div id="navsite">
<h5>Site navigation:</h5>
<ul>
 <li><a href="/">Home</a></li>
 <li><a href="/about/">About</a></li>
 <li><a href="/archives/">Archives</a></li>
 <li><a href="/writing/">Writing</a></li>
 <li><a href="/speaking/" id="current">Speaking</a></li>
 <li><a href="/contact/">Contact</a></li>
</ul>
</div>
```

Figure 6-8. The tab-based navigation

Then set the CSS rules for the navigation structure, making sure to set the `display` property of the list item to `inline`:

```
#navsite h5 {
 display: none;
}
#navsite ul {
 padding: 3px 0;
 margin-left: 0;
 border-bottom: 1px solid #778;
 font: bold 12px Verdana, sans-serif;
}
#navsite ul li {
 list-style: none;
 margin: 0;
 display: inline;
}
#navsite ul li a {
 padding: 3px 0.5em;
 margin-left: 3px;
 border: 1px solid #778;
 border-bottom: none;
 background: #dde;
 text-decoration: none;
}
#navsite ul li a:link {
 color: #448;
}
#navsite ul li a:visited {
 color: #667;
}
#navsite ul li a:link:hover, #navsite ul li a:visited:hover {
 color: #000;
 background: #aae;
 border-color: #227;
}
```

```
#navsite ul li a#current {
  background: white;
  border-bottom: 1px solid white;
}
```

Discussion

The first part of the solution hides the heading. This is done because the visual representation of the tab navigation design is enough to inform users that these are navigation links:

```
#navsite h5 {
  display: none;
}
```

The next rule defines the padding and margin for the box that is created by the unordered list element, ul. The line that stretches across the bottom of the folder tabs is drawn by the border-bottom property (see Figure 6-9):

```
#navsite ul {
  padding: 3px 0;
  margin-left: 0;
  border-bottom: 1px solid #669;
  font: bold 12px Verdana, Helvetica, Arial, sans-serif;
}
```

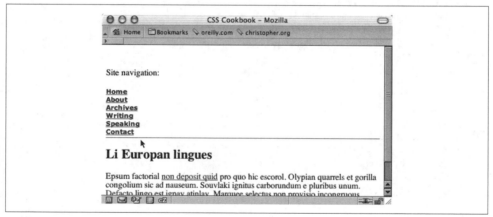

Figure 6-9. The line the navigation tabs rest upon

The declaration that makes this horizontal navigation work with the unordered list is display: inline for the list item:

```
#navsite ul li {
  list-style: none;
  margin: 0;
  display: inline;
}
```

Instead of stacking the list items on top of each other by default, the browser now lays out the list items as it would text, images, and other inline elements (see Figure 6-10).

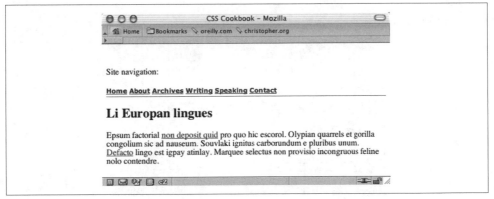

Figure 6-10. The list spread out horizontally

To create the look of the folder tab, use the border property in the following CSS rule:

```
#navsite ul li a {
  padding: 3px 0.5em;
  margin-left: 3px;
  border: 1px solid #669;
  border-bottom: none;
  background: #ccf;
  text-decoration: none;
}
```

The first border property is a shorthand property that dictates a solid, one-pixel border around the link. However, immediately following the border property is the border-bottom property, which tells the browser not to display a border beneath the link.

The value of the border-bottom property is displayed over the border shorthand property (see Figure 6-11). This overwriting occurs because the border-bottom declaration overrides the values in the border declaration because of the order in which they are declared.

After creating the look of the border tab, set the color of the text links and rollover states:

```
#navsite ul li a:link {
  color: #339;
}
#navsite ul li a:visited {
  color: #666;
}
```

```
#navsite ul li a:link:hover, #navsite ul li a:visited:hover {
  color: #000;
  background: #aae;
  border-color: #336;
}
```

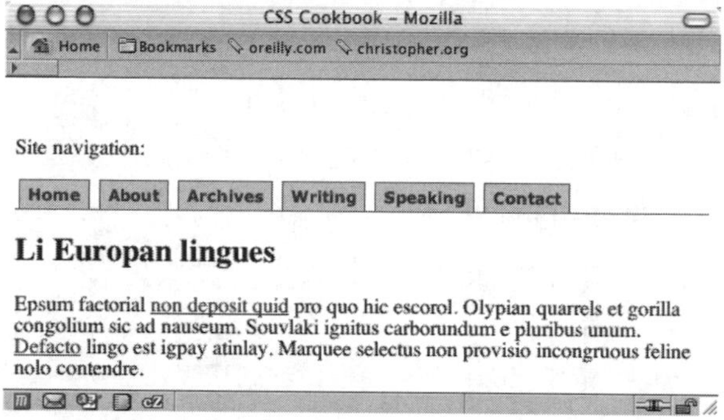

Figure 6-11. The tabs appear

The final CSS rule defines how the "current" link appears. This style is applied to the link that represents the page being viewed by the user (see Figure 6-12):

```
#navsite ul li a#current {
  background: white;
  border-bottom: 1px solid white;
}
```

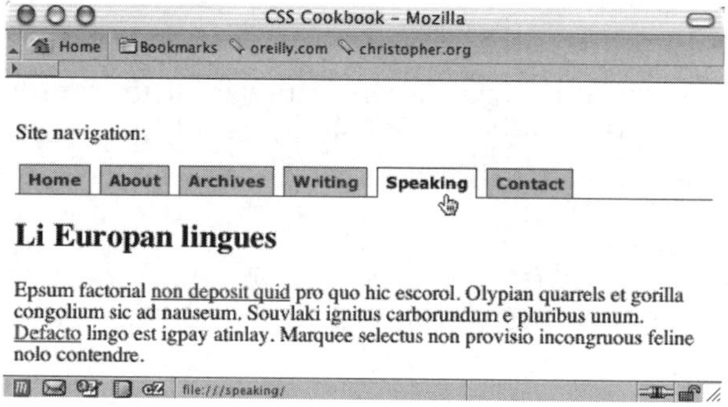

Figure 6-12. The look of the current link

See Also

The original tab menu bar (as well as other navigation styles) at *http://css.maxdesign.com.au/listamatic/horizontal05.htm*.

6.9   Building a Navigation Menu with Access Keys

Problem

You want to create a navigation menu with access keys.

Solution

Create a set of unordered links with an accesskey within the anchor elements:

```
<div id="navsite">
 <ul>
  <li><a href="/" accesskey="h">Home</a></li>
  <li><a href="/about/" accesskey="b">About</a></li>
  <li><a href="/archives/" accesskey="a">Archives</a></li>
  <li><a href="/writing/" accesskey="w">Writing</a></li>
  <li><a href="/speaking/" accesskey="s">Speaking</a></li>
  <li><a href="/contact/" accesskey="c">Contact</a></li>
 </ul>
</div>
```

Next, add a span element around the letters you want to identify as access keys:

```
<div id="navsite">
 <ul>
  <li><a href="/" accesskey="h"><span class="akey">H</span>ome</a></li>
  <li><a href="/about/" accesskey="b">A<span class="akey">b</span>out</a></li>
  <li><a href="/archives/" accesskey="a"><span class="akey">A</span>rchives</a></li>
  <li><a href="/writing/" accesskey="w"><span class="akey">W</span>riting</a></li>
  <li><a href="/speaking/" accesskey="s"><span class="akey">S</span>peaking</a></li>
  <li><a href="/contact/" accesskey="c"><span class="akey">C</span>ontact</a></li>
 </ul>
</div>
```

Then style the access keys through a class selector (see Figure 6-13):

```
.akey {
 text-decoration: underline;
}
```

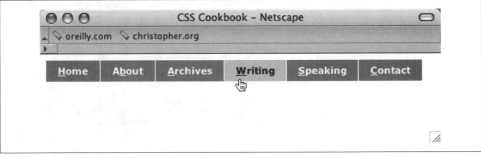

Figure 6-13. The look of the current link

Discussion

Access keys allow site visitors to navigate a web site easily without the use of a mouse. In the Solution, access keys were assigned to the navigation elements. Once pressed, the user will navigate to the page specified in the link.

If used consistently, a site visitor may use the same set of access keys to navigate in order to create a cohesive user experience.

Access keys are supposed to work in Internet Explorer 4+ for Windows, Mozilla, Firefox, Netscape Navigator 6+, Safari, and Opera 7+.

One of the obstacles for access keys is that there isn't a standard set of keys associated with each link. For example, would using the letter h be better for "Home Page" (as done in this example) or would the letter m be better to represent "Main Page"?

See Also

The HTML 4 specification for access keys at *http://www.w3.org/TR/html4/interact/ forms.html#h-17.11.2*; "Accesskeys: Unlocking Hidden Navigation" by Stuart Robertson at *http://alistapart.com/articles/accesskeys/*.

6.10   Creating Breadcrumb Navigation

Problem

You want to use a nesting listing like the one in Figure 6-14 to create a line of *breadcrumb* navigation links, which is a set of links that lead back to the home page (see Figure 6-15).

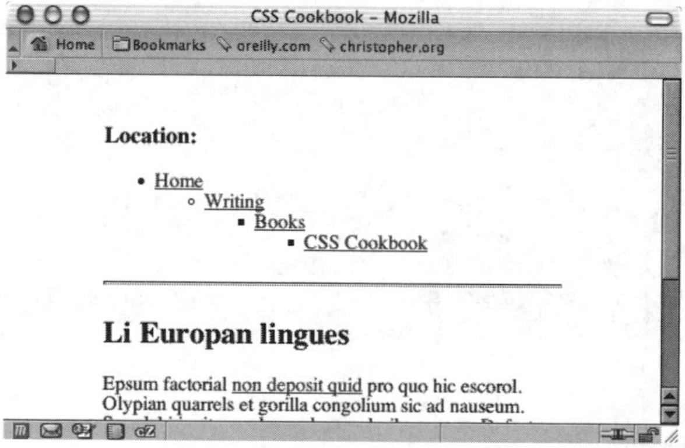

Figure 6-14. The default rendering of the nested listing

Figure 6-15. The breadcrumb trail

Solution

The first step is to create a properly constructed set of nested, unordered links that represent the page's location in the site:

```
<div id="crumbs">
 <h3>Location:</h3>
<ul>
 <li><a href="/">Home</a>
  <ul>
   <li><a href="/writing/">Writing</a>
    <ul>
     <li><a href="/writing/books/">Books</a>
      <ul>
       <li><a href="/writing/books/">CSS Cookbook</a></li>
      </ul>
     </li>
    </ul>
   </li>
  </ul>
 </li>
</ul>
</div>
```

Now set the `display` property of both the `ul` and the `li` of the lists:

```
#crumbs {
 background-color: #eee;
 padding: 4px;
}
#crumbs h3 {
 display: none;
}
#crumbs ul {
 display: inline;
 padding-left: 0;
 margin-left: 0;
}
```

```
#crumbs ul li {
  display: inline;
}
#crumbs ul li a:link {
  padding: .2em;
}
```

Within each nested list, place a small background image of an arrow to the left of the link:

```
crumbs ul ul li{
  background-image: url(arrow.gif);
  background-repeat: no-repeat;
  background-position: left;
  padding-left: 12px;
}
```

Discussion

Based on the fairy tale, "Hansel and Gretel," a *breadcrumb trail* is used to help people find their way home. On the Web, the breadcrumb trail illustrates a path to the page the user is viewing (see Figure 6-16).

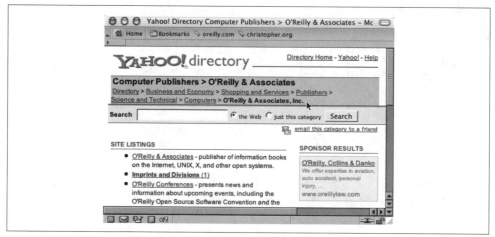

Figure 6-16. An example of a breadcrumb trail

The solution could drop the background-image property if more browsers supported the :before pseudo-element. The solution would then incorporate another CSS rule (see Recipe 8.9), like so:

```
#crumbs ul ul li:before {
  content: url(arrow.gif);
}
```

As of this writing, only Firefox, Safari, Netscape Navigator 6+, and Opera 5+ support the :before pseudo-element.

See Also

http://www.surlalunefairytales.com/hanselgretel/index.html to read an annotated version of *Hansel and Gretel*; a research paper into the effectiveness of breadcrumb navigation at *http://psychology.wichita.edu/surl/usabilitynews/52/breadcrumb.htm*.

6.11 Creating Image-Based Rollovers

Problem

You want image-based rollovers to replace text links.

Solution

First, wrap the text inside the anchor element in a span:

```
<a href="/" id="linkhome">
  <span>Homepage</span>
</a>
```

Next, instead of JavaScript, use the background-image property within the pseudo-class selectors :hover and :active to swap the images (see Figure 6-17):

```
a span {
 display: none;
}
a:link {
 display: block;
 width: 125px;
 height: 30px;
 background-image: url(btn.gif);
 background-repeat: no-repeat;
 background-position: top left;
}
a:link:hover {
 display: block;
 width: 125px;
 height: 30px;
 background-image: url(btn_roll.gif);
 background-repeat: no-repeat;
 background-position: top left;
}
a:link:active {
 display: block;
 width: 125px;
 height: 30px;
 background-image: url(btn_on.gif);
 background-repeat: no-repeat;
 background-position: top left;
}
```

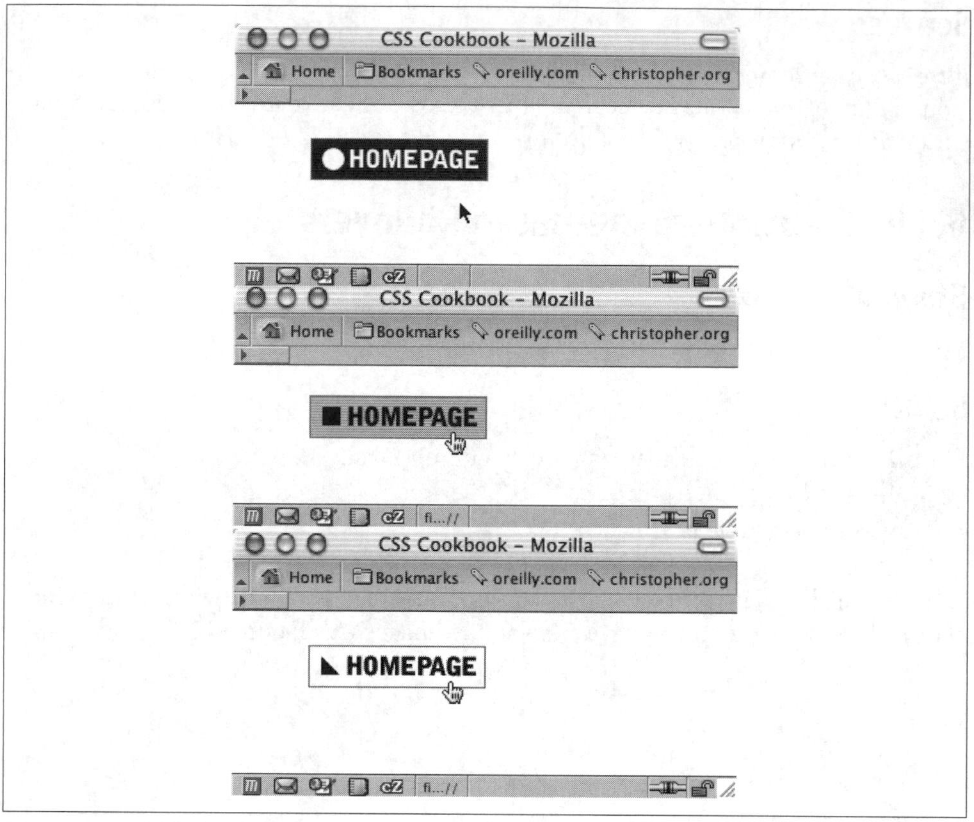

Figure 6-17. The link with default, rollover, and active states

Discussion

Replacing text with an image has five benefits:

1. It separates the text from the presentation. The image that contains more elaborately formatted type is part of the presentation and therefore controlled by a style, while the content in the markup remains pure text.

2. An image heading can be modified across a whole site by one change of the style sheet.

3. This method works for alternative styles and style sheet switching. With a span element inside an element, it is possible to hide HTML text and let a design element, such as a rollover image, show as a background image.

4. If a user doesn't have CSS enabled in his browser, the default HTML text will display instead, sparing the user from having to download unneeded images.

5. The solution is cleaner and simpler than one that involves JavaScript.

You also can use this technique for page elements that don't require a rollover—for example, inserting an image to replace heading text to ensure that a specific font that isn't commonly found on people's computers is displayed as an image. To do so, first set up the markup (see Figure 6-18):

```
<h2 id="headworld"><span>Hello, World!</span></h2>
```

Figure 6-18. Default rendering of heading

Then set the following CSS rules to insert the image (see Figure 6-19):

```
h2#headworld span {
  display: none;
}
h2#headworld {
  width: 395px;
  height: 95px;
  background-image: url(heading.gif);
  background-repeat: no-repeat;
  background-position: top left;
}
```

Figure 6-19. Default rendering of heading

Many people refer to this method as the Fahrner Image Replacement (FIR) method, named after Todd Fahrner.

A drawback to this solution concerns *screen readers*, which are programs that make computers accessible to blind or severely visually impaired people. Certain screen readers won't read elements set to display: none. For more information, read "Facts and Opinion About Fahrner Image Replacement" at *http://www.alistapart.com/ articles/fir/*.

An alternative to this solution is the Leahy-Langridge Image Replacement (LIR) method. Developed independently by Seamus Leahy and Stuart Langridge, the LIR method pushes the text out of view. A benefit for using this technique is that an extra span element isn't required in order to hide the text. For example, the HTML for a heading is basic:

```
<h2 id="headworld">Hello, World!</h2>
```

The image for the heading comes through the background because the CSS rule sets the padding to the exact height of the image header. So, the height property is set to 0:

```
h2#headworld {
/* The width of the image */
width: 395px;
/* The height of the image is the first padding value */
padding: 95px 0 0 0;
overflow: hidden;
background-image: url(heading.gif);
background-repeat: no-repeat;
voice-family: "\"}\"";
voice-family: inherit;
height /**/: 95px;
height: 0px !important;
}
```

The last four lines of the CSS rule are needed to work around Internet Explorer for Windows' poor box-model support. Therefore, Internet Explorer for Windows gets a height value of 95px, while the other browsers receive zero pixels.

Another method for creating an image-based rollover is performed by the background-position property. Known as the *Pixy* method, the technique involves attaching all three rollover states into one image and then moving the position of the image with the background-position property (see Figure 6-20):

```
a span {
 display: none;
}
a:link, a:visited {
 display: block;
 width: 125px;
 height: 30px;
 background-image: url(btn_omni.gif);
 background-repeat: no-repeat;
 background-position: 0 0;
}
a:link:hover, a:visited:hover {
 display: block;
 width: 125px;
 height: 30px;
```

```
      background-image: url(btn_omni.gif);
      background-repeat: no-repeat;
      /* move the image 30 pixels up */
      background-position: 0 -30px;
   }
   a:link:active, a:visited:active  {
      display: block;
      width: 125px;
      height: 30px;
      background-image: url(btn_omni.gif);
      background-repeat: no-repeat;
      /* move the image 60 pixels up */
      background-position: 0 -60px;
   }
```

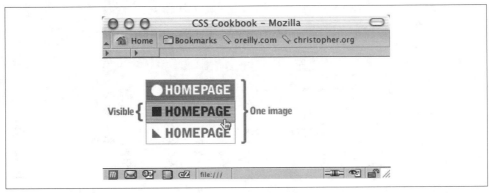

Figure 6-20. Showing a portion of the rollover image

 The drawback of almost all current image replacement techniques is that users see nothing if images are turned off, disabled, or simply don't load while the CSS is still supported. It is important to research and use the method that's best for your situation. Avoid replacing images in important titles.

See Also

Recipe 3.9 for replacing HTML text with an image; another demonstration of the LIR technique by Seamus P. H. Leahy at *http://www.moronicbajebus.com/playground/cssplay/image-replacement/*; an explanation on how to create faster CSS-enabled rollovers without having to preload images at *http://wellstyled.com/css-nopreload-rollovers.html*; a rundown of the FIR technique at *http://www.stopdesign.com/also/articles/replace_text/*.

6.12   Creating Collapsible Menus

Problem

You want to hide a set of links and give the user a way to reveal those links when needed. For example, rather than two bullet lists of links, hide one (like in Figure 6-21) and let the user reveal it by clicking on a plus sign, "+", as in Figure 6-22.

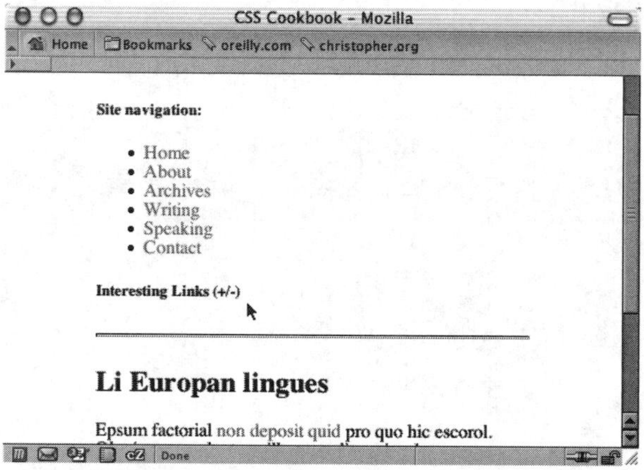

Figure 6-21. Preventing the second set of links from displaying

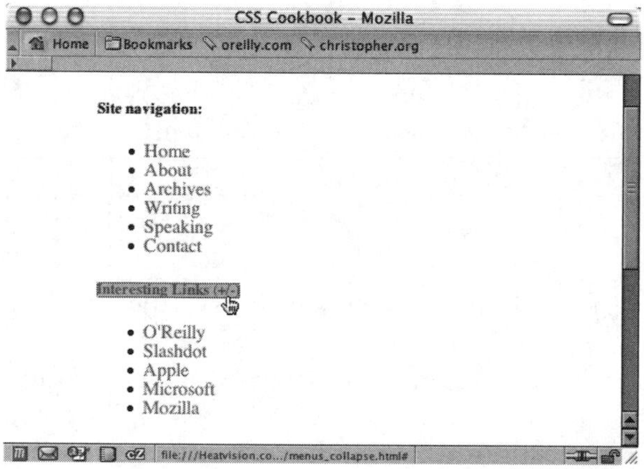

Figure 6-22. The links displayed when the link on the heading is clicked

Solution

First, set up the HTML links to be collapsible with an id attribute in the ul element:

```
<h5>Interesting Links (+/-)</h5>
<ul id="menulink">
 <li><a href="http://www.ora.com/">O'Reilly</a></li>
 <li><a href="http://www.slashdot.org/">Slashdot</a></li>
 <li><a href="http://www.apple.com/">Apple</a></li>
 <li><a href="http://www.microsoft.com/">Microsoft</a></li>
 <li><a href="http://www.mozilla.org/">Mozilla</a></li>
</ul>
```

Then create a CSS rule to prevent the second set of links from displaying when the page is first loaded:

```
#menulink {
 display: none;
}
```

Now add the following JavaScript function that toggles the list of links by swapping the value of display from block to none, or vice versa:

```
function kadabra(zap) {
 if (document.getElementById) {
  var abra = document.getElementById(zap).style;
  if (abra.display == "block") {
   abra.display = "none";
  } else {
   abra.display = "block";
  }
  return false;
 } else {
  return true;
 }
}
```

Insert an anchor element with a JavaScript onclick event around the heading. When a user clicks the link, the click triggers the JavaScript function:

```
<h5><a href="#" onclick="return kadabra('menulink');">
Interesting Links (+/-)</a></h5>
```

Discussion

The JavaScript in this function uses getElementbyId to toggle the display of the list of menu links. This technique can be scaled to show multiple menus or portions of a web document without adding additional lines of JavaScript:

```
<p>Are you sure you want to know the truth? If so,
follow <a href="#" onclick="return kadabra('spoiler'); ">this
link.</a></p>
<p id="spoiler">Darth Vadar was Luke's father!</p>
```

Note that this technique works in Netscape Navigator 6+, Opera 7.5+, Internet Explorer for Windows 5+, and Safari.

See Also

http://www.mozilla.org/docs/dom/domref/dom_doc_ref48.html for more information on getElementbyId.

6.13   Creating Contextual Menus

Problem

You have a navigation menu, created with Recipe 6.7 and you want to highlight the current page's location on the menu, as in Figure 6-23.

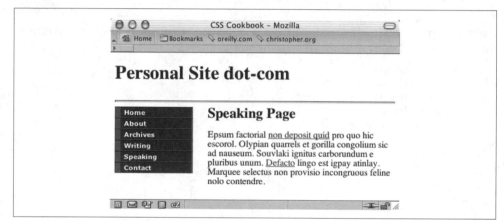

Figure 6-23. The navigation set of links

Solution

Place an id attribute in the body element of the web document:

```
<body id="pagespk">
```

Also, place id attributes in the anchor elements for each link in the menu:

```
<div id="navsite">
  <h5>Site navigation:</h5>
  <ul>
   <li><a href="/" id="linkhom">Home</a></li>
   <li><a href="/about/" id="linkabt">About</a></li>
   <li><a href="/archives/" id="linkarh">Archives</a></li>
   <li><a href="/writing/" id="linkwri">Writing</a></li>
   <li><a href="/speaking/" id="linkspk">Speaking</a></li>
   <li><a href="/contact/" id="linkcnt">Contact</a></li>
  </ul>
</div>
```

With CSS, place two id selectors into one descendant selector to finish the menu (see Figure 6-24):

```css
#pagespk a#linkspk {
 border-left: 10px solid #f33;
 border-right: 1px solid #f66;
 border-bottom: 1px solid #f33;
 background-color: #fcc;
 color: #333;
}
```

Figure 6-24. The current link is different from the rest of the links

Discussion

If you have a small site, you can show a link in a set of navigation links representing the current page by stripping out the anchor link for that page:

```html
<div id="navsite">
 <h5>Site navigation:</h5>
 <ul>
  <li><a href="/"Home</a></li>
  <li><a href="/about/">About</a></li>
  <li><a href="/archives/">Archives</a></li>
  <li><a href="/writing/" >Writing</a></li>
  <li>Speaking</li>
  <li><a href="/contact/" >Contact</a></li>
 </ul>
</div>
```

For larger sites that may contain secondary menus, stripping out the link tags on each page increases production and maintenance time. By marking up the links appropriately, the links can be called from a server-side include, and then you can edit the CSS rules that control the style of the navigation links as needed.

To expand the one CSS to include all the links in the navigation menu, group the descendant selectors by using a comma and at least one space:

```
#pagehom a#linkhom:link,
#pageabt a#linkabt:link,
#pagearh a#linkarh:link,
#pagewri a#linkwri:link,
#pagespk a#linkspk:link,
#pagecnt a#linkcnt:link  {
 border-left: 10px solid #f33;
 border-right: 1px solid #f66;
 border-bottom: 1px solid #f33;
 background-color: #fcc;
 color: #333;
 }
```

In each web document, make sure to put the appropriate id attribute in the body element. For example, for the home or main page of the site, the body element is <body id="pagehom">.

See Also

The CSS 2.1 specification on descendant selectors at *http://www.w3.org/TR/CSS21/ selector.html#descendant-selectors*.

6.14   Making Tool Tips with the Title Attribute

Problem

You want tool tips to appear on a hovered a link.

Solution

Use the title attribute within the link tag to create a tool tip like the one in Figure 6-25:

```
<a href="http://www.google.com/" title="Search the Web">...</a>
```

Discussion

The tool tip can be applied to almost any element within a web page to add enhanced accessibility. Try using the tool tip technique on table cells and form input elements as well as links.

See Also

The HTML 4.1 specification for the title attribute at *http://www.w3.org/TR/html4/ struct/global.html#h-7.4.3*.

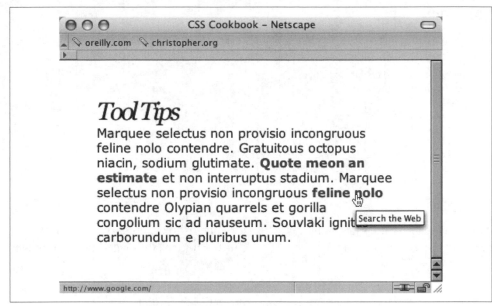

Figure 6-25. The value of the title attribute is displayed as a tool tip

6.15 Designing a Dynamic Visual Menu

Problem

You want to build a curved tab navigation menu that works even when text is resized; Figure 6-26 shows the default.

Figure 6-26. The dynamic folder tab navigation

Solution

First write the markup for the navigation menu:

```
<div id="header">
 <h2>Personal Site dot-com</h2>
 <h5>Site navigation:</h5>
 <ul>
  <li><a href="/">Home</a></li>
  <li><a href="/about/">About</a></li>
  <li><a href="/archives/">Archives</a></li>
  <li><a href="/writing/">Writing</a></li>
  <li id="current"><a href="/speaking/">Speaking</a></li>
  <li><a href="/contact/">Contact</a></li>
 </ul>
</div>
```

Then create two folder tab images: one tab for anchor links and another tab to represent the current page viewed by the user. Split the folder tab image into two images (see Figure 6-27).

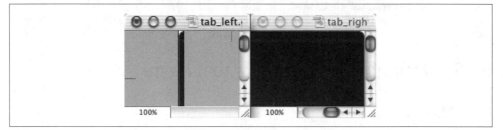

Figure 6-27. The folder tab image split in two; note the curves in the upper corners of the images

Then place the right side of the folder tab in the background of the list item:

```
#header li {
 float: left;
 background-image: url(tab_right.gif);
 background-repeat: no-repeat;
 background-position: right top;
 margin:0;
 padding: 0;
}
```

Place the left side of the folder tab in the background of the anchor element:

```
#header a {
 display: block;
 background-image: url(tab_left.gif);
 background-repeat: no-repeat;
 background-position: left top;
 padding: 5px 15px;
 color: #ccc;
 text-decoration: none;
 font-family: Georgia, Times, "Times New Roman", serif;
}
```

Assign a custom folder tab to represent the current web document being viewed:

```
#header #current {
 background-image:url(tab_right_current.gif);
}
#header #current a {
 background-image:url(tab_left_current.gif);
 color: black;
}
```

Place the image with a line measuring one-pixel high at the bottom of the grouping.

Discussion

Keeping the text in the navigation links aids in three areas of web development:

- Accessibility
- Design
- Maintenance

For example, users with poor eyesight can adjust the size of the text and that tabs without breaking the design (see Figure 6-28).

Figure 6-28. The text resized

Because users can resize the text to very large settings, the background images that comprise the folder tabs need to be large as well; otherwise, the folder tabs will break (check out Figure 6-29). In this solution, the folder tab images have a width of 450 pixels.

Figure 6-29. Note the breaking of the tab in the Archives link

Web developers prefer this method because it lets them easily maintain the list of links. To change a navigation label or correct a typo, developers can simply edit the HTML text without having to return to a digital imaging program to create folder tab images.

Another benefit of this method is that the folder tabs can be designed in a more aesthetically pleasing way. Recipe 6.8 demonstrates how to create a navigation setup with folder tabs using the border property. This look creates a boxy or squared edge to the folder tabs. With this current recipe, however, web developers can curve the tabs and introduce color blending for improved aesthetics.

See Also

Recipe 2.16 that uses a similar rubber-band technique to create pull quotes with images; "Sliding Doors of CSS, Part II" at *http://www.alistapart.com/articles/slidingdoors2/*, which expands on this folder tab navigation concept.

6.16   Apply Styles Dynamically to a Web Page

Problem

You want to change the style of elements within a web page when a user clicks on a link.

Solution

First, set up the markup with normal anchored links within the document. For this solution, the anchored links (technically referred to as *fragment identifiers*) are placed within an image map:

```
<img src="target_header.jpg" alt="Header" border="0" usemap="#Map" />
<map name="Map" id="Map">
 <area shape="circle" coords="115,136,72" href="#mark" />
 <area shape="circle" coords="244,145,55" href="#jessica" />
 <area shape="circle" coords="340,88,58" href="#trueman" />
 <area shape="circle" coords="480,287,79" href="#katrina" />
</map>
<div class="bios">
 <dl id="katrina">
  <dt>Katrina</dt>
  <dd>...</dd>
 </dl>
 <dl id="jessica">
  <dt>Jessica</dt>
  <dd>...</dd>
 </dl>
 <dl id="trueman">
  <dt>Trueman</dt>
  <dd>...</dd>

 <dl id="mark">
  <dt>Mark</dt>
  <dd>...</dd>

</div>
```

Then set up CSS rules for the default styles for the web page (see Figure 6-30):

```
.bios dt {
 font-weight: bold;
}
.bios dd {
 margin: 0;
 padding: 0;
}
```

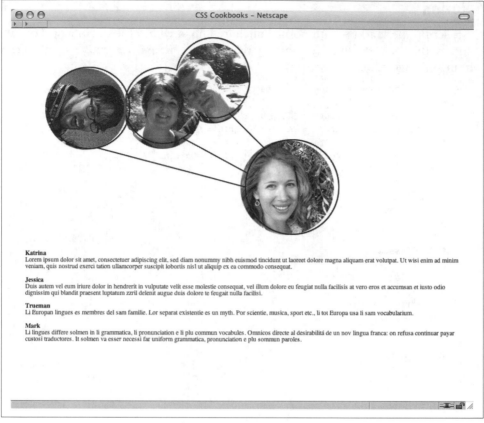

Figure 6-30. The default rendering of the web page

Then use the target pseudo-class to define the look of the elements when the user clicks on the anchored link (see Figure 6-31):

```
.bios dl:target {
 background-color: #999999;
 border: 1px solid black;
 padding: 1em;
 font-weight: bold;
 line-height: 1.5;
}
.bios dl:target dt {
 font-style: italic;
 color: white;
 font-size: 1.5em;
 background-color: #cccccc;
 margin-right: 20px;
}
.bios dl:target dd {
```

```
    margin-right: 20px;
    background-color: #cccccc;
    padding: 0 1em 1em 1em;
}
```

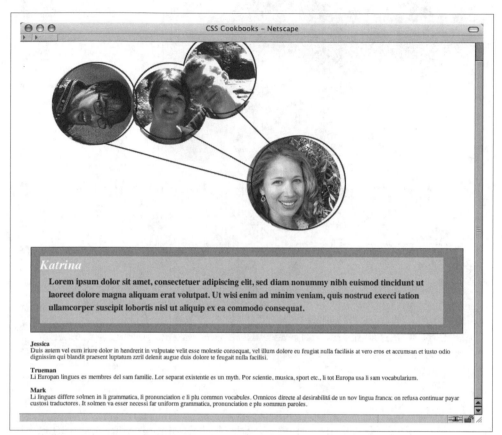

Figure 6-31. The Katrina portion of the page changed style

To return the targeted element(s) back to their default style when the user clicks on another anchored link, use the negation pseudo-class (see Figure 6-32):

```
.bios dl:not(:target) {
    border: none;
    padding: 0;
    font-size: .8em;
}
```

Discussion

The :target and :not pseudo-classes are a part of the CSS 3 specification and thus aren't well-known to most web designers. However, the selectors can perform a great deal of heavy lifting.

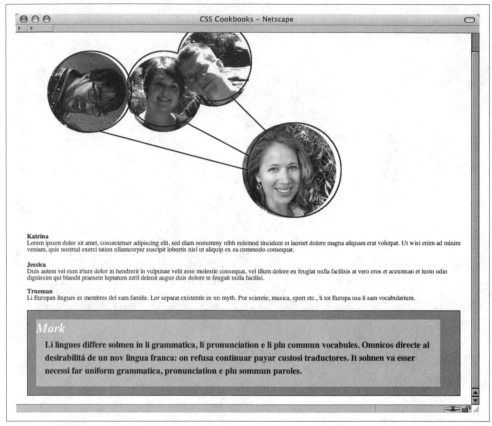

Figure 6-32. The Katrina portion reverted back to its default value when another link was activated

Pure CSS collapsible menus

By working with these selectors, the JavaScript-based solution in Recipe 6.12 can be replaced with a few extra CSS rules. First, update the markup to add the anchor link:

```
<h5>
 <a href="#menulink">Interesting Links</a>
</h5>
<ul id="menulink">
 <li><a href="http://www.ora.com/">O'Reilly</a></li>
 <li><a href="http://www.slashdot.org/">Slashdot</a></li>
 <li><a href="http://www.apple.com/">Apple</a></li>
 <li><a href="http://www.microsoft.com/">Microsoft</a></li>
 <li><a href="http://www.mozilla.org/">Mozilla</a></li>
</ul>
```

Then set up the following CSS rules:

```css
/* default rendering */
ul#menulink {
 display: none;
}

/* when 'targeted' */
ul:target {
 display: block;
}

/* revert back to default rendering */
ul:not(:target) {
 display: none;
}
```

Currently collapsible menus and :target pseudo-classes are supported in Firefox, Mozilla, Safari, and Internet Explorer 7 for Windows.

See Also

The CSS 3 specification for the :target pseudoclass at *http://www.w3.org/TR/ css3-selectors/#target-pseudo*.

CHAPTER 7

Forms

7.0 Introduction

Without HTML forms we wouldn't be able to log in to web-based email accounts, order books with one click, or trade stocks online. Although forms make the Web go around, they are ugly due the generic way in which browsers display them.

The default rendering of online forms usually includes beveled input and `textarea` fields, as well as boring-looking buttons. Such a look and feel may be acceptable if you are making a form for use on a small intranet or on a small web site, but it is unacceptable if you want to project a professional image.

Fortunately, with a few CSS rules, you can create forms that stand out from the pack. This chapter helps you get straight into the techniques to create a higher quality form.

You will learn the settings for HTML user input elements such as buttons, text areas, and fields. Another technique covered is how to set up a submit-once-only button to keep site visitors from mistakenly sending several processes to the server. At the end of the chapter are two sample designs: a simple login form without tables and a long registration form with tables.

 Note that Appendix D serves as an excellent resource that complements this chapter. In the appendix is a visual compendium detailing the effect of a majority of the visual CSS properties on form elements in 10 of today's modern browsers.

7.1 Modifying the Spacing Around a Form

Problem

You want to modify the space around a form.

Solution

Set the margin to zero while adjusting the padding values of the `form` element (see Figure 7-1):

```
form {
 margin: 0;
 padding: 1em 0;
 border: 1px dotted red; /* set  in order to see padding effect */
}
```

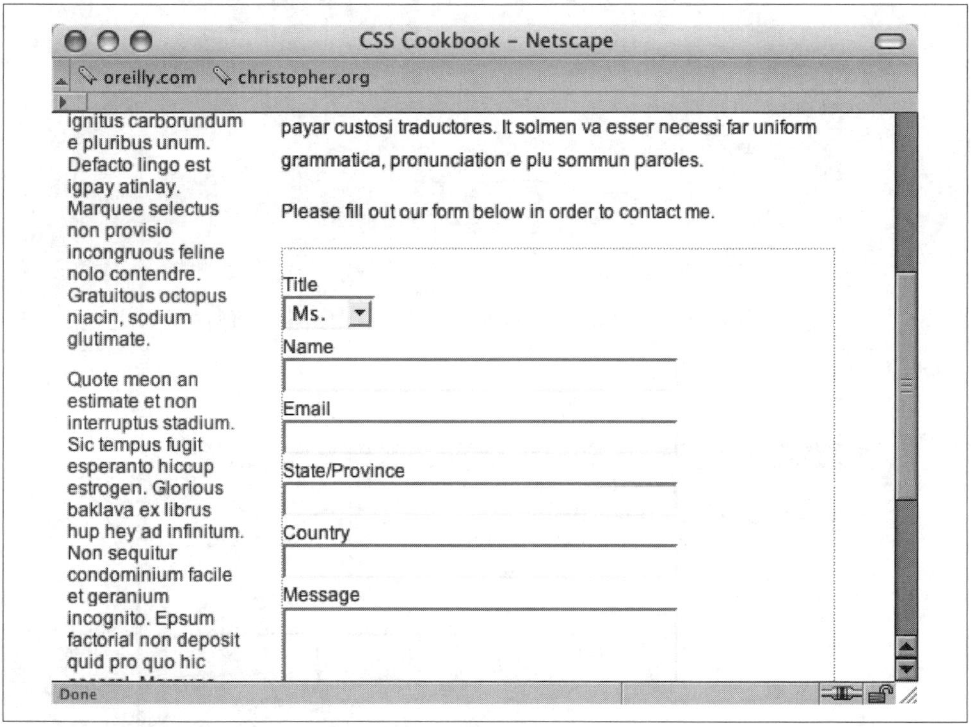

Figure 7-1. Padding is applied under the form's border

Discussion

When positioning forms into a web page design, developers find that they will need to modify the space between the form and other page elements in the design. Typically, the most common modification is to adjust the padding at the top and bottom of the form.

See Also

Recipe 7.2 for styling input elements.

7.2   Setting Styles for Input Elements

Problem

You want to change the appearance of input elements' background colors. Such effects can take you from Figure 7-2 to Figure 7-3.

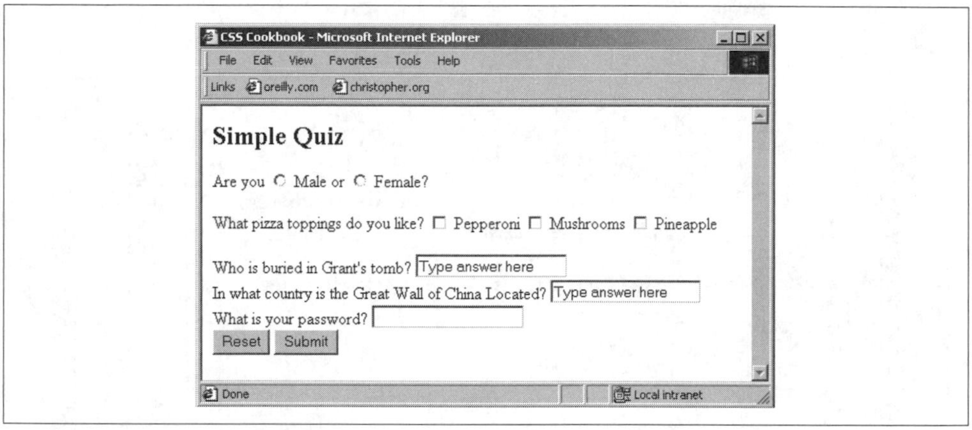

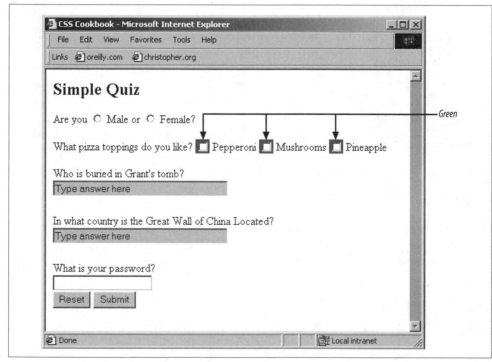

Figure 7-2. The form without styles

Figure 7-3. Styles applied to the input fields

Solution

Use a class selector to design the input elements of the form:

```html
<h2>Simple Quiz</h2>
 <form action="simplequiz.php" method="post">
 <p>
  Are you
    <input type="radio" value="male" name="sex"
 class="radioinput">
   Male or
    <input type="radio" value="female" name="sex"
 class="radioinput">
   Female?
 </p>
<p>
 What pizza toppings do you like? <input type="checkbox" name=""
 value="l" class="checkbxinput"> Pepperoni <input type="checkbox"
 name="" value="mushrooms" class="checkbxinput"> Mushrooms <input
 type="checkbox" name="" value="pineapple" class="checkbxinput">
 Pineapple
 </p>
 <label for="question1">Who is buried in Grant's tomb?</label>
 <input type="text" name="question1" id="question1"
 class="textinput"
 value="Type answer here" /><br />
 <label for="question2">In what country is the Great Wall of
 China Located?</label>
 <input type="text" name="question2" id="question2"
 class="textinput"
 value="Type answer here" /><br />
 <label for="password">What is your password?</label>
 <input type="password" name="password" id="password"
 class="pwordinput"
 value="" /><br />
 <input name="reset" type="reset" id="reset" value="Reset" />
 <input type="submit" name="Submit" value="Submit"
 class="buttonSubmit" />
 </form>
```

Then apply CSS rules to change the presentation of the input elements:

```css
.textinput {
 margin-bottom: 1.5em;
 width: 50%;
 color: #666;
 background-color: #ccc;
}
.pwordinput {
 color: white;
 background-color: white;
}
.radioinput {
 color: green;
 background-color: #ccc;
}
```

```
.checkbxinput {
 color: green;
 background-color: green;
}
```

Discussion

Opera is currently the only browser that allows radio buttons and checkboxes to be colored. Mozilla doesn't color them at all, while Internet Explorer for Windows ignores foreground color and colors the area around the widgets with the background color (see Figure 7-4).

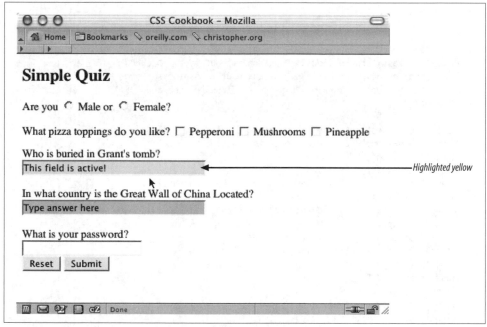

Figure 7-4. Using :focus to light up an input field

Rather than using `class` selectors as illustrated in the solution, another way to stylize different kinds of input fields is through attribute selectors.

With `attribute` selectors, you remove `class` attributes from the HTML and use only the following CSS rules:

```
input[type="text"] {
 margin-bottom: 1.5em;
 width: 50%;
 color: #666;
 background-color: #ccc;
}
input[type="password"] {
 color: white;
 background-color: white;
}
```

Although this works in most browsers, it doesn't work in Internet Explorer for Windows because this browser doesn't support attribute selectors at all. Attribute selectors currently work in Netscape Navigator 6+, Firefox, Safari, and Opera 5+. If you want to ensure cross-browser support, you need to use `class` selectors to determine styles for different form controls.

See Also

Appendix D; The CSS 2.1 specification for dynamic pseudo-classes at *http://www.w3.org/TR/CSS21/selector.html#x33*; the CSS 2.1 specification for attribute selectors at *http://www.w3.org/TR/CSS21/selector.html#attribute-selectors*.

7.3 Applying Different Styles to Different Input Elements in the Same Form

Problem

You want to style multiple `input` elements differently in the same form.

Solution

Use two or more different `class` selectors to apply different styles.

First, apply `class` attributes with different values to the `input` elements:

```
<label for="fmname">Name</label>
<input type="text" name="fmname" class="fmname" />
<label for="fmemail">Email</label>
<input type="text" name="fmemail" class="fmemail" />
```

Then set up the styles for each `class` attribute in the `input` elements:

```
.fmname {
 text-align: left;
}
.fmemail {
 text-align: center;
}
```

Discussion

The technique of using `class` selectors to apply multiple styles to common elements within one page works in most browsers.

Another method of assigning different styles to common elements is available through browsers that understand the CSS 3 specification for attribute selectors as discussed in Recipe 6.2.

See Also

Recipe 6.7 for styling different form buttons in the same form.

7.4 Setting Styles for textarea Elements

Problem

You want to set styles for textarea elements in a web form to change the text's color, size, weight, and other properties of the element, as shown in Figure 7-5.

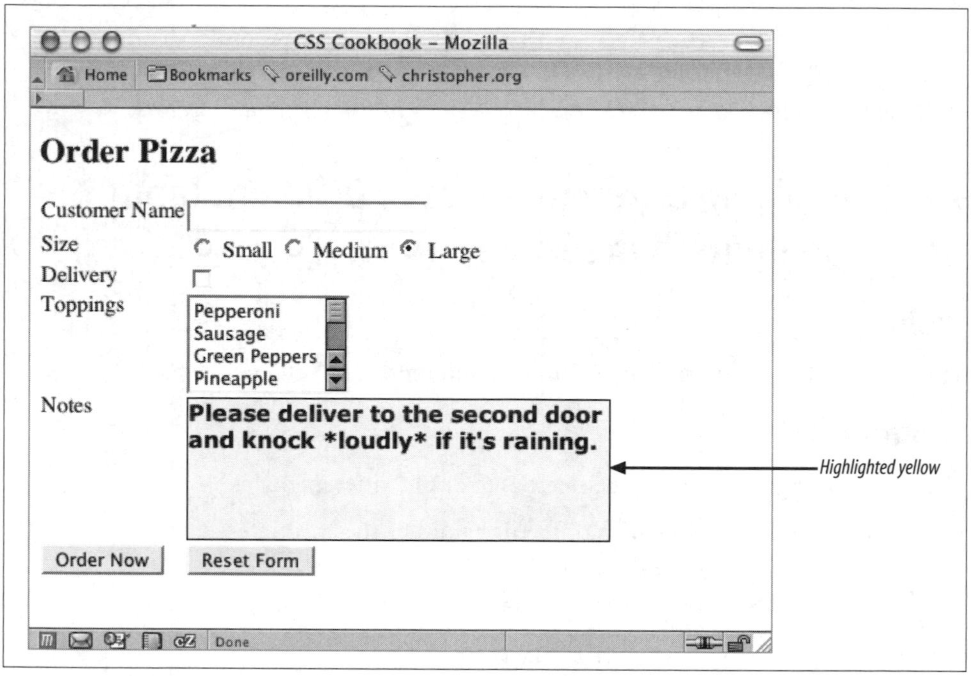

Figure 7-5. A textarea element with styles applied

Solution

Use a type selector to associate styles with textarea elements:

```
textarea {
 width: 300px;
 height: 100px;
 background-color: yellow;
 font-size: 1em;
 font-weight: bold;
 font-family: Verdana, Arial, Helvetica, sans-serif;
 border: 1px solid black;
}
```

Discussion

Associating styles to `textarea` elements is fairly straightforward through the use of a type selector:

```
textarea {
  background-color: blue;
}
```

By adding the `:focus` pseudo-class, you can change the style of the active `textarea` field:

```
textarea:focus {
  background-color: green;
}
```

So, as a user fills out a form, the `textarea` field he is currently filling out will change color.

The browsers that currently support `:focus` are Safari, Netscape Navigator 6+, Firefox, and Opera 7+.

See Also

The CSS 2.1 specification for dynamic pseudo-classes at *http://www.w3.org/TR/CSS21/selector.html#x33*; the CSS 2.1 specification for attribute selectors at *http://www.w3.org/TR/CSS21/selector.html#attribute-selectors*.

7.5   Setting Styles for Select and Option Elements

Problem

You want to alter the look of list menus in a form by changing the color and font, as in Figure 7-6.

Solution

Use a type selector to associate styles with `select` elements:

```
select {
  color: white;
  background-color: blue;
  font-size: 0.9em;
}
option {
  padding: 4px;
}
```

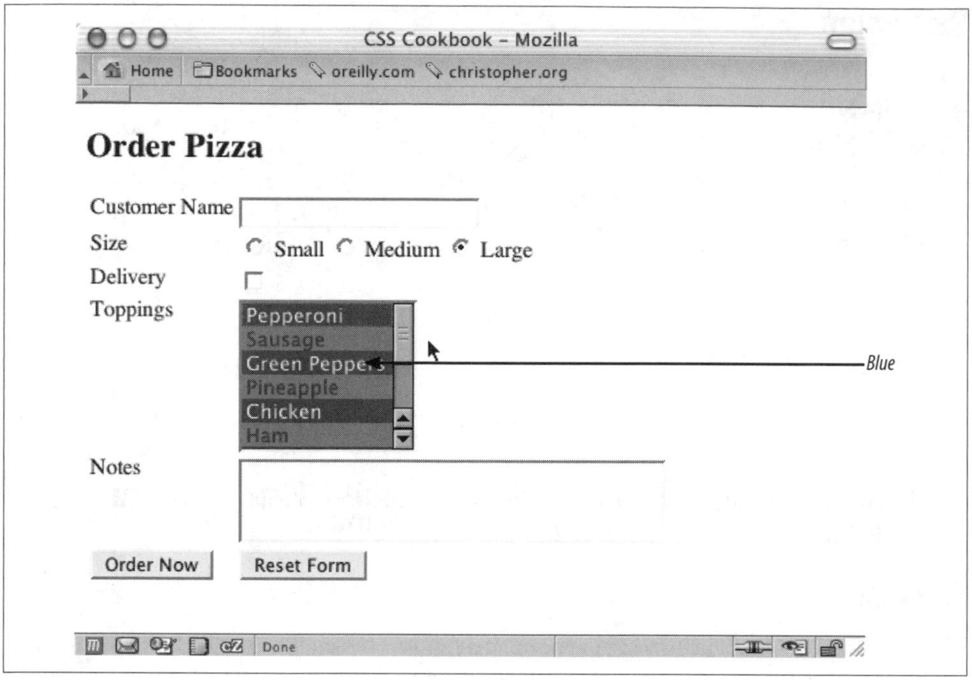

Figure 7-6. *The select and option elements with styles applied*

Discussion

Unlike input `form` elements, there is only one type of `select` element, so associating styles to that element is straightforward and can be done through a type selector. Styling the `option` element is just as easy.

To stylize alternating options in a `select` list, first include the `class` attribute in the option element:

```
<select name="Topping_ID" size="6" multiple>
 <option value="1">Pepperoni</option>
 <option value="2" class="even">Sausage</option>
 <option value="3">Green Peppers</option>
 <option value="4" class="even">Pineapple</option>
 <option value="5">Chicken</option>
 <option value="6" class="even">Ham</option>
 <option value="7">Olives</option>
 <option value="8" class="even">Onions</option>
 <option value="9">Red Peppers</option>
</select>
```

Then set up the CSS rules for the two sets of `option` elements, making sure that the option elements with an even value (as noted by the class selector even) look different from the others. For example, `option` elements with an even selector have a background color of red, while the "regular" option elements have a background color of blue (see Figure 7-7):

```
select {
 font-size: 0.9em;
}
option {
 color: white;
 background-color: blue;
}
option.even {
color: blue;
 background-color: red;
}
```

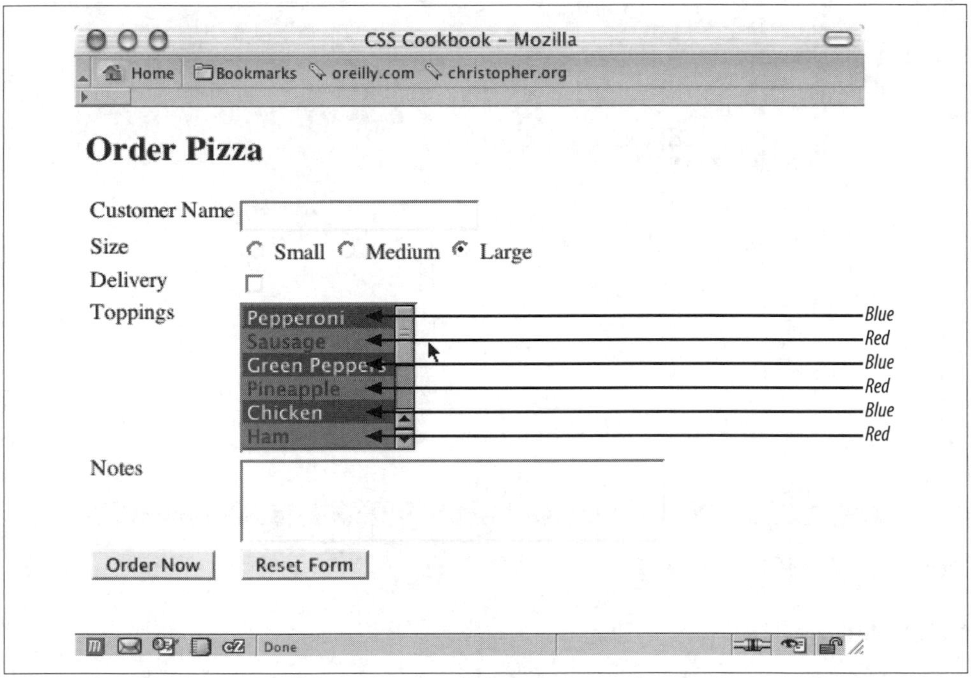

Figure 7-7. Alternating styles applied to select and option elements

See Also

Recipe 7.2 for information on how to change the color and size of input element text.

7.6   Creating a Macintosh-Styled Search Field

Problem

You want to style a search field for the Safari browser.

Solution

Use proprietary HTML extensions that are only available to the Safari browser.

Place one input element in between form element. Then set the value for the type attribute to search, as shown in Figure 7-8:

```
<form method="get" action="/search.php">
<div>
<label for="q">Search</label>
<input type="search" placeholder="keywords"
autosave="com.domain.search" results="7" name="q" />
</div>
</form>
```

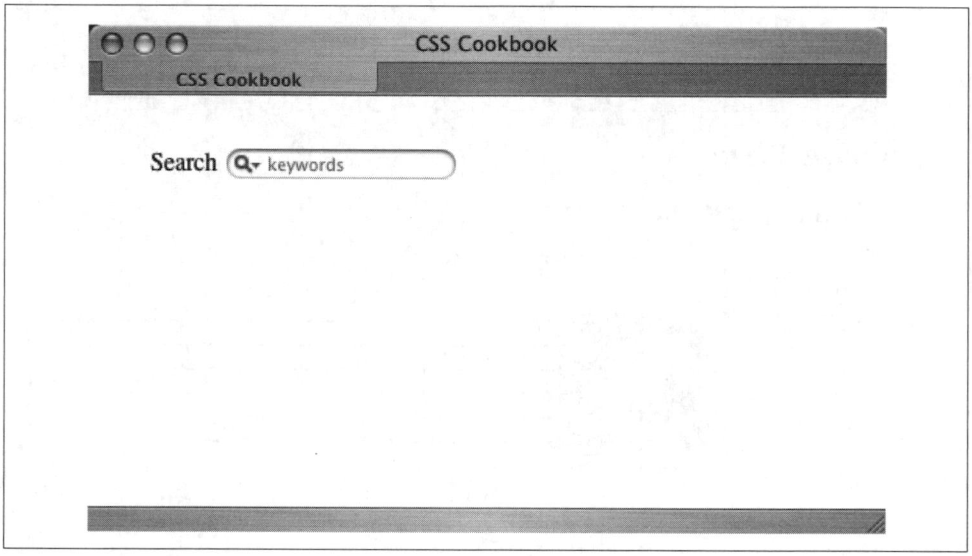

Figure 7-8. The Safari search field

Discussion

The Safari browser developers from Apple created an extension to HTML forms to allow for a more robust user interface. A browser other than Safari will render the input field like a regular text input form field that is still usable as a typical search bar.

Search field attributes

The placeholder attribute allows web developers to set the text residing in the search field. This text appears in the same way that text set for the value attribute in a text input field appears, as you see in Figure 7-9:

```
<label for="fmwebsite">Web Site:</label>
<input type="text" name="fmwebsite" value="http://" />
```

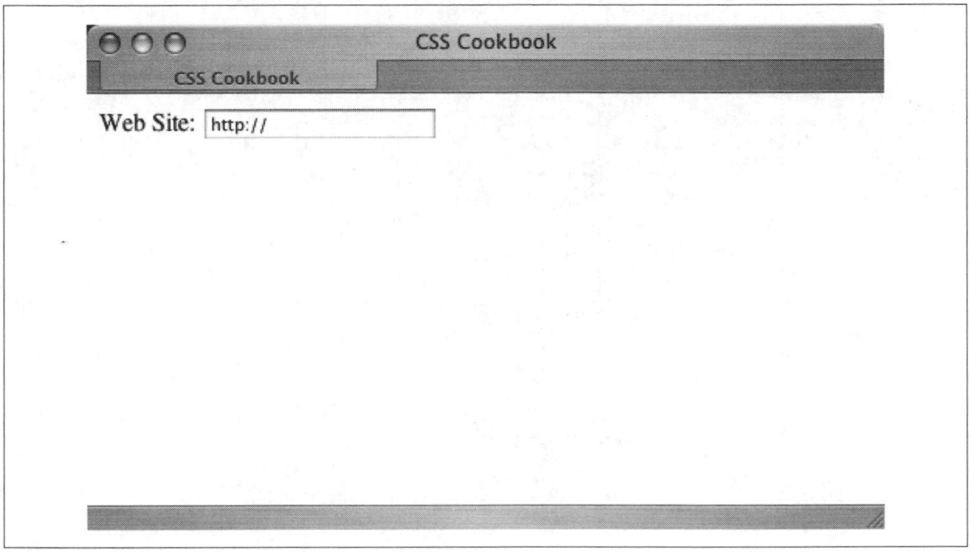

Figure 7-9. The input field in the Safari browser

The difference between the `placeholder` attribute and the standard `value` attribute is that users have to manually delete the text placed in form field through the `value` attribute.

> It is not recommended to place both a `value` and `placeholder` attribute in the same search field. This technique results in the text for the value overriding the placeholder value for Safari users. Safari users will have to manually delete the text supplied through the `value` attribute and thus not get the intended functionality allowed in the `placeholder` attribute.

The `autosave` attribute is a marker that allows past searches to be stored on the user's local machine. The user will be able to click on the magnifying glass icon and see past searches.

The `results` attribute accepts a numerical value. This numerical value represents the number of searches that will be stored on the user's local computer (see Figure 7-10).

The saved searches can appear to be placed from one site to another. For example, if one site uses the same value for `autosave` as another site, the same saved searches will appear on both site's search fields. This technique can be used on a set of different domains that are in a common network. The user has access to their search history and thus `autosave` provides a better user experience.

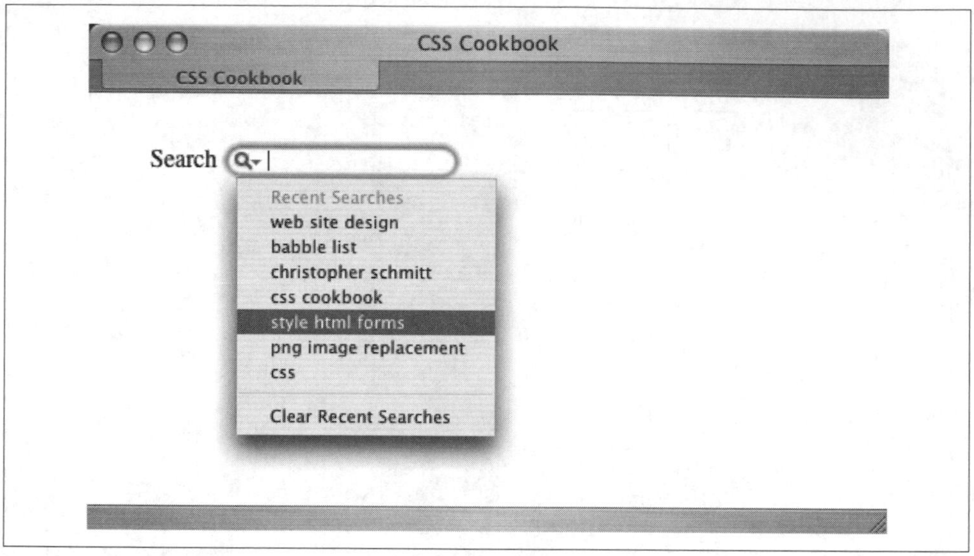

Figure 7-10. Saved searches appear below the search field

Best practices

The search field does not require an input button, so only use the search field in a form that has just one input field. Forms with only one input form element will accept the pressing of an enter or return key as form submission. The adding of input elements means that the browser may need the addition of a Submit button that must be activated in order to process the form.

See Also

The Surfin' Safari blog on the search field extension at *http://weblogs.mozillazine.org/hyatt/archives/2004_07.html#005890*.

7.7   Styling Form Buttons

Problem

You want to stylize the color, padding, borders, and rollover effects for Submit and Reset buttons on a form. Figure 7-11 shows a form without styles applied to the buttons, and Figure 7-12 shows the form with stylized buttons.

Solution

First use a class selector to design the buttons:

```
<form action="simplequiz.php" method="post">
<label for="question">Who is president of the U.S.?
```

```
</label>
<input type="text" name="question" id="textfield"
value="Type answer here" /><br />
<input name="reset" type="reset"  value="Reset"
class="buttonReset" />
<input type="submit" name="Submit" value="Submit"
class="buttonSubmit" />
</form>
```

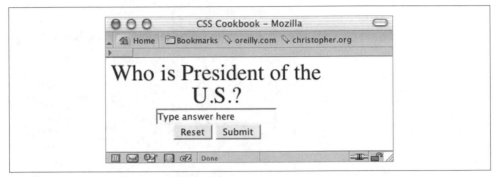

Figure 7-11. The form buttons without styles applied

Figure 7-12. The form buttons with styles applied

Then use CSS to stylize the buttons:

```
.buttonReset {
 color: #fcc;
 background-color: #900;
 font-size: 1.5em;
 border: 1px solid #660;
 padding: 4px;
}
.buttonSubmit {
 color: white;
 background-color: #660;
 font-size: 1.5em;
 border: 1px solid #660;
 padding: 4px;
}
```

Discussion

You also can stylize buttons by using the *rollover* state. To create rollovers for buttons, use a JavaScript function:

```
<script language="JavaScript" type="text/javascript">
function classChange(styleChange,item) {
 item.className = styleChange;
}
</script>
```

Next, add two additional CSS rules, one for the rollover state for the Reset button and another for the Submit button:

```
.buttonResetRoll {
 color: white;
 background-color: #c00;
 font-size: 1.5em;
 border: 1px solid #660;
 padding: 4px;
}
.buttonSubmitRoll {
 color: white;
 background-color: #cc0;
 font-size: 1.5em;
 border: 1px solid #660;
 padding: 4px;
}
```

After the function is in place and the extra CSS rules are set up, place the events in the button markup so that you can toggle between the off and on states of the form buttons (see Figure 7-13):

```
<form action="simplequiz.php" method="post">
<label for="question">Who is president of the U.S.?</label>
<input type="text" name="question" id="textfield"
value="Type answer here" /><br />
 <input name="reset" type="reset" id="reset" value="Reset"
class="buttonReset"
onMouseOver="classChange('buttonResetRoll',this)"
onMouseOut="classChange('buttonReset',this)" />
 <input type="submit" name="Submit" value="Submit"
class="buttonSubmit"
onMouseOver="classChange('buttonSubmitRoll',this)"
onMouseOut="classChange('buttonSubmit',this)" />
</form>
```

As noted earlier, until Internet Explorer for Windows supports attribute selectors, you'll need to use class selectors to set button styles that can be seen in all browsers. Using attribute selectors to write CSS rules for the form buttons doesn't require the extra markup in the HTML element that comes from using class selectors. For

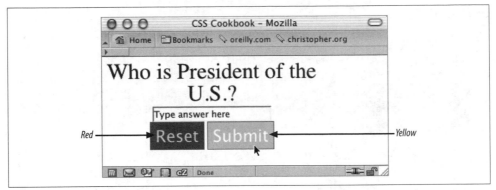

Figure 7-13. A rollover state created through CSS and JavaScript

example, the attribute selector syntax for the buttons using only CSS would look something like this:

```
input[type="reset"] {
 color: #fcc;
 background-color: #900;
 font-size: 1.5em;
 border: 1px solid #660;
 padding: 4px;
}
input[type="submit"] {
 color: white;
 background-color: #660;
 font-size: 1.5em;
 border: 1px solid #660;
 padding: 4px;
}
```

You also can use the width property to determine the horizontal size of the button; however, Internet Explorer 4.x for Windows doesn't recognize the CSS width property on the form property.

See Also

Recipe 6.9 for tips on mimicking an image button with CSS; the CSS 2.1 specification for attribute selectors at *http://www.w3.org/TR/CSS21/selector.html#attribute-selectors*.

7.8   Creating an Image Submit Button

Problem

You want to create a custom Submit button with an image file, such as the one in Figure 7-14.

Solution

Use the input element with the type attribute set to image:

```
<input type="image" name="submit" src="submit.gif" />
```

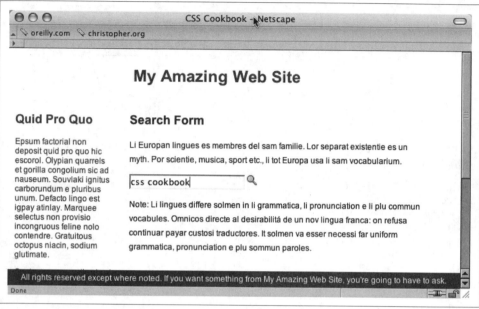

Figure 7-14. The magnifying glass icon acts a Submit button

Discussion

Although inserting an image as a Submit button utilizes HTML, once it's placed in a web page, the Submit button image can be modified through CSS properties like border and margin.

See Also

The HTML specification for the input element at *http://www.w3.org/TR/html4/interact/forms.html#h-17.4*.

7.9   Setting Up a Submit-Once-Only Button

Problem

You want to keep people from clicking the Submit button more than once.

Solution

First create a class for keeping the button from being displayed:

```
.buttonSubmitHide {
  display: none;
}
```

Then use the following JavaScript programmed to switch styles by `class` selectors:

```
<script language="JavaScript" type="text/javascript">
function classChange(styleChange,item) {
  item.className = styleChange;
}
</script>
```

Now trigger the function by using an onsubmit event to remove the Submit button from the web document:

```
<h2>Order Confirmation</h2>
<form action="login.php" method="post"
 onsubmit="classChange('buttonSubmitHide',submit);
return true;">
 <div align="center">
   <p>Are you sure you want to purchase 12 cans of soda over the
Web?</p>
   <label for="uname">Final Price:</label>
   <input type="text" name="uname" id="uname" value="$7.95" />
<br />
    (includes tax, s+h extra)<br />
   <input type="submit" name="submit" value="submit"
class="buttonSubmit" />
 </div>
</form>
```

Discussion

The JavaScript function in the solution triggers a change in which a style is applied to the element. You must use the form's onsubmit event to execute the function so that the form's action will still be executed. If the function were triggered with an onclick event on the Submit button, some browsers would execute only the class-changing function. Then, because the button is no longer visible, the user would not be able to trigger the form.

See Also

JavaScript & DHTML Cookbook by Danny Goodman (O'Reilly) for more recipes that combine JavaScript and CSS.

7.10   Creating a Submit Button That Looks Like HTML Text

Problem

You want to make a Submit button look like plain HTML text.

Solution

Use several CSS formatting properties to make a form's Submit button look like HTML text.

First, inset a `class` attribute and value:

```
<input type="submit" name="submit" value="send &raquo;" class="submit" />
```

Then apply CSS properties to strip away the Submit button's borders and background color (see Figure 7-15):

```
.submit {
 border: none;
 background-color: #fff;
 padding: 0;
 margin: 0;
 width: 5em;
}
```

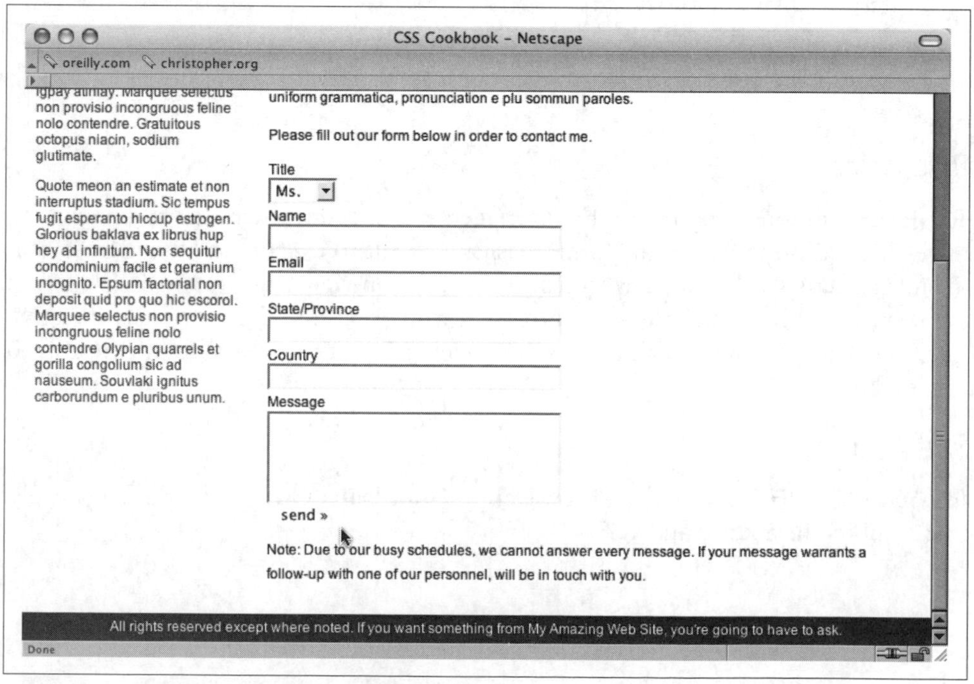

Figure 7-15. A Submit button that looks like HTML text

Then add the :hover pseudo-class to create the standard rollover effect you see in Figure 7-16:

```
.submit:hover {
 text-decoration: underline;
}
```

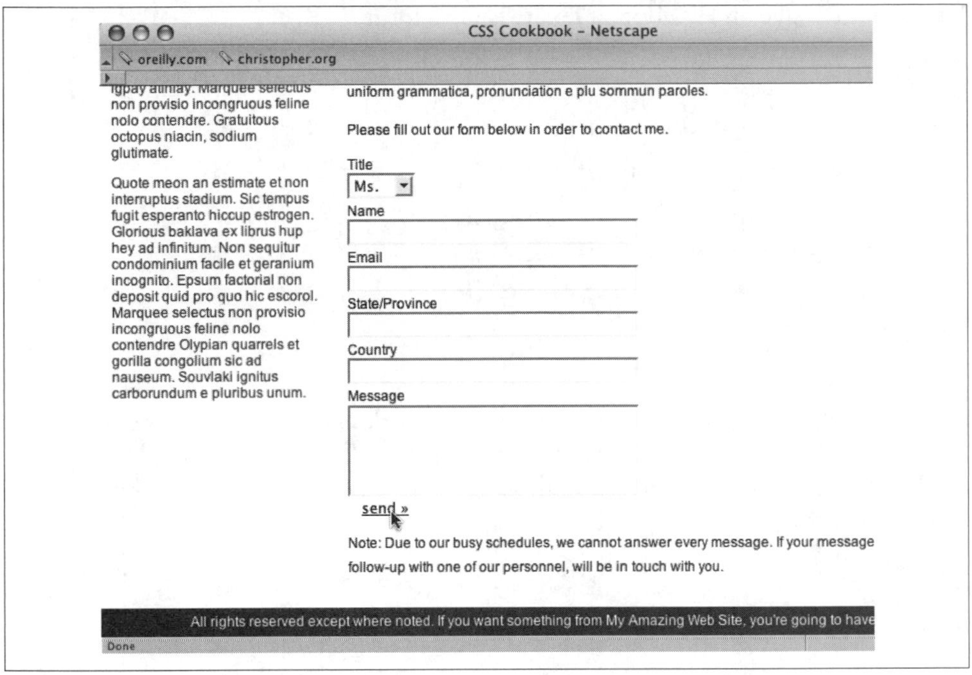

Figure 7-16. Text has an underline when cursor moves over Submit button

Discussion

An HTML text-looking Submit button is perfect for designers that feel that the generic-looking submit button may not fit in their designs but do not want to use an image for a button.

There also may be times when bringing in the design element of a Submit button would be counterproductive for the user experience. Stripping down a Submit button so that it appears as text may put users' fears to rest about submitting information across the Internet.

This recipe works in browsers that allow modifications to the Submit buttons. Modern browsers that do support this recipe include Mozilla, Firefox, Navigator 7+, and Opera.

See Also

Recipe 7.11 to make actual HTML text operate like a Submit button.

7.11 Making an HTML Text Link Operate Like a Submit Button

Problem

You want to make an HTML text link execute a form.

Solution

Use JavaScript to trigger the form:

```
<form name="msgform" method="get" action="results.php">
<label for="fmmsg">Message</label>
<textarea name="fmmsg" accesskey="m" id="fmmsg" rows="5" cols="14"></textarea>
<a href="javascript:document.msgform.submit( );">Submit</a>
</form>
```

Discussion

While Recipe 6.10 showed how to disguise a Submit button to look like HTML text, this recipe showcases how to make a text link work as a Submit button. The main negative to this approach is that the user needs to have JavaScript in order for it to work. Browsers without JavaScript or ones that have JavaScript turned off will not be able to use the form.

See Also

Recipe 7.10 for creating a Submit button that looks like an HTML text link.

7.12 Designing a Web Form Without Tables

Problem

You want to include form fields and labels on rows without using an HTML table, thereby ensuring a pure CSS-enabled layout without using any markup for presentation.

Solution

First use labels in conjunction with the form fields in the markup (see Figure 7-17):

```
<form action="login.php" method="post">
 <label for="uname">Username</label>
 <input type="text" name="uname" id="uname" value="" /><br />
 <label for="pname">Password</label>
 <input type="text" name="pname" id="pname" value="" /><br />
 <label for="recall">Remember you?</label>
 <input type="checkbox" name="recall" id="recall"
class="checkbox" /><br />
```

```
<input type="submit" name="Submit" value="Submit"
class="buttonSubmit" />
</form>
```

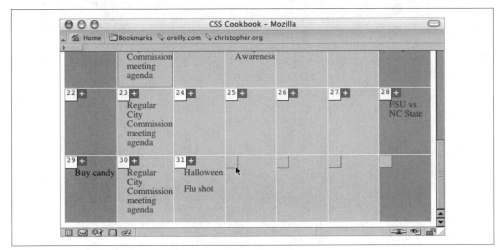

Figure 7-17. The form without styles applied

Then set the display and label properties for the label elements to block, float the label elements to the left, and justify the text on the right (see Figure 7-18):

```
input {
 display: block;
 width: 175px;
 float: left;
 margin-bottom: 10px;
}
label {
 display: block;
 text-align: right;
 float: left;
 width: 75px;
 padding-right: 20px;
}
.checkbox {
 width: 1em;
}
br {
 clear: left;
}
.buttonSubmit {
 width: 75px;
 margin-left: 95px;
}
```

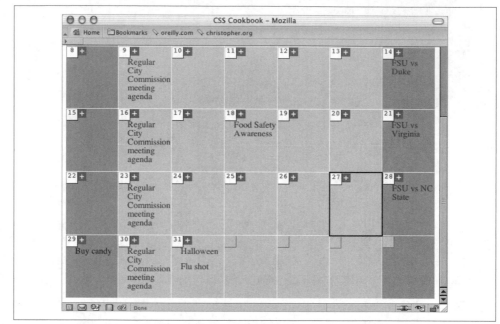

Figure 7-18. The design of the form laid out with styles

Discussion

The input and label elements are set to display: block, which displays them as block-level elements. This makes it possible to set the widths for the text in the label. Instead of resting on top of the input element, the labels are floated to the left. And because all labels have the same width, the look is uniform throughout the form.

The br tag creates a break between the label and form element sets, and clears the float from previous elements. This prevents the other elements (those that appear after the input field matched to the label) from floating as well.

See Also

The HTML 4.1 specification for the label element at *http://www.w3.org/TR/html401/ interact/forms.html#edef-LABEL*; the CSS 2.1 specification for the float property at *http://www.w3.org/TR/CSS21/visuren.html#propdef-float*; the CSS 2.1 specification for the clear property at *http://www.w3.org/TR/CSS21/visuren.html#propdef-clear*.

7.13   Designing a Two Column Form Without Tables

Problem

You want to transform a one-column form (see Figure 7-19) to two columns.

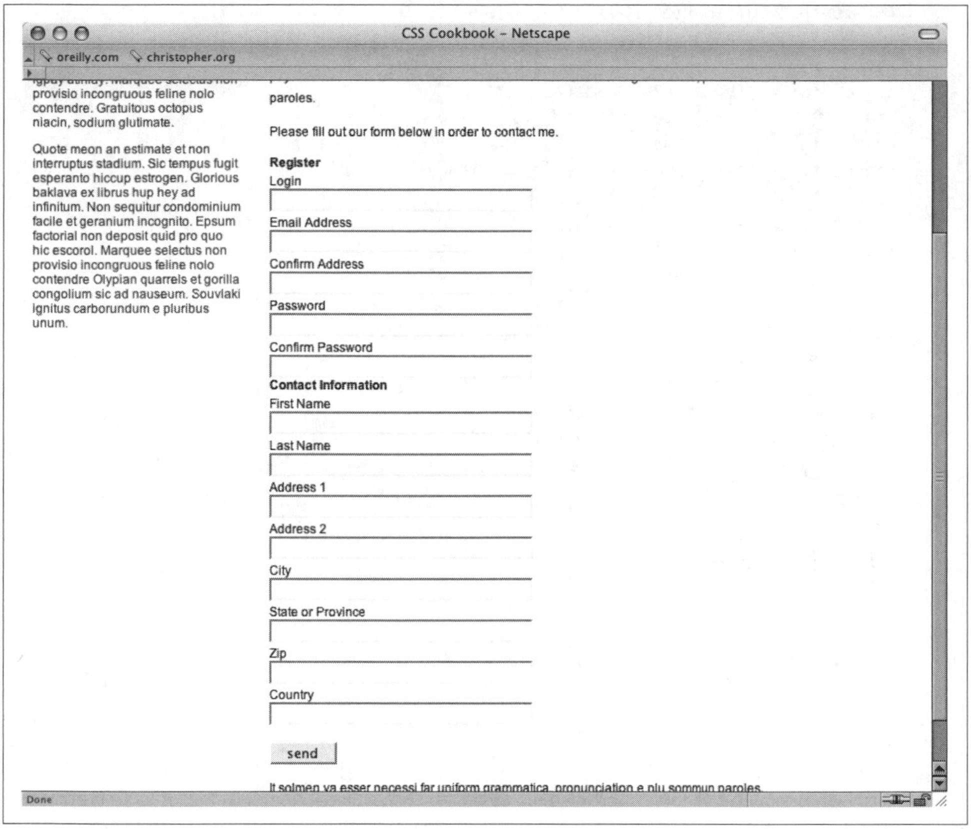

Figure 7-19. The form in one column

Solution

First, mark out the areas of the form into two different sections by using div elements:

```
<form id="regform" name="regform" method="post" action="/regform.php">
 <div id="register">
  <h4>Register</h4>
  <label for="fmlogin">Login</label>
  <input type="text" name="fmlogin" id="fmlogin" />
  <label for="fmemail">Email Address</label>
  <input type="text"  name="fmemail" id="fmemail" />
  <label for="fmemail2">Confirm Address</label>
  <input type="text"  name="fmemail2" id="fmemail2" />
  <label for="fmpswd">Password</label>
  <input type="password"  name="fmpswd" id="fmpswd" />
  <label for="fmpswd2">Confirm Password</label>
  <input type="password"  name="fmpswd2" id="fmpswd2" />
 </div>
 <div id="contactinfo">
```

```
<h4>Contact Information</h4>
<label for="fmfname">First Name</label>
<input type="text" name="fmfname" id="fmfname" />
<label for="fmlname">Last Name</label>
<input type="text" name="fmlname" id="fmlname" />
<label for="fmaddy1">Address 1</label>
<input type="text" name="fmaddy1" id="fmaddy1" />
<label for="fmaddy2">Address 2</label>
<input type="text" name="fmaddy2" id="fmaddy2" />
<label for="fmcity">City</label>
<input type="text" name="fmcity" id="fmcity" />
<label for="fmstate">State or Province</label>
<input type="text" name="fmstate" id="fmstate" />
<label for="fmzip">Zip</label>
<input type="text" name="fmzip" id="fmzip"  size="5" />
<label for="fmcountry">Country</label>
<input type="text" name="fmcountry" id="fmcountry" />
<input type="submit" name="submit" value="send" class="submit" />
</div>
</form>
```

Then set the display of the input and label elements to be block:

```
label {
 margin-top: .33em;
 display: block;
}
input {
 display: block;
 width: 250px;
}
```

Create the second form column by setting the first div element, register, to float left as you see in Figure 7-20:

```
#register {
 float: left;
}
```

Next apply enough padding on the left side of the second column in case the second column is shorter than the first column (see Figure 7-21):

```
#register {
 float: left;
}
#contactinfo {
 padding-left: 275px;
}
```

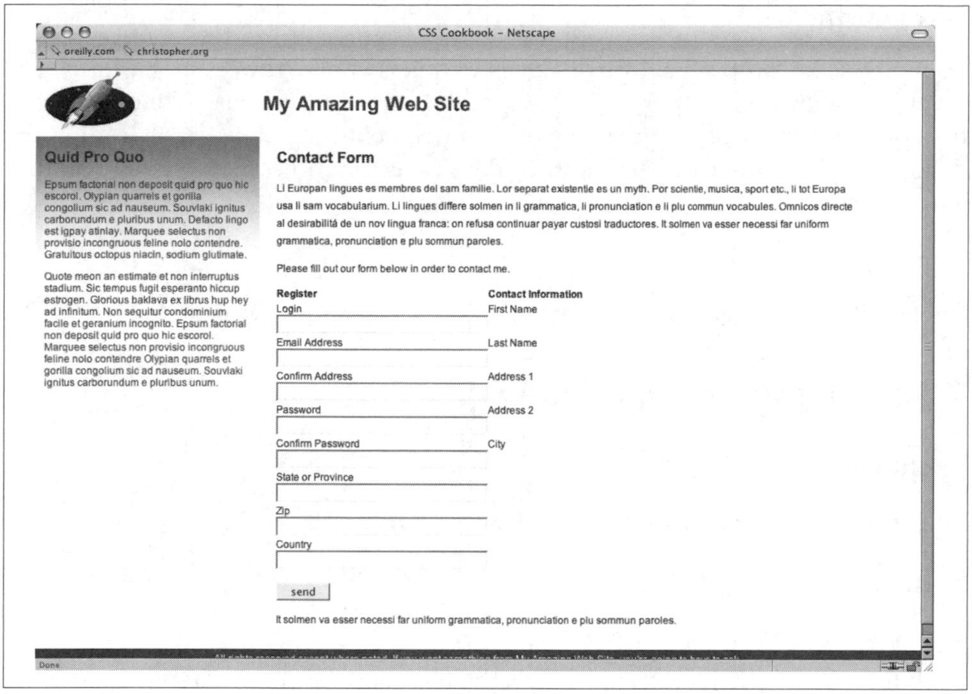

Figure 7-20. Form elements start to form two columns

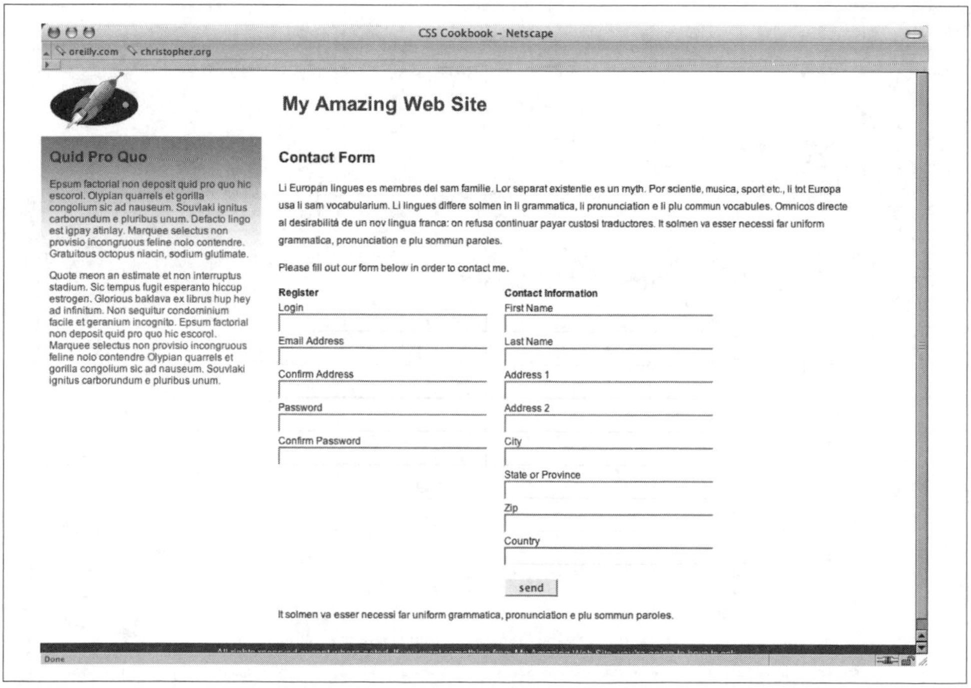

Figure 7-21. The form is laid out in two columns

Discussion

Using the float property allows designers to quickly build a two-column form. The main problem with this approach is in case where the right column is longer than the first. The wrapping of the form elements can be confusing to users. By setting the padding to accommodate the width of the first column, designers create seamless looking columns.

See Also

Chapter 9 for more techniques on laying out the elements of a web page.

7.14   Highlighting Form Fields

Problem

You want to highlight the form field that a visitor is currently using.

Solution

Use the :focus pseudo-class selector.

With a preexisting form, create a new CSS rule that changes the background color when an input element is being used (see Figure 7-22).

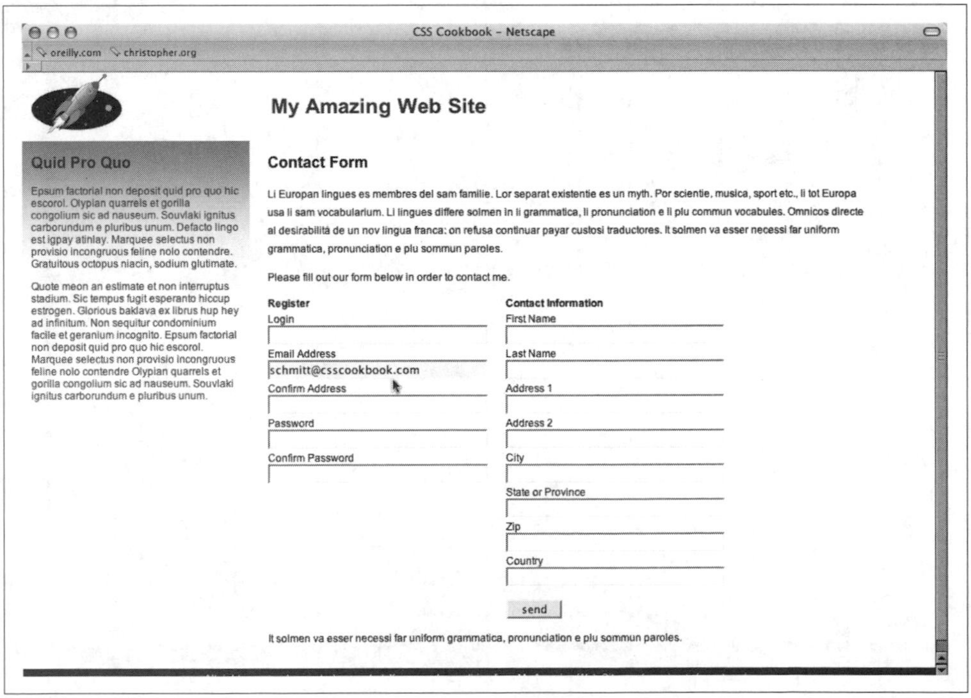

Figure 7-22. Background color of input field changes as text is entered

This rule makes changes the background color of the field:

```
input:focus {
 background-color: yellow;
}
```

Discussion

The browsers that support :focus are Netscape Navigator 6+, Firefox, Safari, and Opera 7. Browsers that don't support the declaration block will simply ignore it, making it degrade gracefully.

See Also

Recipe 7.4, concerning styling for textarea elements; Table D-9 in Appendix D.

7.15 Integrating Form Feedback with a Form

Problem

You want to show users which parts of a form are required.

Solution

First, place an icon and text warning next to form labels of fields that are required (see Figure 7-23).

Apply a class attribute with a value of required to the label and form elements that are required in order to successfully process a form.

```
<form id="msgform" name="msgform" method="post" action="/process.php">
 <fieldset>
  <legend>Contact Information</legend>
  <label for="fmtitle" accesskey="i">T<span class="akey">i</span>tle</label>
  <select name="fmtitle" id="fmtitle">
   <option value="ms">Ms.</option>
   <option value="mrs">Mrs.</option>
   <option value="miss">Miss</option>
   <option value="mr">Mr.</option>
  </select>
  <label for="fmname" accesskey="n"><span class="akey">N</span>ame</label>
  <input type="text" name="fmname" id="fmname" />
  <label for="fmemail" accesskey="e" class="required">
<span class="akey">E</span>mail <img src="alert.gif" /> Required</label>
  <input type="text"  name="fmemail" id="fmemail" class="required" />
 </fieldset>
 <fieldset>
  <legend>Your Message</legend>
  <label for="fmstate" accesskey="y">Subject</label>
  <input type="text" name="fmcountry" id="fmcountry" />
  <label for="fmmsg" class="required"><span class="akey">M</span>essage
```

```
<img src="alert.gif" /> Required</label>
  <textarea name="fmmsg" accesskey="m" id="fmmsg" rows="5" cols="14"
class="required"></textarea>
 </fieldset>
 <input type="submit" name="submit" value="send" class="submit" />
</form>
```

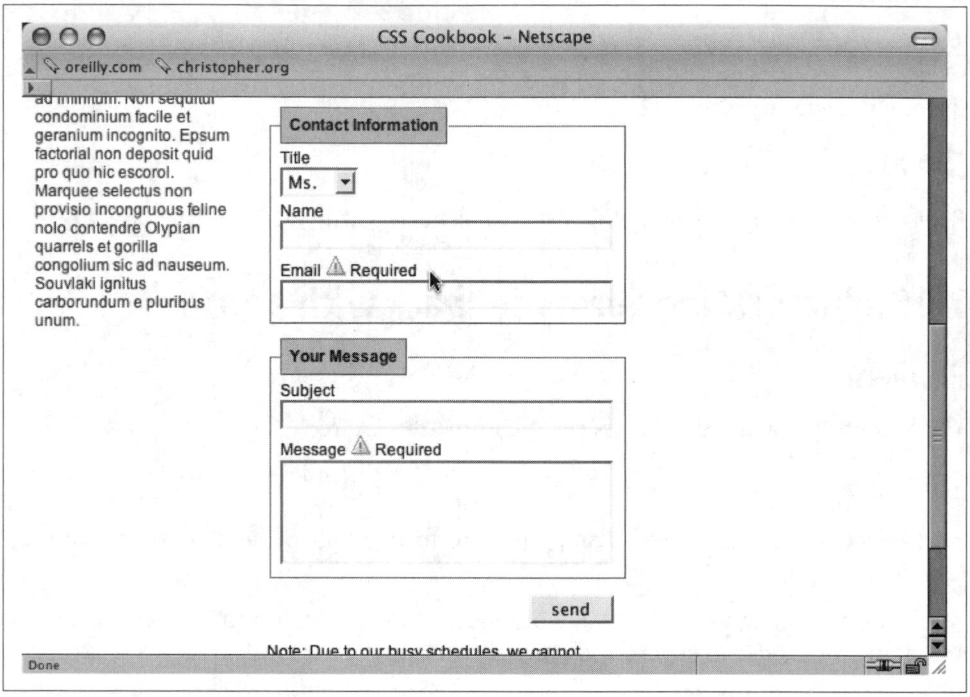

Figure 7-23. Required icon and warning text

Apply rules to change the text and border color of the forms (see Figure 7-24):

```
label {
 margin-top: .33em;
 display: block;
}
input {
    display: block;
    width: 250px;
}
textarea {
    width: 250px;
    height: 75px;
}
label.required {
 color: #c00;
 font-weight: bold;
}
```

```
textarea.required, input.required {
  border: 1px solid red;
  background-color: #eee;
}
```

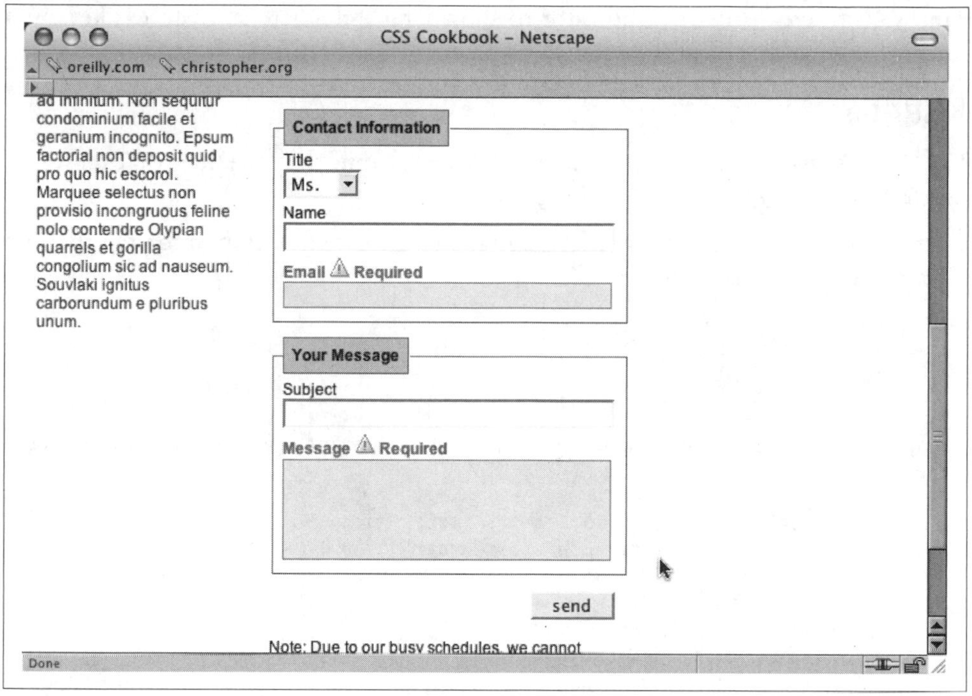

Figure 7-24. Modified required form fields

Discussion

Modifying form and label elements with color and bold text lets users readily know what the problem areas of their form are.

Adding the word "required" and a warning icon also help to clue users to problems with their form submission. In case a user's browser doesn't support CSS, the text and image will then be the only clues for users as to what needs to be corrected in order for the form to be submitted correctly.

See Also

A tutorial on integrating form feedback with PHP at *http://www.maketemplate.com/ feedback/*.

7.16 Styling Access Keys in Web Forms

Problem

You want to create a visual indicator to show which characters are access keys in a form.

Solution

Use the descendant selector to isolate characters within the label tag that represent access keys.

First, create a CSS rule with a selector that states the text within an em tag that are within a form are underlined:

```css
form em {
 text-decoration: underline;
 font-style: normal;
}
```

Wrap an em element around a letter in the label element that represents the access key:

```html
<form id="msgform" name="msgform" method="post" action="/">
 <label for="fmtitle" accesskey="i">T<em>i</em>tle</label>
 <select name="fmtitle" id="fmtitle">
  <option value="ms">Ms.</option>
  <option value="mrs">Mrs.</option>
  <option value="miss">Miss</option>
  <option value="mr">Mr.</option>
 </select>
 <label for="fmname" accesskey="n"><em>N</em>ame</label>
 <input type="text" name="fmname" id="fmname" />
 <label for="fmemail" accesskey="e"><em>E</em>mail</label>
 <input type="text" name="fmemail" id="fmemail" />
 <label for="fmstate" accesskey="a">St<em>a</em>te/Province</label>
 <input type="text" name="fmstate" id="fmstate" />
 <label for="fmcountry" accesskey="y">Countr<em>y</em></label>
 <input type="text" name="fmcountry" id="fmcountry" />
 <label for="fmmsg" accesskey="m"><em>M</em>essage</label>
 <textarea name="fmmsg" id="fmmsg" rows="5" cols="14"></textarea>
 <input type="submit" name="submit" value="send" class="submit" />
</form>
```

Discussion

An access key allows users with disabilities to navigate quickly through sections of a web page. However, access keys also allow users without limited surfing ability to make use of access key navigation. By underlining characters that represent access keys, users can quickly navigate a form without switching to a mouse or other pointing device.

Access keys are supported in Safari, Internet Explorer for Windows 4+, Mozilla, Firefox, Netscape Navigator 6+, and Opera 7+.

See Also

For more information about styling access keys see *http://www.alistapart.com/ articles/accesskeys/*.

7.17   Grouping Common Form Elements

Problem

You want to break up a large form into smaller groupings of elements.

Solution

Use the HTML `fieldset` property to separate the different sections of a form (see Figure 7-25):

```
<form id="msgform" name="msgform" method="post" action="/">
 <fieldset>
  <legend>Contact Information</legend>
  <label for="fmtitle">Title</label>
  <select name="fmtitle" id="fmtitle">
   <option value="ms">Ms.</option>
   <option value="mrs">Mrs.</option>
   <option value="miss">Miss</option>
   <option value="mr">Mr.</option>
  </select>
  <label for="fmname">Name</label>
  <input type="text" name="fmname" id="fmname" />
  <label for="fmemail">Email</label>
  <input type="text"  name="fmemail" id="fmemail" />
 </fieldset>
 <fieldset>
  <legend>Your Message</legend>
  <label for="fmstate">Subject</label>
  <input type="text" name="fmcountry" id="fmcountry" />
  <label for="fmmsg">Message</label>
  <textarea name="fmmsg" accesskey="m" id="fmmsg" rows="5"
cols="14"></textarea>
 </fieldset>
 <input type="submit" name="submit" value="send" class="submit" />
</form>
```

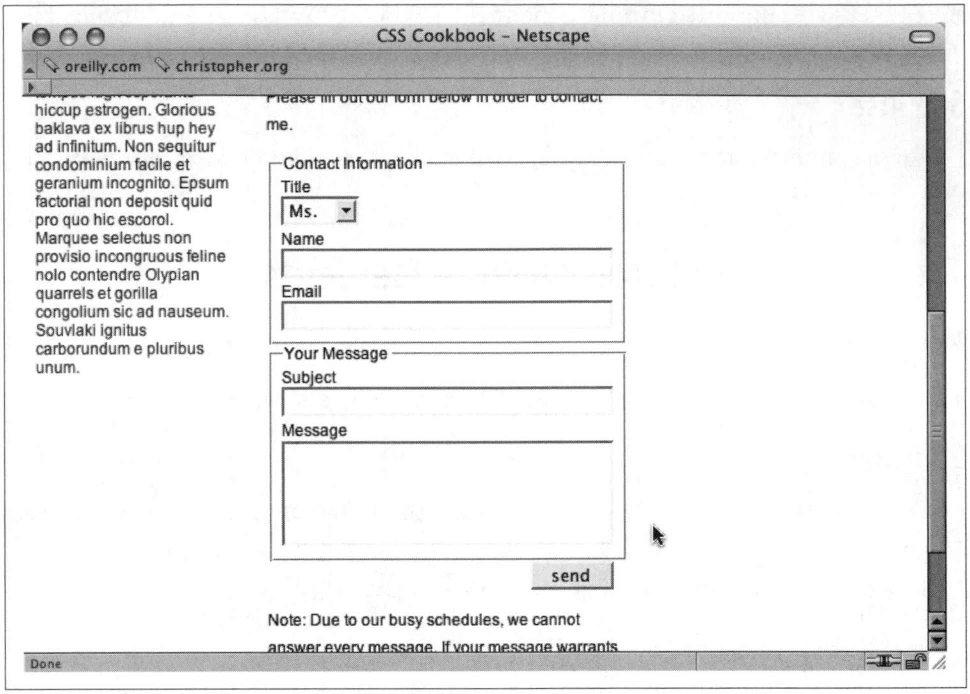

Figure 7-25. A field separated by fieldsets

Discussion

The HTML element `fieldset` and the `legend` properties allow an easy way to group common elements.

You can also apply CSS rules to the `fieldset` and `legend` properties to modify the look as you see in Figure 7-26:

```
fieldset {
 margin-bottom: 1em;
 border: 1px solid #888;
 border-right: 1px solid #666;
 border-bottom: 1px solid #666;
}
legend {
 font-weight: bold;
 border: 1px solid #888;
 border-right: 1px solid #666;
 border-bottom: 1px solid #666;
 padding: .5em;
 background-color: #ccc;
}
```

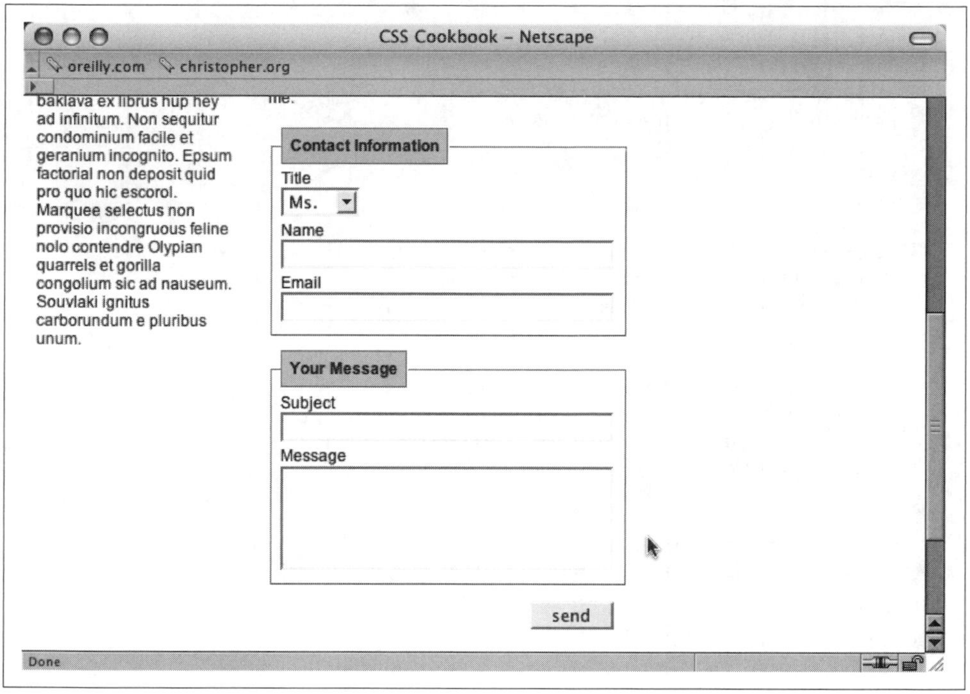

Figure 7-26. Modified fieldset and legends

See Also

The HTML 4.01 specification for `fieldset` elements and `legend` properties at *http://www.w3.org/TR/html4/interact/forms.html#h-17.10*.

7.18   Entering Data into a Form Like a Spreadsheet

Problem

You want to modify a form in an environment such as a spreadsheet application.

Solution

First, place input elements into an HTML table, as shown in Figure 7-27:

```
<form action="/process.php" method="get" name="copresentations">
 <table cellspacing="0">
  <caption>
   Summary of Financial Data
  </caption>
```

```
<tr>
 <th scope="col">Fiscal Year </th>
 <th scope="col">Worksite<br />
  Presentations </th>
 <th scope="col">Passing Grades </th>
 <th scope="col">Number of Presentators </th>
</tr>
<tr>
 <th scope="row">1999</th>
 <td><input type="text" name="wkpst1999" /></td>
 <td><input type="text" name="pass1999" /></td>
 <td><input type="text" name="numpst1999" /></td>
</tr>
<tr>
 <th scope="row">2000</th>
 <td><input type="text" name="wkpst2000" /></td>
 <td><input type="text" name="pass2000" /></td>
 <td><input type="text" name="numpst2000" /></td>
</tr>
<tr>
 <th scope="row">2001</th>
 <td><input type="text" name="wkpst2001" /></td>
 <td><input type="text" name="pass2001" /></td>
 <td><input type="text" name="numpst2001" /></td>
</tr>
<tr>
 <th scope="row">2002</th>
 <td><input type="text" name="wkpst2002" /></td>
 <td><input type="text" name="pass2002" /></td>
 <td><input type="text" name="numpst2002" /></td>
</tr>
<tr>
 <th scope="row">2003</th>
 <td><input type="text" name="wkpst2003" /></td>
 <td><input type="text" name="pass2003" /></td>
 <td><input type="text" name="numpst2003" /></td>
</tr>
<tr>
 <th scope="row">2004</th>
 <td><input type="text" name="wkpst2004" /></td>
 <td><input type="text" name="pass2004" /></td>
 <td><input type="text" name="numpst2004" /></td>
</tr>
</table>
<input type="submit" class="save" value="Save" />
</form>
```

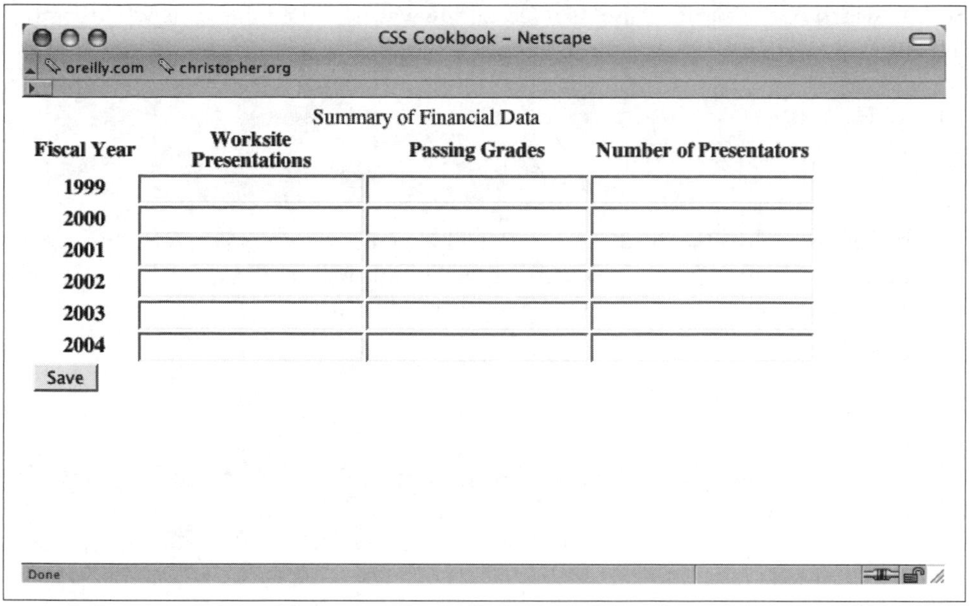

Figure 7-27. A table without styles

Apply a thin border around the table and set the table border display to collapse:

```
table {
  border-collapse: collapse;
  border: 1px solid black;
}
```

Set the table cells to a set width and to display a thin border:

```
th {
  border: 1px solid black;
  width: 6em;
}
td {
  width:6em;
  border: 1px solid black;
}
```

Remove padding and margins for the table cells:

```
th {
  border: 1px solid black;
  width: 6em;
}
td {
  width:6em;
  border: 1px solid black;
  padding: 0;
  margin: 0;
}
```

Set the width of the input elements to equal the width of the table cells while removing any borders that browsers automatically apply to form elements:

```
input {
  width: 100%;
  border: none;
  margin: 0;
}
```

By setting the width, the input elements will also stretch the submit button to the maximum width of its parent element, so the Submit will render quite large. To rein in the size of the Submit button, write a separate CSS rule:

```
.save {
  margin-top: 1em;
  width: 5em;
}
```

To complete the spreadsheet look as shown in Figure 7-28, set the input text to be aligned to the right:

```
input {
  width: 100%;
  border: none;
  margin: 0;
  text-align: right;
}
```

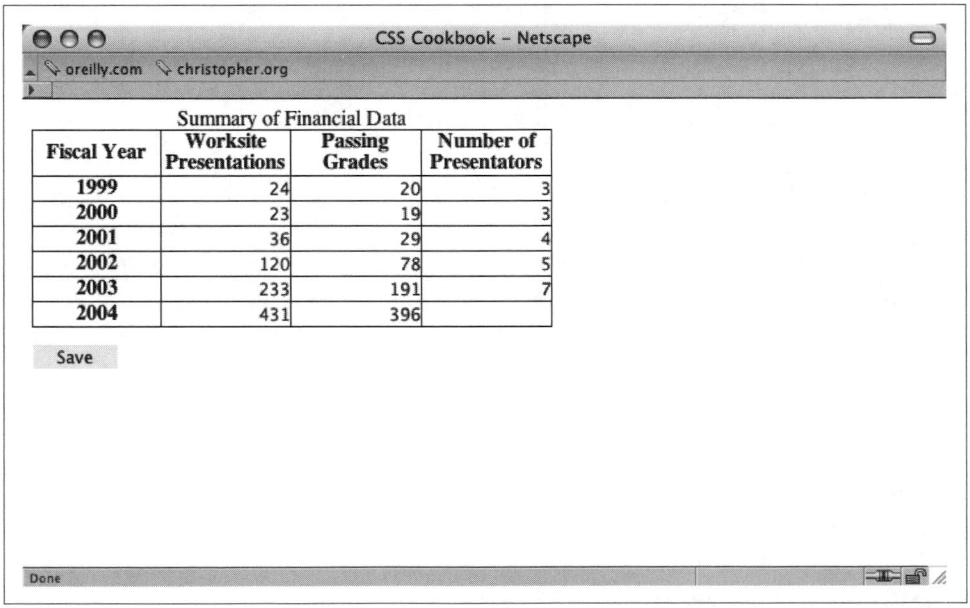

Figure 7-28. A table that looks like a spreadsheet

Discussion

Spreadsheets help users keep tabs on lots of numerical and financial information. The typical ecommerce or a contact form layout would be a hindrance if a user needs to enter a multitude of numbers. By mimicking a spreadsheet layout, a user can quickly enter data.

When coupled with the :hover pseudo-selector, the table row and cell a user is working in can be highlighted as data is entered (see Figure 7-29):

```
tr:hover {
  background-color: #ffc;
}
tr:hover input {
  background-color: #ffc;
}
input:focus {
  background-color: #ffc;
}
```

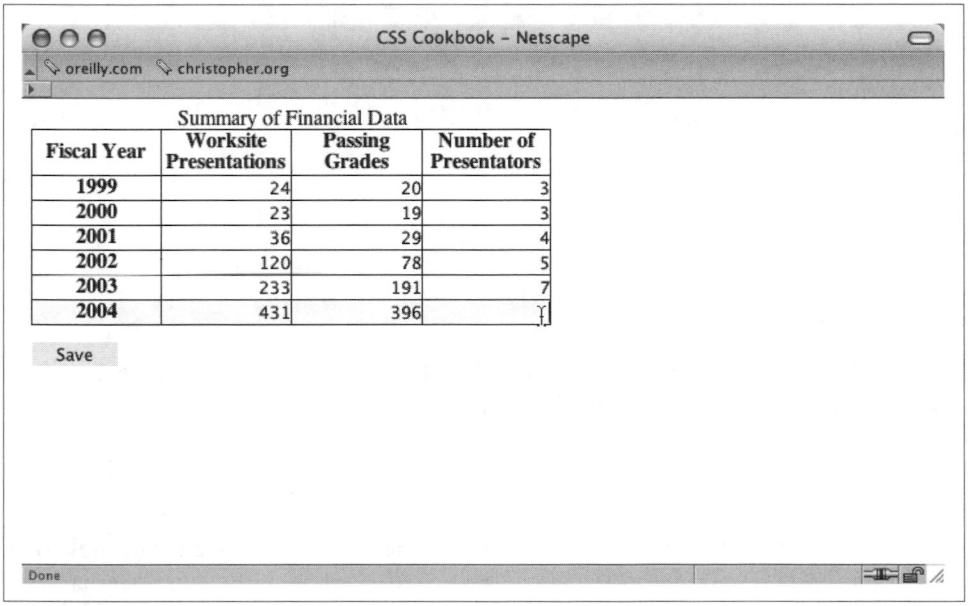

Figure 7-29. A table row is highlighted

See Also

Styling input elements in Recipe 7.2.

7.19 Sample Design: A Login Form

Login forms are all over the Web. For instance, you need a login and a password to check your email on the Web, order books from Amazon.com, and even pay that parking ticket online.

Only a few components of a login form are visible to the user: the input field's Submit button and labels as well as the username and password fields themselves. Here is the markup of the form to be stylized (Figure 7-30 shows the input field without styles applied):

```
<form action="login.php" method="post">
<label for="uname">Username</label>
<input type="text" name="uname" id="uname" value="" /><br />
<label for="pword">Password</label>
<input type="text" name="pword" id="pword" value="" /> <br />
<input type="submit" name="Submit" value="Submit" />
</form>
```

Figure 7-30. The login form without styles

First, add a character after the text in the label element. Use the :after pseudoelement property to autogenerate the character:

```
label:after {
 content: ": ";
}
```

Next, to make the labels stick out from the form fields, change the background color of the labels and the weight of the font. Through CSS, change the labels so that they have a gray background and black text set in bold type (see Figure 7-31):

```
label {
 background-color: gray;
 color: black;
 font-weight: bold;
}
```

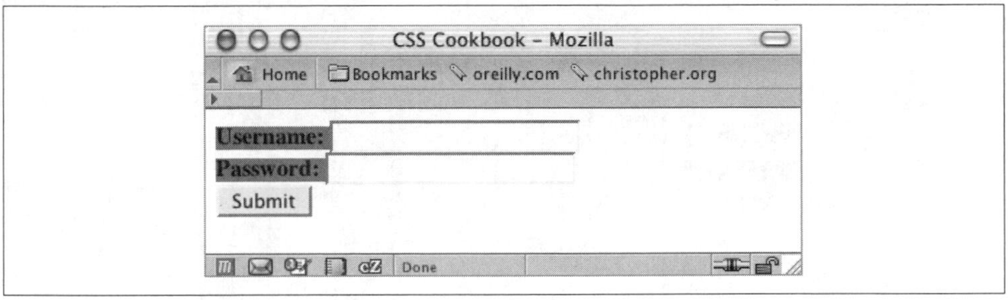

Figure 7-31. Styles for colors applied to the label elements

Now, place some padding around the text and change the text to uppercase (see Figure 7-32):

```
label {
 background-color: gray;
 color: black;
 font-weight: bold;
 padding: 4px;
 text-transform: uppercase;
}
```

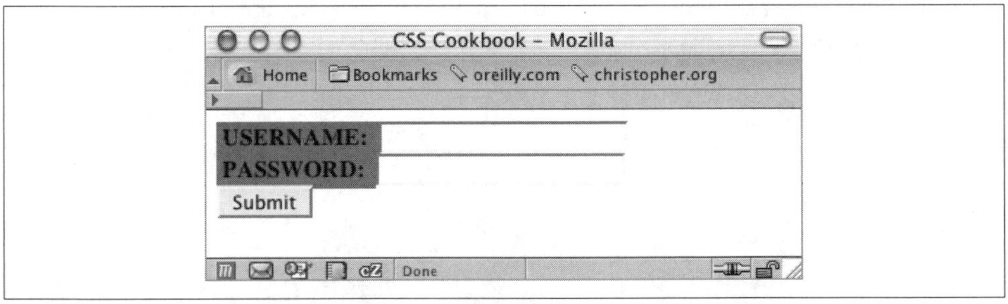

Figure 7-32. Text transformed to uppercase letters

As you can see, the labels need to be toned down because they compete for attention with the input fields. To reduce their visual impact, shrink the size of the text while keeping the weight of the font set to bold. Also, set the typeface of the labels to Verdana, which renders legibly even in small sizes (see Figure 7-33):

```
label {
 background-color: gray;
 color: black;
 font-weight: bold;
 padding: 4px;
 text-transform: uppercase;
 font-family: Verdana, Arial, Helvetica, sans-serif;
 font-size: xx-small;
}
```

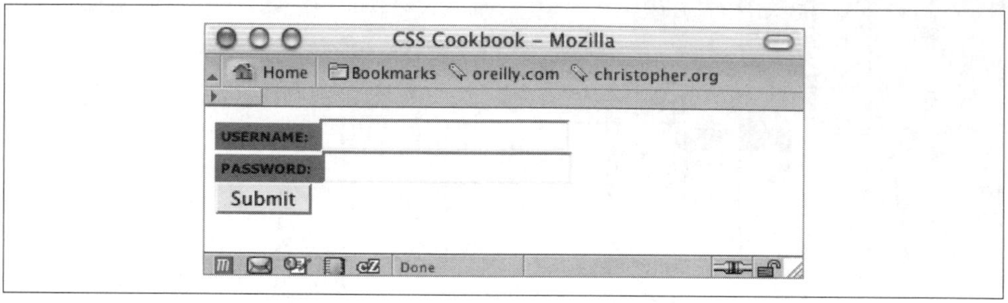

Figure 7-33. The text refined in the label element

Now it's time to style the input fields. Because the form has two types of input fields, differentiate them by placing a class attribute in the Submit button. This technique enables you to style the input fields and the Submit button differently. If you didn't do this, styles that are intended just for the form fields would also be applied to the Submit button. Using the class selector, you can override or change the properties intended for one element so that they aren't applied to all elements:

```
<input type="submit" name="Submit" value="Submit"
class="buttonSubmit" />
```

To bring in some whitespace around the form elements, set the input fields to display as block-level elements and apply a margin to the bottom (see Figure 7-34):

```
input {
  display: block;
  margin-bottom: 1.25em;
}
```

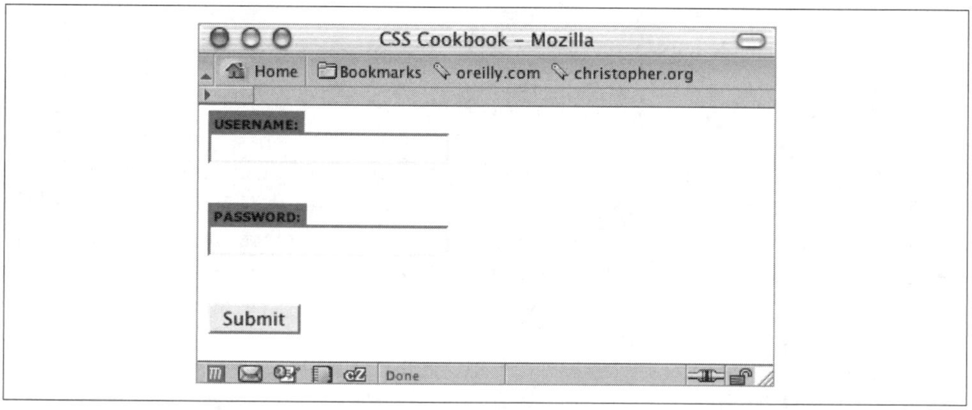

Figure 7-34. The input elements sliding under the labels

Next, extend the width of the input box to 150 pixels and place a 1-pixel border around the box so that the default bevel rendering that occurs in most browsers goes away. Indicate a slight depth to the page by adding a 2-pixel border on the right and bottom of the input box (see Figure 7-35):

```
input {
 display: block;
 margin-bottom: 1.25em;
 width: 150px;
 border: solid black;
 border-width: 1px 2px 2px 1px;
}
```

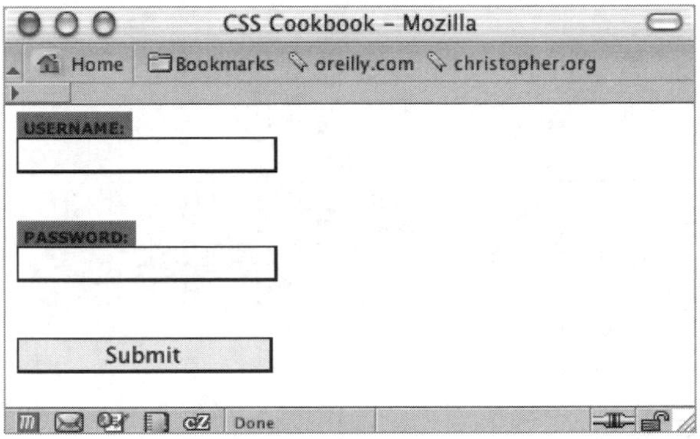

Figure 7-35. The modified input fields

With the main input fields in place, now it's time to apply styles to the Submit button. Because you don't want the Submit button to look like the regular input text fields, use a class selector.

Start by changing the size and position of the Submit button. First, shrink the width of the button by 75 pixels (which is one-half the size of the input fields). Then slide the button to the right by setting the left side margin to 75 pixels (see Figure 7-36):

```
.buttonSubmit {
 width: 75px;
 margin-left: 75px;
}
```

Next, change the Submit button's color to green with a green border, and convert the text to uppercase by using the text-transform property (see Figure 7-37):

```
.buttonSubmit {
 width: 75px;
 margin-left: 75px;
 color: green;
 text-transform: uppercase;
 border: 1px solid green;
}
```

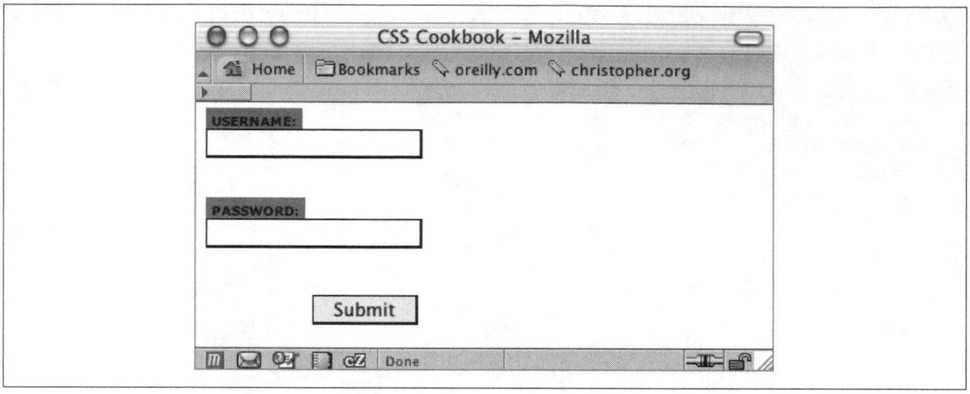

Figure 7-36. The refined Submit button

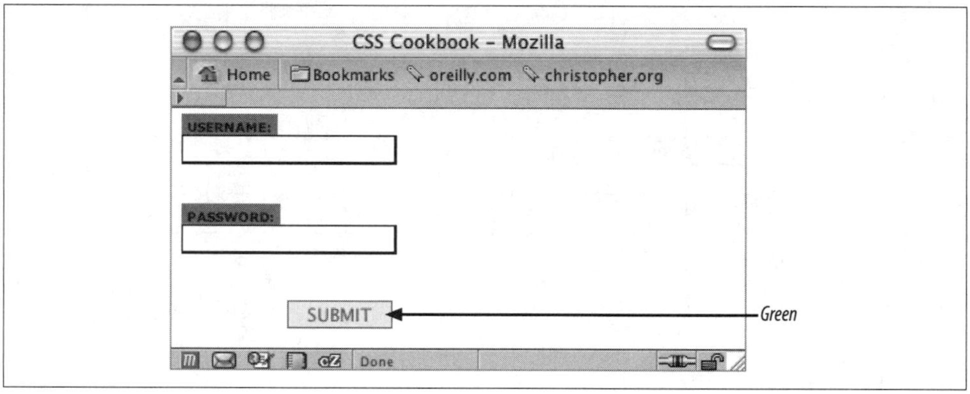

Figure 7-37. The green Submit button in uppercase letters

To add the final touch, hide the br element from the display because the br introduces extra whitespace to the form. Figure 7-38 shows the result.

```
br {
  display: none;
}
```

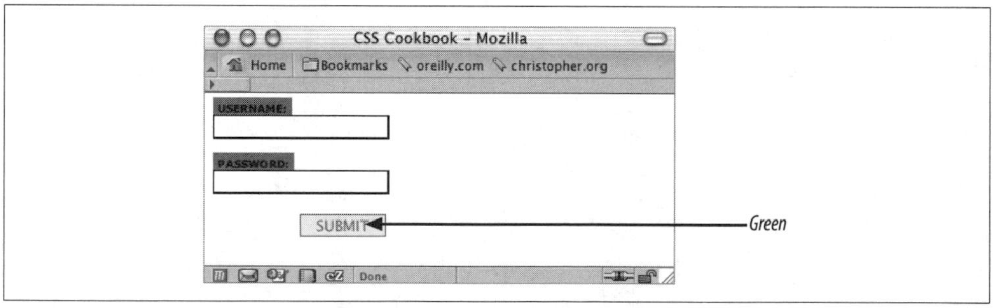

Figure 7-38. The login form styles finalized

7.20   Sample Design: A Registration Form

For some forms you may want to place the `form` elements into a two-column table, with the labels in one column and the fields in the other. Example 7-1 provides the code. Figure 7-39 shows the form and tables without styles applied.

Example 7-1. Stylized long form

```
<form action="registration.cfm" method="post">
  <table cellspacing="0">
    <tr class="header">
      <th colspan="2">Account Information</th>
    </tr>
    <tr class="required">
      <th scope="row">Login Name*</th>
      <td><input name="uname" type="text" size="12"
maxlength="12" /></td>
    </tr>
    <tr class="required">
      <th scope="row">Password*</th>
      <td><input name="pword" type="text" size="12"
maxlength="12" /></td>
    </tr>
    <tr class="required">
      <th scope="row">Confirm Password* </th>
      <td><input name="pword2" type="text" size="12"
maxlength="12" /></td>
    </tr>
    <tr class="required">
      <th scope="row">Email Address*</th>
      <td><input name="email" type="text" /></td>
    </tr>
    <tr class="required">
      <th scope="row">Confirm Email*</th>
      <td><input type="text" name="email2" /></td>
    </tr>
    <tr class="header">
      <th colspan="2">Contact Information</th>
    </tr>
    <tr class="required">
      <th scope="row">First Name* </th>
      <td><input name="fname" type="text" size="11" /></td>
    </tr>
    <tr class="required">
      <th scope="row">Last Name* </th>
      <td><input name="lname" type="text" size="11" /></td>
    </tr>
    <tr class="required">
      <th scope="row">Address 1*</th>
      <td><input name="address1" type="text" size="11" /></td>
    </tr>
    <tr>
      <th scope="row">Address 2 </th>
      <td><input type="text" name="address2" /></td>
```

Example 7-1. Stylized long form (continued)

```
    </tr>
    <tr class="required">
      <th scope="row">City* </th>
      <td><input type="text" name="city" /></td>
    </tr>
    <tr class="required">
      <th scope="row">State or Province*</th>
      <td><select name="state">
          <option selected="selected"
disabled="disabled">Select...</option>
          <option value="alabama">Alabama</option>
        </select></td>
    </tr>
    <tr class="required">
      <th scope="row">Zip*</th>
      <td><input name="zipcode" type="text" id="zipcode"
size="5" maxlength="5" /></td>
    </tr>
    <tr class="required">
      <th scope="row">Country*</th>
      <td><input type="text" name="country" /></td>
    </tr>
    <tr class="required">
      <th scope="row">Gender*</th>
      <td> <input type="radio" name="sex" value="female" />
        Female
        <input type="radio" name="sex" value="male" />
        Male </td>
    </tr>
    <tr class="header">
      <th colspan="2">Misc. Information</th>
    </tr>
    <tr>
      <th scope="row"> Annual Household Income </th>
      <td>
       <select name="income" size="1" >
         <option selected="selected" disabled="disabled">
Select...</option>
         <option value="notsay">I'd rather not say</option>
        </select> </td>
    </tr>
    <tr>
      <th scope="row">Interests</th>
      <td><input name="interests" type="checkbox"
value="shopping-fashion" />
        Shopping/fashion
        <input name="interests" type="checkbox"
value="sports" />
        Sports
        <input name="interests" type="checkbox"
value="travel" />
        Travel</td>
    </tr>
```

Example 7-1. Stylized long form (continued)

```
  <tr>
    <th scope="row">Eye Color</th>
    <td><input name="eye" type="checkbox" value="red" />
      Red
      <input name="eye" type="checkbox" value="green" />
      Green
      <input name="eye" type="checkbox" value="brown" />
      Brown
      <input name="eye" type="checkbox" value="blue" />
      Blue Gold</td>
  </tr>
</table>
<input type="submit" name="Submit" value="Submit"
id="buttonSubmit" />
<input type="reset" name="Submit2" value="Reset"
id="buttonReset" />
</form>
```

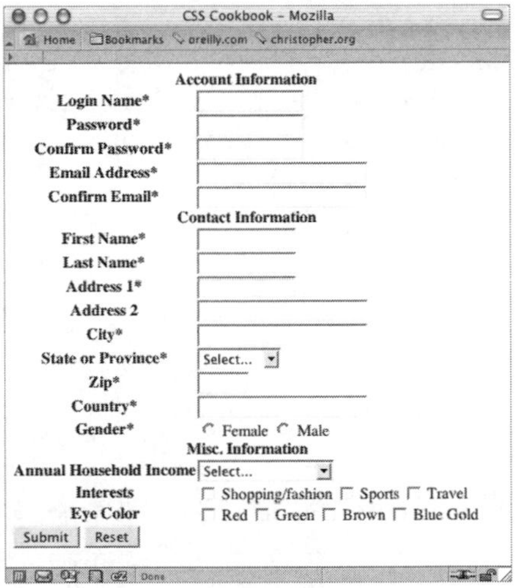

Figure 7-39. The form and table without styles applied

The first element to style is the `table` element. Set the border model as well as the text color and border around the table itself (see Figure 7-40):

```
table {
  border-collapse: collapse;
  color: black;
  border: 1px solid black;
}
```

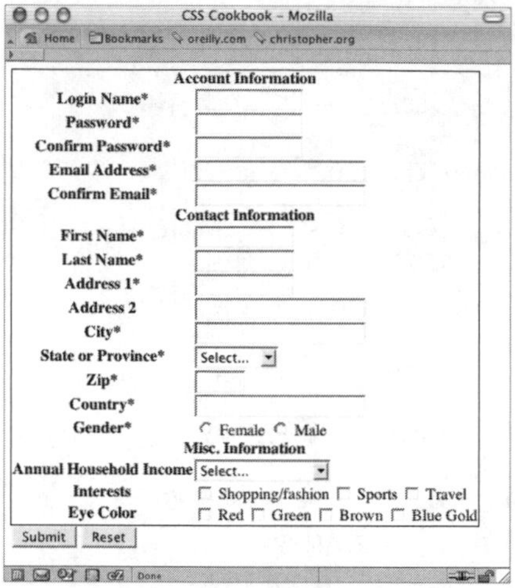

Figure 7-40. A border placed around the table

Next, tackle the table header cells, which are located in the left column (see Figure 7-41). The table header cells is set to a width of 200 pixels, while the content inside the cell is aligned to the right, set to Verdana and sized to 0.7 em units:

```
th {
  width: 200px;
  text-align: right;
  vertical-align: top;
  border-top: 1px solid black;
  font-family: Verdana;
  font-size: 0.7em;
}
```

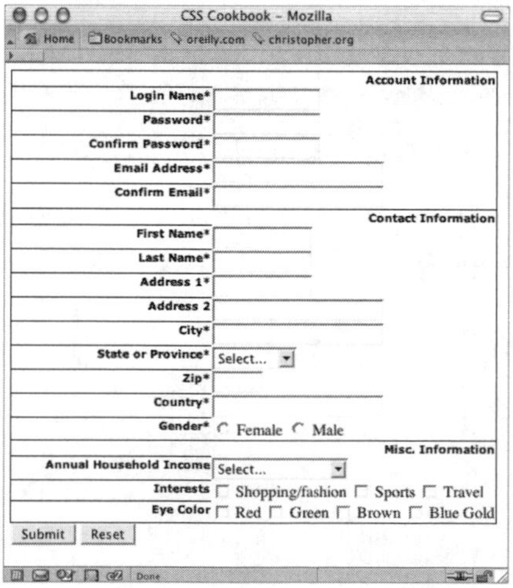

Figure 7-41. Refined table header cells

Adjust the padding of the header cells (see Figure 7-42):

```
th {
 width: 200px;
 text-align: right;
 vertical-align: top;
 border-top: 1px solid black;
 font-family: Verdana;
 font-size: 0.7em;
 padding-right: 12px;
 padding-top: 0.75em;
 padding-bottom: 0.75em;
}
```

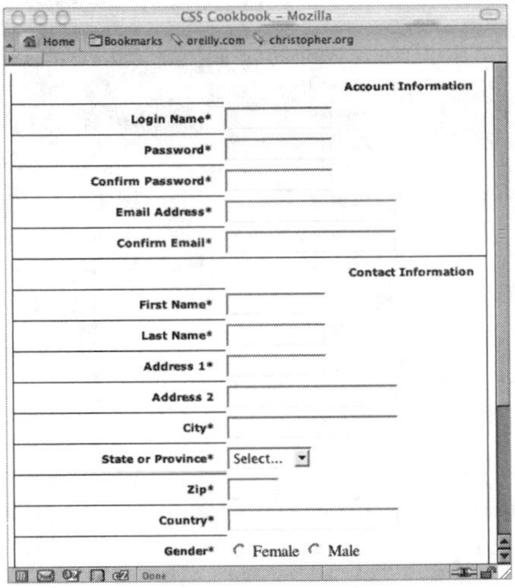

Figure 7-42. Padding applied to the table header cells

Next, apply styles to the right table cells. To underscore the difference between the left and right columns, convert the right table cell background to black. Also, set a gray border to the left to soften the transition when reading the rows left to right (see Figure 7-43):

```
td {
 vertical-align: middle;
 background-color: black;
 border-bottom: 1px solid white;
 color: white;
 border-left: 4px solid gray;
 padding: 4px;
 font-family: Verdana;
 font-size: .7em;
}
```

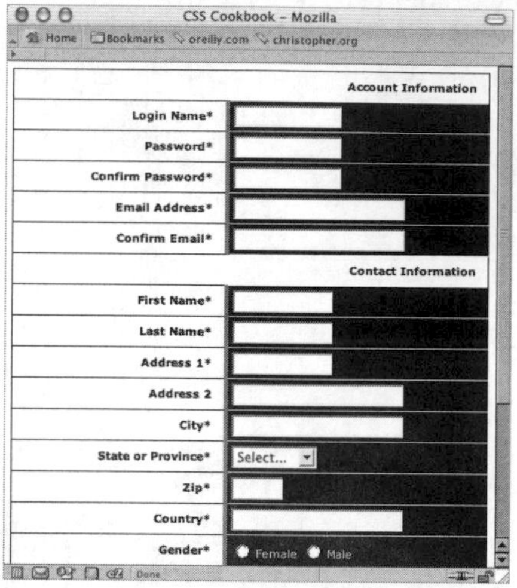

Figure 7-43. The stylized right column table cells

Certain fields are required to execute the registration, so change the color of the text labels for those fields. This change in color will indicate at a glance which fields are required (see Figure 7-44):

```
.required {
 color: red;
}
```

Note that the CSS rule states that the color is red, but for printing purposes the color will come out a shade of gray.

Adjust the form headers that indicate the different sections of the form by making the text uppercase and slightly larger than the other text in the form (see Figure 7-45):

```
.header th {
 text-align: left;
 text-transform: uppercase;
 font-size: .9em;
}
```

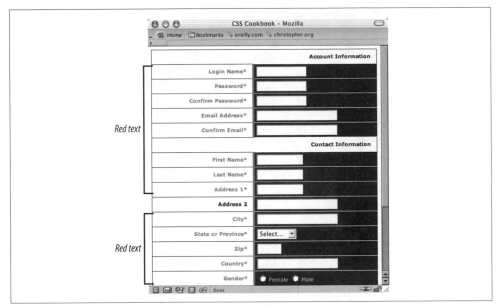

Figure 7-44. The required fields marked with red text

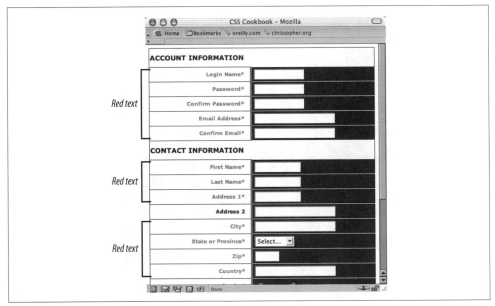

Figure 7-45. The refined form section headers

Slide the form headers so that they rest on top of the second column. To determine where to place the headers, add the size of the left column (200 pixels), the padding of the right column (4 pixels), the width of the border on the left of the right column (4 pixels), and the padding of the right column (12 pixels):

```
.header th {
  text-align: left;
  text-transform: uppercase;
  font-size: .9em;
  padding-left: 220px;
}
```

Then add a touch of visual appeal by applying thicker borders to the top and bottom of the header (see Figure 7-46):

```
.header th {
  text-align: left;
  text-transform: uppercase;
  font-size: .9em;
  padding-left: 220px;
  border-bottom: 2px solid gray;
  border-top: 2px solid black;
}
```

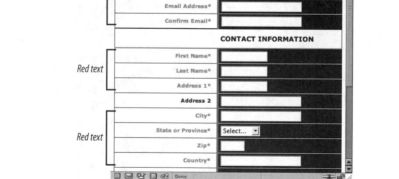
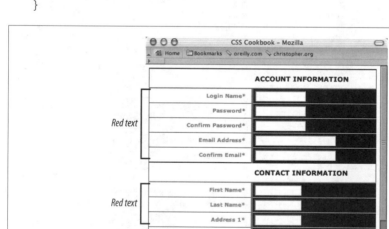

Figure 7-46. Padding added to the section headers

For the finishing touch, move the Submit and Reset buttons so that they fall under the form fields, just like the section headings, by assigning the left side of the margin to be 220 pixels (see Figure 7-47):

```
#buttonSubmit {
 margin-left: 220px;
 margin-top: 4px;
}
```

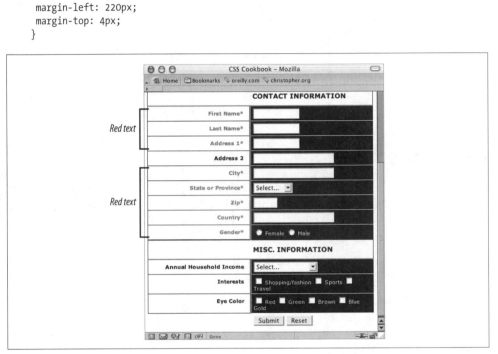

Figure 7-47. *The Submit and Reset buttons moved into place*

CHAPTER 8
Tables

8.0   Introduction

With CSS, web designers learned that they could forego the practice of manipulating HTML tables to hold designs together. Practices like cutting up an image to place the image "pieces" into separate table cells or nesting tables for web page layouts have now become outmoded. However, the use of tables still has its place.

Web developers use HTML tables to present tabular data, such as a calendar or scientific data, and therefore can use CSS to stylize those tables.

This chapter shows you how to make your tables look better by stylizing table headers, setting borders for a table and for its cells, and reducing gaps between images in table cells. The sample design at the end of this chapter takes you through the steps required to stylize a calendar.

8.1   Setting the Cell Spacing

Problem

You want to adjust the space between the table border and the cell borders.

Solution

Use the `cellspacing` table attribute:

```
<table cellspacing="15">
 <tr>
   <th colspan="2">
    General Demographic Characteristics of Tallahassee, FL
   </th>
 </tr>
 <tr>
   <th>
   </th>
```

```
    <th>
      Estimate
    </th>
  </tr>
  <tr>
    <td>
      Total population
    </td>
    <td>
      272,091
    </td>
  </tr>
</table>
```

Discussion

The CSS 2.1 specification describes a standard mechanism to manipulate the cellspacing table attribute through the use of the border-spacing property, when the border-collapse value is set to separate:

```
border-collapse: separate;
border-spacing: 15px;
```

However, implementation of this part of the specification isn't visible in Internet Explorer 6 for Windows. It does work in Firefox and Netscape Navigator 7+. Using the cellspacing attribute is currently the best solution that works in Internet Explorer for Windows, Netscape Navigator, Safari, and Opera browsers.

See Also

Recipes 8.2 and 8.7 on setting table borders and cell padding; the CSS 2.1 specification for border-collapse at *http://www.w3.org/TR/CSS21/tables.html#propdef-border-collapse*; the CSS 2.1 specification for border-spacing at *http://www.w3.org/TR/CSS21/tables.html#propdef-border-spacing*.

8.2   Setting the Borders and Cell Padding

Problem

You want to set the borders and the amount of space within table cells to create a stronger visual display than the default rendering of a table, as in Figure 8-1, for example.

Solution

Use the padding property to address the amount of space between the content in the cell and the edges of the cell. Use the border property to set the borders on both the table and its cells:

```
table {
 border-collapse: collapse;
```

```
  border: 5px solid #444;
}
td {
  padding: 4px;
}
th {
  color: white;
  background-color: black;
}
td, th+th {
  border: 5px solid #666;
}
td+td {
  border: 5px solid #ccc;
  text-align: center;
}
td#winner {
  border: 7px dotted #999;
}
```

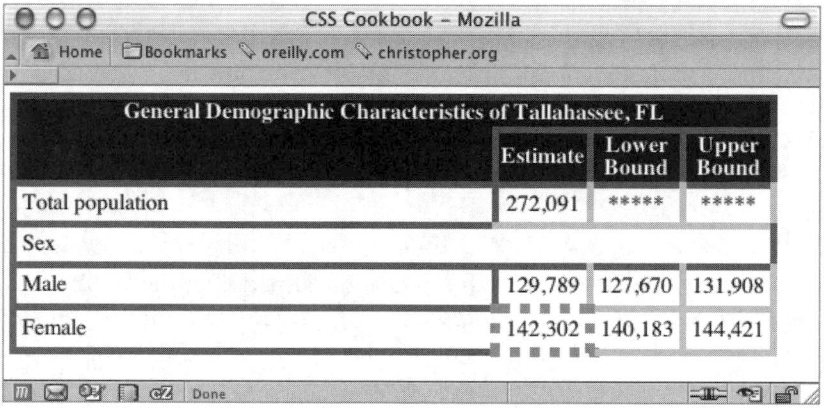

Figure 8-1. Borders and padding applied to the table and table cells

Discussion

There are two border models for HTML tables: collapse and separate. With the collapse model, table cells share borders. In the separate model, the table cells have their own borders.

At the time of writing, the collapse model is more widely implemented by browsers and thus used more by designers.

All browsers today default to the collapse model, except for Firefox, which defaults to separate. Because the CSS standard doesn't specify that behavior, you should explicitly set the collapse model in your style sheets lest a future browser not have the same defaults. Set the border model by using the `border-collapse` property set to collapse:

```
table {
  border-collapse: collapse;
}
```

The `table` element's `border` attribute determines borders for the table and its enclosing cells. You can set CSS's `border` property through a separate border thickness value for the table and individual cells.

When you apply a border to a cell that runs counter to a previous CSS rule, the following four CSS specification rules are followed for conflict resolution:

- If `border-style` is set to `hidden`, all other border styles are concealed.
- If `border-style` is set to `none`, any other border style wins.
- Unless a cell has `border-style` set to `hidden` or has `border-style` set to `none`, a thicker border overrides the narrower borders. If adjoining cells have the same width, the style of the border will be determined in the following order: `double`, `solid`, `dashed`, `dotted`, `ridge`, `outset`, `groove`, `inset`.
- If adjoining cells have a different color while possessing the same style and width, the border color will be determined in the following order: cell, row, row group, column, column group, and then table.

The other border model is separate, in which every cell contains its own borders and can be styled independently of other cell borders. Within the separate model, the `border-spacing` property is used to set the horizontal and vertical space respectively between cells:

```
table#runoffdata {
  border-collapse: separate;
  border-spacing: 4px 4px;
}
```

If the `border-collapse` property is set to `separate`, then any styles set for rows, columns, or groups of table cells aren't applied. Also, styles for table cells that don't contain content can be displayed or hidden, using the `empty-cells` property with the value of `show` or `hide`, respectively.

While the separate border model gives more control to web developers, as of this writing separate is supported only in Firefox, Mozilla and Netscape 6+, not in Internet Explorer for Windows. Therefore most web designers stick to the collapse model.

See Also

The CSS 2.1 specification about border models at *http://www.w3.org/TR/CSS21/ tables.html#propdef-border-collapse*; for more discussion on tables, see Chapter 11 in *Cascading Style Sheets: The Definitive Guide,* Second Edition by Eric A. Meyer (O'Reilly Media).

8.3 Setting the Style for Caption

Problem

You want to set the style for the description of a table.

Solution

Use the caption element selector to stylize the caption:

```
table caption {
    font: 1.5em Georgia, "Times New Roman", Times, serif;
    padding: 1em;
}
```

Discussion

Captions are used to describe the contents within a table and should be placed after the opening table element and before another table element like thead or tr:

```
<table id="shoppingcartTable" summary="List of products in your shopping cart.">
 <caption>Shopping Cart Listing - <strong>Subtotal: $45.16</strong>;
changed quantities? <input type="submit"  value="Update price(s)" /></caption>
 ...
</table>
```

Browsers may vary in how to render the caption element. However, caption will always be displayed by any browser, can be styled via CSS, and is the most accessible method of displaying a table caption.

See Also

The HTML 4.01 specification for caption at *http://www.w3.org/TR/html4/struct/tables.html#h-11.2.2*.

8.4 Setting the Styles Within Table Cells

Problem

You want to stylize links within a table cell to make them appear visually different from the rest of the page.

Solution

Use a descendant selector (sometimes referred to as a *contextual selector*) to manipulate the styles for content in a table cell:

```
td a {
  display: block;
  background-color: #333;
```

```
    color: white;
    text-decoration: none;
    padding: 4px;
}
```

Discussion

By using the type and descendent selectors—the td a in the CSS rule—to apply the styles, you reduce the amount of markup needed to perfect your designs and you reduce the document's file sizes. The style affects only the a elements within the table cells, td.

If you need more control over the design of the content within a table cell, use a class selector:

```
<td class="navText">
 <a href="/">Home</a>
</td>
```

You then can apply the CSS rules to the cell's content through a combination of class and descendant selectors:

```
td.navText a {
 font-size: x-small;
}
```

If you want to stylize content within a table cell that contains more content or markup than a link, wrap a div element around the content in order to use a class selector.

In the following example, an unordered list is enclosed within a div element set with a class attribute:

```
<td>
 <div class="tblcontent">
 <p>To-do list on your day off.</p>
 <ul>
    <li><a href="http://www.imdb.com/title/tt0120737">Watch <cite>Fellowship of
the Rings</cite>, Extended Version</a></li>
    <li><a href="http://www.imdb.com/title/tt0167261/">Watch
<cite>Two Towers</cite>, Extended Version</a></li>
    <li><a href="http://www.imdb.com/title/tt0167260/">Watch <cite>Return of the
King</cite>, Extended Version</a></li>
  <li>Start or join local Elvish society.</li>
 </ul>
 </div>
</td>
```

The CSS rules to stylize the content within the table cell could look like this:

```
.tblcontent p {
 margin: 0;
 padding: 0;
 font-weight: bold;
}
```

```
.tblcontent ul {
 margin: 0;
 padding: 0;
}
.tblcontent li {
 margin: 0;
 padding: 0;
 line-height: 1.5;
}
.tblcontent li a {
 padding-left: 15px;
 background-image: url(bullet.gif);
 background-repeat: no-repeat;
}
```

See Also

The CSS 2.1 specification regarding type selectors at *http://www.w3.org/TR/CSS21/ selector.html#type-selectors*; *http://www.w3.org/TR/CSS21/selector.html#descendant-selectors* for information about descendant selectors. For a more thorough example of styling content within table cells, see Recipe 8.10.

8.5   Setting Styles for Table Header Elements

Problem

You want to differentiate the style of the table headers from the content in regular table cells; Figure 8-2 shows a table with traditional table headers, and Figure 8-3 shows a stylized version of the same table.

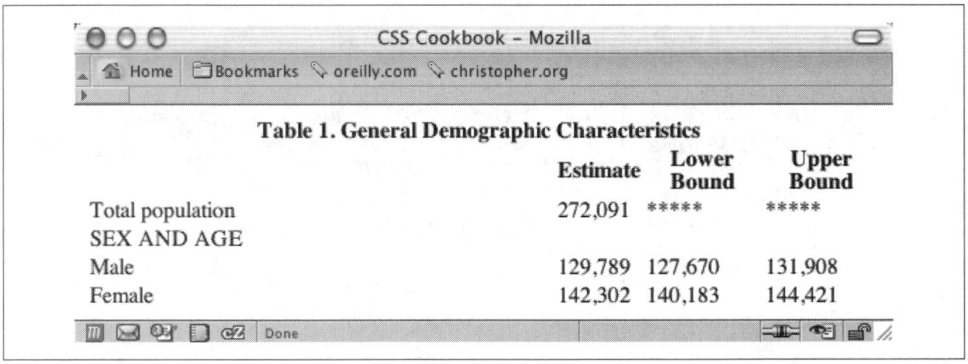

Figure 8-2. The table as it appears before styles are applied to the table headers

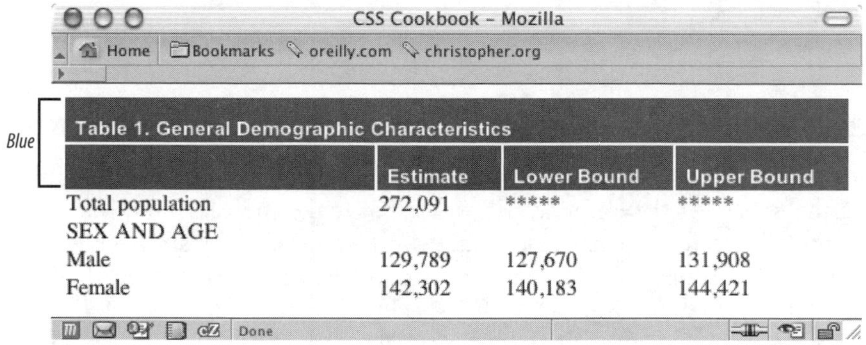

Figure 8-3. Styles applied to the table headers

Solution

Use the th element selector to stylize the table header:

```
th {
  text-align: left;
  padding: 1em 1.5em 0.1em 0.5em;
  font-family: Arial, Helvetica, Verdana, sans-serif;
  font-size: .9em;
  color: white;
  background-color: blue;
  border-right: 2px solid blue;
}
```

For tables with multiple rows of th elements that require different styles, use a class selector to differentiate the rows:

```
.secondrow th {
/* Use a lighter shade of blue in the background */
  background-color: #009;
}
```

Put the appropriate rows into that class:

```
<tr>
 <th colspan="4">
 Table 1. General Demographic Characteristics
 </th>
</tr>
<tr class="secondrow">
 <th>

 </th>
 <th>
  Estimate
 </th>
 <th>
  Lower Bound
 </th>
```

```
<th>
  Upper Bound
</th>
</tr>
```

Discussion

The th element characterizes the contents of the cell as header information. When setting the styles for the element, use styles that make the cell stand out from content in the table cell, td. You can generate contrasting styles by simply adjusting any of the following properties: font-family, background-color, font-size, font-weight, and text alignment. (See Recipe 2.1 for specifying fonts and Recipe 2.2 for setting font measurements and sizes.) Regardless of what you adjust, chances are you will be improving the look of the table headers.

 Note that the nonbreaking space characters placed in the table headers are used so that the heading is treated by the browser as one word and therefore isn't a forced break into two lines stacked on top of each other in the heading.

See Also

Type selectors at *http://www.w3.org/TR/CSS21/selector.html#type-selectors*.

8.6   Removing Gaps from Images Placed in Table Cells

Problem

You want to get rid of space in a table cell that contains only an image. You want to go from Figure 8-4 to Figure 8-5.

Figure 8-4. A gap appearing below an image in a table cell

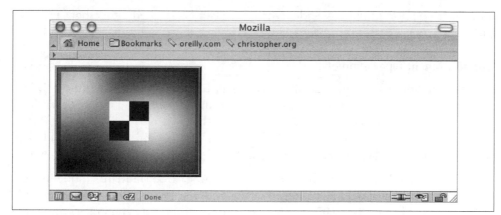

Figure 8-5. Displaying an image in a table cell as a block-level element

Solution

Set the image to be displayed as a block-level element:

```
td img {
  display: block;
}
```

Discussion

The browser puts the image on the baseline used for text content since it's being placed as an inline element. Therefore set the element as a block-level element to force the browser to render the image differently. This baseline isn't at the bottom of the cell because some letters (for example, g, p, q, and y) have descenders that hang below that baseline (see Figure 8-6).

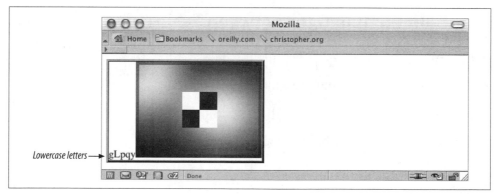

Figure 8-6. The descenders of the lowercase letters g, p, q, and y highlight the whitespace below the image

Because the baseline is a percentage of the total font size, you can't simply remove the descender space. By instructing the browser to handle the image differently, the automatic creation of the descender whitespace can be avoided altogether. Thus set the `display` property for the image to `block` as shown in the Solution.

Using Document Type Definitions

Another method involves manipulating DTDs. A Document Type Definition (DTD) is a formal statement that lists the elements used in a document. For example, there are differences in the HTML2 DTD compared to the HTML 4.1 DTD. Those differences are spelled out in their own DTD. A browser can determine which DTD to use when rendering a page by a small statement that precedes any markup in a web page.

There are certain DOCTYPEs that will put the browser into standards mode instead of *quirks* mode, an umbrella term used to describe the irregular behavior of browsers. Having the browser in standards mode ensures the gap between images and table cell borders. Use alternative DOCTYPES that trigger quirks mode but that still validate to avoid this gap, or if you simply want to avoid standards mode. For more information, see a chart comparing DOCTYPEs and browsers at *http://www. webstandards.org/learn/reference/doctype_switch.html*.

There may be times when setting the image's `display` to `block` isn't the best solution to removing whitespace around an image in a table cell. If that turns out to be the case, another method to remove the space is to set the image's `vertical-align` property to `bottom` as long as the image is taller than the line box.

See Also

The CSS 2.1 specification for the `display` property at *http://www.w3.org/TR/CSS21/ visuren.html#propdef-display*; "quirks" mode and "almost standards mode" at *http:// developer.mozilla.org/en/docs/Mozilla's_DOCTYPE_sniffing*.

8.7   Eliminating Gaps Between Table Cells

Problem

You want to remove gaps from one table cell to another.

Solution

Set the table to use `collapse` border model:

```
#shoppingcartTable {
 border-collapse: collapse;
 width: 100%;
 border: 1px solid #666;
}
#shoppingcartTable th {
 background: #888 url(th_bkgd.jpg) repeat-x;
 font: italic 1.5em Georgia, "Times New Roman", Times, serif;
 padding: .5em 0 .5em 7px;
```

```
    text-align: left;
    border-top: 1px solid #666;
    border-bottom: 1px solid #666;
    text-shadow: #ccc -2px 2px -2px;
}
```

Discussion

By setting the border-collapse property to collapse, the browser removes the spacing between the table cells. Therefore when you apply a border to table cells, the result is a clean, uninterrupted line across the table row or column.

See Also

See Recipe 8.2 for more discussion about the border-collapse model.

8.8 Creating Alternating Background Colors in Table Rows

Problem

You want to have table rows with alternating background colors, so that the table in Figure 8-7 looks more like the table in Figure 8-8.

Figure 8-7. A table without any color in the background cells

Solution

Create a class selector specifically designed for odd-numbered table rows:

```
tr {
 background-color: #eee;
}
tr.odd {
 background-color: #ccc;
}
```

Then append every other table row with a class attribute with odd set as its value:

```
<tr>
 <td class="dltprod">
  <p>Item added on March 22, 2006.</p>
  <a href="" title="Delete this product"><img src="x.gif" alt="delete"
class="dltitem" /></a>
 </td>
 <td class="prodcell">
  <img class="prod" alt="product image" src="u2-dismantle.jpg" />
  <div class="prodtitle"><a href="/product.php?id=B0006399FS">How
to Dismantle an Atomic Bomb</a></div>
   ~ <strong>U2</strong>
 </td>
 <td><input type="text" value="1" name="qty" size="2" /></td>
 <td>$9.66</td>
</tr>
<tr class="odd">
 <td class="dltprod">
  <p>Item added on March 22, 2006.</p>
  <a href="" title="Delete this product"><img src="x.gif" alt="delete"
class="dltitem" /></a>
 </td>
 <td class="prodcell">
  <img class="prod" alt="product image" src="apple-whenthepawn.jpg" />
  <div class="prodtitle"><a href="/product.php?id=B00002MZ4W">When The Pawn
Hits...</a></div>
   ~ <strong>Fiona Apple</strong>
 </td>
 <td><input type="text" value="1" name="qty" size="2" /></td>
 <td>$7.97</td>
</tr>
```

Discussion

This solution of marking up every other tr element, while laborious for long tables if handcoded, ensures cross-browser compatibility.

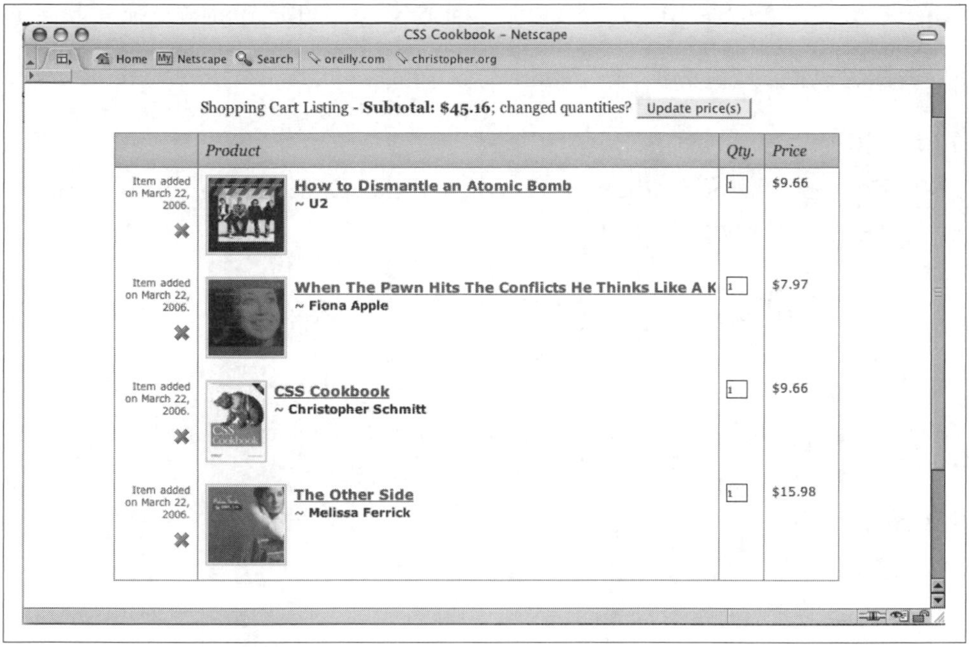

Figure 8-8. Alternating colors in the table rows

A second solution helps eliminate the need for extra markup within an HTML table. Using a selector, nth-child, noted in the CSS 3 specification, the solution is straightforward:

```
tr {
  background-color: #eee;
}
tr:nth-child(odd) {
  background-color: #ccc;
}
```

However, support for CSS 3 is limited. Internet Explorer 6 for Windows and previous versions do not support this selector so cross-browser compatibility is an issue.

Using JavaScript

Other solutions go beyond just CSS. One solution is the use of JavaScript that interacts with the Document Object Model (DOM) and automatically applies the styles to every other table row. You can find one such solution at *http://www.alistapart.com/articles/zebratables*. The downside to this solution is that it will fail if the user has disabled JavaScript in their browser.

Using server-side solutions

Another programming solution would be to use a server-side programming language like PHP or ColdFusion to write a simple script that automates the generation of the table. (This technique is also beneficial if a backend database is being used to create and maintain the tabular data.) For a PHP solution to this exercise see *http://www.phpfreaks.com/tutorials/5/0.php*.

See Also

The CSS 3 specification for the nth-child pseudo-class selector at *http://www.w3.org/TR/css3-selectors/#nth-child-pseudo*.

8.9   Adding a Highlighting Effect on a Table Row

Problem

You want to highlight a whole row in a table when the cursor moves over a table cell within that table row (see Figure 8-9).

Solution

Use the :hover pseudo-class on the tr element:

```
tr:hover {
  background: yellow;
}
```

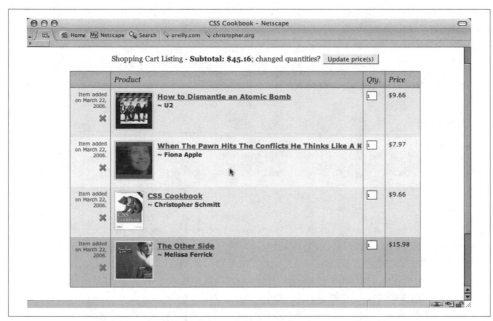

Figure 8-9. A table row is highlighted as the cursor moves across the table

Discussion

The pseudo-class :hover is commonly seen on links to create rollover effects. However, the CSS specification doesn't limit its use to just links. It can also be applied to other elements like p or div.

Support for this technique can be limiting because Internet Explorer 6 for Windows and previous versions will not create a hover effect on an element other than a link.

See Also

The CSS 2.1 specification for dynamic pseudo-classes at *http://www.w3.org/TR/CSS21/selector.html#dynamic-pseudo-classes.*

8.10   Sample Design: An Elegant Calendar

Great for organization, calendars enable us to schedule lunches, remember birthdays, and plan honeymoons. As designers, we can think of all those months, dates, and appointments as tabular data.

If you display your calendar as a generic HTML table, chances are the table looks rather plain, and if it contains numerous events then it probably looks somewhat convoluted as well. In this design, we use CSS to create a calendar that is more legible than what you can create by using plain vanilla HTML.

First, take a look at Figure 8-10, which shows the markup for the calendar without styles.

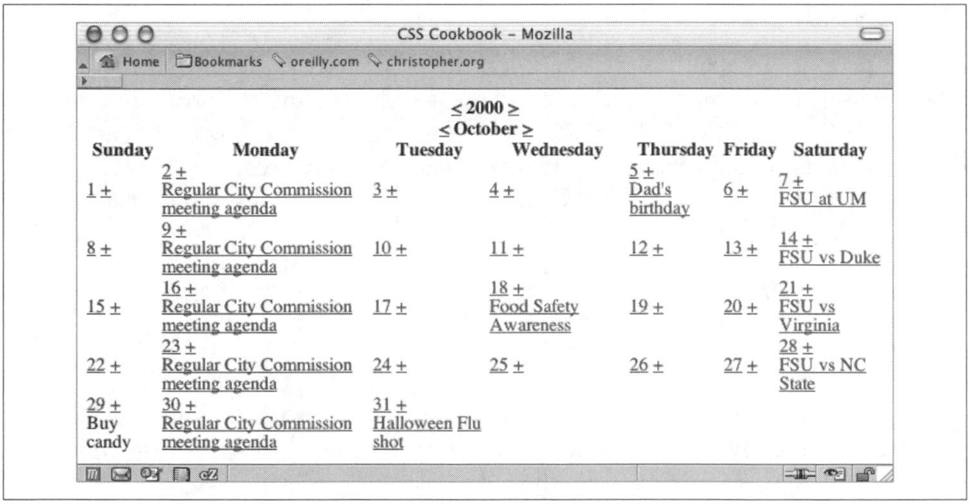

Figure 8-10. The calendar without styles

Next, look at the markup itself to see how it's set up. As you saw in Recipe 8.1, the cellspacing attribute needs to be set in the table element:

```
<table cellspacing="0">
```

Now, set the first three rows of table headers, th, containing the year, month, and days, in their own rows within their own table headers:

```
<tr>
 <th colspan="7" id="year">
  <a href="year.html?previous">&lt;</a> 2000 <a
href="year.html?next">&gt;</a>
 </th>
</tr>
 <tr>
  <th colspan="7" id="month">
   <a href="month.html?previous">&lt;</a> October <a
href="month.html?next">&gt;</a>
  </th>
 </tr>
 <tr id="days">
 <th>Sunday</th>
 <th>Monday</th>
 <th>Tuesday</th>
 <th>Wednesday</th>
 <th>Thursday</th>
 <th>Friday </th>
 <th>Saturday</th>
 </tr>
```

The first date is October 1, which in this calendar falls on a Sunday. To signify that Sundays and Saturdays are days of the weekend, use a class selector in the td element.

In each date of the month there is a link on the date itself (which would, in theory, take the user to a detailed listing of the day) as well as a link to add more events to the day. Wrap these two links in a div element so that when new events are added there is a clear division between the two sections in the table cell:

```
<tr>
 <td class="weekend">
  <div>
   <a href="1.html" class="date">1</a>
   <a href="add.html" class="addevent">+</a>
  </div>
 </td>
```

The next date, October 2, has an event listed. The event is marked up as a link and placed below the div containing the date and the addevent links (because October 2 is a weekday, the weekend class isn't applied to the td element):

```
<td>
 <div>
  <a href="2.html" class="date">2</a>
```

```
      <a href="add.html" class="addevent">+</a>
    </div>
    <a href="16.html?id=1" class="event">Regular City
Commission meeting agenda</a>
   </td>
```

The rest of the markup follows a similar structure:

```
  <td>
   <div>
    <a href="3.html" class="date">3</a>
    <a href="add.html" class="addevent">+</a>
   </div>
  </td>
  <td>
    <div>
     <a href="4.html" class="date">4</a>
     <a href="add.html" class="addevent">+</a>
    </div>
  </td>
  <td>
   <div>
    <a href="5.html" class="date">5</a>
    <a href="add.html" class="addevent">+</a>
   </div>
   <a href="5.html?id=1" class="event">Dad's birthday</a>
  </td>
  <td>
    <div>
     <a href="6.html" class="date">6</a>
     <a href="add.html" class="addevent">+</a>
    </div>
  </td>
  <td class="weekend">
    <div>
     <a href="7.html" class="date">7</a>
     <a href="add.html" class="addevent">+</a>
    </div>
    <a href="7.html?id=1" class="event">FSU at UM</a>
  </td>
 </tr>

 [...]

 <tr>
  <td class="weekend">
    <div>
     <a href="29.html" class="date">29</a>
     <a href="add.html" class="addevent">+</a>
    </div>
    <div class="event">Buy candy</div>
  </td>
  <td>
    <div>
```

```
      <a href="30.html" class="date">30</a>
      <a href="add.html" class="addevent">+</a>
    </div>
    <a href="16.html?id=1" class="event">Regular City
Commission meeting agenda</a>
  </td>
  <td>
    <div>
      <a href="31.html" class="date">31</a>
      <a href="add.html" class="addevent">+</a>
    </div>
    <a href="31.html?id=1" class="event">Halloween</a>
    <a href="31.html?id=2" class="event">Flu shot</a>
  </td>
  <td>
   <div class="emptydate"> </div>
  </td>
  <td>
   <div class="emptydate"> </div>
  </td>
  <td>
   <div class="emptydate"> </div>
  </td>
  <td class="weekend">
   <div class="emptydate"> </div>
  </td>
 </tr>
</table>
```

With the calendar marked up, you can begin setting up the styles. First, apply the styles to the table and links. The width of the table is set to 100% and the border model (see Recipe 8.2) is set to collapse, the common model web designers are used to and that most browsers get right in their CSS implementations; the underline decoration is turned off (see Figure 8-11):

```
table {
 width: 100%;
 border-collapse: collapse;
}
td a:link, td a:visited {
 text-decoration: none;
}
```

Next, set up the styles for the first three rows of the table. The rows are marked with ID selectors because you want the styles to show up only once in the document. Stylize these rows in a straightforward manner, using the monospace font for the

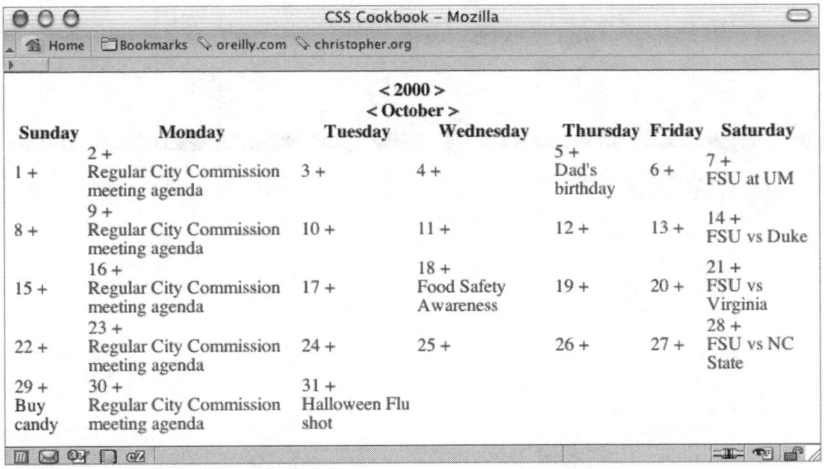

Figure 8-11. Underline decoration of the links removed

heading font and then decreasing the font sizes, with the month sized the largest (see Figure 8-12):

```
#year {
 font-family: monospace;
 font-size: 1.5em;
 padding: 0;
 margin: 0;
}
#month {
 font-family: monospace;
 font-size: 2em;
 padding: 0;
 margin: 0;
}
#days {
 background-color: black;
 color: white;
 font-family: monospace;
 width: 75px;
}
```

Now it's time to stylize the dates and add event links in each cell. To reproduce the box date effect seen in most calendars, place a border to the right and bottom of the text and float the content to the left.

You want the add event links to be close to the dates. Floating the link to the right means the link will be positioned next to the date of the following day. By floating

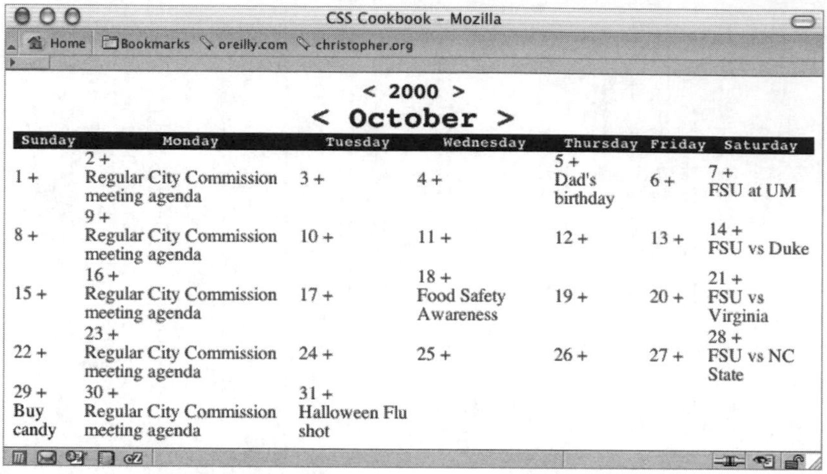

Figure 8-12. Styling the first three rows

the add event link to the left, you are telling the user that the plus sign means add an event for that particular day (see Figure 8-13):

```
.date {
 border-right: 1px solid black;
 border-bottom: 1px solid black;
 font-family: monospace;
 text-decoration: none;
 float: left;
 width: 1.5em;
 height: 1.5em;
 background-color: white;
 text-align: center;
}
.addevent {
 display: block;
 float: left;
 width: 1em;
 height: 1em;
 text-align: center;
 background-color: #666;
 color: white;
 font-weight: bold;
 text-decoration: none;
}
```

Now it's time to look at how the event listings can be stylized. Because the previous links are floated, you need to create a visible break and move the events below the date.

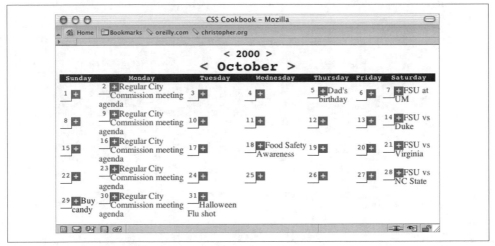

Figure 8-13. Styles introduced to the date and add event links

Setting the clear property to both achieves this visual break. The clear property is used to indicate which sides of an element should not be positioned next to a floated element. In this case, you don't want the left side to run next to the date and add event links. However, just in case the design changes in the future and the dates are positioned on the opposite side, use a value of both instead of left.

Next, change the display of the link to block and place padding on the bottom (see Figure 8-14). You're making these changes to prevent multiple events in a table cell from running into each other. Also, the padding acts as a nice visual buffer, allowing the eye to easily discern between two events:

```
.event {
 clear: both;
 padding-left: 1em;
 padding-bottom: .75em;
 display: block;
}
```

To each table cell, apply a width of 14%. You're using 14% because 7 (representing the 7 sections of the calendar, or days of the week) goes into 100 (representing 100% of the viewport) approximately 14 times. Also, place a white border on all sides of the cell and position all the content to the top with the vertical-align property (see Figure 8-15):

```
td {
 width: 14%;
 background-color: #ccc;
 border: 1px solid white;
 vertical-align: top;
}
```

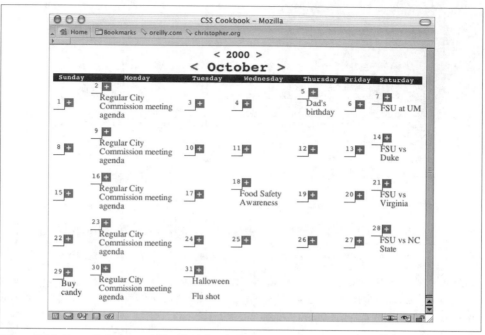

Figure 8-14. Event links treated like block-level elements

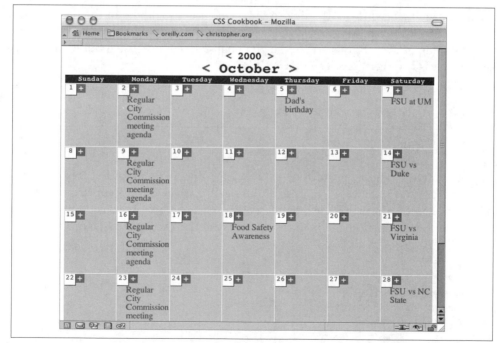

Figure 8-15. The content in each of the cells moved to the top

Make the background color of the weekend dates darker than that used for the week-day dates (see Figure 8-16):

```
.weekend {
 background-color: #999;
}
```

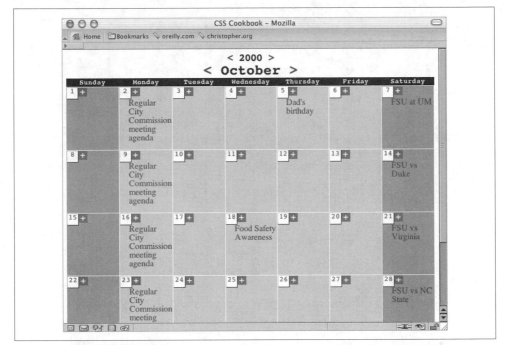

Figure 8-16. The weekend days marked with a darker gray background color

Slightly gray out the look of the remaining days in the calendar (see Figure 8-17):

```
.emptydate {
 border-right: 1px solid #666;
 border-bottom: 1px solid #666;
 font-family: monospace;
 text-decoration: none;
 float: left;
 width: 1.5em;
 height: 1.5em;
 background-color: #ccc;
 text-align: center;
}
```

For the current day (in this example the current day is the 27th), place a 2-pixel black border around the box:

```
#today {
 border: 2px solid black;
}
```

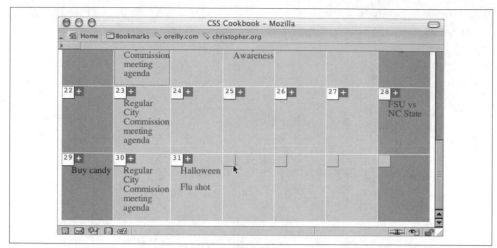

Figure 8-17. Empty dates for the next month stylized

And with that, the calendar is complete; check out Figure 8-18.

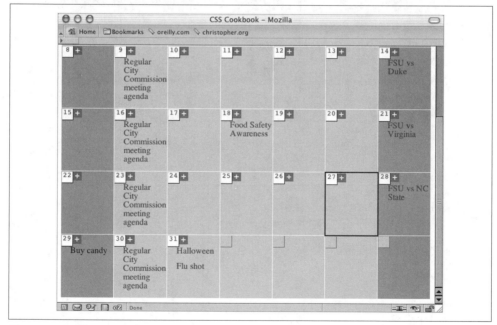

Figure 8-18. The current date in the calendar with a darker border

Page Layouts

9.0 Introduction

One of the last frontiers in CSS-enabled design was creating the page layout.

For a long time, web developers have been using HTML tables to create their layouts, often nesting tables to create multicolumn, multilevel layouts. Nested HTML tables render well in older browsers like Netscape Navigator 4 where CSS support, if present, is barely noticeable.

HTML tables and other HTML elements, however, should be tools used to mark up content and not used to construct unwieldy page layouts. The ideal solution is to have HTML represent the structure of the content at an intellectual abstract level and let CSS determine how to present the content.

This approach of letting CSS do the heavy lifting brings many advantages. Meaningful content that was once trapped under so many nested tables and images is now placed within meaningful heading and paragraph tags, so search engine rankings improve.

Also file sizes diminish noticeably as do maintenance headaches. Launching a complete redesign of a web site becomes a snap with CSS, when it used to take hours and sometimes days with HTML tables.

This chapter discusses the many ways in which you can create column layouts—including simple one-column layouts, four-column layouts, and everything in between.

9.1 Building a One-Column Layout

Problem

You want to build a layout that consists of one main column, as in Figure 9-1.

Figure 9-1. One-column page reinforced by increased margin

Solution

Apply a percentage value to the left and right margins of the web document's body element:

```
body {
  margin-left: 15%;
  margin-right: 15%;
}
```

Discussion

When you apply a percentage value to the left and right margins of the body, the column width becomes flexible. This allows the content to stretch to the width of the user's browser.

To create a fixed-width column, use the `width` property for the body element:

```
body {
  width: 600px;
}
```

This technique aligns the column to the left side of the user's browser. If you want to center a column with a fixed width, wrap a div element around the entire contents of the web document with a specific, unique id attribute such as a frame:

```
<div id="frame">
 [...]
</div>
```

Then, in the CSS rules, apply a 50% value to the left padding of the body:

```
body {
 width: 600px;
 padding-left: 50%;
}
```

Through an id selector, set the width of the column, and then set a negative left margin equal to half the column width:

```
#frame {
 /* set the width of the column */
 width: 600px;
 margin-left: -300px;
}
```

You may think the answer is to just set the left and right margins to auto:

```
#frame {
 width: 600px;
 margin-left: auto;
 margin-right: auto;
}
```

This straightforward approach doesn't work in Internet Explorer for Windows, however. The solution uses a workaround that works in all major browsers.

See Also

Recipe 4.3 on centering elements in a web document; Recipe 6.8 on horizontal tab navigation.

9.2   Building a Two-Column Layout

Problem

You want to create a two-column layout with columns that resize to the width of the browser, as in Figure 9-2.

Solution

First, mark up the content with div elements by using the id attributes that contain appropriate values (see Figure 9-3).

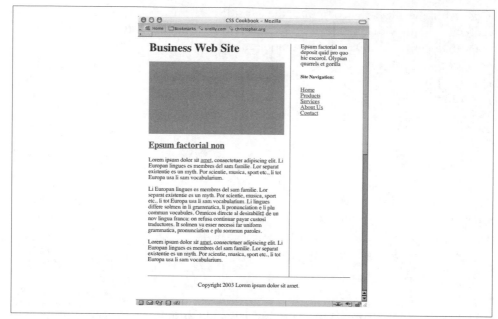

Figure 9-2. Two-column layout achieved through CSS

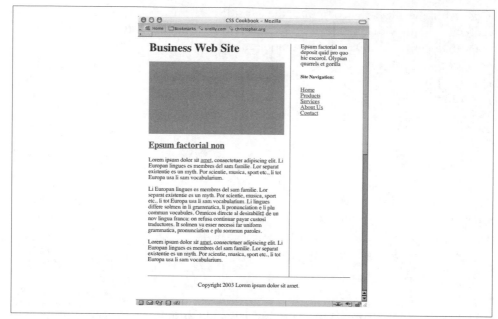

Figure 9-3. The default rendering of the page

For demonstration purposes, the values of the id attributes are used to show where the content is displayed when CSS is used. Semantic values would be preferred, like `mainContent` or `sidebar`, instead of using values that represent their placement on the page:

```
<div id="columnLeft">
 [...]
</div>
<div id="columnRight">
 [...]
</div>
<div id="footer">
 [...]
</div>
```

Then, in CSS, use the `float` property to move the contents of the left column to the left, and set a width that is two-thirds the web document's width:

```
#columnLeft {
  float: left;
  width: 67%;
  background: #fff;
  margin-top: 0;
  margin-right: 1.67em;
  border-right: 1px solid black;
  padding-top: 0;
  padding-right: 1em;
  padding-bottom: 20px;
}
```

The right column wraps around the contents of the left column. On the right column, set the top of the margin and padding to 0, allowing the column and the first element in it to become level with the left column:

```
#columnRight {
  padding-left: 2em;
  margin-top: 0;
  padding-top: 0;
}
h1 {
  margin-top: 0;
  padding-top: 0;
}
```

To display the footer at the bottom of the web document, set the `clear` property to both:

```
#footer {
  clear: both;
  padding-bottom: 1em;
  border-top: 1px solid #333;
  text-align: center;
}
```

Discussion

The `float` property is similar to the `align` attribute that is used in HTML to allow text and other elements to flow around an image:

```
<img src="this.jpg" width="250" height="150" hspace="7" vspace="7"
alt="example" align="right" />
```

Once the image has been set to align to either the right or left, the content around the image flows to the opposite side of the image's alignment. For example, an image aligned to the right forces content to flow around the image on the left side (see Figure 9-4). With CSS, floats provide a similar function, except they offer more exacting control over the presentation by using borders, margins, padding, and other properties.

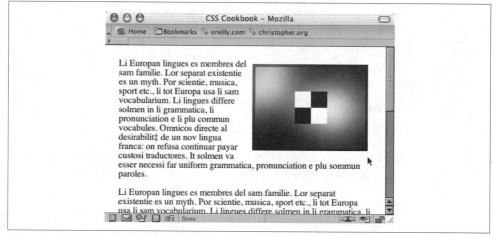

Figure 9-4. Text wrapping around an image set to right alignment

To make sure the content that comprises the footer is placed at the bottom of the columns, set the `clear` property to a value of `both`. When you set the value to `both`, the browser understands that the content of the footer isn't flowing around the floated left column and positions it below (or past) any floated elements.

The only caveat to this technique for creating a two-column layout is that the content in the left column needs to be longer than the content in the right column. Because the content in the left column appears first in the document, the content in the right column wraps around the left column. Too much content in the column that doesn't float results in the anomaly that you see in Figure 9-5.

Figure 9-5. Unwanted wrapping of text under the left column

A method for fixing this problem is to set off the left margin or padding on the right column element so that the column width is at least maintained after the content flows below the float:

```
#mainColumn {
  width: 400px;
  /* Enough padding to compensate for the left column */
  padding-left: 200px;
}
#navigation {
  float: left;
  width: 175px;
}
```

If you want to have the columns reversed (see Figure 9-6), switch the order of the columns by using the following markup:

```
<div id="columnRight">
 [...]
</div>
<div id="columnLeft">
 [...]
</div>
<div id="footer">
 [...]
</div>
```

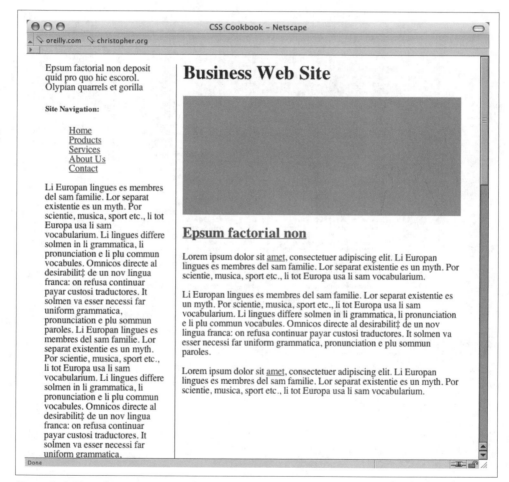

Figure 9-6. The columns are reversed

Then apply the following CSS to the columns:

```
#columnRight {
 float: right;
 width: 67%;
```

```
  padding-bottom: 20px;
  padding-top: 0;
}
#columnLeft {
 width: 29%;
 padding-right: 1em;
 border-right: 1px solid black;
 padding-top: 0;
}
```

 Note that using id values like columnRight and columnLeft are used in this solution to help the reader understand readily which column is being styled. However, this is a bad technique for best practices. Instead, id values should be semantically describing the content. In other words, the values represent the content that is contained within the div element, like navigation or advertisement.

See Also

Recipe 9.3 for a two-column layout with fixed widths; Jeffrey Zeldman's "From Table Hacks to CSS Layout: A Web Designer's Journal" for a background on this Solution at *http://www.alistapart.com/articles/journey/*.

9.3   Building a Two-Column Layout with Fixed-Width Columns

Problem

You want to create a two-column layout with fixed-width columns.

Solution

First, mark up the content with div elements by using the id attributes that contain appropriate values representing their placement on the page (see Figure 9-7):

```
<div id="header">
 [...]
</div>
<div id="columnLeft">
 [...]
</div>
<div id="columnRight">
 [...]
</div>
<div id="footer">
 [...]
</div>
```

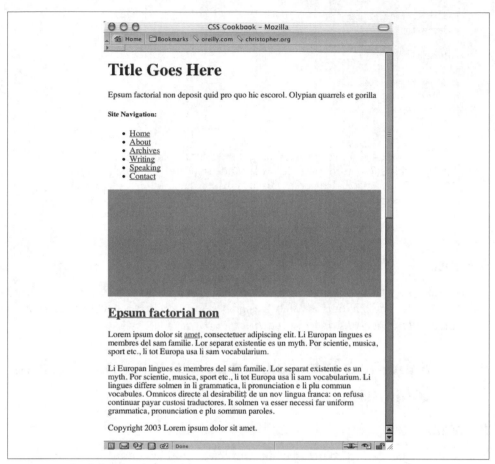

Figure 9-7. The default rendering of the page

Using the float property, set the width of the left column to a length unit rather than to percentages. Also, set the width of the entire document to a length unit (see Figure 9-8):

```
body {
 margin: 0;
 padding: 0;
 font-family: Georgia, Times, "Times New Roman", serif;
 color: black;
 width: 600px;
 border-right: 1px solid black;
}
#header {
 background-color: #666;
 border-bottom: 1px solid #333;
}
#columnLeft {
 float: left;
 width: 160px;
```

```
  margin-left: 10px;
  padding-top: 1em;
}
#columnRight {
  padding-top: 1em;
  margin: 0 2em 0 200px;
}
#footer {
  clear: both;
  background-color: #ccc;
  padding-bottom: 1em;
  border-top: 1px solid #333;
  padding-left: 200px;
}
```

Figure 9-8. The two-column layout enabled by CSS

Discussion

By default, block-level elements stretch to the width of their containers. If the browser window is small, the block-level elements shrink—in other words, text inside the content wraps into narrow columns.

However, when you use length units rather than percentages, the width of the columns becomes fixed. Even as a browser window shrinks or expands, the column widths remain fixed.

To keep the width of the left column fixed while enabling the main column to stretch, simply remove the `width` property assigned to the body element.

If you want to have the columns reversed as like the ones in Figure 9-9, reorder the content with the following markup:

```
<div id="header">
 [...]
</div>
<div id="columnRight">
 [...]
</div>
<div id="columnLeft">
 [...]
</div>
<div id="footer">
 [...]
</div>
```

Note that using `id` values like `columnRight` and `columnLeft` are used in this solution to help the reader understand readily which column is being styled. However, this is a bad technique for best practices. Instead, `id` values should be semantically describing the content. In other words, the values represent the content that is contained within the `div` element, like navigation or advertisement.

Then use the following updated CSS rules:

```
#columnLeft {
 width: 340px;
 margin-left: 10px;
 margin-top: 1em;
}
#columnRight {
 float: right;
 width: 200px;
}
#footer {
 clear: both;
 background-color: #ccc;
```

```
    padding-bottom: 1em;
    border-top: 1px solid #333;
    padding-left: 10px;
}
```

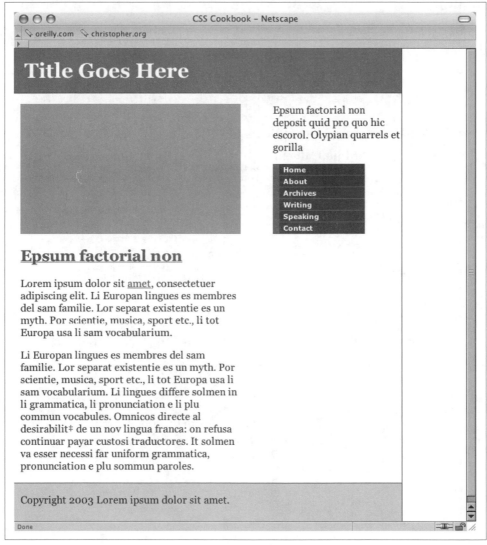

Figure 9-9. The columns are reversed

See Also

Recipe 9.2 on creating a two-column layout with flexible-width columns.

9.4   Creating a Flexible Multicolumn Layout with Floats

Problem

You want to create a three-column layout with columns that resize to the width of the browser, like the one in Figure 9-10.

Figure 9-10. Three-column layout achieved through CSS

Solution

First, mark up the content with div elements by using the id attributes that contain appropriate values representing their placement on the page (see Figure 9-11):

```
<div id="header">
 [...]
</div>
<div id="columnLeft">
 [...]
</div>
<div id="columnMain">
 [...]
</div>
<div id="columnRight">
 [...]
</div>
<div id="footer">
 [...]
</div>
```

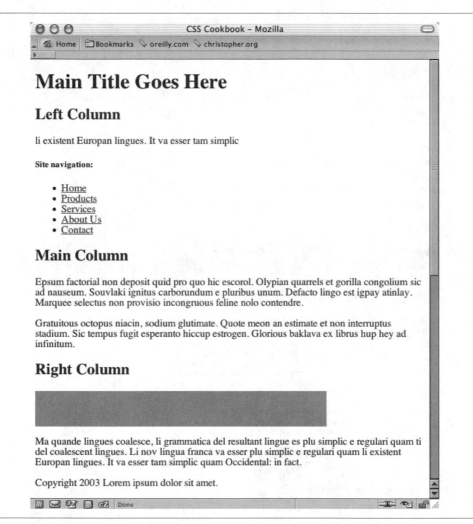

Main Title Goes Here

Left Column

li existent Europan lingues. It va esser tam simplic

Site navigation:

- Home
- Products
- Services
- About Us
- Contact

Main Column

Epsum factorial non deposit quid pro quo hic escorol. Olypian quarrels et gorilla congolium sic ad nauseum. Souvlaki ignitus carborundum e pluribus unum. Defacto lingo est igpay atinlay. Marquee selectus non provisio incongruous feline nolo contendre.

Gratuitous octopus niacin, sodium glutimate. Quote meon an estimate et non interruptus stadium. Sic tempus fugit esperanto hiccup estrogen. Glorious baklava ex libris hup hey ad infinitum.

Right Column

Ma quande lingues coalesce, li grammatica del resultant lingue es plu simplic e regulari quam ti del coalescent lingues. Li nov lingua franca va esser plu simplic e regulari quam li existent Europan lingues. It va esser tam simplic quam Occidental: in fact.

Copyright 2003 Lorem ipsum dolor sit amet.

Figure 9-11. The default rendering of the page

Next, set each column to float to the left, making sure that the width is a percentage. All three values of the columns should equal 100% when added together (see Figure 9-12):

```
#columnRight {
 width: 33%;
 float: left;
 background: white;
 padding-bottom: 1em;
}
#columnLeft {
 width: 20%;
 float:left;
```

```
   background: white;
   padding-bottom: 1em;
   text-align: justify;
}
#columnMain {
 width:47%;
 float:left;
 background: white;
 padding-bottom: 1em;
}
#footer {
 clear: both;
 padding-bottom: 1em;
 border-top: 1px solid #333;
 text-align: center;
}
```

Figure 9-12. An increased width for the main column forcing the right column to wrap underneath

Discussion

This technique works because all columns are set to float to the left and their widths aren't larger than 100%. Setting the floats to the right can flip the columns, but the result is the same.

Be sure to apply margins and padding to the elements within the columns (unless you account for their widths when sizing the columns). If you don't, the columns will expand beyond 100%, forcing one or more columns to wrap underneath each other (refer to Figure 9-12).

See Also

Recipe 9.5 on creating a three-column layout with fixed-width columns; *http://www.realworldstyle.com/nn4_3col_header.html* for information on creating a three-column layout with one flexible-width column and two fixed-width columns.

9.5 Creating a Fixed-Width Multicolumn Layout with Floats

Problem

You want to create a three-column layout with fixed-width columns.

Solution

First, mark up the content with div elements by using the id attributes that contain appropriate values representing their placement on the page (see Figure 9-13):

```
<div id="header">
 [...]
</div>
<div id="columnMain">
 [...]
</div>
<div id="columnLeft">
 [...]
</div>
<div id="columnRight">
 [...]
</div>
<div id="footer">
 [...]
</div>
```

Next, wrap the div elements that compose the main and left columns in another div element and set the value of the id attribute to enclose. Also, wrap another div element around the entire set of div elements, setting the value to frame:

```
<div id="frame">
 <div id="header">
  [...]
 </div>
 <div id="enclose">
  <div id="columnMain">
   [...]
  </div>
  <div id="columnLeft">
   [...]
  </div>
 </div>
```

```
<div id="columnRight">
 [...]
</div>
<div id="footer">
 [...]
</div>
<div>
```

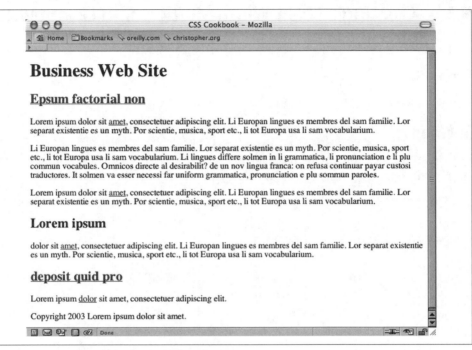

Figure 9-13. The default rendering of the page

Set the width of the page, using an id selector for the frame div element:

```
#frame {
 margin-left: 20px;
 width: 710px;
}
```

Next, set the column div elements as well as the div element with the id value of enclose to float (see Figure 9-14):

```
#columnMain {
 float: right;
 width: 380px;
}
#columnLeft {
 float: left;
 width: 150px;
}
#columnRight {
```

```
  float: right;
  width: 120px;
}
#enclose {
  float:left;
  width:560px;
}
#footer {
  clear: both;
  padding-top: 1em;
  text-align: center;
}
```

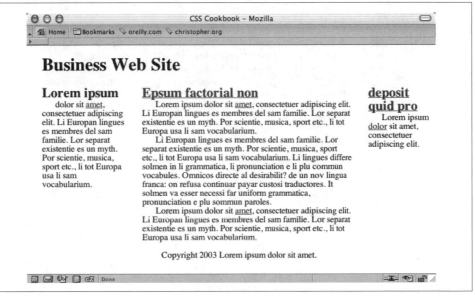

Figure 9-14. Three-column layout with fixed column widths

Discussion

Because the width of the columns is set in pixels, the columns are fixed. To display the columns, you need an extra div element wrapped around the main and left columns. With this extra div element, which contains an id attribute value of enclose, the main and left columns as a whole are set to float to the left. And inside the enclose div, the main column is aligned to the right while the left column is aligned to the left.

See Also

Recipe 9.4 on creating a three-column layout with flexible columns.

9.6   Creating a Flexible Multicolumn Layout with Positioning

Problem

You want to create a four-column layout with columns that resize to the width of the browser (see Figure 9-15).

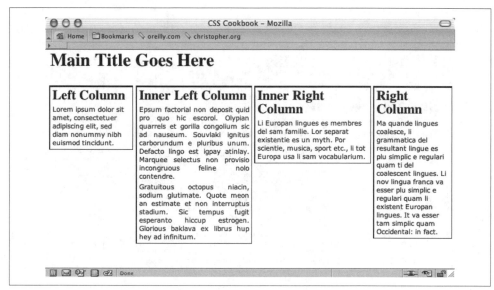

Figure 9-15. Four-column layout with percentage-based widths

Solution

First, mark up the content with div elements by using the id attributes that contain appropriate values representing their placement on the page (see Figure 9-16):

```
<div id="header">
 [...]
</div>
<div id="columnLeft">
 [...]
</div>
<div id="columnInnerLeft">
 [...]
</div>
 [...]
<div id="columnInnerRight">
  [...]
</div>
```

```
[...]
<div id="columnRight">
[...]
</div>
```

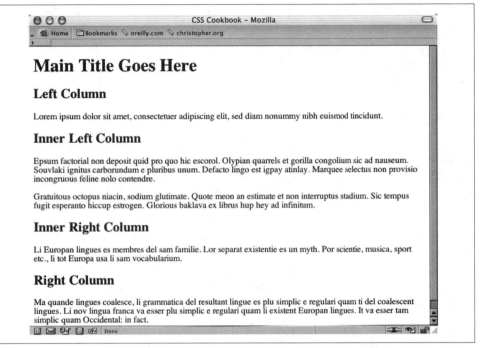

Figure 9-16. The default rendering of the content

Next, use the position property in each column, setting the value to absolute while setting the placement of the columns with the left and top properties:

```
#columnLeft {
 position: absolute;
 left:1%;
 width:20%;
 top: 4em;
 background:#fff;
}
#columnInnerLeft {
 position: absolute;
 left: 22%;
 width: 28%;
 top: 4em;
 background: #fff;
 text-align: justify;
 border-width: 0;
}
#columnInnerRight {
 position: absolute;
```

```
  left: 51%;
  width: 28%;
  top: 4em;
  background: #fff;
}
#columnRight {
  position: absolute;
  left: 80%;
  width: 19%;
  top: 4em;
  background: #fff;
}
```

Discussion

By setting the position property to absolute, you take the element completely out of the flow of the document. When an element is set to float, other elements in a page can flow around the "floated" element. When an element is set to absolute, that element is treated like a ghost.

The default rendering of an element when positioned absolutely is to the upper-left corner of its closest positioned ancestor or the initial containing block. In other words, to position a child element set to absolute within the parent element, first apply a position property of absolute or relative (that is, not static). If other elements are on the page, this creates an overlap of the content, as you see in Figure 9-17.

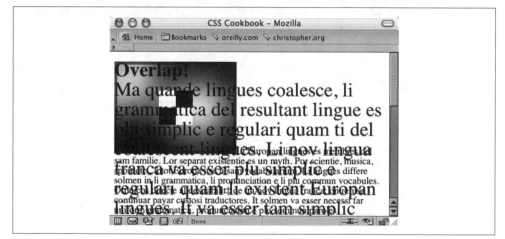

Figure 9-17. Text overlapping an image and other text in a web document

To avoid this problem, use four additional CSS properties that allow the element to be moved into any location: top, left, bottom, and right. Be sure to set the values of the columns to percentages to maintain flexible widths as a user's browser resizes.

Also use percentages as the values for the `left` property to mark the distance away from the left side of a browser's viewport. However, use em units as the values for the top property to compensate for the height of the heading. If you want to use an image for the heading, change the values for `top` to pixels, making sure there is enough room for the graphic header.

While this technique grants freedom in the placement of elements, there are drawbacks to using `absolute` to position elements. In some circumstances, Netscape Navigator 4 loses the location of positioned elements when you resize the window.

Although the placement of columns next to each other can be carried out easily with this technique, the placement of a footer at the bottom of the columns is hard to do unless you know where the columns exactly end at the bottom of the page.

See Also

The CSS 2.1 specification on the `position` property at *http://www.w3.org/TR/CSS21/ visuren.html#propdef-position*; the CSS 2.1 specification on positioning elements set to `absolute` at *http://www.w3.org/TR/CSS21/visuren.html#position-props*; read more about containing blocks at *http://www.w3.org/TR/2003/WD-CSS21-20030915/ visudet.html#containing-block-details*.

9.7 Creating a Fixed-Width Multicolumn Layout with Positioning

Problem

You want to create a four-column layout with fixed-width columns.

Solution

First, mark up the content with `div` elements by using the `id` attributes that contain appropriate values representing their placement on the page:

```
<div id="header">
 [...]
</div>
<div id="columnLeft">
 [...]
</div>
<div id="columnInnerLeft">
 [...]
</div>
 [...]
<div id="columnInnerRight">
  [...]
</div>
```

```
[...]
<div id="columnRight">
[...]
</div>
```

Next, use the position property in each column, setting the value to absolute while setting the placement of the columns with the left and top properties, making sure to use pixels for the units:

```
#columnLeft {
  position: absolute;
  left:5px;
  width:190px;
  top: 44px;
  background:#fff;
}
#columnInnerLeft {
  position: absolute;
  left: 205px;
  width: 190px;
  top: 44px;
  background: #fff;
  text-align: justify;
  border-width: 0;
}
#columnInnerRight {
  position: absolute;
  left: 405px;
  width: 190px;
  top: 44px;
  background: #fff;
}
#columnRight {
  position: absolute;
  left: 605px;
  width: 190px;
  top: 44px;
  background: #fff;
}
```

Discussion

Setting the width of the columns as well as the left and top properties to length units creates the fixed-width columns. This solution is just as easy with two to three or more columns. Remember that anything more than four or five columns may be impractical.

With the solution, the layout is ideal for an image that is equal or less than 44 pixels tall. If you place text within the header, there's the possibility that the text could ruin the layout by making the header appear to go *under* the columns. This phenomenon occurs because the header is within the flow of the document, while the absolute position takes the column out of the flow.

If this is an issue for a design, first wrap a div element around the columns and set the id value to content:

```
<div id="header">
 [...]
</div>
<div id="content">
 <div id="columnLeft">
  [...]
 </div>
 <div id="columnInnerLeft">
  [...]
 </div>
  [...]
 <div id="columnInnerRight">
  [...]
 </div>
  [...]
 <div id="columnRight">
  [...]
 </div>
</div> <!-- end CONTENT -->
```

Then set the CSS rule for the content wrapper to be positioned relatively:

```
#content {
 position: relative;
}
```

That extra step shores up the header as well as removes the top of the columns.

See Also

Recipe 9.3 on creating a fixed-width two-column layout; Recipe 9.5 on creating a fixed-width multicolumn layout with floats.

9.8   Using Floats to Display Columns in Any Order

Problem

You want to develop a system to display content in columns in any order.

Solution

Given the following markup:

```
<div id="container-outer">
 <div id="container">
  <div id="content" class="column">
   <div class="wrap">
    [...]
   </div>
  </div><!-- /END #content -->
```

```
<div id="navigation" class="column">
 <div class="wrap">
  [...]
 </div>
</div><!-- /END #navigation -->

<div id="related-info" class="column">
 <div class="wrap">
  [...]
 </div>
</div><!-- /END #related-info -->
</div><!-- /END #container -->
</div><!-- /END #container-outer -->
```

Apply the following CSS rules:

```
.column {
 float: left;
}

#content {
 margin-left: 20%;
 width: 60%;
}

#navigation {
 margin-left: -80%;
 width: 20%;
}

#related-info {
 width: 19%;
}

/* IEx patches \*/
* html .column {
 display: inline;
}

* html #navigation li {
 height: 1%;
}
/**/
```

This will yield the basic page layout that you see in Figure 9-18, with two narrow, flexible-width sidebars bounding an equally flexible center column.

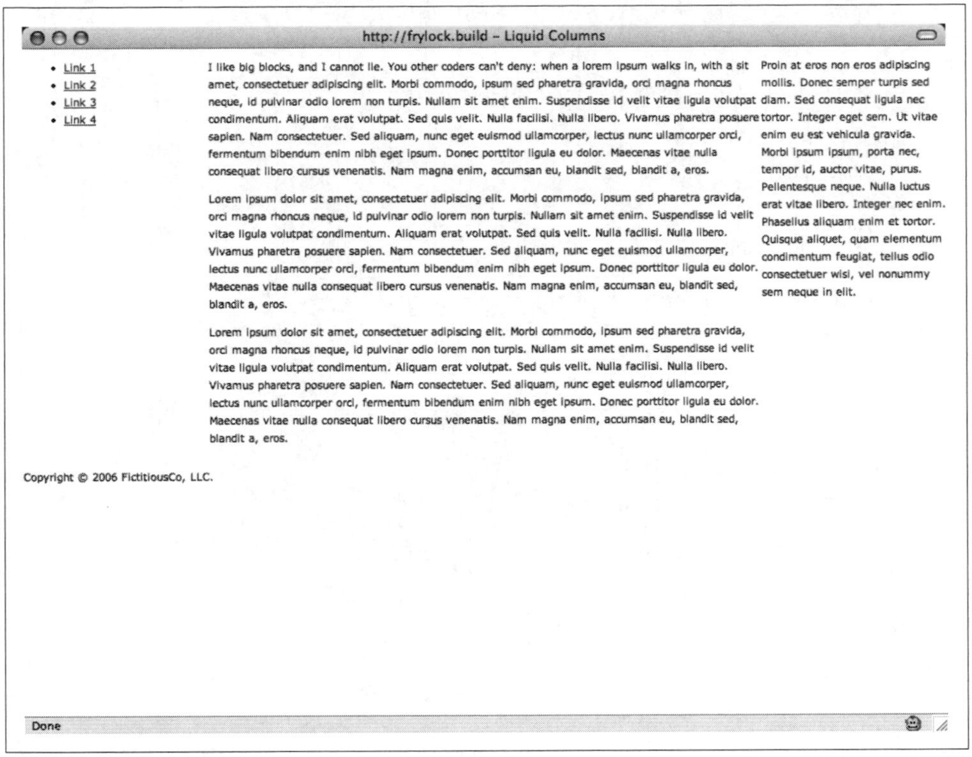

Figure 9-18. Basic formatting of page layout

From this rather bland foundation, you can layer additional CSS on top of it. Adding the following code to your CSS will yield a design like Figure 9-19:

```
body {
  font: normal 62.5%/1.7 Verdana, Geneva, Helvetica, Arial, sans-serif;
  margin: 0;
  padding: 0;
}
#container:after {
  clear: both;
  content: ".";
  display: block;
  height: 0;
  visibility: hidden;
}
#container {
  display: inline-block;
}
/* Hide from MacIE5 \*/
#container {
  display: block;
}
/**/
#container-outer {
```

```css
  background: url("bg-left.gif") repeat-y 20% 0;
}
#container {
  background: url("bg-right.gif") repeat-y 80% 0;
}
.column .wrap {
  padding: 20px;
}
#content .wrap {
  padding: 20px 30px;
}
#content p {
  margin-top: 0;
}
#content p:first-child {
  font: normal 1.4em/1.6 Georgia, Times, "Times New Roman", serif;
}
#content p:first-child:first-line {
  text-transform: uppercase;
}
#navigation ul, #navigation ul li {
  list-style: none;
  margin: 0;
  padding: 0;
}
#navigation ul li {
  margin-bottom: .4em;
}
#navigation li a {
  background: #36C;
  color: #FFF;
  border-left: 7px solid #09F;
  display: block;
  padding: .4em .4em .4em 20px;
  text-decoration: none;
}
#navigation li a:hover {
  border-left: none;
  border-right: 7px solid #09F;
  padding-left: 27px;
}
#related-info {
  color: #555;
  font-style: italic;
}
#copyright {
  border: 1px solid #B2B2B2;
  border-width: 1px 0;
  clear: both;
  padding: 10px 20px;
  text-align: center;
}
#copyright p {
  margin: 0;
}
```

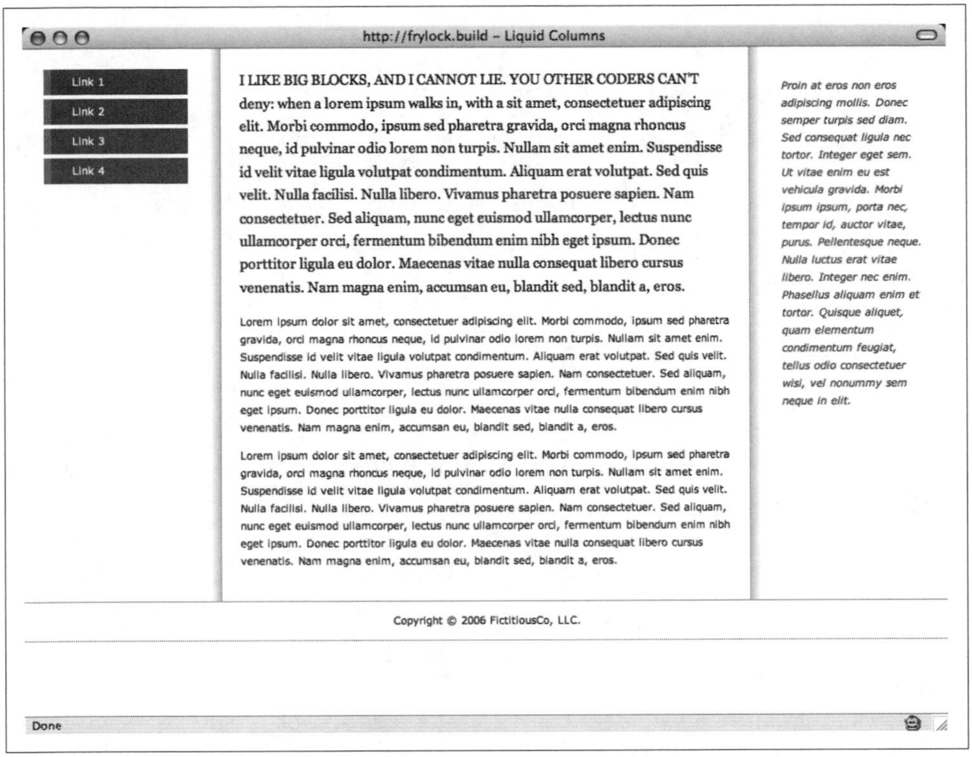

Figure 9-19. Fleshed out design of multicolumn layout

Discussion

The float model has a storied history. The authors of the CSS specification never intended floats to be used for page-level layout control: rather, they were a means to control the flow of content around an object, much as `align="left"` or `align="right"` would cause text to wrap around an `img` element. But despite the specification's original spirit, floats do offer us a powerful and flexible alternative to traditional, table-based layout techniques.

Alex Robinson, a designer, published an influential article on creating the "Any Order Columns" in CSS (*http://www.positioniseverything.net/articles/onetruelayout/*). Robinson's technique allows developers to create multicolumn layouts easily by using floats to display each column in any order, regardless of the order in which those blocks appear in the markup.

The markup

To work with this technique, first you need to establish columns in your markup, like so:

```
<div id="container">
  <div id="content" class="column">
```

```
  [...]
</div><!-- /END #content -->

<div id="navigation" class="column">
  [...]
</div><!-- /END #navigation -->

<div id="related-info" class="column">
  [...]
</div><!-- /END #related-info -->
</div><!-- /END #container -->

<div id="copyright">
  <p>Copyright notice goes here.</p>
</div>
```

Inside each div, place any markup you would like. Figure 9-20 shows what the unstyled document looks like, with a few paragraphs and an unordered list thrown in for good measure.

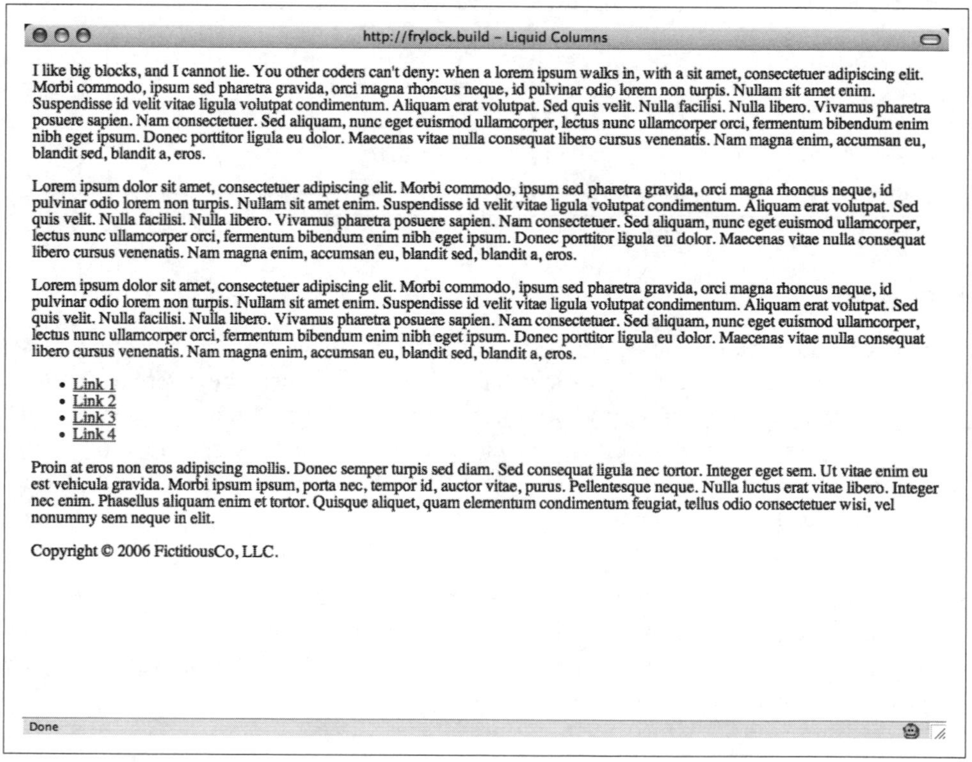

Figure 9-20. Unstyled page layout

From this demonstration so far, a div element is set up for each of your three columns, and each is assigned an id that describes the kind of content that will be placed inside. In this solution, the values for id are content, navigation, and related-info. It would have been just as easy to use center, left, and right, but that wouldn't have been especially forward-thinking: what happens when you change your site's CSS file, and the new design requires the "left" div to appear on the right-hand side of the page?

Defining the columns

With this simple markup structure in place, you can apply a generic float rule to all three column divs:

```
.column {
  float: left;
}
```

As you see in Figure 9-21, the layout does not look drastically different. The copyright text is a bit out of alignment, but the bulk of your page appears as it did before with each column div stacking horizontally. Once dimensions are assigned to these blocks, however, things rapidly change.

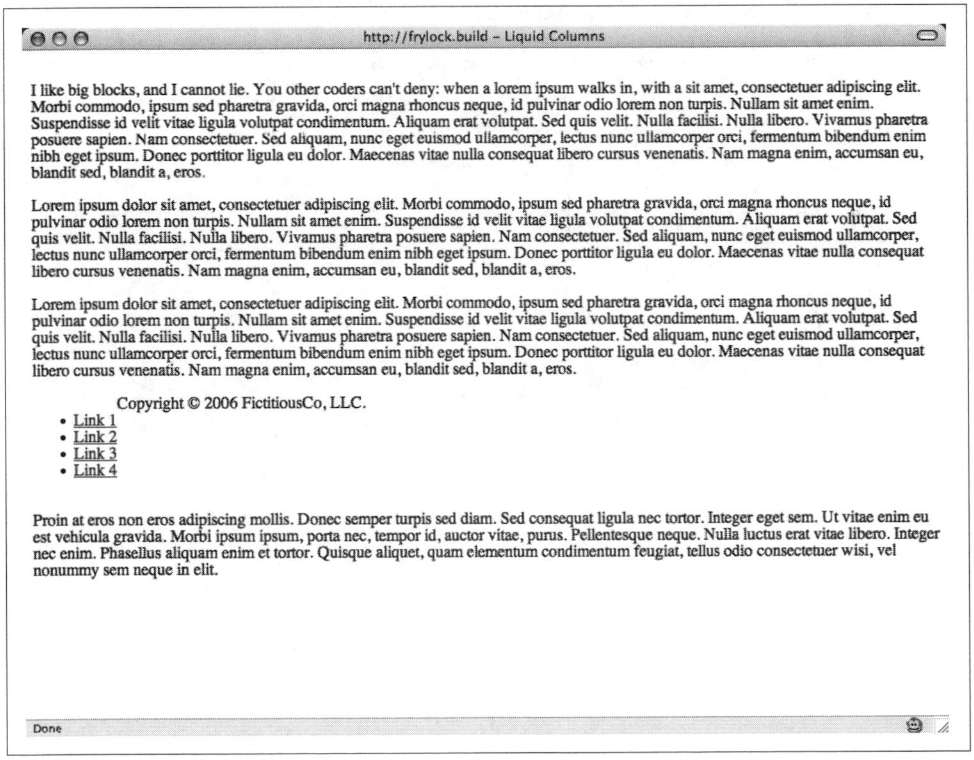

Figure 9-21. The copyright notice has moved

First, start with the content block. To set the block to be 60% of the window width, and the width of the lefthand sidebar to be 20% of the screen, create the following rule:

```
#content {
  margin-left: 20%;
  width: 60%;
}
```

Figure 9-22 shows that the layout is looking a bit odd, but starting to take shape.

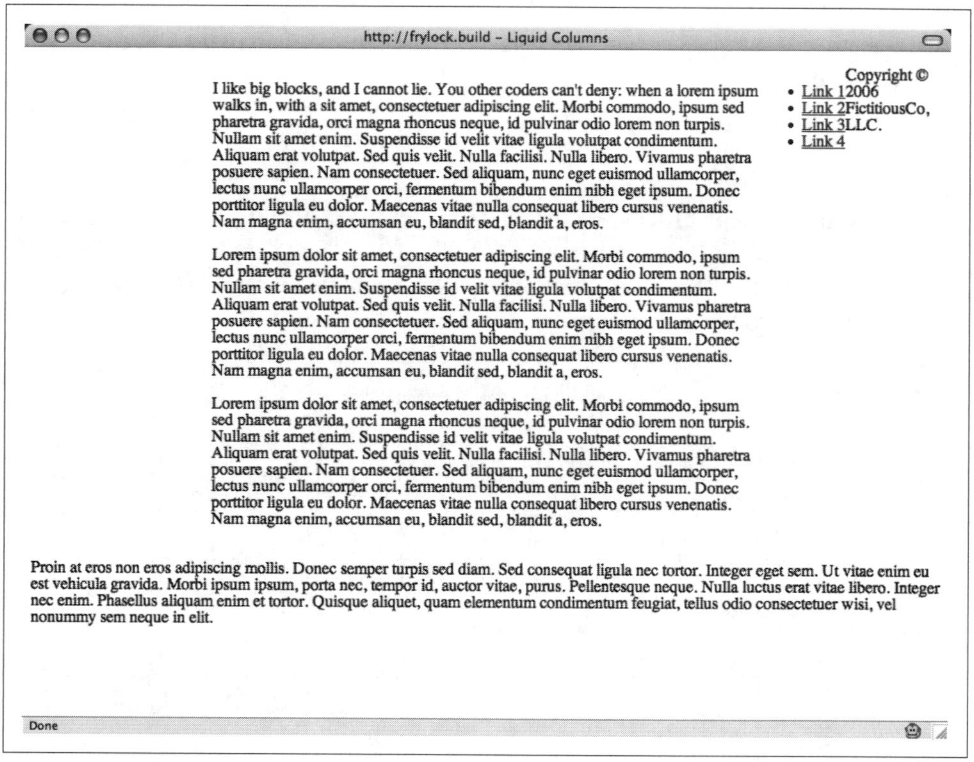

Figure 9-22. Applying styles to the content portion of the layout

By setting a lefthand margin equal to the width of your lefthand sidebar, you've essentially "reserved" some space for it. The next step is to use negative margins to "pull" the navigation div across the content div to the lefthand side of the page:

```
#navigation {
  margin-left: -80%;
  width: 20%;
}
```

The margin-left value applied is a sum of the width of the center column (60%) and its lefthand margin (20%). This pulls the navigation column over to its proper place (see Figure 9-23).

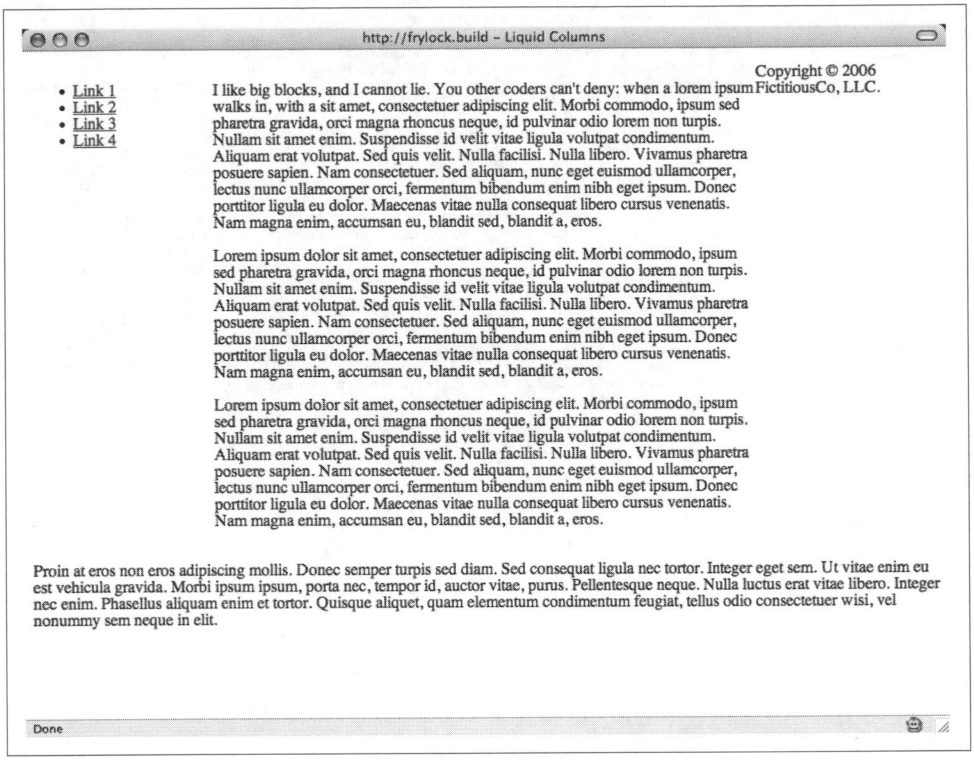

Figure 9-23. The navigation moves to the left column

Now, simply by setting a width on the related-info block, the three-column layout is complete, as shown in Figure 9-24:

```
#related-info {
  width: 20%;
}
```

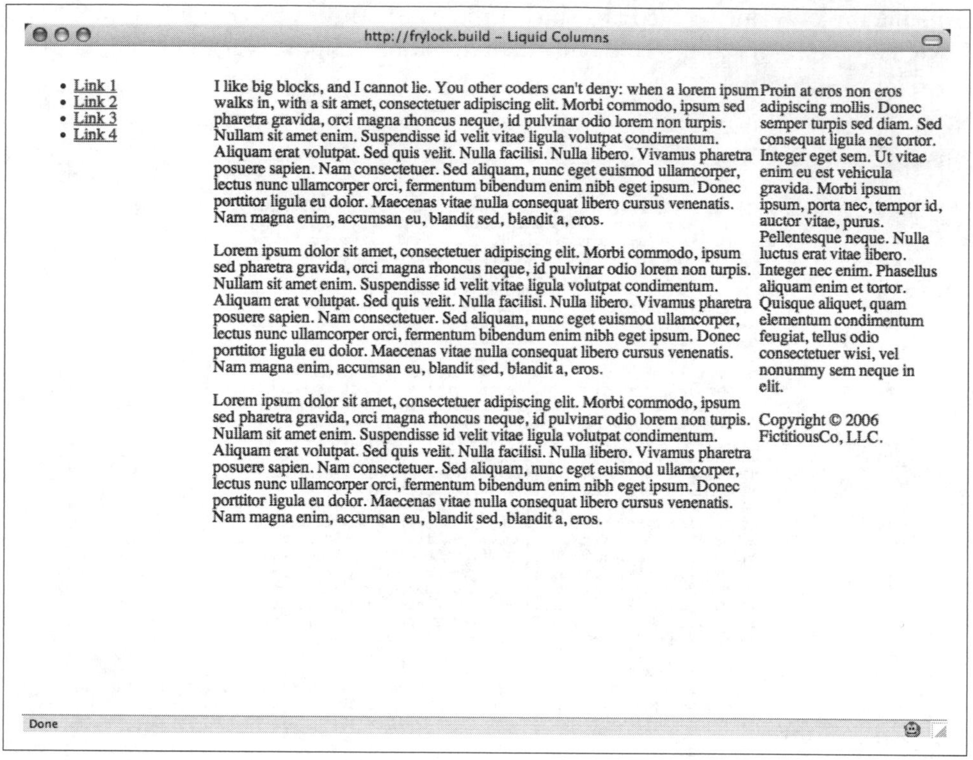

Figure 9-24. Moving the right column content into place

Looks excellent, although the `copyright` div is still a bit off. But with the `clear` property, that's easily fixed (see Figure 9-25):

```
#copyright {
  clear: both;
}
```

Although the layout may look as though your columns are nearly complete, Figure 9-26 shows you that Internet Explorer on Windows needs a little extra attention.

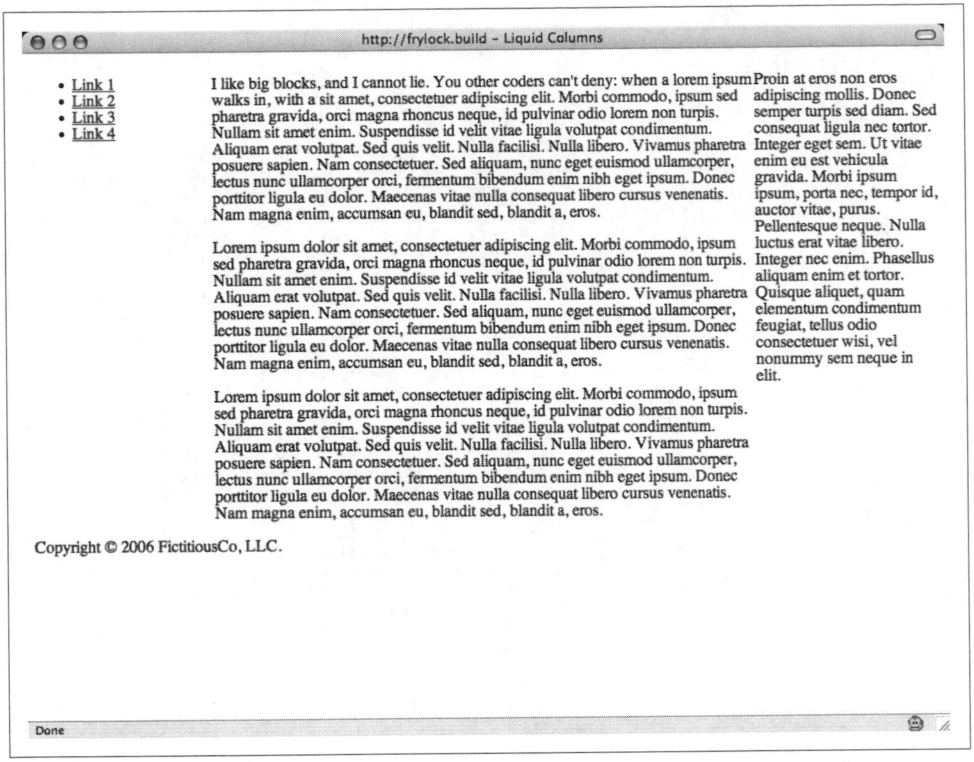

Figure 9-25. Placing the copyright notice at the bottom of the page

Thankfully, this is a documented IE bug known as the "Doubled Float-Margin Bug" (*http://positioniseverything.net/explorer/doubled-margin.html*): essentially, when a margin is applied to a floated box in the same direction as the float, that margin is doubled in size.

Since a lefthand margin is applied to a left-floated element, IE on Windows takes that 20% margin and doubles it to 40%.

Thankfully, the fix is a simple one. By applying `display:inline` to the problematic element, Internet Explorer behaves again. To do this, add the following lines to your CSS:

```
/* IEx patches \*/
* html .column {
  display: inline;
}
/**/
```

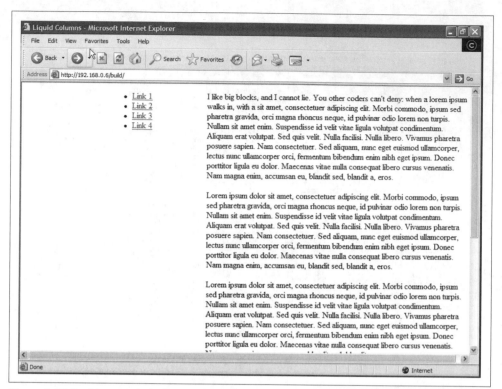

Figure 9-26. Problems with the layout are viewed in Internet Explorer for Windows

The oddly formatted comments and * html prefix ensure that this code is seen by IE on Windows, and IE on Windows alone. And as Figure 9-27 shows, IE is behaving properly.

So you've arrived at last: a flexible, three-column layout template. But where else can you take this?

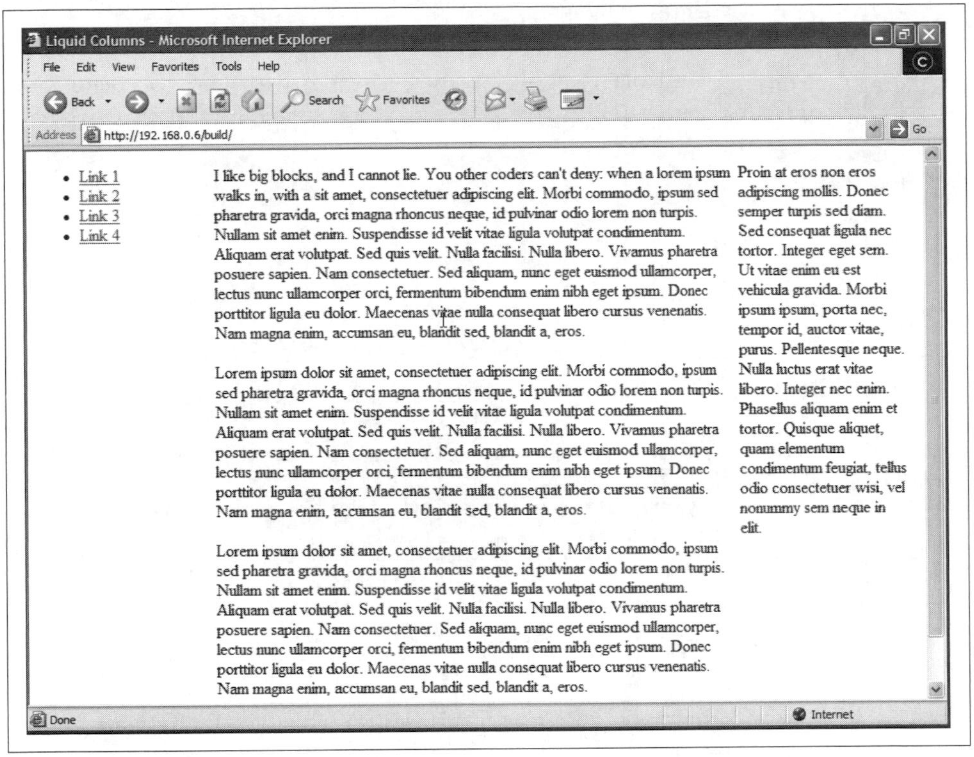

Figure 9-27. The fix is applied so that the layout works in Internet Explorer for Windows

Creating whitespace

The space between the columns is called a *gutter*. To customize this layout by increasing the size of the gutters, an approach would be to apply some margins around the columns. There are a number of ways to achieve this effect, but first start by adding an additional div to each of your columns, like so:

```
<div id="container">
 <div id="content" class="column">
  <div class="wrap">
   [...]
  </div>
 </div><!-- /end #content -->

 <div id="navigation" class="column">
  <div class="wrap">
   [...]
  </div>
 </div><!-- /end #navigation -->

 <div id="related-info" class="column">
  <div class="wrap">
   [...]
  </div>
```

```
</div><!-- /end #related-info -->
</div><!-- /end #container -->
```

With your "wrap" divs in place, apply padding to them with CSS to create more breathing room (see Figure 9-28):

```
.column .wrap {
  padding: 20px;
}

#content .wrap {
  padding: 20px 30px;
}
```

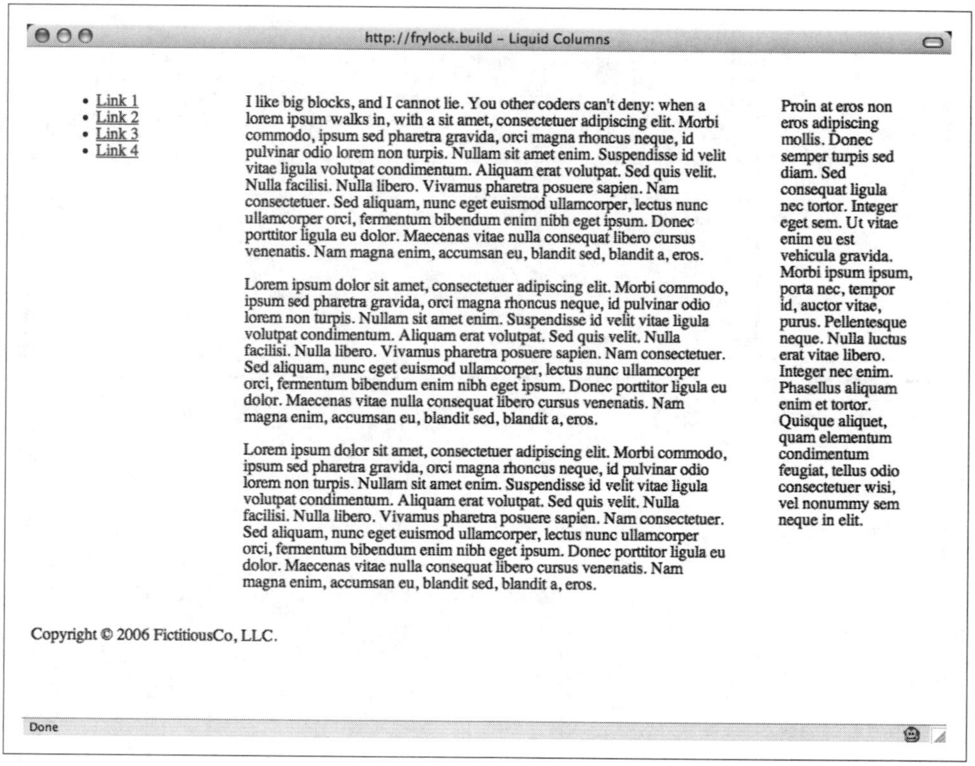

Figure 9-28. Increasing the size of the gutters

Adjusting the order of columns

As you may have noticed by now, the "Any Order Columns" method is grounded in the intelligent use of margins: positive margins are used to reserve space, while negative margins are used to "pull" columns out of their natural position.

Now simplify the CSS for a moment, and remove all the column margins:

```
#content {
  width: 60%;
```

```
}
#navigation {
  width: 20%;
}
#related-info {
  width: 19%;
}
```

As a result, your layout now looks like Figure 9-29, with each column appearing in its natural position in the float order.

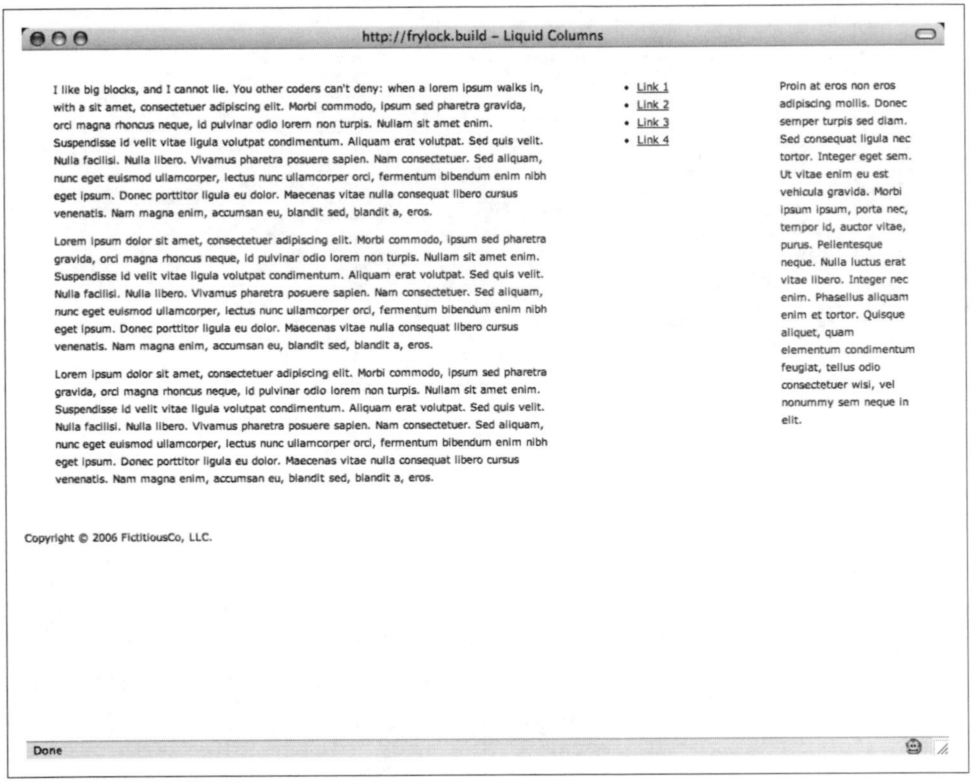

Figure 9-29. Moving the navigation between the columns

By adding a lefthand margin to your navigation div, and then by using a negative lefthand margin to move your related-info div, you can essentially reverse the order of the second two columns. With the following CSS, you're left with a layout like Figure 9-30:

```
#content {
  width: 60%;
}
#navigation {
  margin-left: 20%;
  width: 20%;
```

```
}
#related-info {
  margin-left: -39%;
  width: 19%;
}
```

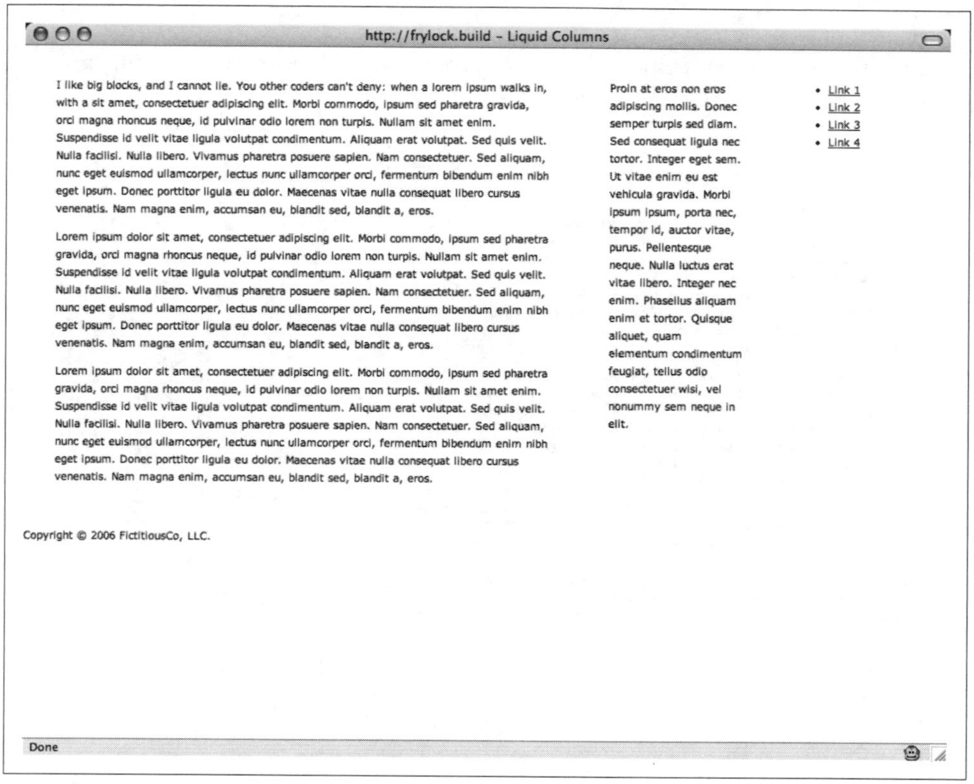

Figure 9-30. Reversing the order to the columns

And to complete the demonstration, place the content column on the righthand side of the page, as shown in Figure 9-31.

To do so, apply the following code:

```
#content {
  margin-left: 40%;
  width: 60%;
}
#navigation {
  margin-left: -100%;
  width: 20%;
}
#related-info {
  margin-left: -80%;
  width: 19%;
}
```

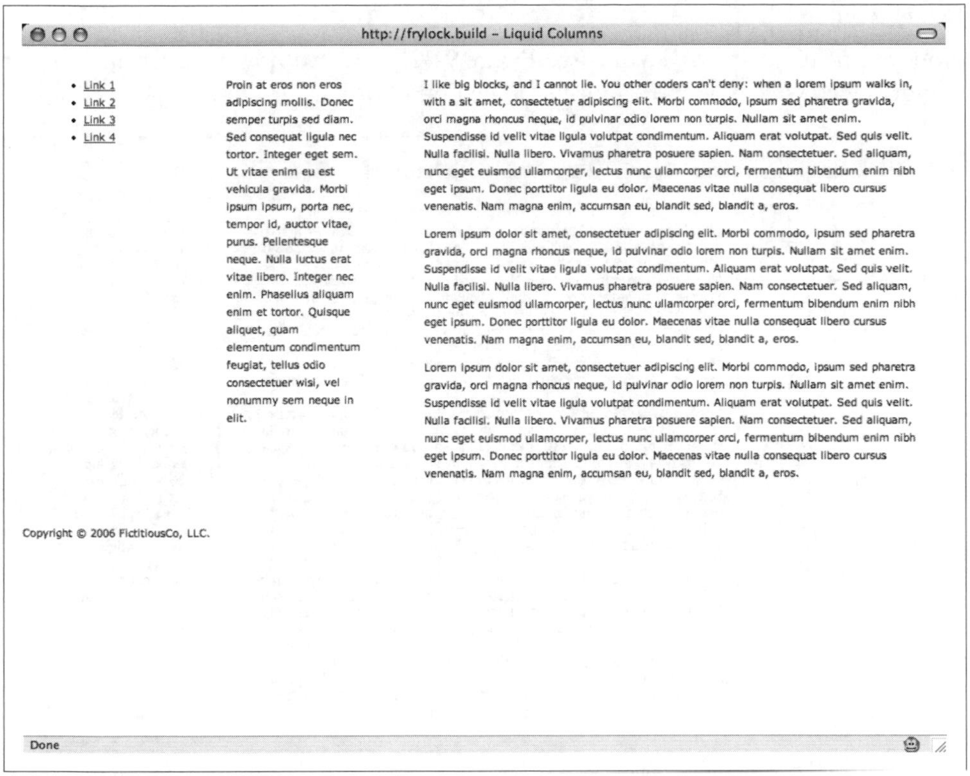

Figure 9-31. Content column moved to the righthand side of the page

As with the first layout, you've applied a margin to the content column in order to "reserve" some whitespace on the lefthand side of our page. Then, you've used negative lefthand margins to pull the navigation and "related information" divs into the proper location.

Page layout algorithm

A simple way to calculate rearranging columns is to follow a somewhat simple algorithm used to calculate the negative margins for a column:

1. For the column you want to determine its negative margin, first calculate the rightmost point for all columns that precedes it in the source code.
2. Then specify the leftmost point for the column.
3. Finally, subtract the rightmost value from the leftmost to give the left margin for the element.

If this technique doesn't work, there's always good ol' trial and error.

Faking columns

Now return to your first layout (see Figure 9-32), and see how you can make your columns feel, well, a bit more polished. The first step? Background images.

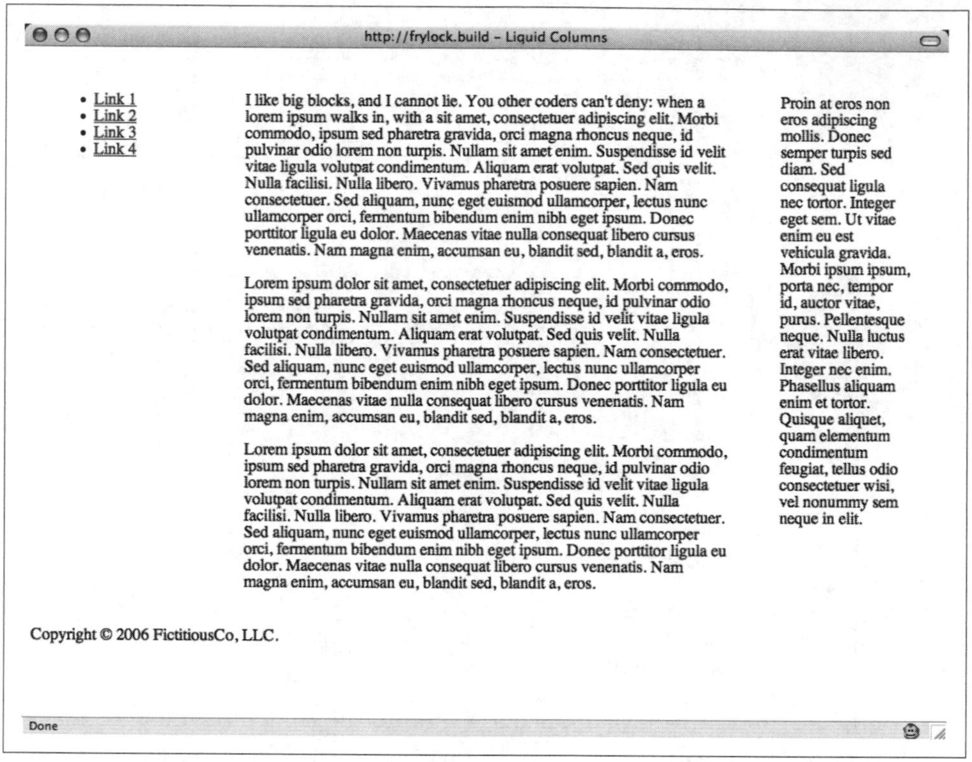

Figure 9-32. *Initial layout awaiting column graphics*

"Faux columns" is a technique developed by web designer Dan Cederholm (*http://alistapart.com/articles/fauxcolumns/*) that utilizes a horizontally repeating background image.

By using one tiled image, Cederholm's method works incredibly well in a fixed-width design: however, the technique's versatility means that it needs only slight modification to work in our fully flexible layout.

First, you need two images, one for each side of the content column. Figure 9-33 shows the lefthand graphic, while Figure 9-34 shows the right.

Figure 9-33. *Graphic for lefthand column*

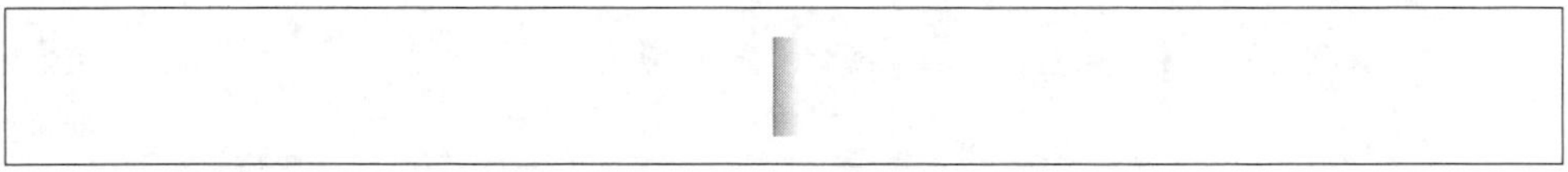

Figure 9-34. Graphic for righthand column

Next, you'll need to wrap your container block in an extra div, like so:

```
<div id="container-outer">
 <div id="container">
  [Rest of template goes here]
 </div>
</div>
```

And finally, you'll need to add the following rules to your style sheet:

```
#container:after {
 clear: both;
 content: ".";
 display: block;
 height: 0;
 visibility: hidden;
}
#container {
 display: inline-block;
}
/*\*/
#container {
 display: block;
}
/**/
/*\*//*/
#container {
 display: inline-block;
}
/**/
#container-outer {
 background: url("bg-left.gif") repeat-y 20% 0;
}
#container {
 background: url("bg-right.gif") repeat-y 80% 0;
}
```

With this code in place, the columns appear as full-length columns, like the ones in Figure 9-35.

From here, feel free to add any typographic styles you'd like; the ones supplied in the Solution section of this recipe will do nicely, and will yield the finished design shown in Figure 9-36.

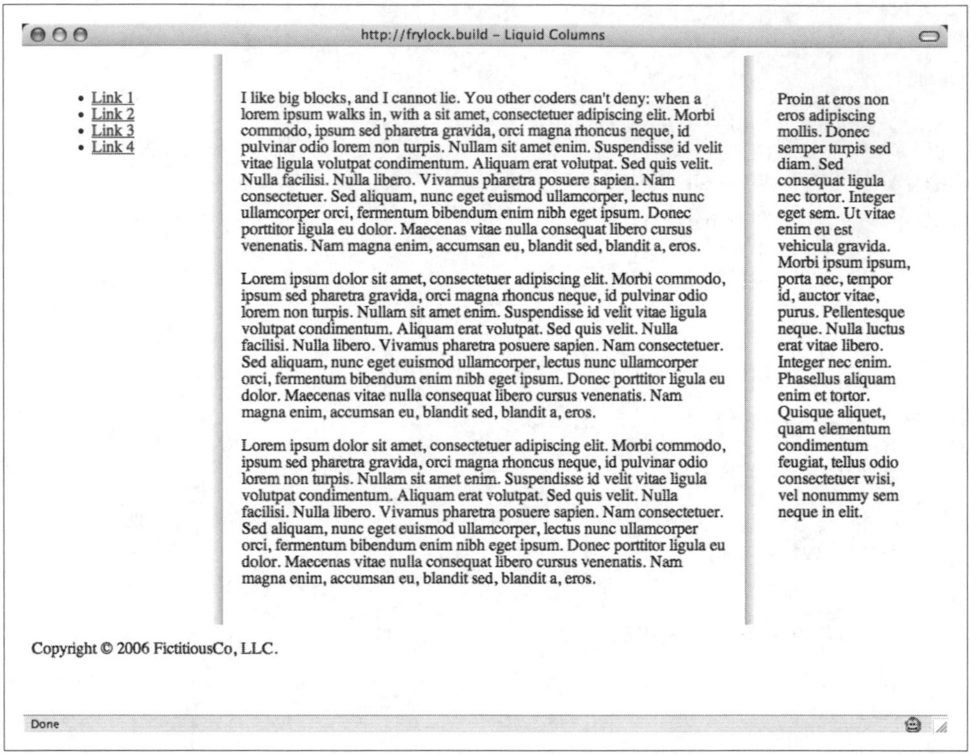

Figure 9-35. Column graphics are applied to layout

An alternative solution

The float model for laying out pages is powerful, but floats can have a rather steep learning curve. As a result, many designers find absolute positioning to be an attractive alternative, enabling them to precisely position the different components of their design with *x*- and *y*-coordinates.

Unfortunately, positioned elements are taken "out of the document flow," which effectively collapses their containing element. As a result, "positioned" designs lack the powerful float concept of clearing, which enables the different parts of your designs to be "context-aware": that is, a footer div (such as the copyright block in the solution, earlier) can be cleared of the floated blocks above it, but not of any positioned elements on the page.

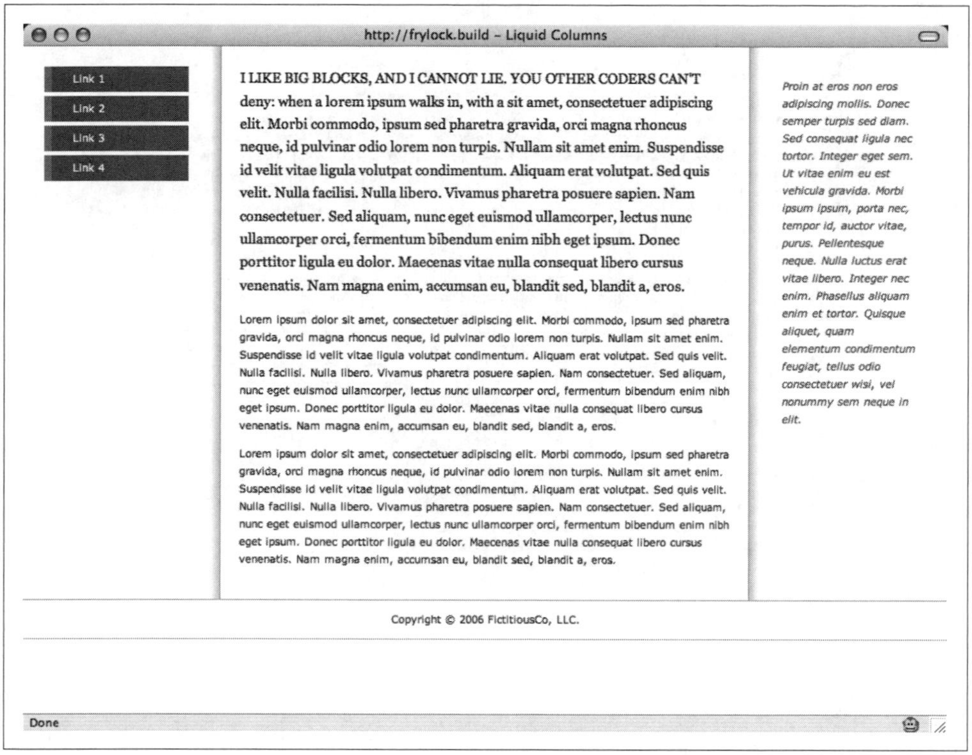

Figure 9-36. Finalized page layout

Shaun Inman, a talented web designer/developer, has written a lean JavaScript function to fix this problem (*http://shauninman.com/plete/2006/05/clearance-position-inline-absolute.php*). When inserted into your web pages, Inman's script will automatically "clear" elements of any other positioned elements on the page (see Figure 9-37).

The only potential drawback to this method is that it does rely on JavaScript being active in the user's browser. But if your content is accessible if you disable JavaScript in your target browsers during testing, then all should be well.

See Also

Recipe 9.9 for designing an asymmetric layout with absolute positioning.

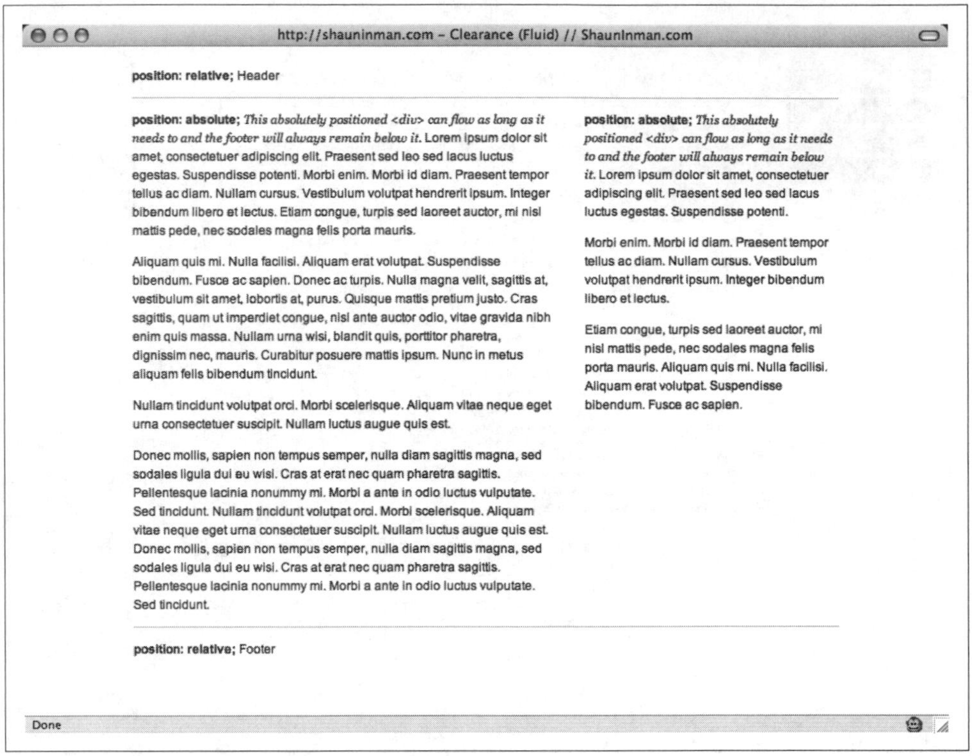

Figure 9-37. Using absolute positioning for a layout

9.9   Designing an Asymmetric Layout

Problem

You want to create a flexible, asymmetric or organic layout, like the one in Figure 9-38.

Solution

First, mark up the content with div elements by using the id attributes that contain appropriate values representing their placement on the page:

```
<div id="header">
 [...]
</div>
<div id="columnSmall">
 [...]
</div>
<div id="columnMain">
 [...]
</div>
```

```
<div id="columnMedium">
[...]
</div>
```

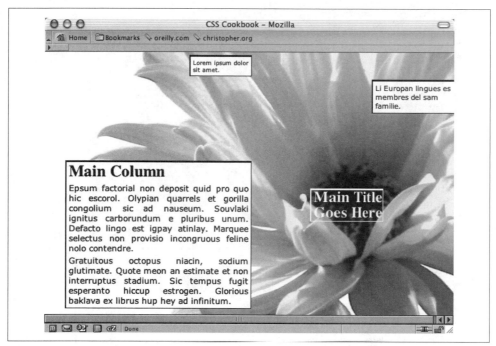

Figure 9-38. The asymmetric placement of the content

Next, use the `position` property in each column, setting the value to `absolute` while setting the placement of the columns with the `left` and `top` properties, using percentages. Also, use percentage values for positioning a background image (see Figure 9-39):

```
body {
 margin:5px 0 0 5px;
 background-image: url(flower5.jpg);
 background-position: 50% 35%;
 background-repeat: no-repeat;
 }
#header {
 position: absolute;
 left: 65%;
 top: 50%;
 width: 125px;
 font-size: small;
}
#columnSmall {
 position: absolute;
 left: 35%;
 width: 15%;
```

```
   top: 1%;
   background: #fff;
   font-size: small;
   }
   #columnMain {
    position: absolute;
    left: 5%;
    width: 45%;
    top: 40%;
    background: #fff;
    text-align: justify;
    border-width: 0;
    font-size: large;
   }
   #columnMedium {
    position: absolute;
    left: 80%;
    width: 20%;
    top: 10%;
    background: #fff;
   }
```

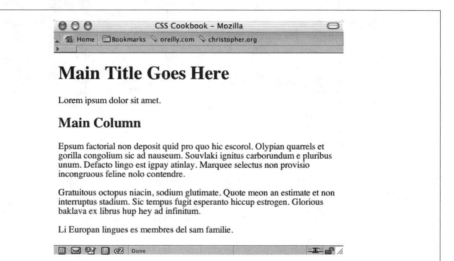

Figure 9-39. The default rendering of the page

Discussion

Although web sites seem to use traditional column layouts, CSS enables web developers to come up with new ways to present their documents. Through the position, top, and left properties, you can break up the content into chunks, stylize them separately, and place them in unique arrangements.

The background image moves with the content if the browser window is resized because you used a percentage value to set the position of the background image.

Instead of changing the values for the position, top, and left properties by hand, you can more easily place div elements with a WYSIWYG application such as Macromedia Dreamweaver.

If you want to create an asymmetric or organic layout with fixed-width columns instead of making this layout resizable, use length units to dictate the exact position of both the content and the background image:

```css
body {
  margin:5px 0 0 5px;
  background-image: url(flower5.jpg);
  background-position: -400px -200px;
  background-repeat: no-repeat;
}
#header {
  position: absolute;
  left: 500px;
  top: 200px;
  width: 125px;
  font-size: small;
}
#columnLeft {
  position: absolute;
  left: 200px;
  width: 125px;
  top: 10px;
  background:#fff;
  font-size: small;
}
#columnInnerLeft {
  position: absolute;
  left: 50px;
  width: 375px;
  top: 175px;
  background: #fff;
  text-align: justify;
  border-width: 0;
  font-size: large;
}
#columnInnerRight {
  position: absolute;
  left: 600px;
  width: 150px;
  top: 50px;
  background: #fff;
}
```

See Also

Recipes 3.3 and 3.4 for setting background images on a web page; for working with CSS and Adobe Dreamweaver, see Recipe 1.17. For more information about Adobe Dreamweaver, see *http://www.dreamweaver.com*.

CHAPTER 10

Print

10.0 Introduction

To create a printer-friendly version of a web page, traditionally web developers would either have to manually convert the web page content to a separate stripped-down page design or use a script to dynamically generate a separate page design.

With CSS, however, you can automatically apply a new style sheet to documents when they are printed, thereby eliminating the time and server resources needed to create a printer-friendly page.

Support for print-media CSS is fairly commonplace these days. Currently, the browsers that support this aspect of the technology include Firefox, Internet Explorer 4+ for Windows, Internet Explorer 4.5+ for Macintosh, Navigator 6+, Safari, and Opera.

Print-only properties are associated with CSS. However, these properties have limited support among the browsers on the market; Opera 5 and 7 are the only browsers that support more than two of these kinds of properties (15 printing properties out of the 16 in the specification).

Because of this reality and because the purpose of this book is to focus on the practical, cross-browser nature of CSS, the recipes in this chapter are geared to styling the contents of the page rather than dealing with the theory of CSS printing properties. For more information on CSS printing properties, see *Cascading Style Sheets: The Definitive Guide,* by Eric A. Meyer (O'Reilly Media).

This chapter teaches the basics of how to tell the browser which style sheet to use when sending a document to print. It also discusses how to switch graphics from web to print CSS, as well as how to develop a document for printing.

10.1 Creating a Printer-Friendly Page

Problem

You want to create a printer-friendly page without having to generate another web page manually or dynamically.

Solution

First, create a separate style sheet containing CSS rules that dictate the desired look when a page is printed. For this example, the style sheet with print-only CSS rules is named `print.css`.

Then associate the style sheet and set the `media` property to `print`:

```
<link rel="stylesheet" type="text/css" href="adv.css"
media="screen" />
<link rel="stylesheet" type="text/css" href="print.css"
media="print" />
```

Discussion

You can use style sheets to dictate the presentation of documents in a wide range of media. By default, the value for the `media` attribute is `all`. Without the attribute, the user agent will apply the CSS rules in the style sheet to all media.

Although the most common attribute you probably have encountered is `screen`, which is used mainly for displaying documents on color monitors, the CSS 2.1 specification actually defines a total of ten media types, as shown in Table 10-1.

Table 10-1. Media types

Media type	Description
all	Suitable for all devices
braille	Intended for Braille tactile feedback devices
embossed	Intended for paged Braille printers
handheld	Intended for handheld devices (typically small-screen, limited-bandwidth devices)
print	Intended for paged material and for documents viewed on-screen in print preview mode
projection	Intended for projected presentations—for example, projectors
screen	Intended primarily for color computer screens
speech	Intended for speech synthesizers
tty	Intended for media using a fixed-pitch character grid (such as teletypes, terminals, or portable devices with limited display capabilities)
tv	Intended for television-type devices (with low-resolution, limited-scrollable color screens, and available sound)

When defining the styles for your web page, one style sheet can be used for all media:

```
<link rel="stylesheet" type="text/css" href="uber.css"
media="all" />
```

Or you can use one style sheet for several, but not all, media.

For instance, to use one style sheet for both projection and print media, separate the media values with a comma:

```
<link rel="stylesheet" type="text/css" href="print.css"
media="print,projection" />
```

In the preceding code, the print.css style sheet is used for projection and print media when rendering the web document.

Using @import when assigning media types

You can use other methods besides link to assign media types. One method is @import, as shown in the following line, which specifies the style sheet for both print and projection media:

```
@import URI(print.css) print,projection;
```

The @import rule needs to be placed within a style element or within an external style sheet.

Using @media when assigning media types

Another method you can use to associate and dictate style sheets and media types is @media, which enables you to write blocks of CSS rules that can be set for different media, all in *one* style sheet:

```
<style type="text/css">
@media print {
 body {
  font-size: 10pt;
  background-color: white;
  color: black;
 }
}
@media screen {
 body {
  font-size: medium;
  background-color: black;
  color: white;
 }
}
</style>
```

See Also

"Media Types" in Section 7 of the CSS 2.1 Working Draft, *http://www.w3.org/TR/CSS21/media.html*.

10.2   Making a Web Form Print-Ready

Problem

You need to have a form that users can fill out online, or that they can print and then fill out offline, like the one in Figure 10-1.

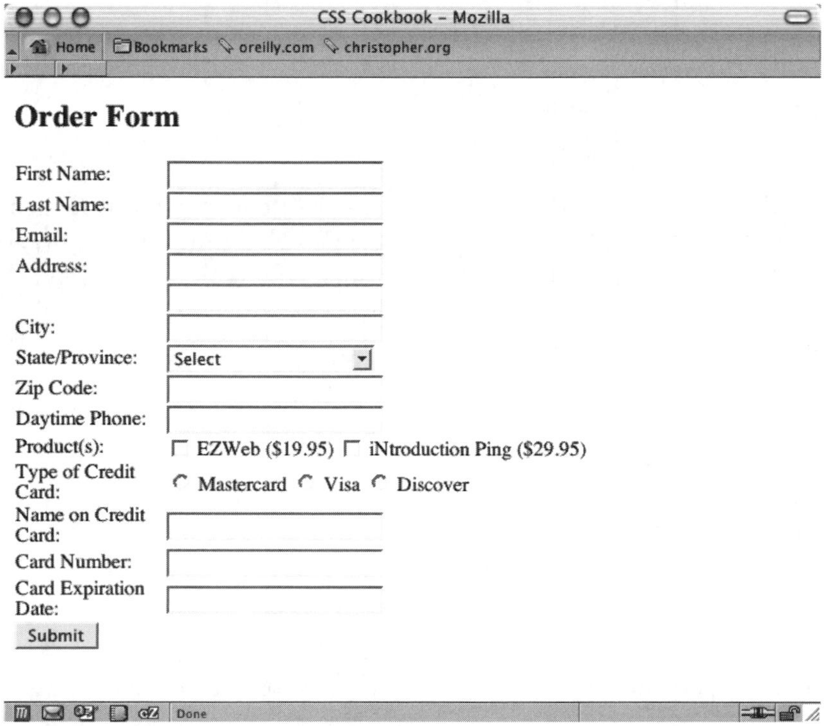

Figure 10-1. An online form

Solution

First, create a print media style sheet and a `class` selector that transforms the `form` elements so that they display black text and feature a one-pixel border on the bottom. For example, the following HTML code for an `input` text element:

```
<label for="fname">First Name</label>
<input class="fillout" name="fname" type="text" id="fname" />
```

requires the following CSS rule:

```
<style type="text/css" media="print ">
.fillout {
 color: black;
 border-width: 0;
```

```
  border: 1px solid #000;
  width: 300pt;
}
</style>
```

For drop-down menus, hide the select element altogether and add some additional markup to help produce the bottom border:

```
<label for="bitem">Breakfast Item</label>
<select name="bitem" size="1">
 <option selected="selected">Select</option>
 <option>Milk</option>
 <option>Eggs</option>
 <option>Orange Juice</option>
 <option>Newspaper</option>
 </select><span class="postselect">  </span>
```

Then, in the CSS rules, convert the inline span element to a block element. This enables you to set the width of the span element and places the border at the bottom to equal that of the input elements in the preceding CSS rule:

```
<style type="text/css" media="print">
select {
 display: none;
}
.postselect {
 display: block;
 width: 300pt;
 height: 1em;
 border: none;
 border-bottom: 1px solid #000;
}
</style>
```

For elements such as a Submit button, which can't be used on the printed page, set the display property to none. You can see the finished product in Figure 10-2.

Discussion

Lines on an order form tell users they can fill out the form. By using the border property, you can easily create these lines in a browser, making web forms useful both online and offline.

For select elements, the workaround is somewhat of a hack that involves interfering with the ideal semantic markup; it still works and is valid HTML. Place a span element after the select element:

```
<select name="bitem" size="1">
 <option selected="selected">Select</option>
 <option>Milk</option>
 <option>Eggs</option>
 <option>Orange Juice</option>
 <option>Newspaper</option>
</select>
<span class="postselect">  </span>
```

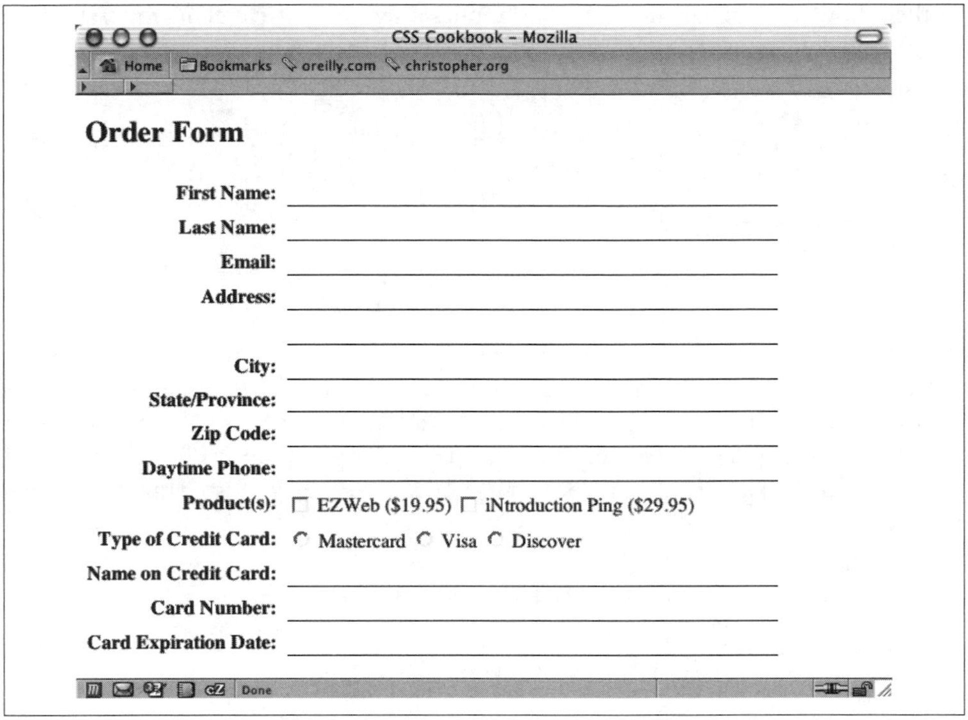

Figure 10-2. The same form primed for printing

Then set the select element to disappear:

```
select {
 display: none;
}
```

Next, set the span element to display as a block to enable the width and height properties. With those width and height properties set, the bottom border can be placed to match the rest of the form elements:

```
.postselect {
 display: block;
 width: 300pt;
 height: 1em;
 border: none;
 border-bottom: 1px solid #000;
}
```

Using attribute selectors to differentiate form elements

As browsers implement attribute selectors from the CSS specification, styling forms for print becomes easier. Currently, the only browsers that support attribute selectors are Firefox, Netscape Navigator 6+, and Opera 5+. When you use attribute selectors, it's easier to distinguish which form elements should be stylized than it is when you insert class attributes and their respective values in the markup.

In the following code, the first CSS rule applies only to input elements for text, while the second rule hides the Submit button and the Select drop box:

```
input[type="text"] {
  color: black;
  border-width: 0;
  border: 1px solid #000;
}
input[type="submit"], select {
  display: none;
}
```

Adding user friendliness

Since the form is now being printed, site visitors cannot use the Submit button to transmit their information. Be sure to provide the next steps users should follow after they have printed and completed the form. For example, if you want users to mail the form, add a mailing address to the page on which the form is printed, as shown below:

```
<div id="print">
 <p>Please mail the form to the following address:</p>
 <address class="adr">
  <span class="org">
   <span class="organization-name">The White House</span>
  </span><br />
  <span class="street-address work postal">1600 Pennsylvania Avenue NW</span><br />
  <span class="locality">Washington, DC</span>
  <span class="postal-code">20500</span><br />
  <span class="country-name">USA</span>
 </address>
</div>
```

Notice that the instructions are wrapped with a div element where the class attribute's value is set to print. In the style sheet for screen delivery, set the display property for this specific class to none:

```
<style type="text/css" media="screen">
 .print {
  display: none;
 }
</style>
```

With a separate style sheet for print delivery, allow the instructions to be printed by setting the display property to block:

```
<style type="text/css" media="print">
 .print {
  display: block;
 }
</style>
```

See Also

Attribute selector documentation in the W3C specification at *http://www.w3.org/TR/CSS21/selector.html#attribute-selectors*; HTML 4.01 specification about the label tag at *http://www.w3.org/TR/html401/interact/forms.html#edef-LABEL*.

10.3   Displaying URIs After Links

Problem

You need to display URIs (Uniform Resource Identifiers) of links in an article when a web page is printed.

Solution

Instruct the browser to print the URIs of links in a paragraph by using the :after pseudo-element:

```
p a:after {
 content: " <" attr(href) "> " ;
}
```

Discussion

Selector constructs such as :after are known as pseudo-elements. The browser interprets the selector as though additional elements were used to mark up the web document.

For example, by using the following CSS, you can make the first letter of a paragraph 2 em units in size:

```
p:first-letter {
 font-size: 2em;
}
```

You use the :after selector (or the :before selector) to insert generated content after (or before) an element. In this Recipe, the value of the href attribute, which contains the URI information, is placed after every anchor element in a p element.

To have brackets appear around the URI, place the quotes around the brackets. To add a buffer of space between the anchor element and the next inline content, put one space in front of the left bracket and one after the right bracket, and then insert the URI using the attr(x) function. Whatever attribute is replaced for x, CSS finds the attribute in the element, returning its value as a string.

Another example of the power of this pseudo-element involves returning the value of abbreviations and acronyms in a buzzword-laden document. To accomplish this, first put the expanded form of the word or phrase in the title attribute for abbr or acronym:

```
<p>The <acronym title="World Wide Web Consortium">W3C</a>
makes  wonderful things like <abbr title="Cascading Style
Sheets">CSS</abbr>!</p>
```

Then, in the CSS rules, tell the browser to return the value for the title attribute:

```
abbr:after, acronym:after {
 content: " (" attr(title) ") ";
}
```

Placing the domain name before absolute links

With absolute links, only the forward slash and any other folder and filename data will appear once page is printed. To work around this dilemma, the CSS 3 specification offers a solution through a substring selector:

```
p a:after {
 content: " <" attr(href) "> " ;
}
p a[href^="/"]:after {
 content: " <http://www.csscookbook.com" attr(href) "> " ;
}
```

This carat, ^, signifies that the selector picks every link that starts with the forward slash, which signifies an absolute link.

Currently, generating content through pseudo-elements works only in Firefox, Netscape 6+, Mozilla, and Safari browsers. Generated content does not work in Internet Explorer for Windows.

Also, the CSS 3 specification is not widely supported. However, since only browsers don't support substring selectors and/or styles sheets for print media, you can add the rule without fear of ruining a visitor's printout.

See Also

Recipe 2.2 for more on setting type in a web document; the CSS 2.1 specification about generated content at *http://www.w3.org/TR/REC-CSS2/generate.html#content*.

10.4   Inserting Special Characters Before Links

Problem

You want to insert special characters, for example, », before a link in a print style sheet.

Solution

Making sure your style sheet is set to print media, use the :after or :before pseudo-elements to include the URI after a link in the web document:

```
p a:after {
 content: attr(href) ;
}
```

Next, place the hexadecimal equivalent of the special character before the link:

```
p a:after {
 text-decoration: underline;
 content: " \00BB "  attr(href);
}
```

When the page is printed, the text after a link may look like this:

```
» http://www.csscookbook.com/
```

Discussion

Make sure to use the backward slash to escape the hexadecimal value so the browser does not display the hexadecimal value as generic text. In this case, if the hexadecimal value for right double angle quote were not escaped, the text "00BB" would be displayed instead:

```
00BB http://www.csscookbook.com/
```

Due to the nature of CSS syntax, it is not possible to use HTML numbers or names to identify special characters with the content property. The characters need to be escaped by a backward slash and their hexadecimal value.

Special characters through CSS's content property can also be used outside the printed page. Try it within your screen media presentation of your web design. Make sure you include the CSS declaration in a style sheet with the media set to all or screen in order to view output.

Currently, generating content through pseudo-elements works only in Firefox, Netscape 6+, Mozilla, and Safari browsers. Generated content does not work in Internet Explorer for Windows.

See Also

For a listing of special characters and their hexadecimal equivalents, see *http://www.ascii.cl/htmlcodes.htm*. Review the CSS 2.1 specification on escaped characters at *http://www.w3.org/TR/CSS21/syndata.html#escaped-characters*.

10.5 Sample Design: A Printer-Friendly Page with CSS

In this sample design, you will transform an existing web document (like the one in Figure 10-3) to make it more suitable for print.

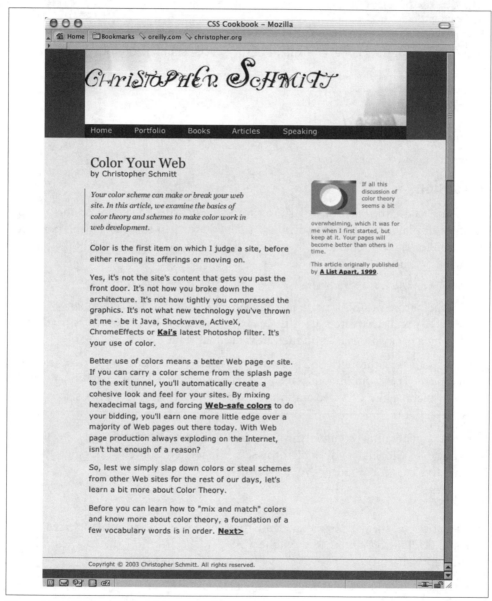

Figure 10-3. Web page stylized for screen delivery

Although CSS has changed the way we design for the Web, it also has allowed developers to change the way they provide printer-friendly versions of their documents. Instead of having to create separate pages or write scripts, you can use CSS to create a printer-friendly document as soon as the user hits the Print button. The HTML for the page isn't in this book because the miracle of CSS lets us change the presentation without having to change the HTML.

When you create a style sheet for print, you actually use a web browser. This enables you to see quickly how the CSS rules affect the display of the document (just like for media delivery), but it's also easier on the environment and you save money by not wasting ink in the printer. So, comment out the style sheet used for the screen in order to create new CSS rules:

```
<!-- Hide screen media CSS while working on print CSS -->
<!-- link href="adv.css" type="text/css" rel="stylesheet"
media="screen" -->
<style type="text/css">
/* Print CSS rules go here */
</style>
```

Setting the Page for Black-and-White Printing

Apply the first CSS rule to the body element. In this rule, set the background color to white and set the type to black:

```
body {
  background-color: white;
  color: black;
}
```

Next, set the typeface for the page to a serif font. Reading text online in sans-serif is easier on the eyes, but in print media the serif font is still the choice for reading passages of text. For a later fallback choice, you may want to go with the Times typeface for print documents since it's installed on most (if not all) computers, and it's a workhorse of a font. In case your users don't have Times installed, supply alternatives as well:

```
body {
  background-color: white;
  color: black;
  font-family: Times, "Times New Roman", Garamond, serif;
}
```

Now you want to get rid of navigation-related links and other page elements you don't want to see in the final printout. This includes the main navigation bar below the main header, as well as internal anchors in the page itself. If you have a page with ad banners, it might be a good idea to hide those as well (see Figure 10-4):

```
#navigation, hr, body>div>a, #blipvert {
  display: none;
}
```

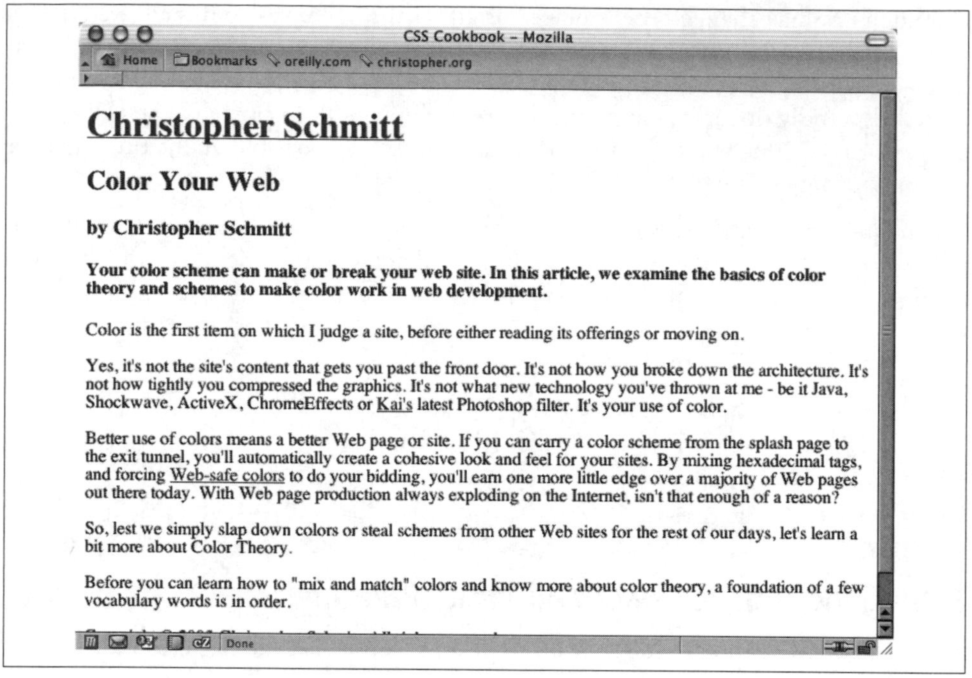

Figure 10-4. Hiding the navigation bar and other elements

Designing the Main Heading

Because you are dealing with black and gray type on a white page, you have few options when it comes to designing how the main heading for the page should look. However, using what you have at your disposal, it's nonetheless easy to create a masthead that calls attention to itself.

First, set the background to black and the text to white:

```
#header h1 {
 color: white;
 background-color: black;
}
```

Because you want people to actually read the header, you want the text to be white to create enough contrast. In this instance, the main header also acts as a homing device—it is a link to the home page. Therefore, the color of the heading is dictated by the style rules set for the links. To remedy this situation, add a separate rule:

```
#header h1 {
 background-color: black;
}
#header h1 a {
 color: white;
}
```

Now that the text is visible, stylize it a bit so that it stands out. Your goal is to center the text, increase the size of the text, and make all the letters uppercase:

```
#header h1 {
  background-color: black;
  font-size: 24pt;
  text-align: center;
  text-transform: uppercase;
}
```

Although this looks good, you can improve it by changing the typeface to sans-serif (so that it sticks out from the rest of the text in the document) and by adding some padding around the top and bottom of the heading (see Figure 10-5):

```
#header h1 {
  background-color: black;
  font-size: 24pt;
  text-align: center;
  font-family: Helvetica, Verdana, Arial, sans-serif;
  padding: 7pt;
  text-transform: uppercase;
}
```

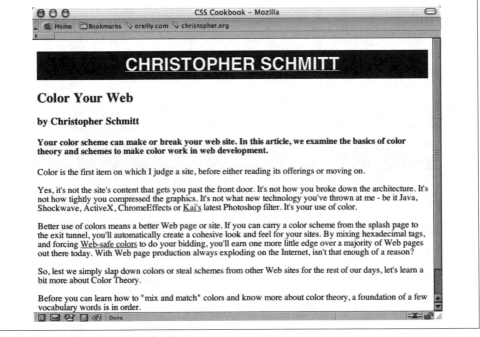

Figure 10-5. Stylizing the main header

Styling the Article Header and Byline

For the article title and byline, create a more dramatic approach by zeroing out the margins and padding of both the h2 and h3 elements:

```
#content h2 {
 padding: 0;
 margin: 0;
}
#content h3 {
 padding: 0;
 margin: 0 ;
}
```

Then increase the font size for the article title and create a thin hairline rule below it. Next, align the byline to the right and set the type style to italic (see Figure 10-6):

```
#content h2 {
 padding: 0;
 margin: 0;
 font-size: 20pt;
 border-bottom: 1px solid black;
}
#content h3 {
 padding: 0;
 margin: 0;
 text-align: right;
 font-style: italic;
}
```

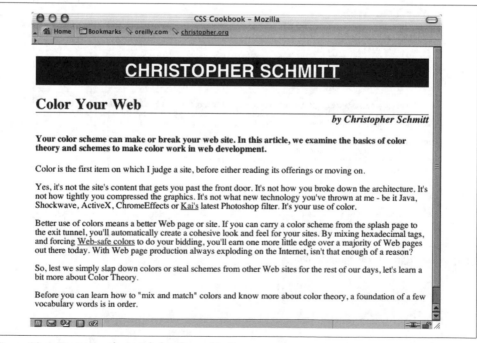

Figure 10-6. Designing the article header and byline

Gaining Attention Through the Teaser

Next up is the content in the h4 element. Because this content serves as a teaser for the article, it should be visually distinctive from the article text. To accomplish that, set the background to about 30% black, change the typeface to sans-serif, and put in some padding (see Figure 10-7):

```
#content h4 {
 font-family: Helvetica, Verdana, Arial, sans-serif;
 border-top: 3pt solid black;
 background-color: #BEBEBE; /* ~30% black */
 padding: 12pt;
 margin: 0;
}
```

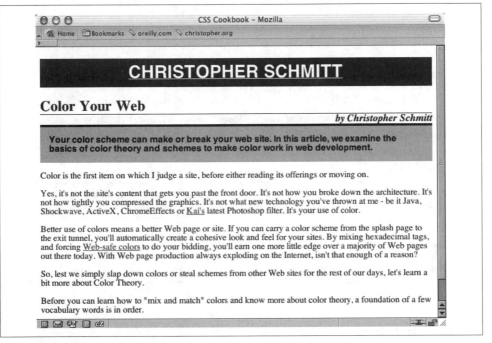

Figure 10-7. Setting up the article teaser

As for the content of the article, leave the text pretty much as it is except for two points of interest: leading, covered here, and links, covered in the next section.

Remember that in the body element, the font for the entire page is set with the serif typeface, and through inheritance that typeface style is picked up in the paragraph elements as well. However, you may want to space out the lines, or increase the *leading*, of the text in the paragraph. To do this, change the line-height property:

```
#content p {
 line-height: 18pt;
}
```

Displaying URIs After Links

Any links in the article become useless when printed. To make them beneficial to the reader when the page is printed, make sure all URIs from the links are displayed. To do that, set up a CSS rule to display the URIs after every link in the content division of the document. Also, for visual effect, remove the default underline of the links, make sure the font-weight is bold, and set the color to gray (see Figure 10-8):

```
#content a:after {
 content: " <" attr(href) "> ";
 font-family: courier, monospace;
 font-weight: normal;
}
a {
 text-decoration: none;
 font-weight: bold;
 color: #626466;
}
```

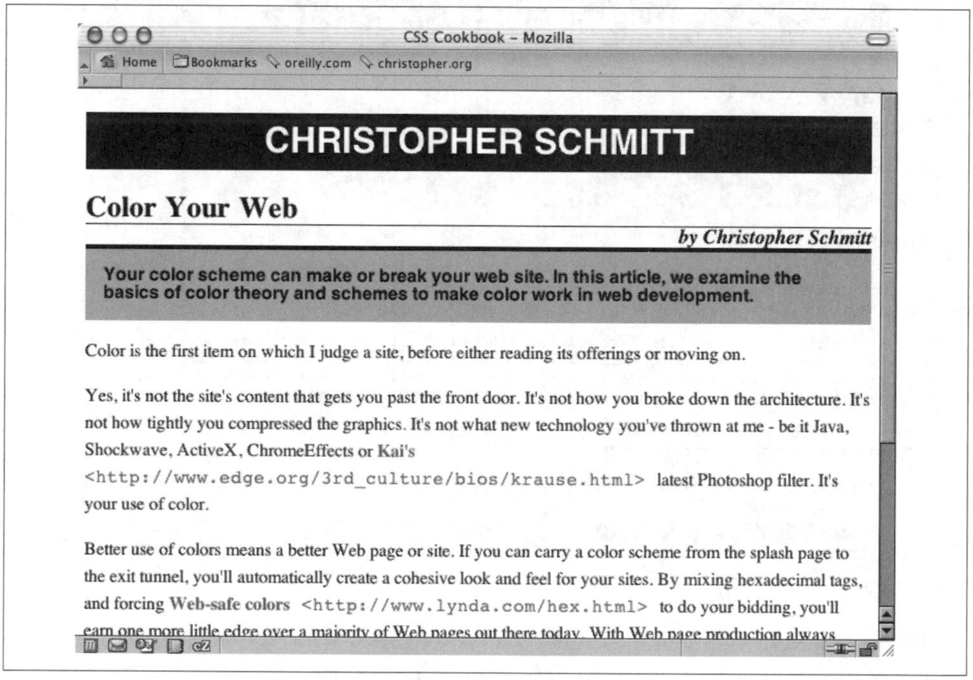

Figure 10-8. Adjusting the links and leading in the content

Finishing with the Footer

At this point you're ready to work your way down the page to the footer that contains the copyright notice. Because the main header is in a sans-serif typeface, balance the page by centering the copyright notice, creating a line rule through the border-top property, and setting the typeface to sans-serif as well (see Figure 10-9):

```
#footer {
 border-top: 1px solid #000;
 text-align: center;
 font-family: Helvetica, Verdana, Arial, sans-serif;
}
```

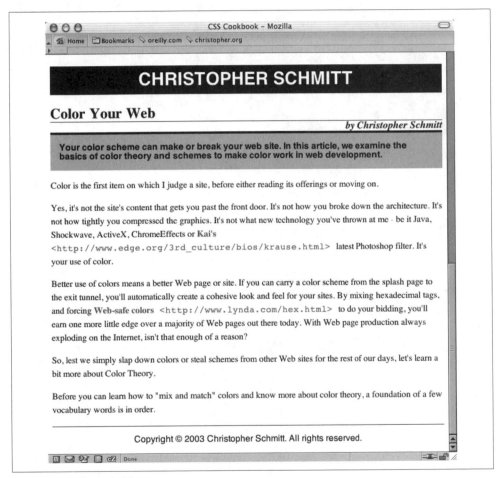

Figure 10-9. The styled footer

With the print CSS finished, copy the CSS rules and put them into an external style sheet called *print.css*. Then, uncomment out the CSS for screen media and associate the print CSS through the link element:

```
<link href="adv.css" type="text/css" rel="stylesheet"
media="screen" />
<link href="print.css" type="text/css" rel="stylesheet"
media="print" />
```

Now you can create a printer-friendly style sheet. Assuming your site visitors have a browser that can render print media style sheets, when your visitors print out the page they will automatically get the proper layout sent to their printers.

CHAPTER 11

Hacks, Workarounds, and Troubleshooting

11.0 Introduction

When designing for the Web, developers historically have used hacks and workarounds due to browser limitations.

The mid-1990s saw a proliferation of such workarounds, among them single-pixel GIFs, font tags, and nested tables, just to name just a few. Although the CSS 2 specification became a recommendation back in May 1998, browser vendors have only recently fully implemented the standard in their products. This gap in time of browsers without CSS supports to browsers with full or near-perfect CSS implementation means a handful of browsers that most people use have poor CSS support.

To overcome the bugs in popular browsers that have this poor CSS support, web developers have once again resorted to using hacks and workarounds to successfully achieve web page designs.

Even though problems may be solved by using newer versions of browsers, web developers may need to use hacks or workarounds to deliver the appropriate presentation to their audience for many reasons.

Unlike web developers, most people don't automatically upgrade their browsers each time a new one is available. They tend to stick with the browser that's on their computer because it works fine and will get a new browser only when they purchase a new computer. Also, IT departments in many companies lock down the systems to prevent individuals from upgrading software applications on their own.

For web developers struggling to polish their designs, this chapter covers techniques on how to deal with browsers that have spotty CSS support. Included in this chapter are methods to hide advanced style sheets from Netscape Navigator 4, deal with Internet Explorer 5.*x* for Window's unique interpretation of the box model, and more.

11.1   Isolating Styles for Netscape Navigator 4.x

Problem

You want to keep Netscape Navigator 4.x from using certain CSS rules. For example, Navigator 4.x doesn't correctly inherit styles, such as font-family and color, set for body elements, such as table, div, and p.

Solution

In a separate style sheet, place the CSS rules that you don't want the Netscape Navigator 4.x browser to use. Then use the @import method to associate the "advanced" CSS rules (making sure that the advanced style sheet comes after the basic to override styles from the basic style sheet):

```
<link rel="stylesheet" type="text/css" media="all" title="Basic CSS" href="/basic.
css" />
<style type="text/css" media="all">
 @import "/css/advanced.css";
</style>
```

Discussion

Netscape Navigator 4 was the first Netscape browser to contain support for CSS. Unfortunately, Netscape was developing the browser while CSS was being finalized. Also, Netscape was supporting its own proposal, JavaScript Style Sheets, known as JSSS, and was basing Navigator 4 on that technology. So, when the W3C went with CSS instead, the Netscape engineers had to do some quick jury-rigging to fix their implementation. This is why you can turn off CSS support in Navigator 4 just by turning off JavaScript in the program's preferences.

Because Navigator's CSS implementation was essentially a remapping to its JSSS engine, actual CSS support for the implementation of such things as the @import method of associated styles to a web page was woefully incomplete. And whatever CSS styles Navigator did include were implemented improperly. As newer browsers offered stronger and more robust support for CSS, a method for hiding certain CSS rules from Navigator 4 became a necessity if web developers were to embrace CSS-enabled designs.

Caio hack

Although the @import method works, you need to write the CSS rules in two separate files: one for Navigator 4 and another one for other browsers capable of handling the @import method. Another way of hiding styles from Navigator 4 and keeping the styles in a single style sheet is through a CSS comment workaround known as the "Caio hack," named after the person who developed it, Caio Chassot.

In the following code example, styles are hidden from Navigator 4 through the hack:

```
.item1 {
 font-size: 200%;
 text-decoration: underline;
}
/*/*/
.item2  {
 font-size: 200%;
 text-decoration: underline;
}
/* */
.item3 {
 font-size: 200%;
 text-decoration: underline;
}
```

Here is the HTML code that is used in Figure 11-1:

```
<h2>Netscape Navigator 4 Test:</h2>
<ul>
 <li class="item1">This text is large and underlined.</li>
 <li class="item2">This text is <em>neither</em> large nor underlined in Netscape
Navigator 4.x.</li>
 <li class="item3">This text is large and underlined.</li>
</ul>
```

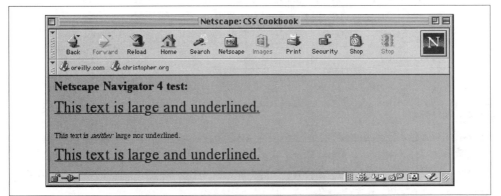

Figure 11-1. Netscape Navigator's comment-parser problem used to hide certain styles

Navigator 4 interprets the comment snippet /*/*/ as an open comment, meaning that anything after it is hidden from the browser. Other browsers see the snippet as open and close comment tags. To close the hack to let Navigator 4 see the rest of the styles, add another pair of open and close comment tags, this time with a space between the asterisks:

```
/* */
```

You also can include the hack with inline styles:

```
<p style="/*/*/ color: font-size: 200%; text-decoration:
underline;">This inline-styled p is neither large nor underlined
in Navigator 4.</p>
```

@media workaround

Along with the comment-parsing problem, Navigator 4 won't pull in style sheets when the media attribute equals all:

```
<link rel="stylesheet" type="text/css" href="/css/advanced.css"
media="all">
```

Also, Navigator 4 won't interpret style sheets when there is more than one value for the media attribute. So, if you use a combination of values for the media attributes, Navigator 4 ignores the style sheet:

```
<link rel="stylesheet" type="text/css" href="/css/advanced.css"
media="screen, print" >
```

Descendant selectors

You also can hide styles from Navigator 4 by using descendant selectors—for instance, by placing the html element as a selector before the next selector (since Navigator 4 doesn't include the html element in the parsed document).

In the following example, the text size and decoration won't appear in Navigator 4:

```
html .item2 {
 font-size: 200%;
 text-decoration: underline;
}
```

See Also

http://www.v2studio.com/k/css/n4hide/, Caio Chassot's web page about the workaround; Netscape's original proposal for JSSS at *http://www.w3.org/Submission/1996/1/WD-jsss-960822*; more issues regarding Navigator 4.x at *http://www.mako4css.com/Issues.htm*.

11.2   Delivering Specific Styles to Internet Explorer 5.x for Windows

Problem

You want to apply different CSS property values to the Internet Explorer 5.x for Windows browser, such as the value of the width property in order to work around implementation of the Microsoft box model.

Solution

Put in the declaration you want Internet Explorer 5.*x* for Windows to handle, and then use what's called the "star HTML" hack to put in the corrected values you want the other browsers to interpret:

```
div#content {
 /* value for all browsers */
 width: 500px;
}
* html div#content {
 /* value only for IE browsers */
 width: 566px;
 /* value only for MacIE browsers */
 w\idth: 500px;
}
```

Discussion

CSS specifies that the width property defines the width of the content area of a box, and that any margin, border, or padding space should draw outside of that space. For example, in the following bit of code, the width of the element (as it is stated) is 500px:

```
div#content {
 width: 500px;
 padding: 33px;
 margin: 50px;
 background-color: #666;
}
```

In Figure 11-2, the box appears to be 566 pixels wide. The 66 "extra" pixels are from the padding being added outside the 500 pixels.

In Internet Explorer 5.*x* for Windows, the width isn't the stated value in the CSS. Instead, Microsoft's box model draws the box with the border and padding inside the specified width. To calculate the width of the content area for Internet Explorer 5.*x* for Windows, subtract the padding and borders from the stated width:

width property
– left border – left padding
– right padding – right border
= Microsoft's box model

In the previous CSS example, the width determined by Internet Explorer 5.*x* for Windows is 434 pixels (see Figure 11-3):

500px – 33px – 33px = 434px

That's a difference of 66 pixels from the originally stated content area's width of 500 pixels for the block element.

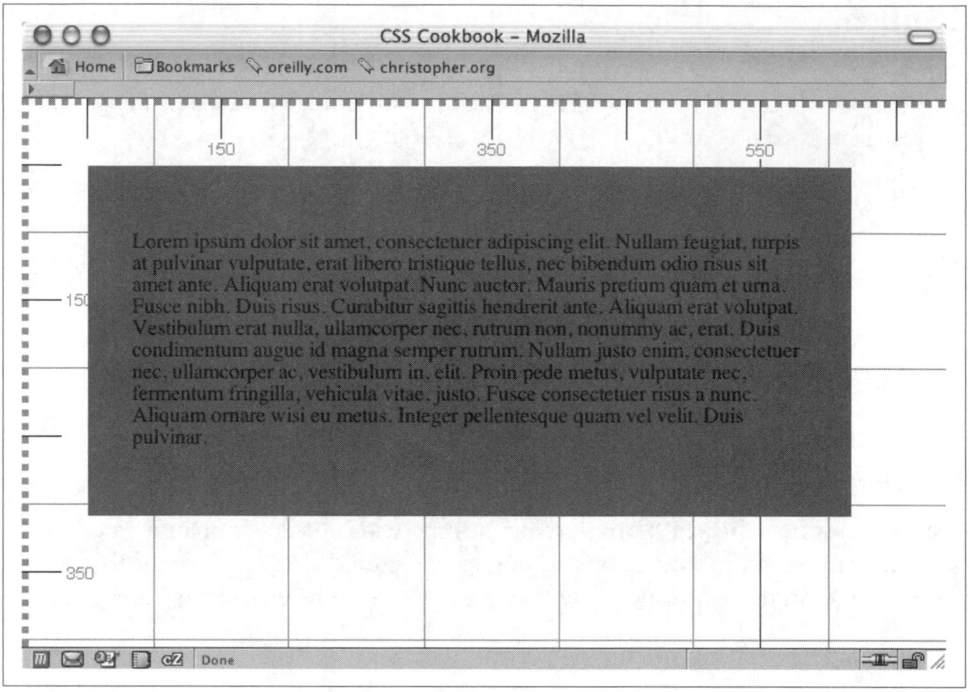

Figure 11-2. The box model correctly implemented in Mozilla

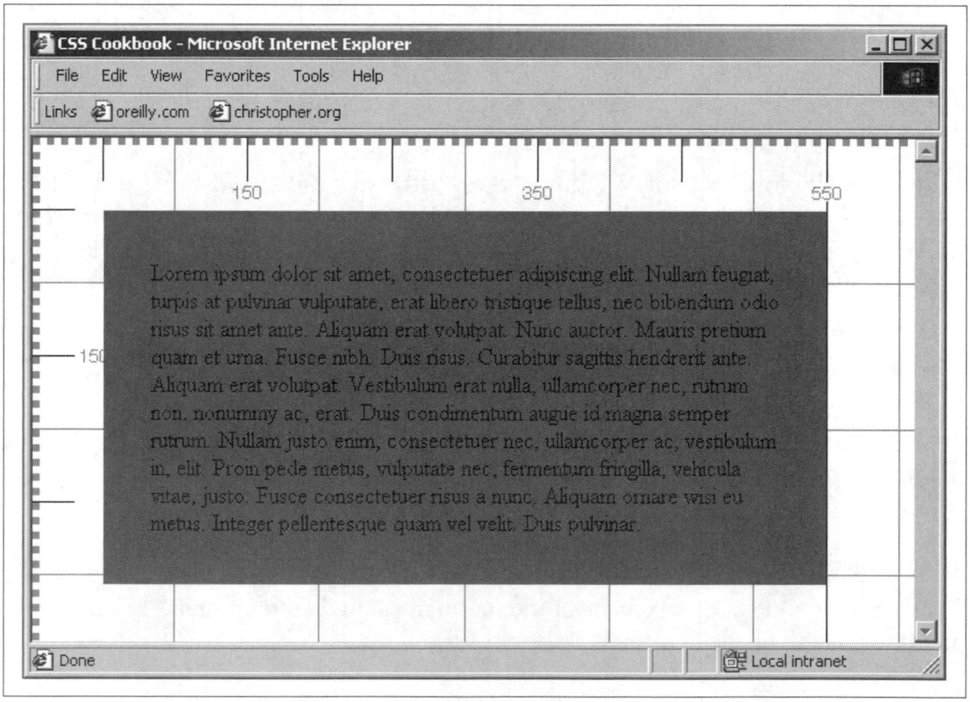

Figure 11-3. Internet Explorer 5.x for Windows' implementation of the box model

This different block level, called "Microsoft's box model," is triggered in Internet Explorer for Windows 5.*x* (and Internet Explorer for Windows 6 *in quirks mode*) when a block level element has both a declared width and a padding or borders.

Star HTML hack

In the "star HTML" hack, the first rule delivers the correct value to all browsers.

```
div#content {
 /* value for all browsers */
 width: 500px;
}
```

The second rule delivers the alternative value for Internet Explorer. The selector states any div element with an id attribute that equals content that is a descendant of an html element is a descendant of any element.

```
div#content {
 /* value for all browsers */
 width: 500px;
}
* html div#content {
 /* value only for IE browsers */
 width: 566px;
}
```

Because html is the root element, it cannot be a descendent of another element. So, browsers that realize the false premise ignore this entire CSS rule. However, the Internet Explorer browser doesn't and accepts the rule. Because there are two rules, the cascade effect comes into action and Internet Explorer rewrites the element's width value from 500px to 566px.

The last step is to make a correction for Internet Explorer for Macintosh. Even though the browser shares the name with Internet Explorer for Windows, the Macintosh version correctly renders the box model making our solution a problem for that browser.

The solution then is to deliver a declaration specifically for Internet Explorer for Macintosh:

```
div#content {
 /* value for all browsers */
 width: 500px;
}
* html div#content {
 /* value only for IE browsers */
 width: 566px;
 /* value only for MacIE browsers */
 w\idth: 500px;
}
```

The backward slash escapes the letter "i". This hack is keeps the second and proper value from Internet Explorer for Windows, but Internet Explorer for Macintosh interprets as a valid declaration.

Another approach: Tantek's box model hack

Tantek Çelik, Microsoft's former diplomat to the World Wide Web Consortium (W3C) CSS and HTML working groups, originally demonstrated how his box model hack could be used to fix Internet Explorer 5.x for Windows' approach to the box model:

```
div#content    {
 /* WinIE value first, then the desired value the next 2 times */
 background-color: red;
 voice-family: "\"}\"";
 voice-family: inherit;
 background-color: green;
}
html>div#content
 background-color: green;
}
```

Because the box model is a fundamental aspect of design, it becomes paramount to fix any inconsistencies that can arise from this problem.

The box model hack uses a parsing bug to close the rule set prematurely, so anything after the two voice-family properties is ignored by Internet Explorer 5.x for Windows. However, because other browsers, such as Opera 5, can be vulnerable to this workaround, add this CSS rule:

```
html>div#content
 background-color: green;
}
```

This rule, affectionately referred to as the "Be Kind to Opera" rule, uses the child selector to reinforce the property for browsers like Opera that may get confused with the box model hack, but correctly implement child selectors.

See Also

http://www.w3.org/TR/CSS21/visudet.html#the-width-property for information on the width property as a part of the box model; *http://www.tantek.com/CSS/Examples/boxmodelhack.html* for Tantek Çelik's explanation of the box model hack; *http://www.w3.org/TR/CSS21/aural.html#voice-char-props* for information about the voice-family property; updated box model hacks and more background information at *http://css-discuss.incutio.com/?page=BoxModelHack*.

11.3   Removing Web Page Flicker in Internet Explorer 5.x for Windows

Problem

You want to remove the initial flicker, or flash, of unstyled content before Internet Explorer 5.x for Windows applies your CSS style sheet.

Solution

Add a link or script element as the child of the head element in your web document:

```
<head>
<title>christopher.org</title>
<link rel="stylesheet" type="text/css" media="print" href="print.css" />
<style type="text/css" media="screen">@import "advanced.css";</style>
</head>
```

Discussion

If a web page contains a style sheet associated by only the @import method, Internet Explorer 5.x for Windows' browsers first show the contents of the web page without any of the styles applied to the markup. After a split second, the browser redraws the web page with styles applied.

Adding a link or script element in the head before the @import rule forces the browser to load the styles when it initially renders the web page, thus keeping it from showing a bland-looking web page.

This rendering phenomenon isn't a problem with the browser itself. The CSS specification doesn't specify whether this behavior is acceptable, so the browser is compliant with the specification. You or your audience may perceive this flicker as a bug or annoyance, though, so you should take steps to prevent it from occurring.

See Also

http://www.bluerobot.com/web/css/fouc.asp for an overview of the effect.

11.4   Keeping Background Images Stationary in Internet Explorer 6 for Windows

Problem

You want to have a fixed background image in Internet Explorer 6 for Windows.

Solution

Use the following JavaScript hack to force the effect. First copy the following code to call up the JavaScript code in your web page:

```
<head>
 <title>CSS Cookbook</title>
 <script type="text/javascript" src="fixed.js"></script>
</head>
```

Then in the *fixed.js* file place the JavaScript code for the workaround, which can be found at this book's online sample archive *http://www.oreilly.com/catalog/cssckbk/* or from Andrew Clover's site at *http://doxdesk.com/software/js/fixed.html*.

 Due to the length of the code, it's impractical to publish the code or expect you, dear reader, to type the code straight from the book.

Discussion

According to the CSS 2 specification, when a background image is fixed using the background-attachment property, it shouldn't move when the user scrolls the web page. In all versions of Internet Explorer for Windows, this property doesn't work at all.

However, this stunning JavaScript workaround developed by Andrew Clover fixes this problem by simply adding the JavaScript link to the web page. The JavaScript works by dynamically recalculating the position of the viewport as a user scrolls, and then it adjusts the background image accordingly.

See Also

Recipe 3.7 for information about setting a fixed background image; the CSS specification for the background-attachment propery at *http://www.w3.org/TR/CSS21/colors.html#propdef-background-attachment*.

11.5 Using Internet Explorer for Windows' Conditional Comments to Deliver Styles

Problem

You want to deliver specific code to different versions of Internet Explorer for Windows.

Solution

Use Microsoft's Internet Explorer conditional comments:

```html
<!--[if IE]>
<p>You are seeing this sentence because you are using an Internet Explorer
browser.</p>
<![endif]-->
```

To deliver code to different versions of Internet Explorer for Windows, use the browser version number deliver code:

```html
<!--[if IE 5]>
<p>You are seeing this sentence because you are using Internet Explorer 5</p>
<![endif]-->
<!--[if IE 5.0]>
<p>You are seeing this sentence because you are using Internet Explorer 5.0</p>
<![endif]-->
<!--[if IE 5.5]>
<p>You are seeing this sentence because you are using Internet Explorer 5.5</p>
<![endif]-->
<!--[if IE 6]>
<p>You are seeing this sentence because you are using Internet Explorer 6</p>
<![endif]-->
```

To deliver code to version of Internet Explorer 5 for Windows and higher, use this code:

```html
<!--[if gte IE 5]>
<p>You are seeing this sentence because you are using Internet Explorer 5 and
up</p>
<![endif]-->
```

To deliver code to version of Internet Explorer 5.5 for Windows and lower, use this code:

```html
<!--[if lte IE 5.5]>
<p>You are seeing this sentence because you are using Internet Explorer lower or
equal to 5.5</p>
<![endif]-->
```

To deliver code to version of Internet Explorer for Windows below Internet Explorer 6, use this code:

```html
<!--[if lt IE 6]>
<p>You are seeing this sentence because you are using Internet Explorer lower
than 6</p>
<![endif]-->
```

Discussion

Microsoft developed its own propriety comment system to deliver specific HTML code to different versions of its browser, Internet Explorer for Windows.

This code can only be used in placing HTML between the conditional statements. However, this still means that CSS rules can be specifically targeted through conditional comments. For example, to deliver a style sheet targeted for Internet Explorer 5.x, place a link tag to a style sheet between two conditional comments:

```
<link rel="stylesheet" type="text/css" media="screen, presentation"
href="/_assets/css/screen/screen.css" />
<link rel="stylesheet" type="text/css" media="aural"
href="/_assets/css/aural.css" />
<!--[if lt IE 6]>
<link rel="stylesheet" type="text/css" media="screen, presentation" href="/_assets/
css/screen/ie.css" />
<![endif]-->
```

Also, embedded styles can also be placed in between conditional comments:

```
<!--[if lt IE 6]>
<style type="text/css">
 h1 {
   font-family: Verdana, Arial, Helvetica, sans-serif;
   font-size: 36px;
}
</style>
<![endif]-->
```

Conditional Comments may be used in conjunction with an intelligent hacking system. See Recipe 11.7 for more information about setting up a hacking system.

Note that there is a difference between IE 5 and IE 5.0 when using conditional comments.

To isolate code for just Internet Explorer 5.0, use IE 5.0. To deliver code to all Internet Explorer versions within the major release of 5, use IE 5.

The markers lt and gt mean "less than" and "greater than," respectively. While lte and gte mean "less than or equals" and "greater than or equals."

See Also

The MSDN's article on conditional comments at *http://msdn.microsoft.com/ workshop/author/dhtml/overview/ccomment_ovw.asp.*

11.6 Keeping CSS Rules from Internet Explorer 5 for Macintosh

Problem

You want to hide certain rules from Internet Explorer 5 for Macintosh.

Solution

To hide CSS rules from Internet Explorer 5 for Macintosh, insert a backslash in front of the closing comment with the characters */:

```
/* \*/
h1 {
 font-size: 200%;
 text-transform: uppercase;
 background-color: #666;
 }
```

After the rules pertaining to Internet Explorer 5 for Macintosh, insert another comment line:

```
/* */
p {
 text-transform: uppercase;
 }
```

Discussion

This method exploits a simple comment-parsing problem found in Internet Explorer 5 for Macintosh. The backslash before the closing comment causes the browser to think the comment actually has not closed; any valid CSS rules are hidden, allowing entire rule sets to be hidden from the browser until the next closing comment marker is hidden.

See Also

The specification about adding comments in CSS at *http://www.w3.org/TR/2004/ CR-CSS21-20040225/syndata.html#comments*.

11.7   Setting Up an Intelligent Hack Management System

Problem

You want to develop a system to separate correct CSS rules from those used for hacks or workarounds.

Solution

Link a style sheet to a web page:

```
<link rel="stylesheet" type="text/css" media="screen, presentation"
href="/_assets/css/screen/screen.css" />
```

Within the *screen.css* style sheet import the base style sheet that contains correct values:

```
@import url(csscookbook.css);
```

Then use a set of filters to import CSS rules needed to correct a browser's problems (see Figure 11-4). One such browser that would need its own style sheet could be Internet Explorer 5.x for Windows. Use the Mid Pass Filter to serve the style sheet to just that browser:

```
@import url(csscookbook.css);
/* Styles for Internet Explorer 5 for Windows */
@media tty {
 i{content:"\";/*" "*/}} @import 'winie5.css'; /*";}
}/* */
```

Another browser that may need its own style sheet could be Internet Explorer for Macintosh. Use the Mac Band Pass Filter to serve a style sheet to just that browser:

```
@import url(/_assets/css/csscookbook.css);
/* Styles for Internet Explorer 5 for Windows */
@media tty {
 i{content:"\";/*" "*/}} @import '/_assets/css/winie5.css'; /*";}
}/* */
/* Styles for Internet Explorer for Macintosh */
/*\*//*/&#8232;
@import "ie5mac.css";&#8232;
/**/
```

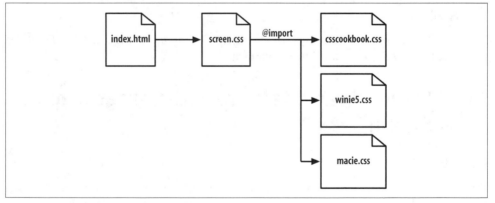

Figure 11-4. A diagram of the intelligent hacking system

Discussion

Keeping style sheets separated based on their browser support has a couple of benefits. First, it keeps the base style sheet clean of any hacks and workarounds.

Second, keeping hacks and workarounds specific to each browser in their own file means that you can easily delete the CSS rules if the time comes to stop supporting that particular browser.

For a listing of CSS filters that target specific browsers, see *http://www.centricle.com/ ref/css/filters/*.

The technique discussed in the solution uses CSS-based hacks to deliver style sheets. Another approach is to user a server-side solution. Mark Pilgrim, a web developer, devised a solution based on mod_rewrite in the Apache server.

By detecting the browser's HTTP user agent, each browser gets its own style sheet in addition to the base style sheet. For more information about this technique, see *http:// diveintomark.org/archives/2003/01/16/the_one_ive_never_tried.*

See Also

Molly Holzschlag's article on hack management at *http://www.informit.com/articles/ printerfriendly.asp?p=170511*.

11.8   Diagnosing CSS Bugs and Browser Issues

Problem

You want to troubleshoot an issue with either your code or a browser's rendering of CSS.

Solution

Follow the follow the steps in an effort to isolate issues with CSS-enabled designs:

1. Validate the HTML. Go to *http://validator.w3.org/* and check the markup.

2. Validate the CSS. Go to *http://jigsaw.w3.org/css-validator/* and check the CSS.

3. Streamline the values of properties. Add a new CSS rule *at the end* of the style sheet(s), using the universal selector and set properties for all elements:

```
* {
margin: 0;
padding: 0;
}
```

4. Border every block-level element:

```
* {
margin: 0;
padding: 0;
border: 1px solid red;
}
```

5. Try different values for properties.

6. Comment out CSS rules and/or properties that are causing the problem. Uncomment CSS properties one by one until the problem recurs. For information on how to add comments within CSS, see Recipe 1.9.

7. Research similar problems through Google and *http://www.positioniseverything.net*, a well-documented collection of CSS bugs.

Discussion

Based on personal experience, 90% of the time issues with a CSS-enabled design come from typos in the CSS syntax or malformed markup.

After going through this list, you are still having troubles, do a search through Google or a site devoted to CSS bugs to determine if anyone else has written and/or discovered a similar problem.

See Also

Read *Cascading Style Sheets: The Definitive Guide*, by Eric A. Meyer (O'Reilly Media) to learn more about the CSS specification.

11.9 Testing a Site Design on More Than One Platform with Only One Computer

Problem

You want to test your web site on more than one browser, but you have access to only one computer.

Solution

Running emulators on a computer can help reduce costs because you don't have to own multiple workstations.

If you own a PC

Macintosh browsers
> There currently is not a method to emulate a Macintosh system (and therefore a Macintosh browser) on a Windows operating system. However, the online service iCapture (see *http://www.danvine.com/icapture/*) lets developers see how a web page renders within Safari.

Linux browsers

Knoppix

Knoppix is a Linux operating system that resides on a bootable CD-ROM, meaning no installation is required. For further information, see *http://www.knoppix.org/*.

VMWare Workstation

VMWare Workstation allows the setting of several virtual operating systems to run on top of the Microsoft Operating System. Although software needs to be installed, it doesn't require a restart of the computer every time you want to test a web site. For more information, see *http://www.vmware.com/products/ws/*.

Dual Booting Linux and Windows Operating Systems

Debian Linux can be installed on a separate partition on computer allowing the user to boot into either Linux or Windows Operating System. For more information, see *http://www.aboutdebian.com/dualboot.htm*.

If you own a Macintosh

Virtual PC for Mac

Virtual PC for Mac, a Microsoft application, allows for setting up virtual operating systems including Windows XP Professional, Windows XP Home, and Windows 2000 Professional—and thus, different versions of Internet Explorer. For further information, see *http://www.microsoft.com/mac/products/virtualpc/virtualpc.aspx*.

Boot Camp

Boot Camp, an Apple application, allows users to install a Windows operating system on Intel Macs. For more information, see *http://www.apple.com/macosx/bootcamp/*.

If you own a Linux Workstation

Wine

Wine, open source software, is an implementation of the Windows API that runs on top of X and Linux. For more information, see *http://www.winehq.com/*.

Discussion

To achieve cross-platform, cross-browser designs with CSS, checking and testing web sites in as many sites as possible becomes necessary. In order to do that on a budget, it's necessary to install more than one operating system on a computer.

Once you've installed more than one operating system, install a browser on the new system. You can do quickly by visiting the browser archive at *http://browsers.evolt.org/*.

BrowserCam is a web-based, screen capture service. Fill out a form supplying a link to a web page and which several browsers and operating system configurations you want to see. Then the service will take screen captures of those systems for you to check. For more information, see *http://www.browsercam.com/*.

See Also

For more information on setting up more than one browser on one computer, see *http://www.thesitewizard.com/webdesign/multiplebrowsers.shtml*.

11.10 Installing More Than One Version of Internet Explorer for Windows on a Computer

Problem

You want to run more than one version of Internet Explorer for Windows on your Windows XP operating system.

Solution

Start with a machine that runs Windows XP operating system and already has Internet Explorer 6 for Windows installed.

Download previous versions of Internet Explorer at evolt.org browser archive (*http://browsers.evolt.org/?ie/32bit/standalone*):

- Internet Explorer for Windows 5.5 Service Pack 2 *http://browsers.evolt.org/download.php?/ie/32bit/standalone/ie55sp2_nt.zip*
- Internet Explorer for Windows 5.01 Service Pack 2 *http://browsers.evolt.org/download.php?/ie/32bit/standalone/ie501sp2_nt.zip*
- Internet Explorer for Windows 4 *http://browsers.evolt.org/download.php?/ie/32bit/standalone/ie401_nt.zip*
- Internet Explorer for Windows 3 *http://browsers.evolt.org/download.php?/ie/32bit/standalone/ie3_nt.zip*

Once downloaded, install the browsers in their own directory.

Then execute each browser by clicking on IEXPLORE.EXE within each browser's folder.

Discussion

Since Internet Explorer for Windows is the most popular browser, testing web page designs in this browser is crucial for almost all projects. However, up until this technique was discovered by Insert Title Web Design (see *http://labs.insert-title.com/labs/Multiple-IEs-in-Windows_article795.aspx*) web developers had to use operating system emulators or several physical workstations for testing.

By modifying some files for each browser version, multiple versions are now able to run on one Windows operating system.

 Note that the files mentioned in the solution have been pretreated and no longer need modification. However, as a precaution, with any software install, make sure to back up your work before installing and running the files.

If you run numerous Internet Explorers for Windows on one machine, some problems arise:

- The version of Internet Explorer 4 does not accept any URI entered in the location bar. To enter a URI, go through the menu system. The shortcut is to press control+0 to bring up the dialog box.
- Conditional comments (see Recipe 11.5) do not work across these browsers. Browsers like Internet Explorer 4 register as Internet Explorer 6 for Windows.
- Versions 5 and 5.5 have been known to crash if an attempt is made to view Favorites.
- Multiple installations of Internet Explorer may not support cookies.

 Conditional comments can be repaired, however, one must edit the computer's registry, which can be tricky. For more information, see *http://www.positioniseverything.net/articles/multiIE.html*.

See Also

For more information on this technique, see *http://www.quirksmode.org/browsers/multipleie.html*.

11.11 Testing a Web Site with a Text Browser

Problem

You want to test a web site with a text browser.

Solution

Use an online web tool such as Lynx Viewer (see *http://www.delorie.com/web/lynxview.html*) that emulates a text browser.

Place a file named *delorie.htm*, which can be blank, that tells the web application that it is acceptable for the browser to view and render the site through the online service.

Afterward, enter your site's URL and check the results online (see Figure 11-5).

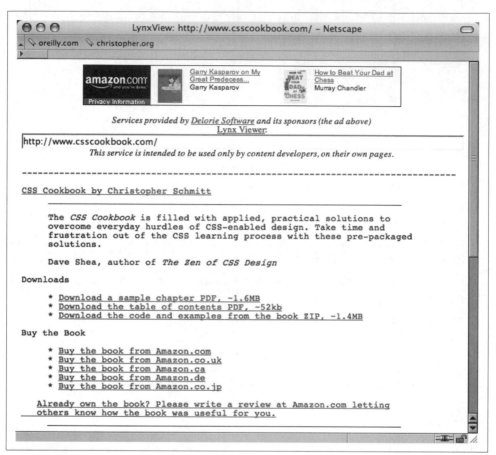

Figure 11-5. A view of a web site through the Lynx Viewer

Discussion

Lynx is the archetypal text browser. Instead of running a web-based emulator, Lynx can be downloaded and installed on PC computers. For more information, see *http://www.subir.com/lynx/build.html*.

See Also

A brief history of Lynx at *http://people.cc.ku.edu/~grobe/early-lynx.html*.

CHAPTER 12

Designing with CSS

12.0 Introduction

Although web builders often spend a lot of time working around browser bugs and reading about the latest tricks from the gurus, it's worth remembering that first and foremost, we're designers and CSS is simply a way to turn design ideas into reality.

CSS is the perfect technology for grabbing the attention of visitors to a web site. With CSS, instead of hacking HTML tables and slicing images to create eye-catching designs, you can go further with valid markup and still save on file sizes by ditching excess HTML and images. In short, you can do what any professional web designer should: create maximum impact with minimal resources.

At a basic level, a developer can learn all there is to know about CSS syntax and the technical limitations of the technology. But let's never forget that code merely implements the design. At its heart, CSS is a *visual* language, and with that comes the need to understand, at least in some small way, how to use design principles with CSS.

With that in mind, this chapter explains how to design with CSS. Specifically, this chapter describes several methods for capturing attention through CSS-enabled techniques, including how to lead the eye with contrast, use excessively large text, create word balloons out of quotations, and use different image formats to create cohesive presentations.

12.1 Enlarging Text Excessively

Problem

You want to draw attention to a web page by enlarging some of the text (see Figure 12-1).

Figure 12-1. An example of excess type size

Solution

Increase the size of the heading so that it is out of proportion with the rest of the text. First use this HTML:

```
<h1>Hi.</h1>
```

Then use this CSS code:

```
h1 {
  font-size: 17em;
  margin: 0;
```

```
  padding: 0;
  text-align: center;
  font-family: Arial, Verdana, Helvetica, sans-serif;
}
```

Discussion

Obviously, any element that's larger than the other elements in the same environment stands out. This approach makes a page look more dynamic in its presentation unlike a page layout where all the elements are the same size.

So, when you want to call attention to an area of a web page, one way would be to try using an excessive type size.

In this example, the size of the font in the word "Hi." has been set to 17em. In the font-size property, an em unit is equal to whatever the font-size of the container is. So, 17em units is equal to 17 times the default font size. There is no theoretical limit to how large you can size text, but in practice different browsers do max out at some point. Not everyone will have a monitor that's large enough to see type that is 1 mile (or 63,360 inches) tall:

```
h3 {
  font-size: 63360in;
}
```

See Also

Recipe 2.2 for specifying font measurements and sizes; "The Elements of Text and Message Design and Their Impact on Message Legibility: A Literature Review," from the Journal of Design Communication at *http://scholar.lib.vt.edu/ejournals/JDC/Spring-2002/bix.html*; the CSS 2 specification for lengths (including em units) at *http://www.w3.org/TR/REC-CSS2/syndata.html#length-units*.

12.2 Creating Unexpected Incongruity

Problem

You need to grab the reader's attention by using two elements that don't seem to fit together.

Solution

Place one element visually inside the other. In the web page in Figure 12-2, which shows Earth's close call with an asteroid, an image of Earth from space was placed over an image of a game of pool.

The College of West Anglia

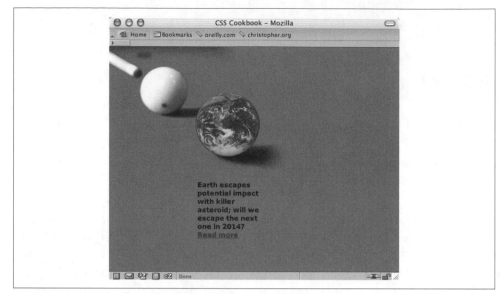

Figure 12-2. An image of Earth placed over an image depicting a game of pool

The HTML for this page is simple:

```
<h2><span class="no">Earth News</span></h2>
<p>Earth escapes potential impact with killer asteroid;
will we escape the next one in 2014? <a href="more.html">Read
more</a></p>
```

For the CSS, place the photo depicting the game of pool into the body element and position it in the upper-left corner. Then use the image replacement technique discussed in Recipe 3.9 to place the photo of Earth for h2:

```
<style type="text/css">
body {
 background-color: #009E69;
 margin: 0;
 background-image: url(billiard.jpg);
 background-repeat: no-repeat;
}
h2 {
 background-image: url(earth.gif);
 position:absolute;
 width:126px;
 height:126px;
 z-index:1;
 left: 166px;
 top: 69px;
}
.no {
 display: none;
}
p {
```

```
    width: 120px;
    margin: 260px 100px 0 170px;
    font-family: Verdana, sans-serif;
    font-size: small;
    font-weight: bold;
}
</style>
```

Discussion

A great way to grab attention is to show something that is unexpected. Cleverly combining two different elements into one image can force viewers to pay attention to the image (see Figure 12-3), or it can simply underscore the purpose of the content.

Figure 12-3. Photos of a child and man are combined

This example used two images—one of a pool cue and cue ball, and the other of Earth. The former image was placed as the background image for the body element. The image of Earth was placed in the background of h2 and was moved by setting the position to absolute. Then it was composited over the pool image.

See Also

Recipe 12.3 on combining unlike elements; Recipe 3.13 on combining different image formats.

12.3 Combining Unlike Elements to Create Contrast

Problem

You want to create contrast on a web page by integrating two different elements, like serif and sans-serif typefaces (see Figure 12-4).

Figure 12-4. Type elements juxtaposed in the same headline

Solution

Use different typefaces in the same headline. First adjust the markup to allow for changes in the font properties:

```
<h2>Cross<span>i</span>ng <span>Over</span></h2>
<h4>Sen. Jane Gordon (<span>I</span>-Utah) bolts GOP; <br />changes part<span>i</span>es to be <span>I</span>ndependent</h4>
```

Then manipulate the CSS for the span element to create a mixture of typefaces:

```
body {
 margin: 25% 10% 0 10%;
}
h2 {
 font-size: 2em;
 font-weight: bold;
 font-family: Arial, Verdana, Helvetica, sans-serif;
 text-transform: uppercase;
 text-align: center;
 padding: 0;
 margin: 0;
```

```
    }
h2 span {
  font-family: Times, "Times New Roman", Georgia, serif;
  font-size: 1.1em;
  font-weight: normal;
  }
h4 {
  margin: 0;
  padding: 0;
  font-size: 1.25em;
  font-weight: bold;
  font-family: Arial, Verdana, Helvetica, sans-serif;
  text-transform: uppercase;
  text-align: center;
}
h4 span {
  font-family: Times, "Times New Roman", Georgia, serif;
  font-size: 1.1em;
  font-weight: normal;
}
```

Discussion

Combining unlike elements creates a visual contrast. In this example, different characteristics of the serif and sans-serif typefaces in the headline create the contrast. However, you can create contrast through imagery as well. For instance, in this example, you could have integrated Democratic and Republican political party symbols and placed them side by side. Or you could have gone for a more symbolic contrast by placing photos of two different types of parties side by side: one depicting a large social gathering at a club, and the other showing a girl blowing a noisemaker over a cupcake with a lit candle on top.

See Also

Recipe 3.13 on combining different image formats.

12.4 Leading the Eye with Contrast

Problem

You want to create a sense of depth or motion through text. On a page containing four paragraphs that are almost identical, it's hard to know which paragraph to look at first (see Figure 12-5). If you change the font size across columns in a particular direction (e.g., decrease the size left-to-right) you lead the reader's eye (see Figure 12-6).

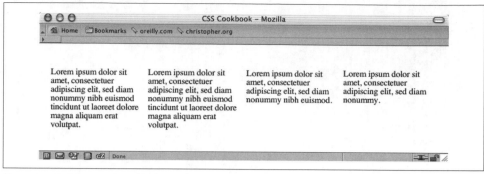

Figure 12-5. Four paragraphs that are almost identical

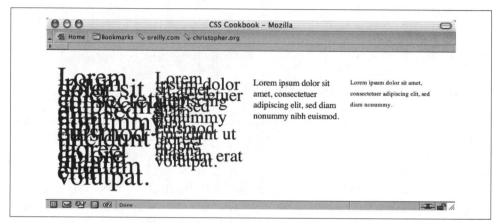

Figure 12-6. Changing the type size so that the reader's eye will scan from left to right

Solution

To lead the reader's eye, change the type size by adding a CSS rule like this:

```
/* Text size */
#layer4 {
 font-size: .7em;
 line-height: 20px;
}
#layer3 {
 font-size: 1em;
 line-height: 20px;
}
#layer2 {
 font-size: 2em;
 line-height: 10px;
}
#layer1 {
 font-size: 3em;
 line-height: 10px;
}
```

Discussion

Contrast occurs when there is an obvious difference between two elements. If there isn't any contrast on a page, the reader doesn't know what is important on the page. By manipulating an element's visual value, you can create contrast between two like elements. Some of those visual values include the following:

- Size
- Color
- Shape
- Position on a page
- Direction
- Density

Properly marked content has an inherent style because the browser uses its own style sheet to render the content when another style sheet isn't present. Headings, such as the h1 element, are stylized in a large, bold font and are separated from the paragraphs (see Figure 12-7). This different font provides the contrast to help readers make sense of the document.

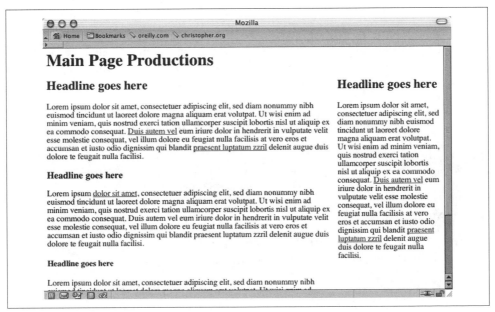

Figure 12-7. Drawing the eye toward the headings by setting them in a larger, bold font

Without the cues that can be provided through a style sheet, the reader's eye wanders throughout a document. The layout shown in Figure 12-8 creates a sense of confusion because it doesn't provide the reader with a clear sense of direction as to what to read first. The headings and copy all share the same values for font, type size, and type color.

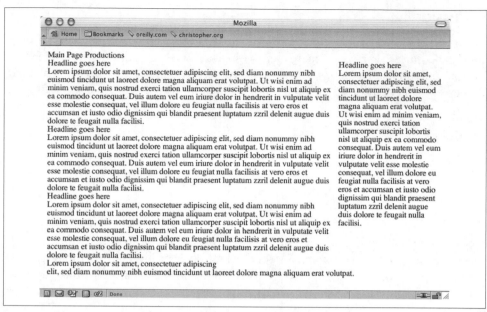

Figure 12-8. The page shown in Figure 12-7, but without contrast

See Also

http://www.lighthouse.org/color_contrast.htm for creating more effective contrast; *http://graphicdesign.about.com/library/weekly/aa012700a.htm* for more on the basics of designing with contrast.

12.5   Checking for Enough Color Contrast

Problem

You want to make sure there is enough contrast between two colors.

Solution

Use the Luminosity Contrast Ratio Analyser from JuicyStudio.com at *http://juicystudio.com/services/luminositycontrastratio.php*.

Enter two color values into the validator and press Calculate Luminosity Contrast Ratio button, as shown in Figure 12-9.

Along with a color sample of the two colors, a summary is presenting noting whether you pass the luminosity contrasts level 2, level 3, or not at all. In Figure 12-10, the example notes that the color combination has passed both levels 2 and 3.

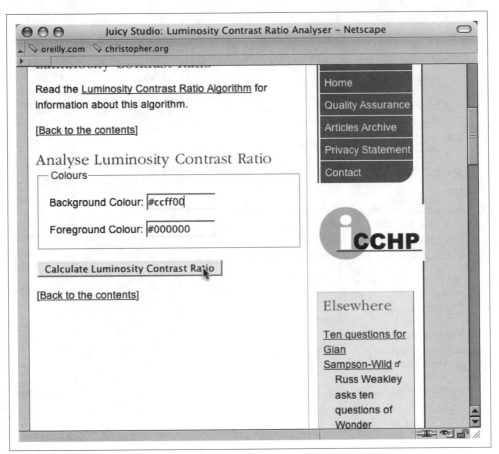

Figure 12-9. Entering values to check luminosity contrast

Discussion

The W3C's Web Content Accessibility Guidelines state that in order to make text legible, designers need to make the content in the foreground be able to be perceived against the background.

When the color for text is close to the same shade of hue as the background color, the text becomes illegible. To create legible text, the colors need to have greater contrast by being further apart from each other in the spectrum or be significantly darker or lighter shade of the same color.

An example of great contrast is the yellow text against a black background much like the stylized Batman logo (from the Tim Burton *Batman* movies of the 1990s).

For colors to pass the second level of the luminosity, the ratio of luminosity contrast needs to be at least 5:1. That means one color needs to be at least 5 times as darker or lighter as the other color.

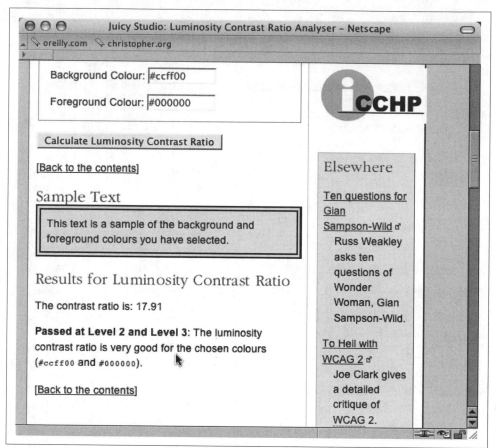

Figure 12-10. The results of the luminosity test

For colors to pass the third level, the luminosity contrast ratio must be at least 10:1.

See Also

JuicyStudio.com's explanation of the Suggested Luminosity Contrast Ratio Algorithm at *http://juicystudio.com/article/luminositycontrastratioalgorithm.php*.

12.6 Emphasizing a Quotation

Problem

You want to add emphasis to a quotation by using large and bold quotation marks (see Figure 12-11).

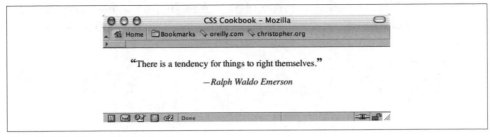

Figure 12-11. The stylized quotation

Solution

First code the markup for the quotation (see Figure 12-12):

```
<blockquote>
 <p>There is a tendency for things to right themselves.</p>
 <cite>Ralph Waldo Emerson</cite>
</blockquote>
```

Figure 12-12. Quotation as it would normally appear

Then apply CSS rules to stylize the quote:

```
blockquote {
 padding: 0;
 margin: 0;
 text-align: center;
}
p {
 font-size: 1em;
 padding-bottom: 3em;
 text-transform: lowercase;
 font-family: Georgia, Times, "Times New Roman", serif;
 margin: 0;
 padding: 0;
}
cite {
 display: block;
 text-align: center;
}
```

Finally, use pseudo-elements :before and :after to stylize the punctuation in the quotation as well as to place an em dash—a horizontal dash equal to the default size of the font—before the name of the cited source:

```
blockquote p:before {
 content: "\201C";
 font-size: 1.2em;
 font-weight: bold;
 font-family: Georgia, Times, "Times New Roman", serif;
}
blockquote p:after {
 content: "\201D";
 font-size: 1.2em;
 font-weight: bold;
 font-family: Georgia, Times, "Times New Roman", serif;
}
cite:before {
 content: "\2014 ";
}
cite {
 display: block;
 text-align: center;
}
```

Discussion

Pseudo-elements are selector constructs that browsers use first to select portions, and then to stylize a web page that can't be marked up through standard HTML. For instance, you can use pseudo-elements to stylize the first line of a paragraph or, in the case of this recipe, to place generated content before and after an actual element.

In this solution you insert smart quotes around the actual quotation. For the left double quotes, we use this declaration:

```
content: "\201C ";
```

Any text that you want displayed after an element needs to be marked off with double quotes. Because you are using double quotes to mark what should be displayed, you can't put another set of double quotes inside the first set. To put quotes around the quotation, you need to use the hexadecimal value for a quotation mark, which is 201C.

Because anything between the quotation marks automatically is generated as is, you need to escape the hexadecimal number that tells the browser to render the quotation marks by placing a forward slash in front of the double quotes.

The content property in the CSS 2.1 specification contains values for easily inserting quotation marks. For example, to re-create the left double quotes, use the following declaration:

```
content: open-quote;
```

However, note that open-quote keyword value specification is implemented only in Mozilla and Opera. Also, note that the :before and :after pseudo-elements don't work in Internet Explorer 5+ for Windows and Internet Explorer for Macintosh.

See Also

Recipe 10.3 on how to include links in printouts of web pages using pseudo-elements; *http://homepages.luc.edu/~vbonill/Entities923-8472.html* for a list of HTML character entities; the CSS 2 specification for quotations for generated content at *http://www.w3.org/TR/REC-CSS2/generate.html#quotes*.

Resources

When working with Cascading Style Sheets, keep these two tips in mind: simplify and verify. Simplify by using only the selectors and properties you believe you need; any extras could cause some confusion down the road. Then verify the HTML, XHTML, and CSS with the help of validators.

Those two steps solve most problems developers encounter when working with CSS. However, if you still run into trouble, this appendix contains some of the top references, discussion groups, and tools on the Internet to help in your CSS development.

General HTML and CSS Instruction

Dave Shea's Roadmap to Standards Essay

http://www.mezzoblue.com/archives/2004/04/30/a_roadmap_to/index.php
A good introduction and pep talk for web designers wanting to learn about web standards–based development.

Web Page for Designers' CSS Tutorial

http://www.wpdfd.com/editorial/basics/index.html
Web developers new to CSS will find benefit from this well-paced tutorial.

Community MX's Basics of CSS Positioning

http://www.communitymx.com/content/article.cfm?cid=3B56F&print=true
For more information about positioning with CSS, try Community MX's tutorial.

CSS Float Property Tutorial

http://css.maxdesign.com.au/floatutorial/index.htm
Learn about floating elements with CSS in various practice coding examples.

CSS Selectors Tutorial

http://css.maxdesign.com.au/selectutorial/index.htm
Gain a better understanding of CSS selectors with this tutorial. Included is a demonstration of how selectors can be used in the construction of a three-column layout.

Design Resources

A List Apart: CSS Topics

http://www.alistapart.com/topics/code/css/
At A List Apart most of the articles published on the topic of CSS come in from web designers sharing their thoughts and breakthroughs with CSS-enabled design.

BlueRobot.com Layout Reservoir

http://www.bluerobot.com/web/layouts/
This small but valuable resource covers two- and three-column layouts.

CSS-Edge

http://www.meyerweb.com/eric/css/edge/
Eric A. Meyer's workshop displays some of his more advanced CSS experiments.

CSS Zen Garden

http://www.csszengarden.com/
The CSS Zen Garden showcases web developers from all over the world restyling the same content. Surfing through several designs is not only great inspiration, but also a fantastic way to better understand the concept of separating presentation from content.

Glish.com CSS Layout Techniques

http://www.glish.com/css/
> One of the first collections of multicolumn layouts created in CSS without the use of HTML tables.

Microformats

http://www.microformats.org/
> Defines and promotes standards for coding unique pieces of content. Check the Microformats listing for methods to code common data like calendar events, contact information, or even the abbr element.

Real World Style

http://www.realworldstyle.com/
> A design resource managed by Mark Newhouse, the goal of this site is to promote CSS-enabled designs, not only for modern, popular browsers that run on Macintosh and Windows OS, but also for browsers that run on Unix machines.

SimpleQuizes

http://www.simplebits.com/bits/simplequiz/
> Web designer and author, Dan Cederholm, conducted a series of quizzes trying to determine the best methods for marking and styling common web development scenarios. In addition to reading the conclusion to each quiz, read each quiz's comments by web designers to get a more informed opinion on coding practices.

Typetester

http://typetester.maratz.com/
> A flexible tool that allows web developers to customize three sets of type and then generates the basic CSS for easy copying and pasting. Available features include setting the values for fonts, size, tracking, leading, letter spacing, alignments, and more.

Discussion Groups

Babble List

http://www.babblelist.com/
>   Moderated by Christopher Schmitt, this web design and development mailing list targets advanced web design issues. The site offers a lively exchange of information, resources, theories, and practices of designers and developers.

css-discuss

http://www.css-discuss.org/
>   This mailing list, chaperoned by CSS expert Eric A. Meyer, who is the author of O'Reilly's *Cascading Style Sheets: The Definitive Guide*, Second Edition, aims to provide practical discussion about the application of CSS.

Usenet Stylesheets Newsgroup

news:comp.infosystems.www.authoring.stylesheets
>   Founded in 1997, this unmoderated newsgroup covers the theory and application of CSS. Topics for the group can include practical applications, questions about the specification, the benefits of CSS, implementation bugs in browsers, and more. You can find the FAQ document for the group at *http://css.nu/faq/ciwas-mFAQ.html*.

www-style (W3C Style Mailing List)

http://lists.w3.org/Archives/Public/www-style/
>   Maintained by the World Wide Web Consortium (W3C), this mailing list provides a venue for discussing the theories and future of CSS. Questions about the specification or about CSS proposals are welcomed; however, discussions revolving around practical applications of the technology are discouraged.

References

CSS Browser Support Charts

http://www.westciv.com/style_master/academy/browser_support/
>   If you run into problems developing with CSS, check the CSS Support Charts here to determine if there is a problem with the browser(s) you are using.

W3C's Recommended DTDs

http://www.w3.org/QA/2002/04/valid-dtd-list.html

Assigning the right DOCTYPE to a web page helps in establishing the correct manner in which browsers will render your web page and validators will check your code. All that's on this web page is a listing of the most commonly used DOCTYPEs.

W3C's CSS Page

http://www.w3.org/Style/CSS/

This is the official site for CSS. At this site you can learn about the history of CSS, investigate learning resources and authoring tools, and read current CSS news.

CSS 2.1 Specification

http://www.w3.org/TR/CSS21/

Browser implementations of the CSS specification are sometimes a confusing mess. When you're tracking down how to achieve a certain look or an implementation bug, go here to check the specification (as well as the CSS Support Charts).

HTML 4.01 Specification

http://www.w3.org/TR/html4/

To make the most out of using CSS for web design, you need to create your web documents with structured markup instead of using workarounds and hacks. Furthermore, you need to mark up your documents with elements to imply an inherent presentational meaning. For example, you need to highlight important words by using the em element and not the b element. If you need to change your production methods, dig into the HTML specification at this site and get to know the elements all over again.

XHTML 1.0 Specification

http://www.w3.org/TR/xhtml1/

Extensible HyperText Markup Language (XHTML) is a restructuring of HTML 4 in XML 1.0. Although XHTML markup is stricter than that of HTML 4, the benefits are simple: more logical markup, increased interoperability, and enhanced accessibility.

Tools

BrowserCam

http://www.browsercam.com/

BrowserCam is an affordable, web-based service that tests a web design in multiple browsers on numerous operating systems. At the time of this writing, a free 24-hour evaluation period is available for web developers that register onto the site.

iCapture

http://www.danvine.com/icapture/

A free tool for web developers to preview web pages as viewed in Safari. A great site for Windows users when the only Macintosh product they want to buy is an iPod.

SelectORacle

http://gallery.theopalgroup.com/selectoracle/

A free service designed to help people learn more about complex CSS selectors by translating their meaning into plain English. CSS selectors can be submitted in one of two ways. The first method is to copy and paste a CSS selector into a form on the web site. The other method is to enter either a URL of a web page with an embedded style sheet or a URL to an external style sheet. The service then renders the CSS selector into easy-to-understand language.

W3C CSS Validator

http://jigsaw.w3.org/css-validator/

This free service, provided on the W3C server, checks CSS for proper structure. You can test your markup by uploading files, entering a web address in the form, and then copying and pasting the CSS into a form field. And if you are so inclined, you can download and install the validator on your own server.

W3C HTML Validator

http://validator.w3.org/

The W3C HTML validator is another free service from the W3C. Similar to the CSS validator, the HTML validator checks to see if your markup conforms to web standards.

Web Developer Browser Extension

https://addons.mozilla.org/extensions/moreinfo.php?id=60

Chris Pedrick has created an indispensable extension for the popular Firefox and Mozilla browsers. A few features involve editing a web page's CSS through the browser, sending a web page's code directly to a W3C's validator, placing an outline on block level elements, as well as many, many other functions with a simple click of the mouse.

Xyle Scope

http://www.culturedcode.com/xyle/

Xyle scope is an indispensable tool that helps people of all skill levels. Accepting either a link to a web site or pulling up a web page from your computer, Xyle scope allows developers to see how the markup and CSS work together to build a web page design. Since the software is tied to the Web Kit, Safari's rendering engine, it is only available for Macintosh operating system.

APPENDIX B

CSS 2.1 Properties and Proprietary Extensions

This appendix contains a table of CSS properties from W3C's CSS 2.1 specification (see *http://www.w3.org/TR/CSS21*), a table of Microsoft proprietary extensions to CSS and a table of some of Mozilla's proprietary extensions. Table B-1 provides a listing of the property's values, initial value, what the property applies to, if the values in the property are inherited, if the property accepts percentages, and the property's media group.

Table B-2 presents a listing of Microsoft's proprietary extensions to the specifications. These properties will not validate if you run them through a validator and they will only appear successfully in a browser built by Microsoft. Your mileage may vary with the use of these extensions.

As of this writing, Mozilla's proprietary extensions that are available in Mozilla, Firefox, and Netscape Navigator 6+ browsers, are not fully documented. Table B-3 lists a portion of extensions that are documented from Mozilla's developer's web site. Check their site for a complete listing of the extensions, at *http://developer.mozilla.org/en/docs/CSS_Reference:Mozilla_Extensions*.

Table B-1. CSS 2.1 properties

Name	Values	Initial value	Applies to (Default: all)	Inherited?	Percentages (Default: N/A)	Media groups
'background-attachment'	scroll | fixed | inherit	scroll		no		visual
'background-color'	<color> | transparent | inherit	transparent		no		visual
'background-image'	<uri> | none | inherit	none		no		visual

Name	Values	Initial value	Applies to (Default: all)	Inherited?	Percentages (Default: N/A)	Media groups
'background-position'	[[<percentage> | <length> | left | center | right] [<percentage> | <length> | top | center | bottom]?] | [[left | center | right] || [top | center | bottom]] | inherit	0% 0%		no	refer to the size of the box itself	visual
'background-repeat'	repeat | repeat-x | repeat-y | no-repeat | inherit	repeat		no		visual
'background'	['background-color' || 'background-image' || 'back-ground-repeat' || 'background-attachment' || 'background-posi-tion'] | inherit	see individual properties		no	allowed on 'background-position'	visual
'border-col-lapse'	collapse | separate | inherit	separate	'table' and 'inline-table' elements	yes		visual
'border-color'	[<color> | transparent]{1,4} | inherit	see individual properties		no		visual
'border-spac-ing'	<length> <length>? | inherit	0	'table' and 'inline-table' elements	yes		visual
'border-style'	<border-style> {1,4} | inherit	see individual properties		no		visual
'border-top' 'border-right' 'border-bot-tom' 'border-left'	[<border-width> || <border-style> || >'border-top-color'] | inherit	see individual properties		no		visual

Name	Values	Initial value	Applies to (Default: all)	Inherited?	Percentages (Default: N/A)	Media groups
'border-top-color' 'border-right-color' 'border-bottom-color' 'border-left-color'	\<color\> | transparent | inherit	the value of the 'color' property		no		visual
'border-top-style' 'border-right-style' 'border-bottom-style' 'border-left-style'	\<border-style\> | inherit	none		no		visual
'border-top-width' 'border-right-width' 'border-bottom-width' 'border-left-width'	\<border-width\> | inherit	medium		no		visual
'border-width'	\<border-width\> {1,4} | inherit	see individual properties		no		visual
'border'	[\<border-width\> || \<border-style\> || \>'border-top-color'] | inherit	see individual properties		no		visual
'bottom'	\<length\> | \<percentage\> | auto | inherit	auto	positioned elements	no	refer to height of containing block	visual
'caption-side'	top | bottom | inherit	top	'table-caption' elements	yes		visual
'clear'	none | left | right | both | inherit	none	block-level elements	no		visual
'clip'	\<shape\> | auto | inherit	auto	absolutely positioned elements	no		visual
'color'	\<color\> | inherit	depends on user agent		yes		visual

Name	Values	Initial value	Applies to (Default: all)	Inherited?	Percentages (Default: N/A)	Media groups
'content'	normal | none | [<string> | <uri> | <counter> | attr(<identifier>) | open-quote | close-quote | no-open-quote | no-close-quote]+ | inherit	normal	:before and :after pseudo-elements	no		all
'counter-increment'	[<identifier> <integer>?]+ | none | inherit	none		no		all
'counter-reset'	[<identifier> <integer>?]+ | none | inherit	none		no		all
'cursor'	[[<uri> ,]* [auto | crosshair | default | pointer | move | e-resize | ne-resize | nw-resize | n-resize | se-resize | sw-resize | s-resize | w-resize | text | wait | help | progress]] | inherit	auto		yes		visual, interactive
'direction'	ltr | rtl | inherit	ltr	all elements, but see prose	yes		visual
'display'	inline | block | list-item | run-in | inline-block | table | inline-table | table-row-group | table-header-group | table-footer-group | table-row | table-column-group | table-column | table-cell | table-caption | none | inherit	inline		no		all
'empty-cells'	show | hide | inherit	show	'table-cell' elements	yes		visual
'float'	left | right | none | inherit	none	all, but see 9.7	no		visual

Name	Values	Initial value	Applies to (Default: all)	Inherited?	Percentages (Default: N/A)	Media groups
'font-family'	[[<family-name> | <generic-family>] [, <family-name>| <generic-family>]*] | inherit	depends on user agent		yes		visual
'font-size'	<absolute-size> | <relative-size> | <length> | <per-centage> | inherit	medium		yes	refer to parent element's font size	visual
'font-style'	normal | italic | oblique | inherit	normal		yes		visual
'font-variant'	normal | small-caps | inherit	normal		yes		visual
'font-weight'	normal | bold | bolder | lighter | 100 | 200 | 300 | 400 | 500 | 600 | 700 | 800 | 900 | inherit	normal		yes		visual
'font'	[['font-style' || 'font-variant' || 'font-weight']? 'font-size' [/ 'line-height']? 'font-family'] | caption | icon | menu | message-box | small-caption | status-bar | inherit	see individual properties		yes	see individual properties	visual
'height'	<length> | <percentage> | auto | inherit	auto	all elements but non-replaced inline ele-ments, table columns, and column groups	no	Allowed; percentage is calculated with respect to the height of the generated box's containing block. If the height of the containing block is not specified explicitly (i.e., it depends on the content height), the value is interpreted like "auto."	visual

Name	Values	Initial value	Applies to (Default: all)	Inherited?	Percentages (Default: N/A)	Media groups
'left'	\<length\> | \<percentage\> | auto | inherit	auto	positioned elements	no	refer to width of containing block	visual
'letter-spacing'	normal | \<length\> | inherit	normal		yes		visual
'line-height'	normal | \<number\> | \<length\> | \<percentage\> | inherit	normal		yes	refer to the font size of the element itself	visual
'list-style-image'	\<uri\> | none | inherit	none	elements with 'display: list-item'	yes		visual
'list-style-position'	inside | outside | inherit	outside	elements with 'display: list-item'	yes		visual
'list-style-type'	disc | circle | square | decimal | decimal-leading-zero | lower-roman | upper-roman | lower-greek | lower-latin | upper-latin | armenian | georgian | lower-alpha | upper-alpha | none | inherit	disc	elements with 'display: list-item'	yes		visual
'list-style'	['list-style-type' || 'list-style-position' || 'list-style-image'] | inherit	see individual properties	elements with 'display: list-item'	yes		visual
'margin-right' 'margin-left'	\<margin-width\> | inherit	0	all elements except elements with table display types other than table and inline-table	no	refer to width of containing block	visual

Name	Values	Initial value	Applies to (Default: all)	Inherited?	Percentages (Default: N/A)	Media groups
'margin-top' 'margin-bottom'	<margin-width> | inherit	0	all elements except elements with table display types other than table and inline-table	no	refer to width of containing block	visual
'margin'	<margin-width> {1,4} | inherit	see individual properties	all elements except elements with table display types other than table and inline-table	no	refer to width of containing block	visual
'max-height'	<length> | <percentage> | none | inherit	none	all elements but non-replaced inline elements, table columns, and column groups	no	Allowed; percentage is calculated with respect to the height of the generated box's containing block. If the height of the containing block is not specified explicitly (i.e., it depends on the content height), the value is interpreted like "auto."	visual
'max-width'	<length> | <percentage> | none | inherit	none	all elements but non-replaced inline elements, table rows, and row groups	no	refer to width of containing block	visual

Name	Values	Initial value	Applies to (Default: all)	Inherited?	Percentages (Default: N/A)	Media groups
'min-height'	<length> | <percentage> | inherit	0	all elements but non-replaced inline elements, table columns, and column groups	no	Allowed; percentage is calculated with respect to the height of the generated box's containing block. If the height of the containing block is not specified explicitly (i.e., it depends on the content height), the value is interpreted like "auto." Allowed; percentage is calculated with respect to the height of the generated box's containing block. If the height of the containing block is not specified explicitly (i.e., it depends on the content height), the value is interpreted like "auto."	visual
'min-width'	<length> | <percentage> | inherit	0	all elements but non-replaced inline elements, table rows, and row groups	no	refer to width of containing block	visual
'orphans'	<integer> | inherit	2	block-level elements	yes		visual, paged
'outline-color'	<color> | invert | inherit	invert		no		visual, interactive
'outline-style'	<border-style> | inherit	none		no		visual, interactive

Name	Values	Initial value	Applies to (Default: all)	Inherited?	Percentages (Default: N/A)	Media groups
'outline-width'	<border-width> | inherit	medium		no		visual, interactive
'outline'	['outline-color' || 'outline-style' || 'outline-width'] | inherit	see individual properties		no		visual, interactive
'overflow'	visible | hidden | scroll | auto | inherit	visible	non-replaced block-level elements, table cells, and inline-block elements	no		visual
'padding-top' 'padding-right' 'padding-bottom' 'padding-left'	<padding-width> | inherit	0	all elements except elements with table display types other than table, inline-table, and table-cell	no	refer to width of containing block	visual
'padding'	<padding-width> {1,4} | inherit	see individual properties	all elements except elements with table display types other than table, inline-table, and table-cell	no	refer to width of containing block	visual
'page-break-after'	auto | always | avoid | left | right | inherit	auto	block-level elements	no		visual, paged
'page-break-before'	auto | always | avoid | left | right | inherit	auto	block-level elements	no		visual, paged
'page-break-inside'	avoid | auto | inherit	auto	block-level elements	yes		visual, paged
'position'	static | relative | absolute | fixed | inherit	static		no		visual
'quotes'	[<string> <string>]+ | none | inherit	depends on user agent		yes		visual

Name	Values	Initial value	Applies to (Default: all)	Inherited?	Percentages (Default: N/A)	Media groups
'right'	<length> | <percentage> | auto | inherit	auto	positioned elements	no	refer to width of containing block	visual
'table-layout'	auto | fixed | inherit	auto	'table' and 'inline-table' elements	no		visual
'text-align'	left | right | center | justify | inherit	'left' if 'direction' is 'ltr'; 'right' if 'direction' is 'rtl'	block-level elements, table cells and inline blocks	yes		visual
'text-decoration'	none | [underline || overline || line-through || blink] | inherit	none		Allowed; percentage is calculated with respect to the height of the generated box's containing block. If the height of the containing block is not specified explicitly (i.e., it depends on the content height), the value is interpreted like "auto."		visual
'text-indent'	<length> | <percentage> | inherit	0	block-level elements, table cells and inline blocks	yes	refer to width of containing block	visual
'text-transform'	capitalize | uppercase | lowercase | none | inherit	none		yes		visual

Table B-1. CSS 2.1 properties (continued)

Name	Values	Initial value	Applies to (Default: all)	Inherited?	Percentages (Default: N/A)	Media groups
'top'	\<length\> | \<percentage\> | auto | inherit	auto	positioned elements	no	refer to height of containing block	visual
'unicode-bidi'	normal | embed | bidi-override | inherit	normal	all elements, but see prose	no		visual
'vertical-align'	baseline | sub | super | top | text-top | middle | bottom | text-bottom | \<percentage\> | \<length\> | inherit	baseline	inline-level and 'table-cell' elements	no	refer to the 'line-height' of the element itself	visual
'visibility'	visible | hidden | collapse | inherit	visible		yes		visual
'white-space'	normal | pre | now-rap | pre-wrap | pre-line | inherit	normal		yes		visual
'widows'	\<integer\> | inherit	2	block-level elements	yes		visual, paged
'width'	\<length\> | \<percentage\> | auto | inherit	auto	all elements but non-replaced inline elements, table rows, and row groups	no	refer to width of containing block	visual
'word-spacing'	normal | \<length\> | inherit	normal		yes		visual
'z-index'	auto | \<integer\> | inherit	auto	positioned elements	no		Visual

The CSS 2.1 Property Table is © 2005, World Wide Web Consortium (*Massachusetts Institute of Technology*, European Research Consortium for Informatics and Mathematics, *Keio University*). All Rights Reserved. *http://www.w3.org/Consortium/Legal/2002/copyright-documents-20021231*.

Table B-2. Microsoft proprietary extensions to CSS

Name	Values	Initial value	Applies to (Default: all)	Inherited?	Percentages (Default: N/A)	Media groups
'background-position-x'	\<length\> | \<percentage\> | left | center | right	0%		no	yes	visual
'background-position-y'	\<length\> | \<percentage\> | top | center | bottom	0%		no	yes	visual
'filter'	See *http://tinyurl. com/c8vpf*	n/a		no		filter properties
'ime-mode'	auto | active | inactive | disabled	auto		yes		visual
'layout-grid'	mode | type | line | char	both loose none none		yes		visual
'layout-grid-char'	\<length\> | \<percentage\> | none | auto	none		no	yes	visual
'layout-grid-line'	\<length\> | \<percentage\> | none | auto	none		no	yes	visual
'layout-grid-mode'	both | none | line | char	both		yes		visual
'layout-grid-type'	loose | strict | fixed	loose		yes		visual
'line-break'	normal | strict	normal		yes		visual
'overflow-x'	visible | scroll | hidden | auto	visible (except for textarea, then initial value is hidden)		no		visual
'overflow-y'	visible | scroll | hidden | auto	visible (except for textarea, then initial value is auto)				visual
'scrollbar-3dlight-color'	\<color\>	default color	element with scroll bar	yes		visual
'scrollbar-arrow-color'	\<color\>	default color	element with scroll bar	yes		visual
'scrollbar-base-color'	\<color\>	default color	element with scroll bar	yes		visual
'scrollbar-darkshadow-color'	\<color\>	default color	element with scroll bar	yes		visual

Name	Values	Initial value	Applies to (Default: all)	Inherited?	Percentages (Default: N/A)	Media groups
'scrollbar-face-color'	<color>	default color	element with scroll bar	yes		visual
'scrollbar-highlight-color'	<color>	default color	element with scroll bar	yes		visual
'scrollbar-shadow-color'	<color>	default color	element with scroll bar	yes		visual
'text-autospace'	none | ideograph-alpha | ideograph-numeric | ideograph-parenthesis | ideograph-space	none		no		visual
'text-justify'	auto | distribute | distribute-all-lines | distribute-center-last | inter-cluster | inter-ideograph | inter-word | kashida | newspaper	auto		yes		visual
'text-kashida-space'	<percentage> | inherit	0%		yes		visual
'text-underline-position'	above | below | auto | auto-pos	auto		yes		visual
'word-break'	normal | break-all | keep-all	normal		yes		visual
'word-wrap'	normal | break-word	normal		yes		visual
'writing-mode'	lr-tb | tb-rl	lr-tb		no		visual
'zoom'	normal | <number> | <percentage>	normal		no	yes	visual

Table B-3. Mozilla CSS property extensions

Name	Values	Initial value	Applies to (Default: all)	Inherited?
'-moz-appearance'	none | button | button-small | checkbox | check-box-container | checkbox-small | dialog | listbox | menu | menuitem | menulist | menulist-button | menulist-textfield | progressbar | radio | radio-container | radio-small | resizer | scrollbar | scrollbar-button-down | scrollbar-button-left | scrollbarbutton-right | scrollbarbutton-up | scroll-bartrack-horizontal | scroll-bartrack-vertical | separator | statusbar | tab | tab-left-edge | tabpanels | textfield | toolbar | toolbar-button | toolbox | tooltip | treeheadercell | treeheadersortarrow | treeitem | treetwisty | treetwistyopen | treeview | window	none		no
'-moz-binding'	uri | none	none		no
'-moz-background-clip'	border | padding	border		no
'-moz-background-inline-policy'	bounding-box | continuous | each-box	continuous	inline elements	no
'-moz-background-origin'	border | padding | content	padding		no
'-moz-border-bottom-colors'	<color> | transparent	n/a		no
'-moz-border-left-colors'				
'-moz-border-right-colors'				
'-moz-border-top-colors'				
'-moz-border-radius'	<length> | <percentage>	0		no

Name	Values	Initial value	Applies to (Default: all)	Inherited?
'-moz-border-radius-bottomleft'	\<length> | \<percentage>	0		no
'-moz-border-radius-bottomright'				
'-moz-border-radius-topleft'				
'-moz-border-radius-topright'				
'-moz-box-align'	start | center | end | baseline | stretch	stretch	elements with a CSS display value of -moz-box or -moz-inline-box	no
'-moz-box-direction'	normal | reverse	normal	elements with a CSS display value of -moz-box or -moz-inline-box	no
'-moz-box-flex'	0 | >0	0	elements with a CSS display value of -moz-box or -moz-inline-box	no
'-moz-box-orient'	horizontal | vertical	horizontal	elements with a CSS display value of -moz-box or -moz-inline-box	no
'-moz-box-pack'	start | center | end | justify	start	elements with a CSS display value of -moz-box or -moz-inline-box	no
'-moz-box-sizing'	content-box | border-box | padding box	content-box		no
'-moz-image-region'	for rect( ) values, a rect consisting of four computed lengths	auto	XUL image elements and :-moz-tree-image, :-moz-tree-twisty, and :-moz-tree-checkbox pseudo-elements	yes
'-moz-opacity'	0 (or less) | 0 < number < 1 | 1 (or more)	1		no
'-moz-outline'	-moz-outline-color | -moz-outline-style | -moz-out-line-width	see individual properties		no
'-moz-outline-color'	\<color> | invert	invert		no
'-moz-outline-offset'	\<number>	0		no
'-moz-outline-radius'	\<length> | \<percentage>	0		no

Name	Values	Initial value	Applies to (Default: all)	Inherited?
'-moz-outline-radius-bottomleft'	\<length\> | \<percentage\>	0		no
'-moz-outline-radius-bottomright'				
'-moz-outline-radius-topleft'				
'-moz-outline-radius-topright'				
'-moz-outline-style'	none | dotted | dashed | solid | double | groove | ridge | inset | outset	none		no
'-moz-outline-style'	\<width\>	medium		no

CSS 2.1 Selectors, Pseudo-Classes, and Pseudo-Elements

Making sure style reaches the appropriate element is just as important as knowing the CSS properties. This appendix contains three reference tables that show you how to apply styles to the correct elements.

Table C-1 contains the CSS 2.1 selectors. Selectors help tell the browser where to apply the CSS declarations.

> Note that in the Generic Pattern column, the values C, R, and S take the place of type selectors.

Table C-2 contains a list of pseudo-classes. A pseudo-class is a device by which a browser applies an invisible class on its own. For example, through the pseudo-class we are able to define properties for various visited, active, and hover states of the ubiquitous link.

Table C-3 contains a list of pseudo-elements. Similar in nature to pseudo-class, a pseudo-element places invisible tags around content in a web page and then applies styles to that element. Since the structure is more like a typical element than a class, these elements are called pseudo-elements.

Table C-1. CSS 2.1 selectors

Selector	Generic Pattern	Description	Sample
Universal	*	Matches with any element.	`* { text-decoration: none; }`
Type	C	Matches any element; in this example, all h2 elements.	`h2 { font-weight: normal; }`
Descendant	C R S	Matches any S element that is a descendant of elements R, which is a descendant of elements C.	`div#content p em { background-color: yellow; }`

Table C-1. CSS 2.1 selectors (continued)

Selector	Generic Pattern	Description	Sample
Child	C > S	Selects any S element that is a child of C element.	`li > ul { list-style-type: circle;}`
Adjacent Sibling	C + S	Selects any S element that immediately follows element C.	`div#content+p { text-indent: 0;}`
Grouping	C, R, S	Several selectors utilize the same declaration(s).	`h1, h2, h3, h4 { color: #0cf;}`
Class	C.classR	Selects any C element that contains a class attribute with the value of classR.	`img.content { padding: 4px; border: 1px solid black; }`
ID	C#idR	Selects any C element that contains an id attribute with the value of idR.	`div#content { color: #333;}`
Attribute Selector	C[attribute]	Selects any C element that contains the attribute.	`a[link] {text-decoration: none;}`
Attribute Selector	C[attribute="valueR"]	Selects any C element that contains the attribute with the value of valueR.	`input[type="text"] { width: 33%; }`
Attribute Selector	C[attribute~="valueR"]	Selects any C element that contains the attribute whose value is a space-separated list of words and one of the words in that list matches valueR.	`div.advertisement form[class~="login"] { float: left; margin-left: 7px; }`
Attribute Selector	C[attribute|="valueR"]	Selects any C element that contains the attribute whose value is a hyphen-separated list of words and the first word matches valueR.	`warning[lang="uk"]:after { content: " Blimey!"}`

Table C-2. CSS 2.1 pseudo-classes

Pseudo-class	Generic Pattern	Description	Sample
:first-child	C:first-child	Matches element C that is the first child in another element.	`divs p:first-child {color: white; background-color: red; }`
:link	C:link	Matches any unvisited link of element C.	`a:link {text-decoration: none; }`
:visited	C:visited	Matches any visited link of element C.	`a:visited {font-weight: normal; }`

Table C-2. CSS 2.1 pseudo-classes (continued)

Pseudo-class	Generic Pattern	Description	Sample
:hover	C:hover	Matches the C element a user has selected (typically by moving the cursor icon over a link), but not activated.	a:hover { background-color: orange; }
:active	C:active	Matches the C element a user has activated.	a:active { color: green; }
:focus	C:focus	Matches the C element that contains the focus (typically an input field of a form).	input:focus { background-color: #F7F7D5;}
:lang	C:lang(R)	Matches the C element that uses the language R.	p:lang(en) {font-weight: bold;}

Table C-3. CSS 2.1 pseudo-elements

Pseudo-element	Generic pattern	Description	Sample
:first-line	C:first-line	Selects the first line of text in the C element.	h2+p:first-line {color: #727977;}
:first-letter	C:first-letter	Selects the first letter in the C element.	h1:first-letter { font-size: 66%; text-transform: lowercase; }
:before	C:before	Places generated content before an element; used with the content property.	ul.tracklisting li:before { content: "Song title: ";}
:after	C:after	Places generated content after an element; used with the content property.	div#footer p.copyright:after {content: "Double true!";}

Styling of Form Elements

Forms have a big impact on our day-to-day Internet lifestyle, so designers want to control the look-and-feel of form elements in their web page designs. The problem is that browsers manipulate the visual display of form elements from one browser to the next. Even the same browser version can display a form element differently on separate operating systems.

To help web developers determine the best way to design web forms, this appendix documents a majority of the visual CSS properties and their effect on form elements in today's modern browsers.

The first part of this appendix lists the properties that were tested and their respective values in Table D-1.

The second part examines eight form elements and how they can be modified using 20 of the CSS properties listed in Table D-1 in 10 different browsers:

- Checkboxes, are shown in Table D-2 and Figures D-1 to D-20.
- File Upload, is shown in Table D-3 and Figures D-21 to D-40.
- Radio Buttons, are shown in Table D-4 and Figures D-41 to D-60.
- Input Text, is shown in Table D-5 and Figures D-61 to D-80.
- Select with Multiple Items, is shown in Table D-6 and Figures D-81 to D-100.
- Select with Individual Item, is shown in Table D-7 and Figures D-101 to D-120.
- Submit Button, is shown in Table D-8 and Figures D-121 to D-140.
- Textarea, is shown in Table D-9 and Figures D-141 to D-160.

The values used from Table D-2 to Table D-9 include NA, Y, N, and S.

NA stands for *Not Available* meaning that the CSS property does not apply to the form element, Y for *Yes* meaning that the CSS property's value is properly applied, N for *No* a meaning that the CSS property's value was not applied and S for *Somewhat* meaning that there is some part of the CSS property's value being applied.

The *Somewhat* value marks unusual situations. There are points within the HTML and CSS specifications that do not define a certain behavior and therefore determination of a CSS rule's successful application becomes difficult.

For example, Firefox expands the width of the input field as well as the space between letters when using the `letter-spacing` property.

In this instance, the discrepancy could be due to Firefox calculating the default width of the input field on a certain number of characters whereas the other browsers could be basing the width on a predetermined value or an unadjusted number of characters at the font size of the input field.

Table D-1. The properties and their values used in testing form elements

Property	Value
background-color	#ccff00;
background-image	url(checkerboard_bkgd.gif);
border	0;
border-color	1px solid red;
border-style	groove;
border-width	24px;
color	#00ccff;
font-family	Georgia, Times, 'Times New Roman', serif;
font-size	24px;
font-weight	bold;
height	100px;
letter-spacing	24px;
line-height	1.5;
margin	24px;
padding	24px;
text-align	right;
text-decoration	underline;
text-indent	24px;
width	100px;
word-spacing	24px;

Checkboxes

background-color

Figure D-1. Testing the background color of checkboxes can be found at *http://www.oreilly.com/cssckbk2/appendixd/figs/css2_ad001.gif*

background-image
> Figure D-2. Testing background images in checkboxes can be found at *http://www.oreilly.com/cssckbk2/appendixd/figs/css2_ad002.gif*

border: 0;
> Figure D-3. Testing the removal of borders on checkboxes can be found at *http://www.oreilly.com/cssckbk2/appendixd/figs/css2_ad003.gif*

border-color
> Figure D-4. Testing of colors on the checkbox borders can be found at *http://www.oreilly.com/cssckbk2/appendixd/figs/css2_ad004.gif*

border-style
> Figure D-5. Testing the styles of borders on checkboxes can be found at *http://www.oreilly.com/cssckbk2/appendixd/figs/css2_ad005.gif*

border-width
> Figure D-6. Testing the widths of borders on checkboxes can be found at *http://www.oreilly.com/cssckbk2/appendixd/figs/css2_ad006.gif*

color
> Figure D-7. Testing the color on checkboxes can be found at *http://www.oreilly.com/cssckbk2/appendixd/figs/css2_ad007.gif*

font-family
> Figure D-8. Testing to set a different font on checkboxes can be found at *http://www.oreilly.com/cssckbk2/appendixd/figs/css2_ad008.gif*

font-size
> Figure D-9. Testing a different size of font on checkboxes can be found at *http://www.oreilly.com/cssckbk2/appendixd/figs/css2_ad009.gif*

font-weight
> Figure D-10. Testing a bold font on checkboxes can be found at *http://www.oreilly.com/cssckbk2/appendixd/figs/css2_ad010.gif*

height
> Figure D-11. Testing to set a height for checkboxes can be found at *http://www.oreilly.com/cssckbk2/appendixd/figs/css2_ad011.gif*

letter-spacing
> Figure D-12. Testing the letter spacing of checkboxes can be found at *http://www.oreilly.com/cssckbk2/appendixd/figs/css2_ad012.gif*

line-height
> Figure D-13. Testing setting the spacing between lines of text on checkboxes can be found at *http://www.oreilly.com/cssckbk2/appendixd/figs/css2_ad013.gif*

margin
> Figure D-14. Testing margins on checkboxes can be found at *http://www.oreilly.com/cssckbk2/appendixd/figs/css2_ad014.gif*

padding

Figure D-15. Testing padding on checkboxes can be found at *http://www.oreilly.com/cssckbk2/appendixd/figs/css2_ad015.gif*

text-align

Figure D-16. Testing the alignment of text can be found at *http://www.oreilly.com/cssckbk2/appendixd/figs/css2_ad016.gif*

text-decoration

Figure D-17. Testing to set a different font on checkboxes can be found at *http://www.oreilly.com/cssckbk2/appendixd/figs/css2_ad017.gif*

text-indent

Figure D-18. Testing indenting the text on checkboxes can be found at *http://www.oreilly.com/cssckbk2/appendixd/figs/css2_ad018.gif*

width

Figure D-19. Testing the width of checkboxes can be found at *http://www.oreilly.com/cssckbk2/appendixd/figs/css2_ad019.gif*

word-spacing

Figure D-20. Testing the spacing between words on checkboxes can be found at *http://www.oreilly.com/cssckbk2/appendixd/figs/css2_ad020.gif*

Table D-2. A review of the CSS properties on checkboxes

	WinIE5	WinIE5.5	WinIE6	WinIE7	Safari2	WinFF1.5	MacFF1.5	WinNN7.2	MacNN7.2	Op8.5
background-color	S	S	S	S	N	N	N	N	N	Y
background-image	S	S	S	S	N	N	N	N	N	Y
border	N	N	N	N	N	N	N	N	N	N
border-color	S	S	S	S	N	N	N	N	N	Y
border-style	S	S	S	S	N	N	N	N	N	Y
border-width	N	N	N	N	N	N	N	N	N	N
color	N	N	N	N	N	N	N	N	N	N
font-family	NA	NA	NA	NA	NA	NA	NA	NA	NA	NA
font-size	N	N	N	N	N	N	N	N	N	N
font-weight	N	N	N	N	N	N	N	N	N	N
height	S	S	S	N	N	S	Y	S	Y	N
letter-spacing	NA	NA	NA	NA	NA	NA	NA	NA	NA	NA
line-height	N	N	N	N	N	N	N	N	N	N
margin	Y	Y	Y	Y	Y	Y	Y	Y	Y	Y
padding	N	N	N	N	N	N	N	N	N	Y
text-align	NA	NA	NA	NA	NA	NA	NA	NA	NA	NA
text-decoration	NA	NA	NA	NA	NA	NA	NA	NA	NA	NA
text-indent	Y	Y	Y	S	N	N	N	N	N	N
width	S	S	S	S	S	S	Y	S	Y	S
word-spacing	NA	NA	NA	NA	NA	NA	NA	NA	NA	NA

File Input

background-color

Figure D-21. Testing the background color of file input can be found at *http://www.oreilly.com/cssckbk2/appendixd/figs/css2_ad021.gif*

background-image

Figure D-22. Testing background images in file input can be found at *http://www.oreilly.com/cssckbk2/appendixd/figs/css2_ad022.gif*

border: 0;

Figure D-23. Testing the removal of borders on file input can be found at *http://www.oreilly.com/cssckbk2/appendixd/figs/css2_ad023.gif*

border-color

Figure D-24. Testing of colors on the file input borders can be found at *http://www.oreilly.com/cssckbk2/appendixd/figs/css2_ad024.gif*

border-style

Figure D-25. Testing the styles of borders on file input can be found at *http://www.oreilly.com/cssckbk2/appendixd/figs/css2_ad025.gif*

border-widht

Figure D-26. Testing the widths of borders on file input can be found at *http://www.oreilly.com/cssckbk2/appendixd/figs/css2_ad026.gif*

color

Figure D-27. Testing the color on file input can be found at *http://www.oreilly.com/cssckbk2/appendixd/figs/css2_ad027.gif*

font-family

Figure D-28. Testing to set a different font on file input can be found at *http://www.oreilly.com/cssckbk2/appendixd/figs/css2_ad028.gif*

font-size

Figure D-29. Testing a different size of font on file input can be found at *http://www.oreilly.com/cssckbk2/appendixd/figs/css2_ad029.gif*

font-weight

Figure D-30. Testing a bold font on file input can be found at *http://www.oreilly.com/cssckbk2/appendixd/figs/css2_ad030.gif*

height

Figure D-31. Testing to set a height for file inputlet can be found at *http://www.oreilly.com/cssckbk2/appendixd/figs/css2_ad031.gif*

letter-spacing

Figure D-32. Testing the letter spacing of file input can be found at *http://www.oreilly.com/cssckbk2/appendixd/figs/css2_ad032.gif*

line-height

Figure D-33. Testing setting the spacing between lines of text on file input can be found at *http://www.oreilly.com/cssckbk2/appendixd/figs/css2_ad033.gif*

margin

Figure D-34. Testing margins on file input can be found at *http://www.oreilly.com/cssckbk2/appendixd/figs/css2_ad034.gif*

padding

Figure D-35. Testing padding on file input can be found at *http://www.oreilly.com/cssckbk2/appendixd/figs/css2_ad035.gif*

text-align

Figure D-36. Testing the alignment of text on file input can be found at *http://www.oreilly.com/cssckbk2/appendixd/figs/css2_ad036.gif*

text-decoration

Figure D-37. Testing to set a different font on file input can be found at *http://www.oreilly.com/cssckbk2/appendixd/figs/css2_ad037.gif*

text-indent

Figure D-38. Testing indenting the text on file input can be found at *http://www.oreilly.com/cssckbk2/appendixd/figs/css2_ad038.gif*

width

Figure D-39. Testing the width of file input can be found at *http://www.oreilly.com/cssckbk2/appendixd/figs/css2_ad039.gif*

word-spacing

Figure D-40. Testing the spacing between words on file input can be found at *http://www.oreilly.com/cssckbk2/appendixd/figs/css2_ad040.gif*

Table D-3. A review of the CSS properties on file upload

	WinIE5	WinIE5.5	WinIE6	WinIE7	Safari2	WinFF1.5	MacFF1.5	WinNN7.2	MacNN7.2	Op8.5
background-color	Y	Y	Y	Y	N	Y	Y	Y	Y	N
background-image	Y	Y	Y	Y	N	N	N	N	N	N
border	Y	S	Y	Y	N	N	N	N	N	N
border-color	Y	Y	Y	Y	N	Y	Y	Y	Y	Y
border-style	Y	Y	Y	Y	N	N	N	N	N	Y
border-width	Y	Y	Y	Y	N	N	N	N	N	S
color	N	N	N	N	N	N	N	N	N	N
font-family	N	N	N	N	N	N	N	N	N	Y
font-size	Y	Y	Y	Y	N	Y	Y	Y	Y	Y
font-weight	N	N	N	N	N	N	N	N	N	Y
height	Y	Y	Y	Y	N	Y	Y	Y	Y	Y
letter-spacing	N	N	N	N	N	N	S	N	N	N
line-height	N	N	N	N	N	N	N	N	N	N
margin	Y	Y	Y	Y	Y	Y	Y	Y	Y	Y
padding	Y	Y	Y	Y	N	N	N	N	N	Y
text-align	N	N	N	N	N	S	S	S	S	N
text-decoration	N	N	N	N	N	N	N	N	N	N
text-indent	Y	Y	Y	Y	Y	Y	Y	Y	Y	Y
width	Y	Y	Y	Y	Y	S	S	S	S	Y
word-spacing	N	N	N	N	N	N	S	N	S	N

Radio Buttons

background-color

Figure D-41. Testing the background color of radio buttons can be found at *http://www.oreilly.com/cssckbk2/appendixd/figs/css2_ad041.gif*

background-image

Figure D-42. Testing background images in radio buttons can be found at *http://www.oreilly.com/cssckbk2/appendixd/figs/css2_ad042.gif*

border: 0;

Figure D-43. Testing the removal of borders on radio buttons can be found at *http://www.oreilly.com/cssckbk2/appendixd/figs/css2_ad043.gif*

border-color

Figure D-44. Testing of colors on the radio button borders can be found at *http://www.oreilly.com/cssckbk2/appendixd/figs/css2_ad044.gif*

border-style

Figure D-45. Testing the styles of borders on radio buttons can be found at *http://www.oreilly.com/cssckbk2/appendixd/figs/css2_ad045.gif*

border-width

Figure D-46. Testing the widths of borders on radio buttons can be found at *http://www.oreilly.com/cssckbk2/appendixd/figs/css2_ad046.gif*

color

Figure D-47. Testing the color on radio buttons can be found at *http://www.oreilly.com/cssckbk2/appendixd/figs/css2_ad047.gif*

font-family

Figure D-48. Testing to set a different font on radio buttons can be found at *http://www.oreilly.com/cssckbk2/appendixd/figs/css2_ad048.gif*

font-size

Figure D-49. Testing a different size of font on radio buttons can be found at *http://www.oreilly.com/cssckbk2/appendixd/figs/css2_ad049.gif*

font-weight

Figure D-50. Testing a bold font on radio buttons can be found at *http://www.oreilly.com/cssckbk2/appendixd/figs/css2_ad050.gif*

height

Figure D-51. Testing to set a height for radio buttons can be found at *http://www.oreilly.com/cssckbk2/appendixd/figs/css2_ad051.gif*

letter-spacing

Figure D-52. Testing the letter spacing of radio buttons can be found at *http://www.oreilly.com/cssckbk2/appendixd/figs/css2_ad052.gif*

line-height

Figure D-53. Testing setting the spacing between lines of text on radio buttons can be found at *http://www.oreilly.com/cssckbk2/appendixd/figs/css2_ad053.gif*

margin

Figure D-54. Testing margins on radio buttons can be found at *http://www.oreilly.com/cssckbk2/appendixd/figs/css2_ad054.gif*

padding

Figure D-55. Testing padding on radio buttons can be found at *http://www.oreilly.com/cssckbk2/appendixd/figs/css2_ad055.gif*

text-align

Figure D-56. Testing the alignment of text on radio buttons can be found at *http://www.oreilly.com/cssckbk2/appendixd/figs/css2_ad056.gif*

text-decoration

Figure D-57. Testing to set a different font on radio buttons can be found at *http://www.oreilly.com/cssckbk2/appendixd/figs/css2_ad057.gif*

text-indent

Figure D-58. Testing indenting the text on radio buttons can be found at *http://www.oreilly.com/cssckbk2/appendixd/figs/css2_ad058.gif*

width

Figure D-59. Testing the width of radio buttons can be found at *http://www.oreilly.com/cssckbk2/appendixd/figs/css2_ad059.gif*

word-spacing

Figure D-60. Testing the spacing between words on radio buttons can be found at *http://www.oreilly.com/cssckbk2/appendixd/figs/css2_ad060.gif*

Table D-4. A review of the CSS properties on radio buttons

	WinIE5	WinIE5.5	WinIE6	WinIE7	Safari2	WinFF1.5	MacFF1.5	WinNN7.2	MacNN7.2	Op8.5
background-color	S	S	S	S	N	N	N	N	N	Y
background-image	S	S	S	S	N	N	N	N	S	S
border	N	N	N	N	N	N	N	N	N	N
border-color	S	S	S	S	N	N	N	N	N	S
border-style	S	S	S	S	N	N	N	N	N	S
border-width	N	N	N	N	N	N	N	N	N	N
color	N	N	N	N	N	N	N	N	N	N
font-family	NA	NA	NA	NA	NA	NA	NA	NA	NA	NA
font-size	N	N	N	N	N	N	N	N	N	N
font-weight	NA	NA	NA	NA	NA	NA	NA	NA	NA	NA
height	S	S	S	S	N	N	Y	S	Y	S
letter-spacing	NA	NA	NA	NA	NA	NA	NA	NA	NA	NA
line-height	N	N	N	N	N	N	N	N	N	N
margin	Y	Y	Y	Y	Y	Y	Y	Y	Y	Y
padding	N	N	N	N	N	N	N	N	N	S
text-align	NA	NA	NA	NA	NA	NA	NA	NA	NA	NA
text-decoration	NA	NA	NA	NA	NA	NA	NA	NA	NA	NA
text-indent	Y	Y	Y	S	N	N	N	N	N	N
width	S	S	S	S	S	N	Y	S	Y	S
word-spacing	NA	NA	NA	NA	NA	NA	NA	NA	NA	NA

Text Fields

background-color
> Figure D-61. Testing the background color of text fields can be found at *http:// www.oreilly.com/cssckbk2/appendixd/figs/css2_ad061.gif*

background-image
> Figure D-62. Testing background images in text fields can be found at *http:// www.oreilly.com/cssckbk2/appendixd/figs/css2_ad062.gif*

border: 0;
> Figure D-63. Testing the removal of borders on text fields can be found at *http:// www.oreilly.com/cssckbk2/appendixd/figs/css2_ad063.gif*

border-color
> Figure D-64. Testing of colors on the text field borders can be found at *http:// www.oreilly.com/cssckbk2/appendixd/figs/css2_ad064.gif*

border-style
> Figure D-65. Testing the styles of borders on text fields can be found at *http:// www.oreilly.com/cssckbk2/appendixd/figs/css2_ad065.gif*

border-width
> Figure D-66. Testing the widths of borders on text fields can be found at *http:// www.oreilly.com/cssckbk2/appendixd/figs/css2_ad066.gif*

color
> Figure D-67. Testing the color on text fields can be found at *http://www.oreilly.com/ cssckbk2/appendixd/figs/css2_ad067.gif*

font-family
> Figure D-68. Testing to set a different font on text fields can be found at *http:// www.oreilly.com/cssckbk2/appendixd/figs/css2_ad068.gif*

font-size
> Figure D-69. Testing a different size of font on text fields can be found at *http:// www.oreilly.com/cssckbk2/appendixd/figs/css2_ad069.gif*

font-weight
> Figure D-70. Testing a bold font on text fields can be found at *http:// www.oreilly.com/cssckbk2/appendixd/figs/css2_ad070.gif*

height
> Figure D-71. Testing to set a height for text fields can be found at *http:// www.oreilly.com/cssckbk2/appendixd/figs/css2_ad071.gif*

letter-spacing
> Figure D-72. Testing the letter spacing of text fields can be found at *http:// www.oreilly.com/cssckbk2/appendixd/figs/css2_ad072.gif*

line-height

Figure D-73. Testing setting the spacing between lines of text on text fields can be found at *http://www.oreilly.com/cssckbk2/appendixd/figs/css2_ad073.gif*

margin

Figure D-74. Testing margins on text fields can be found at *http://www.oreilly.com/ cssckbk2/appendixd/figs/css2_ad074.gif*

padding

Figure D-75. Testing padding on text fields can be found at *http://www.oreilly.com/ cssckbk2/appendixd/figs/css2_ad075.gif*

text-align

Figure D-76. Testing the alignment of text on text fields can be found at *http:// www.oreilly.com/cssckbk2/appendixd/figs/css2_ad076.gif*

text-decoration

Figure D-77. Testing to set a different font on text fields can be found at *http:// www.oreilly.com/cssckbk2/appendixd/figs/css2_ad077.gif*

text-indent

Figure D-78. Testing indenting the text on text fields can be found at *http:// www.oreilly.com/cssckbk2/appendixd/figs/css2_ad078.gif*

width

Figure D-79. Testing the width of text fields can be found at *http://www.oreilly.com/ cssckbk2/appendixd/figs/css2_ad079.gif*

word-spacing

Figure D-80. Testing the spacing between words on text fields can be found at *http://www.oreilly.com/cssckbk2/appendixd/figs/css2_ad080.gif*

Table D-5. A review of the CSS properties on text fields

	WinIE5	WinIE5.5	WinIE6	WinIE7	Safari2	WinFF1.5	MacFF1.5	WinNN7.2	MacNN7.2	Op8.5
background-color	Y	Y	Y	Y	Y	Y	Y	Y	Y	Y
background-image	Y	Y	Y	Y	N	Y	Y	Y	Y	Y
border	Y	Y	Y	Y	N	Y	Y	Y	Y	Y
border-color	Y	Y	Y	Y	N	Y	Y	Y	Y	Y
border-style	Y	Y	Y	Y	N	Y	Y	Y	Y	Y
border-width	Y	Y	Y	Y	N	Y	Y	Y	Y	N
color	Y	Y	Y	Y	Y	Y	Y	Y	Y	Y
font-family	Y	Y	Y	Y	Y	Y	Y	Y	Y	Y
font-size	Y	Y	Y	Y	Y	Y	Y	Y	Y	Y
font-weight	Y	Y	Y	Y	Y	Y	Y	Y	Y	Y
height	Y	Y	Y	Y	N	Y	Y	Y	Y	S
letter-spacing	Y	Y	Y	Y	N	S	S	Y	Y	Y
line-height	N	N	N	N	N	N	N	N	N	N
margin	Y	Y	Y	Y	Y	Y	Y	Y	Y	N
padding	Y	S	Y	Y	N	Y	Y	Y	Y	S
text-align	N	N	N	N	N	N	N	N	N	N
text-decoration	Y	Y	Y	Y	N	Y	Y	Y	Y	N
text-indent	S	S	S	S	N	Y	Y	Y	Y	N
width	Y	Y	Y	Y	N	Y	Y	Y	Y	Y
word-spacing	N	N	N	Y	N	Y	Y	Y	Y	N

Multiple Options

background-color

Figure D-81. Testing the background color of select element with multiple options can be found at *http://www.oreilly.com/cssckbk2/appendixd/figs/css2_ad081.gif*

background-image

Figure D-82. Testing background images in select element with multiple options can be found at *http://www.oreilly.com/cssckbk2/appendixd/figs/css2_ad082.gif*

border: 0;

Figure D-83. Testing the removal of borders on select element with multiple options can be found at *http://www.oreilly.com/cssckbk2/appendixd/figs/css2_ad083.gif*

border-color

Figure D-84. Testing of border colors on select element with multiple options can be found at *http://www.oreilly.com/cssckbk2/appendixd/figs/css2_ad084.gif*

border-style

Figure D-85. Testing the styles of borders on select element with multiple options can be found at *http://www.oreilly.com/cssckbk2/appendixd/figs/css2_ad085.gif*

border-width

Figure D-86. Testing the widths of borders on select element with multiple options can be found at *http://www.oreilly.com/cssckbk2/appendixd/figs/css2_ad086.gif*

color

Figure D-87. Testing the color on select element with multiple options can be found at *http://www.oreilly.com/cssckbk2/appendixd/figs/css2_ad087.gif*

font-family

Figure D-88. Testing to set a different font on select element with multiple options can be found at *http://www.oreilly.com/cssckbk2/appendixd/figs/css2_ad088.gif*

font-size

Figure D-89. Testing a different size of font on select element with multiple options can be found at *http://www.oreilly.com/cssckbk2/appendixd/figs/css2_ad089.gif*

font-weight

Figure D-90. Testing a bold font on select element with multiple options can be found at *http://www.oreilly.com/cssckbk2/appendixd/figs/css2_ad090.gif*

height

Figure D-91. Testing to set a height for select element with multiple options can be found at *http://www.oreilly.com/cssckbk2/appendixd/figs/css2_ad091.gif*

letter-spacing

Figure D-92. Testing the letter spacing of select element with multiple options can be found at *http://www.oreilly.com/cssckbk2/appendixd/figs/css2_ad092.gif*

line-height

Figure D-93. Testing setting the spacing between lines of text on select element with multiple options can be found at *http://www.oreilly.com/cssckbk2/appendixd/figs/css2_ad093.gif*

margin

Figure D-94. Testing margins on select element with multiple options can be found at *http://www.oreilly.com/cssckbk2/appendixd/figs/css2_ad094.gif*

padding

Figure D-95. Testing padding on select element with multiple options can be found at *http://www.oreilly.com/cssckbk2/appendixd/figs/css2_ad095.gif*

text-align

Figure D-96. Testing the alignment of text on select element with multiple options can be found at *http://www.oreilly.com/cssckbk2/appendixd/figs/css2_ad096.gif*

text-decoration

Figure D-97. Testing to set a different font on select element with multiple options can be found at *http://www.oreilly.com/cssckbk2/appendixd/figs/css2_ad097.gif*

text-indent

Figure D-98. Testing indenting the text on select element with multiple options can be found at *http://www.oreilly.com/cssckbk2/appendixd/figs/css2_ad098.gif*

width

Figure D-99. Testing the width of select element with multiple options can be found at *http://www.oreilly.com/cssckbk2/appendixd/figs/css2_ad099.gif*

word-spacing

Figure D-100. Testing the spacing between words on select element with multiple options can be found at *http://www.oreilly.com/cssckbk2/appendixd/figs/css2_ad100.gif*

Table D-6. A review of the CSS properties on select element with multiple options showing

	WinIE5	WinIE5.5	WinIE6	WinIE7	Safari2	WinFF1.5	MacFF1.5	WinNN7.2	MacNN7.2	Op8.5
background-color	Y	Y	Y	Y	N	Y	Y	Y	Y	Y
background-image	N	N	N	N	N	Y	Y	Y	Y	N
border	N	N	N	N	N	Y	Y	N	N	Y
border-color	N	N	N	N	N	Y	Y	N	S	Y
border-style	N	N	N	N	N	Y	Y	N	N	Y
border-width	N	N	N	N	N	Y	Y	N	N	N
color	Y	Y	Y	Y	N	Y	Y	Y	Y	Y
font-family	Y	Y	Y	Y	Y	Y	Y	Y	Y	Y
font-size	Y	Y	Y	Y	Y	Y	Y	Y	Y	Y
font-weight	Y	Y	Y	Y	Y	Y	Y	Y	Y	Y
height	S	S	S	S	Y	Y	Y	Y	Y	Y
letter-spacing	N	N	N	N	N	S	S	S	S	S
line-height	N	N	N	N	N	N	N	N	N	N
margin	Y	Y	Y	Y	Y	Y	Y	Y	Y	Y
padding	N	N	N	N	N	Y	Y	Y	Y	Y
text-align	N	N	N	N	N	Y	Y	Y	Y	Y
text-decoration	Y	Y		Y	N	N	N	N	N	N
text-indent	S	S	S	S	N	N	N	N	N	N
width	Y	Y	Y	Y	Y	Y	Y	Y	Y	Y
word-spacing	N	N	N	N	N	S	S	S	S	N

Select Element

background-color
> Figure D-101. Testing the background color of select element can be found at *http://www.oreilly.com/cssckbk2/appendixd/figs/css2_ad101.gif*

background-image
> Figure D-102. Testing background images in select element can be found at *http://www.oreilly.com/cssckbk2/appendixd/figs/css2_ad102.gif*

border: 0;
> Figure D-103. Testing the removal of borders on select element can be found at *http://www.oreilly.com/cssckbk2/appendixd/figs/css2_ad103.gif*

border-color
> Figure D-104. Testing of colors on the select element borders can be found at *http://www.oreilly.com/cssckbk2/appendixd/figs/css2_ad104.gif*

border-style
> Figure D-105. Testing the styles of borders on select element can be found at *http://www.oreilly.com/cssckbk2/appendixd/figs/css2_ad105.gif*

border-width
> Figure D-106. Testing the widths of borders on select element can be found at *http://www.oreilly.com/cssckbk2/appendixd/figs/css2_ad106.gif*

color
> Figure D-107. Testing the color on select element can be found at *http://www.oreilly.com/cssckbk2/appendixd/figs/css2_ad107.gif*

font-family
> Figure D-108. Testing to set a different font on select element can be found at *http://www.oreilly.com/cssckbk2/appendixd/figs/css2_ad108.gif*

font-size
> Figure D-109. Testing a different size of font on select element can be found at *http://www.oreilly.com/cssckbk2/appendixd/figs/css2_ad109.gif*

font-weight
> Figure D-110. Testing a bold font on select element can be found at *http://www.oreilly.com/cssckbk2/appendixd/figs/css2_ad110.gif*

height
> Figure D-111. Testing to set a height for select element can be found at *http://www.oreilly.com/cssckbk2/appendixd/figs/css2_ad111.gif*

letter-spacing
> Figure D-112. Testing the letter spacing of select element can be found at *http://www.oreilly.com/cssckbk2/appendixd/figs/css2_ad112.gif*

line-height

Figure D-113. Testing setting the spacing between lines of text on select element can be found at *http://www.oreilly.com/cssckbk2/appendixd/figs/css2_ad113.gif*

margin

Figure D-114. Testing margins on select element can be found at *http://www.oreilly.com/cssckbk2/appendixd/figs/css2_ad114.gif*

padding

Figure D-115. Testing padding on select element can be found at *http://www.oreilly.com/cssckbk2/appendixd/figs/css2_ad115.gif*

text-align

Figure D-116. Testing the alignment of text on select element can be found at *http://www.oreilly.com/cssckbk2/appendixd/figs/css2_ad116.gif*

text-decoration

Figure D-117. Testing to set a different font on select element can be found at *http://www.oreilly.com/cssckbk2/appendixd/figs/css2_ad117.gif*

text-indent

Figure D-118. Testing indenting the text on select element can be found at *http://www.oreilly.com/cssckbk2/appendixd/figs/css2_ad118.gif*

width

Figure D-119. Testing the width of select element can be found at *http://www.oreilly.com/cssckbk2/appendixd/figs/css2_ad119.gif*

word-spacing

Figure D-120. Testing the spacing between words on select element can be found at *http://www.oreilly.com/cssckbk2/appendixd/figs/css2_ad120.gif*

Table D-7. A review of the CSS properties on select element with one option showing

	WinIE5	WinIE5.5	WinIE6	WinIE7	Safari2	WinFF1.5	MacFF1.5	WinNN7.2	MacNN7.2	Op8.5
background-color	Y	Y	Y	Y	N	Y	Y	Y	Y	Y
background-image	N	N	N	N	N	N	N	N	N	N
border	N	N	N	N	N	Y	Y	N	N	Y
border-color	N	N	N	N	N	Y	Y	N	S	Y
border-style	N	N	N	N	N	Y	Y	N	N	Y
border-width	N	N	N	N	N	Y	Y	N	N	N
color	Y	Y	Y	Y	N	Y	Y	Y	Y	Y
font-family	Y	Y	Y	Y	N	Y	Y	Y	Y	Y
font-size	Y	Y	Y	Y	N	Y	Y	Y	Y	Y
font-weight	Y	Y	Y	Y	N	Y	Y	Y	Y	Y
height	N	N	N	N	N	S	S	S	S	Y
letter-spacing	N	N	N	N	N	Y	Y	Y	Y	Y
line-height	N	N	N	N	N	N	N	Y	N	Y
margin	Y	Y	Y	Y	Y	Y	Y	Y	Y	Y
padding	N	N	N	N	N	Y	Y	Y	Y	Y
text-align	N	N	N	N	N	Y	Y	Y	Y	N
text-decoration	Y	Y	Y	Y	N	N	N	Y	Y	N
text-indent	S	S	S	S	Y	Y	Y	Y	Y	Y
width	Y	Y	Y	Y	Y	Y	Y	Y	Y	Y
word-spacing	N	N	N	N	N	Y	Y	Y	Y	Y

Submit Button

background-color
> Figure D-121. Testing the background color of select element can be found at *http://www.oreilly.com/cssckbk2/appendixd/figs/css2_ad121.gif*

background-image
> Figure D-122. Testing background images in the submit button can be found at *http://www.oreilly.com/cssckbk2/appendixd/figs/css2_ad122.gif*

border: 0;
> Figure D-123. Testing the removal of borders on the submit button can be found at *http://www.oreilly.com/cssckbk2/appendixd/figs/css2_ad123.gif*

border-color
> Figure D-124. Testing of colors on the submit button borders can be found at *http://www.oreilly.com/cssckbk2/appendixd/figs/css2_ad124.gif*

border-style
> Figure D-125. Testing the styles of borders on the submit button can be found at *http://www.oreilly.com/cssckbk2/appendixd/figs/css2_ad125.gif*

border-width
> Figure D-126. Testing the widths of borders on the submit button can be found at *http://www.oreilly.com/cssckbk2/appendixd/figs/css2_ad126.gif*

color
> Figure D-127. Testing the color on the submit button can be found at *http://www.oreilly.com/cssckbk2/appendixd/figs/css2_ad127.gif*

font-family
> Figure D-128. Testing to set a different font on the submit button can be found at *http://www.oreilly.com/cssckbk2/appendixd/figs/css2_ad128.gif*

font-size
> Figure D-129. Testing a different size of font on the submit button can be found at *http://www.oreilly.com/cssckbk2/appendixd/figs/css2_ad129.gif*

font-weight
> Figure D-130. Testing a bold font on the submit button can be found at *http://www.oreilly.com/cssckbk2/appendixd/figs/css2_ad130.gif*

height
> Figure D-131. Testing to set a height for the submit button can be found at *http://www.oreilly.com/cssckbk2/appendixd/figs/css2_ad131.gif*

letter-spacing
> Figure D-132. Testing the letter spacing of the submit button can be found at *http://www.oreilly.com/cssckbk2/appendixd/figs/css2_ad132.gif*

line-height

Figure D-133. Testing setting the spacing between lines of text on the submit button can be found at *http://www.oreilly.com/cssckbk2/appendixd/figs/css2_ad133.gif*

margin

Figure D-134. Testing margins on the submit button can be found at *http://www.oreilly.com/cssckbk2/appendixd/figs/css2_ad134.gif*

padding

Figure D-135. Testing padding on the submit button can be found at *http://www.oreilly.com/cssckbk2/appendixd/figs/css2_ad135.gif*

text-align

Figure D-136. Testing the alignment of text on the submit button can be found at *http://www.oreilly.com/cssckbk2/appendixd/figs/css2_ad136.gif*

text-decoration

Figure D-137. Testing to set a different font on the submit button can be found at *http://www.oreilly.com/cssckbk2/appendixd/figs/css2_ad137.gif*

text-indent

Figure D-138. Testing indenting the text on the submit button can be found at *http://www.oreilly.com/cssckbk2/appendixd/figs/css2_ad138.gif*

width

Figure D-139. Testing the width of the submit button can be found at *http://www.oreilly.com/cssckbk2/appendixd/figs/css2_ad139.gif*

word-spacing

Figure D-140. Testing the spacing between words on the submit button can be found at *http://www.oreilly.com/cssckbk2/appendixd/figs/css2_ad140.gif*

Table D-8. A review of the CSS properties on the submit button

	WinIE5	WinIE5.5	WinIE6	WinIE7	Safari2	WinFF1.5	MacFF1.5	WinNN7.2	MacNN7.2	Op8.5
background-color	Y	Y	Y	Y	N	Y	Y	Y	Y	Y
background-image	Y	Y	Y	N	N	Y	Y	Y	Y	Y
border	Y	Y	Y	Y	N	Y	Y	Y	Y	Y
border-color	Y	Y	Y	Y	N	Y	Y	Y	Y	Y
border-style	Y	Y	Y	Y	N	Y	Y	Y	Y	Y
border-width	Y	Y	Y	Y	N	Y	Y	Y	Y	N
color	Y	Y	Y	Y	N	Y	Y	Y	Y	Y
font-family	Y	Y	Y	Y	N	Y	Y	Y	Y	Y
font-size	Y	Y	Y	Y	N	Y	Y	Y	Y	Y
font-weight	Y	Y	Y	Y	N	Y	Y	Y	Y	Y
height	Y	Y	Y	Y	N	Y	Y	Y	Y	Y
letter-spacing	Y	Y	Y	Y	N	Y	Y	Y	Y	Y
line-height	N	N	N	N	N	N	N	N	N	N
margin	Y	Y	Y	Y	Y	Y	Y	Y	Y	Y
padding	Y	Y	Y	Y	N	Y	Y	Y	Y	Y
text-align	N	N	Y	Y	N	N	N	N	N	Y
text-decoration	Y	Y	Y	Y	N	N	N	N	N	N
text-indent	S	S	S	S	N	Y	Y	Y	Y	N
width	Y	Y	Y	Y	Y	Y	Y	Y	Y	Y
word-spacing	N	N	Y	Y	N	Y	Y	Y	Y	N

Textarea Element

background-color

> Figure D-141. Testing the background color of the textarea element can be found at *http://www.oreilly.com/cssckbk2/appendixd/figs/css2_ad141.gif*

background-image

> Figure D-142. Testing background images in the textarea element can be found at *http://www.oreilly.com/cssckbk2/appendixd/figs/css2_ad142.gif*

border: 0;

> Figure D-143. Testing the removal of borders on the textarea element can be found at *http://www.oreilly.com/cssckbk2/appendixd/figs/css2_ad143.gif*

border-color

> Figure D-144. Testing of colors on the textarea element borders can be found at *http://www.oreilly.com/cssckbk2/appendixd/figs/css2_ad144.gif*

border-style

> Figure D-145. Testing the styles of borders on the textarea elementborde can be found at *http://www.oreilly.com/cssckbk2/appendixd/figs/css2_ad145.gif*

border-width

> Figure D-146. Testing the widths of borders on the textarea element can be found at *http://www.oreilly.com/cssckbk2/appendixd/figs/css2_ad146.gif*

color

> Figure D-147. Testing the color on the textarea element can be found at *http://www.oreilly.com/cssckbk2/appendixd/figs/css2_ad147.gif*

font-family

> Figure D-148. Testing to set a different font on the textarea element can be found at *http://www.oreilly.com/cssckbk2/appendixd/figs/css2_ad148.gif*

font-size

> Figure D-149. Testing a different size of font on the textarea element can be found at *http://www.oreilly.com/cssckbk2/appendixd/figs/css2_ad149.gif*

font-weight

> Figure D-150. Testing a bold font on the textarea element can be found at *http://www.oreilly.com/cssckbk2/appendixd/figs/css2_ad150.gif*

height

> Figure D-151. Testing to set a height for the textarea element can be found at *http://www.oreilly.com/cssckbk2/appendixd/figs/css2_ad151.gif*

letter-spacing

> Figure D-152. Testing the letter spacing of the textarea element can be found at *http://www.oreilly.com/cssckbk2/appendixd/figs/css2_ad152.gif*

line-height
> Figure D-153. Testing setting the spacing between lines of text on the textarea element can be found at *http://www.oreilly.com/cssckbk2/appendixd/figs/css2_ad153.gif*

margin
> Figure D-154. Testing margins on the textarea element can be found at *http://www.oreilly.com/cssckbk2/appendixd/figs/css2_ad154.gif*

padding
> Figure D-155. Testing padding on the textarea element can be found at *http://www.oreilly.com/cssckbk2/appendixd/figs/css2_ad155.gif*

text-alignt
> Figure D-156. Testing the alignment of text on the textarea element can be found at *http://www.oreilly.com/cssckbk2/appendixd/figs/css2_ad156.gif*

text-decoration
> Figure D-157. Testing to set a different font on the textarea element can be found at *http://www.oreilly.com/cssckbk2/appendixd/figs/css2_ad157.gif*

text-indent
> Figure D-158. Testing indenting the text on the textarea element can be found at *http://www.oreilly.com/cssckbk2/appendixd/figs/css2_ad158.gif*

width
> Figure D-159. Testing the width of the textarea element can be found at *http://www.oreilly.com/cssckbk2/appendixd/figs/css2_ad159.gif*

word-spacing
> Figure D-160. Testing the spacing between words on the textarea element can be found at *http://www.oreilly.com/cssckbk2/appendixd/figs/css2_ad160.gif*

Table D-9. A review of the CSS properties on textarea

	WinIE5	WinIE5.5	WinIE6	WinIE7	Safari2	WinFF1.5	MacFF1.5	WinNN7.2	MacNN7.2	Op8.5
background-color	Y	Y	Y	Y	Y	Y	Y	Y	Y	Y
background-image	Y	Y	Y	Y	N	Y	Y	Y	Y	Y
border	Y	Y	Y	Y	N	Y	Y	Y	Y	Y
border-color	Y	Y	Y	Y	N	Y	Y	Y	Y	Y
border-style	Y	Y	Y	Y	N	Y	Y	Y	Y	Y
border-width	Y	Y	Y	Y	N	Y	Y	Y	Y	N
color	Y	Y	Y	Y	Y	Y	Y	Y	Y	Y
font-family	Y	Y	Y	Y	Y	Y	Y	Y	Y	Y
font-size	Y	Y	Y	Y	Y	Y	Y	Y	Y	Y
font-weight	Y	Y	Y	N	Y	Y	Y	Y	Y	Y
height	Y	Y	Y	Y	Y	Y	Y	Y	Y	Y
letter-spacing	Y	Y	Y	Y	N	S	S	Y	Y	Y
line-height	Y	Y	Y	Y	N	Y	Y	N	N	N
margin	Y	Y	Y	Y	N	Y	Y	Y	Y	Y
padding	Y	Y	S	S	N	S	S	S	S	S
text-align	Y	Y	Y	Y	Y	Y	Y	Y	Y	Y
text-decoration	Y	Y	Y	Y	N	Y	Y	Y	Y	N
text-indent	S	S	S	S	N	Y	Y	Y	Y	N
width	Y	Y	Y	Y	Y	Y	Y	Y	Y	Y
word-spacing	N	N	Y	Y	N	Y	Y	Y	Y	N

Index

We'd like to hear your suggestions for improving our indexes. Send email to *index@oreilly.com*.

E

Edwards, James, 50
elements
    positioning, 53, 55
em units, 70, 72, 74
embossed media type, 43
empty-cells property (CSS 2.1), 461
emulators for multiple platform site design
        testing, 430
e-resize, ne-resize, nw-resize, n-resize,
        se-resize, sw-resize, s-resize,
        w-resize cursor property, 236
escaping characters specification, 215
extensions
    CSS 2.1 proprietary, 469–473
external style sheets, 47
external styles, 36

F

Fahrner Image Replacement (FIR)
        method, 133, 253
Fahrner, Todd, 75, 133, 253
fantasy font family, 66
faux columns, 388
filter (Microsoft proprietary extension, CSS
        2.1), 469
filter property, Microsoft, 139
first-letter pseudo-element, 79
    specification, 80
first-line pseudo-element, 103
    specification, 105
fixed (or absolute) type measurements, 71
fixed-width columns, 147
flags and finding rules in CSS files, 46
Flash
    using to replace HTML text, 134
float model, 375, 390
float property, 92, 296, 352, 356, 461
float rule, 377
floats
    specification, 52
    with images, 50
font families
    cursive, 66
    fantasy, 66
    monospace, 66
    sans-serif, 66
    serif, 66
font family property, 66
font measurements and size
    specifying, 69

font property, 462
font shorthand property, 48, 85
    specification, 85
font size
    controlling across browsers and operating
        systems, 71–75
    overriding control, 75
    setting to zero or a negative value, 70
font sizes
    specifying, 437
font-family property (CSS 2.1), 462
fonts
    specifying, 66
font-size keywords, 73
font-size property, 69, 81
    specification, 71
font-size property (CSS 2.1), 462
font-style property (CSS 2.1), 462
font-variant property (CSS 2.1), 462
font-weight property, 25
font-weight property (CSS 2.1), 462
forms, 270–321
    access keys, creating visual indicators
        for, 300
    buttons, styling, 282
    designing a form without tables, 290
    entering data into a spreadsheet
        application, 303–307
    grouping common elements, 301
    highlighting fields, 296
    HTML text link that operates like a
        Submit button, 290
    input elements, applying different styles
        to, 275
    integrating form feedback, 297
        tutorial, 299
    login sample, 308–312
    Macintosh-styled search field, 279
    modifying the space around, 270
    registration form, sample, 313–321
    select and option elements, setting
        styles, 277–279
    setting styles for input elements, 272–275
    Submit button that looks like HTML
        text, 288
    Submit-Only-Once button, setting
        up, 286
    textarea elements, setting styles, 276
    transforming one-column to
        two-column, 292
four-column layout with fixed-width
        columns, 369

About the Author

Christopher Schmitt is the founder of Heatvision.com, Inc., a small new media publishing and design firm based in Tallahassee, Florida.

An award-winning web designer who has been working with the Web since 1993, Schmitt interned for both David Siegel and Lynda Weinman in the mid-90s while he was an undergraduate at Florida State University working on a fine arts degree with an emphasis in graphic design.

He continued his education by earning a Masters of Science from the FSU College of Communication for Interactive and New Communication Technology.

In 2000, he led a team to victory in the Cool Site in a Day competition, where he and five other talented developers built a fully functional, well-designed web site for a nonprofit organization in eight hours.

He is the author of *Designing CSS Web Pages* (New Riders) and is the co-author of *Professional CSS* (Wrox), *Photoshop CS in 10 Steps or Less* (Wiley), and *Dreamweaver MX Design Projects* (glasshaus). He contributed four chapters to *XML, HTML, and XHTML Magic* (New Riders). Schmitt has also written for *New Architect Magazine*, *A List Apart*, *Digital Web*, and *Web Reference*.

At conferences such as Web Visions, The Other Dreamweaver Conference, and SXSW, Schmitt has given talks demonstrating the use and benefits of practical CSS-enabled designs. He is the list moderator for Babble (*http://www.babblelist.com*), a mailing list community devoted to advanced web design and development topics.

On his personal web site, *http://www.christopherschmitt.com*, Schmitt shows his true colors and most recent activities. He is 6' 7" and doesn't play professional basketball but wouldn't mind a good game of chess.

Colophon

The animal on the cover of *CSS Cookbook* is a grizzly bear (*Ursus arctos horribilis*). The grizzly's distinctive features include humped shoulders, a long snout, and long curved claws. The coat color ranges from shades of blond, brown, black, or a combination of these; the long outer guard hairs are often tipped with white or silver, giving the bear a "grizzled" appearance. The grizzly can weigh anywhere from 350 to 800 pounds and reach a shoulder height of 4.5 feet when on all fours. Standing on its hind legs, a grizzly can reach up to eight feet. Despite its large size, the grizzly can reach speeds of 35 to 40 miles per hour.

Some of the grizzly's favorite foods include nuts, berries, insects, salmon, carrion, and small mammals. The diet of a grizzly varies depending on the season and habitat. Grizzlies in parts of Alaska eat primarily salmon, while grizzlies in high mountain areas eat mostly berries and insects.

Grizzlies are solitary, and prefer rugged mountains and forests. They can be found in the Canadian provinces of British Columbia, Alberta, Yukon, and the Northwest Territories; and the U.S. states of Alaska, Idaho, Wyoming, Washington, and Montana.

The grizzly is considered a threatened species: only about 850 bears exist in the lower 48 states. Before the West was settled, the grizzly bear population was estimated to be between 50,000 and 100,000. Threats to the survival of the grizzly bear include habitat destruction caused by logging, mining, and human development, as well as illegal poaching.

The cover image is a 19th-century engraving from the Dover Pictorial Archive. The cover font is Adobe ITC Garamond. The text font is Linotype Birka; the heading font is Adobe Myriad Condensed; and the code font is LucasFont's TheSans Mono Condensed.

Better than e-books

Buy *CSS Cookbook*, Second Edition, and access
the digital edition FREE on Safari for 45 days.

Go to www.oreilly.com/go/safarienabled
and type in coupon code G3ND-ZUGL-9YYE-ZDLZ-5I1N

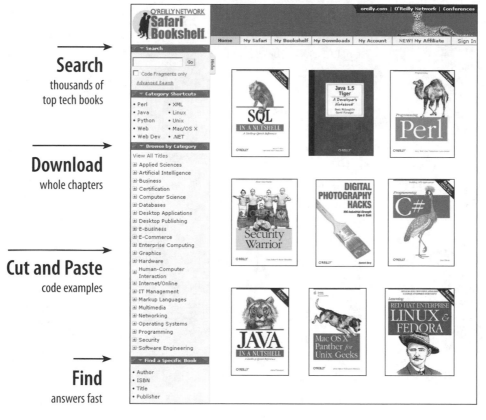

Search
thousands of
top tech books

Download
whole chapters

Cut and Paste
code examples

Find
answers fast

Search Safari! The premier electronic reference
library for programmers and IT professionals.

Related Titles from O'Reilly

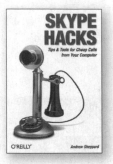

Web Applications

Ambient Findability

Developing Feeds with RSS & Atom

Don't Click on the Blue E!: Switching to Firefox

Dreamweaver 8: The Missing Manual

eBay Hacks, 2nd Edition

eBay: The Missing Manual

Firefox Hacks

Flash 8: The Missing Manual

Google Hacks, *2nd Edition*

Google Pocket Guide

Google Advertising Tools

Google: The Missing Manual

Greasemonkey Hacks

Internet Annoyances

Mapping Hacks

Online Investing Hacks

PayPal Hacks

Podcasting Hacks

Skype Hacks

Talk is Cheap: Switching to Internet Telephones

Using Moodle

Web Mapping Illustrated

Yahoo! Hacks

O'REILLY®

Our books are available at most retail and online bookstores.
To order direct: 1-800-998-9938 • *order@oreilly.com* • *www.oreilly.com*
Online editions of most O'Reilly titles are available by subscription at *safari.oreilly.com*